Leadership in Safety Management

LEADERSHIP IN SAFETY MANAGEMENT

JAMES R. THOMEN
Modern Management Associates
Wilmington, Delaware

A Wiley-Interscience Publication
JOHN WILEY & SONS, INC.
New York / Chichester / Brisbane / Toronto / Singapore

Library of Congress Cataloging in Publication Data:

Thomen, James R.

Leadership in Safety Management / by James R. Thomen.

p. cm.

"A Wiley-Interscience publication."

Includes bibliographical references

1. Industrial Safety—Management. I. Title.

HD7262.T43 1991 91-16849

658.4'08—dc20 CIP

ISBN 0-471-53326-2

Printed in the United States of America

10 9 8 7 6 5 4

To
Lydia

Management cannot provide
a safe place in which to work.
It can provide an environment
in which employees work safely.

CONTENTS

PREFACE

This book is intended to serve as a road map leading to the improvement of safety performance for all who work for a living, although the ideas and practices presented are useful also for those who do not "work."

The need for a book such as this became very clear to me during the years I spent assisting the Du Pont Company[1] in its safety consulting business. Many of my clients are Fortune 500 companies, both non-U.S. companies operating around the world, as well as domestic companies. All have sought to improve their safety and health performance. Most have done so out of genuine concern for the well-being of employees; others as a result of prodding from external forces, primarily governments. Whatever their reasons or motivations, they came to Du Pont seeking advice and guidance regarding the improvement of employee safety and health performance. Why Du Pont? Du Pont has been extraordinarily successful in managing the safety, health and environmental aspects of its business. Peters and Austin have recognized this in their book, "A Passion for Excellence."[2] In addition, Du Pont has been willing to share its experience and view regarding safety.

The company has consistently challenged itself and other organizations to improve their safety performance out of concern for people—both employees and the public at large. Responsible conduct in the area of safety has become increasingly recognized as morally sound, financially rewarding, and necessary to avert or diminish third party (government, media, etc.) intervention which, while normally well-meaning, has often been off-the-mark in effectiveness.

This book is not a Du Pont book, however; it represents solely my current understanding regarding effective and efficient management behavior which leads to improvements in safety performance. It includes the results of 32 years of Du Pont employment, 18 of which were in plant/site management assignments, in addition to several years of outside Du Pont consulting.

The difference between the way Du Pont management behaves regarding safety and the way their counterparts in most other organizations behave is striking. It is the purpose of this book to illustrate efficient and effective managerial behavior patterns through which safety excellence can be achieved as well as to suggest organizational arrangements that facilitate the implementation of these behavior patterns. This is a how-to-do book. Sprinkled in amongst the how-tos you may find some principles and applied psychology, but the book is primarily a presentation of pragmatic procedures and management practices that work. These provide the framework from which ordinary individuals can develop the leadership skills necessary to achieve extraordinary results.

SAFE PEOPLE VERSUS SAFE PLACE

Contrary to the requirements of the U.S. Occupational Health and Safety Act of 1970 and many corporate safety policy statements, it is not possible to provide a safe workplace—a workplace free of recognized hazards. A workplace is neither safe nor unsafe, nor does it possess varying degrees of safety between these two extremes. It is people who are safe or unsafe, or more or less safe. It is the behavior of people, not a characteristic of the workplace, that determines the frequency and degree of personal injuries; or damage to health, the environment, or property. I have never encountered an injury or instance of damage to health, the environment or property that was not the result of human behavior.

To illustrate the point, consider the common household or office door. There are two serious pinch-points, recognized hazards, associated with doors—one at the hinge edge and the other along the opposite edge, or latch edge. People who place their hands or fingers in the open hinge area while talking to a fellow employee are someday going to get their fingers smashed—it is just a matter of time. Likewise, people who close doors by grabbing the edge of the door instead of the door knob are someday going to fail to extricate their hand quickly enough, resulting in a smashed finger. Blackened fingernails are common as a result of automobile door closings. Because of these hazards, I once considered that doors were inherently unsafe, with no practical ways of rendering them safe (the hinged area can be guarded by enclosure with a flexible covering). I have since changed by mind, along with my understanding of safety. I have come to recognize that doors do not possess the attribute of being safe or unsafe. They simply exist. It is how a door is used by people that has the attribute of safety. Safety is not an attribute of an inanimate object or set of objects, however complex. It is what animate individuals do or do not do, that determines the attribute of safety.

This is the central truth, some may say hypothesis, upon which this book is based. Its content is devoted to elucidating organizational ways by which behavior can be continually directed toward more safe behavior and away from less safe behavior. The behavior in question is not limited to the behavior of the injured individual, but also includes the behavior of fellow workers, design engineers, plant location specialists, plant managers, C.E.O.s and others. No one is immune to behaving unsafely. I have attempted to emphasize this concept throughout the text.

DU PONT PERFORMANCE

What has Du Pont accomplished? Figure 1 shows Du Pont's safety performance since 1912. The data of the main graph have been substantially "smoothed" by plotting data only for each eighth year in order to keep the focus on the continuing improvement that has taken place. There have been only two major deviations from this continuous improvement. The first was during World War I, and the second in the 1924–28 time period when the company embarked upon a major new plant construction program. World War II did not result in a deterioration in safety performance, even though employee numbers doubled under wartime conditions. This was validation that the "safety system" worked. The complete data from 1956 to 1989, Figure 2, reveals actual fluctuations in year-to-year performance.

In 1989, The Lost Workday Case frequency rate was 0.024. This reflects 27 lost workday cases for an average employment of 110,000 employees. There were no employee fatalities in 1989. The total OSHA recordable injuries (Lost Workday Cases, Restricted Workday Cases, and Medical Treatment Cases) frequency rate in 1989 was 0.565. The Off-the-Job Lost Workday Case rate was 0.439. Such a performance would not have been achieved without the recognition by the Du Pont "family" of the moral and economic implications of safety in the early years which continues to the present time.

JAMES R. THOMEN

June, 1991
Wilmington, DE

NOTES

1. E. I. Du Pont de Nemours & Company, Inc.
2. T. J. Peters and Nancy K. Austin, *A Passion for Excellence*, Random House, reprinted by Warner Books, Inc. New York, 1986, p. 332–334.

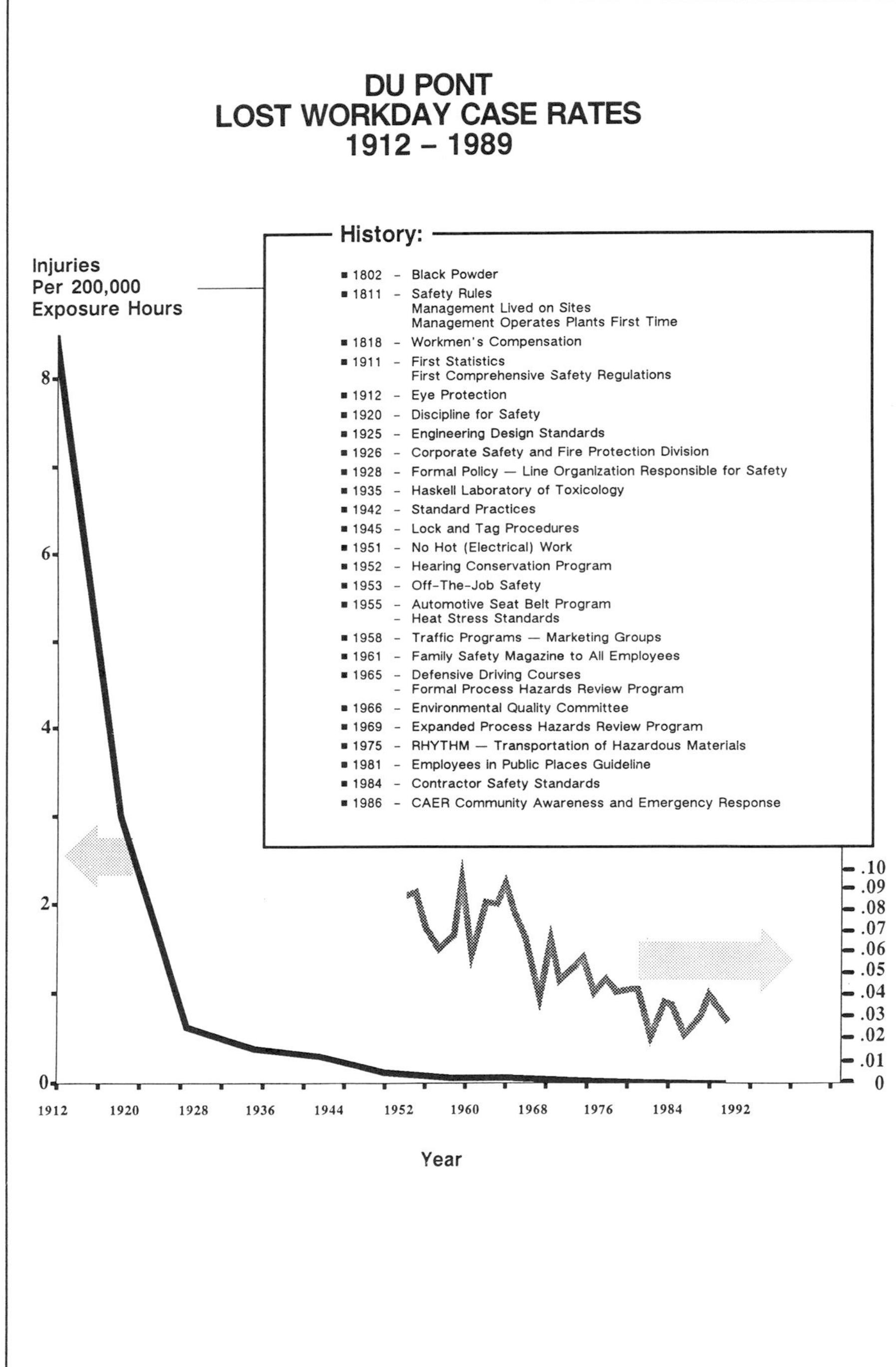
DU PONT
LOST WORKDAY CASE RATES
1912 – 1989
History:
■ 1802 – Black Powder
■ 1811 – Safety Rules
Management Lived on Sites
Management Operates Plants First Time
■ 1818 – Workmen's Compensation
■ 1911 – First Statistics
First Comprehensive Safety Regulations
■ 1912 – Eye Protection
■ 1920 – Discipline for Safety
■ 1925 – Engineering Design Standards
■ 1926 – Corporate Safety and Fire Protection Division
■ 1928 – Formal Policy — Line Organization Responsible for Safety
■ 1935 – Haskell Laboratory of Toxicology
■ 1942 – Standard Practices
■ 1945 – Lock and Tag Procedures
■ 1951 – No Hot (Electrical) Work
■ 1952 – Hearing Conservation Program
■ 1953 – Off-The-Job Safety
■ 1955 – Automotive Seat Belt Program
– Heat Stress Standards
■ 1958 – Traffic Programs — Marketing Groups
■ 1961 – Family Safety Magazine to All Employees
■ 1965 – Defensive Driving Courses
– Formal Process Hazards Review Program
■ 1966 – Environmental Quality Committee
■ 1969 – Expanded Process Hazards Review Program
■ 1975 – RHYTHM — Transportation of Hazardous Materials
■ 1981 – Employees in Public Places Guideline
■ 1984 – Contractor Safety Standards
■ 1986 – CAER Community Awareness and Emergency Response
Injuries
Per 200,000
Exposure Hours
8
6
4
2
0
.10
.09
.08
.07
.06
.05
.04
.03
.02
.01
0
1912
1920
1928
1936
1944
1952
1960
1968
1976
1984
1992
Year

Figure 1

Du Pont

LOST WORKDAY CASE RATES

Year Ending	Year Ending	Year Ending
1912-8.63	1956-.094	1973-.072
1920-3.00	1957-.085	1974-.047
1928-.640	1958-.074	1975-.052
1936-.404	1959-.080	1976-.058
1944-.322	1960-.088	1977-.043
1952-.144	1961-.090	1978-.055
1960-.088	1962-.071	1979-.040
1968-.084	1963-.062	1980-.051
1976-.058	1964-.067	1981-.044
1984-.032	1965-.105	1982-.020
1992-	1966-.065	1983-.035
	1967-.085	1984-.032
	1968-.084	1985-.020
	1969-.097	1986-.026
	1970-.079	1987-.041
	1971-.066	1988-.031
	1972-.043	1989-.024

Figure 2

ACKNOWLEDGEMENTS

The substance of this book is largely derived from work done at E.I. du Pont de Nemours & Co., Inc.—hereafter referred to simply as Du Pont—the world's largest (sales) chemical company based in Wilmington, Delaware, U.S.A., but truly a multinational company with plants and marketing organizations throughout the world. I was an employee of Du Pont during 1953–1985. From 1968 to retirement, I was employed as a plant or site manager. Since retirement I have worked as an independent contractor to Du Pont's Safety Management Services organization, consulting with Du Pont clients around the world engaged in a large variety of activities. This book reflects these experiences along with Du Pont's know-how in managing safety and my conviction that what Du Pont has accomplished, others can also accomplish—given their desire to do so.

The Du Pont family has put its indelible imprint upon the company and its employees. I want, therefore, to acknowledge fully the contribution which generations of Du Ponters have made to the company's understanding of safety management. I take full responsibility for my interpretation of this understanding as represented in this book. For Du Pont, safety is, indeed, a cultural imperative. I have liberally and unashamedly used Du Pont sources throughout the book. What I have learned about managing safety, I have learned though Du Pont. However, Du Pont has no responsibility for the content of the book. I am solely responsible for what has been included or excluded.

CLIENTS' CONTRIBUTION

To my clients, I am indebted for the realization that Du Pont's safety management process is sufficiently different from other safety management efforts to warrant recognition as a separate species. Beyond this, I am also indebted to my clients for the realization that this safety management process can be successfully transplanted into any organization which sincerely has the interests of its employees, its customers, its neighbors and the environment as a fundamental tenet of its business principles. After the successful transplant, those clients have also recognized that successfully managing safety is in the stockholder's interest. Where these interests have not been really adopted as fundamental tenets, the transplant is rejected. Fortunately for me, these cases have been few and have, in fact, occurred only in the public sector. This is not to suggest that somehow the public sector cannot improve safety performance. One of my most successful clients is in the public sector. The key ingredient which is necessary for a successful transplant is genuine dedication to achieving improvement, not whether the organization is public or private.

EDITORS' CONTRIBUTION

Several editors—Barbara Conover, Ellen Acosta, Tom Loid—have struggled with my writing. To each of them I have a debt that only I, my wife and daughter, and they can fully appreciate. Only we saw the original manuscript! Because of the many figures I have included in this book and the variety of sources from which they came, much editorial work was required. I am grateful to have had their indispensable assistance, skill, knowledge, and dedication to the end result. Thank you all.

FAMILY CONTRIBUTION

To my wife, Lydia, belongs the fundamental credit for this book. She has endured long periods of coping alone while I enjoyed the stimulus and exhilaration of new experiences with new processes, new environments and cultures, and new friends. Upon returning home we would discuss my experiences, and out of these discussions and her insight I came to recognize fully that good men and women in country after country, plant after plant, were sincerely trying to reduce the pain, suffering and costs related to employee injuries/illnesses. I came to recognize that Du Pont's methods worked outside Du Pont. I came to recognize that poor performance was not necessarily a result of lack of desire for improvement, but rather lack of knowledge of how to turn desire into results.

To my wife also goes the credit for encouraging me to pursue work after retirement, and safety management consulting, in particular, which has led to the writing of this book. To her also goes the credit for learning WordPerfect and for turning my hand writing into something legible.

Our daughter, Ellen, also typed a substantial part of my handwritten manuscript. I understand that she and her family have repaired the damage caused by arguments over "who is going to use the computer tonight?" To her husband, John, I owe a debt beyond measurement because of his patient, persistent coaching of his mother-in-law in the intricacies of learning to use a computer for word processing by long distance telephone.

JAMES R. THOMEN

COPYRIGHTS AND PERMISSIONS

The illustrative figures in this book came from a variety of sources, cited in the list below. I am grateful for the permission to use them.

Chapter 1

Page 4, Figure 1-1: E. G. Jefferson, "Safety Is Good Business," *Chemical & Engineering News*, November 17, 1986, p. 2. Reprinted with permission.

Pages 5-19, Figures 1-2 to 1-15: From *Accident Facts*, National Safety Council, 1990.

Pages 21-22, Figure 1-16: From Albert R. Karr et al., "OSHA Seeks to Fine Phillips Petroleum $5.7 Million Over Texas Explosions," *The Wall Street Journal*, April 27, 1990, p. A7. Reprinted with permission by *The Wall Street Journal*, (c) 1990 Dow Jones & Company, Inc. All rights reserved worldwide.

Pages 24-25, Figure 1-17: From John Mendeloff, "The Hazards of Rating Workplace Safety," *The Wall Journal*, February 11, 1988, p. A30. Reprinted with permission by *The Wall Street Journal*, (c) 1988 Dow Jones & Company, Inc. All rights reserved worldwide.

Chapter 2

Pages 36-37, Figure 2-1: From Peter F. Drucker, "Leadership: More Doing Than Dash," *The Wall Street Journal*, January 6, 1988, Op-Ed page. Reprinted with permission by *The Wall Street Journal*. (c) Dow Jones & Company, Inc. All rights reserved.

Page 38, Figure 2-2: From Vermont Royster, "Life with Barney at *The Wall Street Journal*," *The Wall Street Journal*, March 16, 1987, editorial page. Reprinted with permission of *The Wall Street Journal*. (c) 1987 Dow Jones & Company, Inc. All rights reserved worldwide.

Chapter 13

Page 344, Figure 13-1: From C. R. Reagan, "Choosing a Crew That'll Stay the Course," *The Wall Street Journal*, August 8, 1983, Editorial Page. Reprinted with permission of *The Wall Street Journal*. (c) 1983 Dow Jones & Company, Inc. All rights reserved.

Page 348, Figure 13-2: From Philip A. Alper, "A Doctor's View of Disability Claims," *The Wall Street Journal*, March 17, 1987, Op-Ed page. Reprinted with permission of *The Wall Street Journal*. (c) 1987 Dow Jones & Company, Inc. All rights reserved.

CHAPTER 1

WHY SAFETY?

SAFETY PAYS

Indeed, why safety? If you ask the average worker why he or she—or a fellow worker—gets injured, the worker will tell you "because we made some dumb mistake." If employees become injured "because of some dumb mistake" made by a worker, why should (note *should*, not *do*) employers become concerned about safety? Why should employers divert organizational assets—time and money—from the bottom line in order to try to keep an employee from making some "dumb mistake"? The only answer to this question is that "it is good business to do so!" That is, the bottom line is not diminished by "diverting" time, money, and conviction to the cause of safety, but rather the bottom line is enhanced. Of course, stating so does not prove the point. To some it may not be possible to prove the point.

The connection between "safety" performance and the input costs is not a simple one. Efforts taken today may not yield results until years later, and the results may not be recognized as being linked to the previous action taken years before. Calculations of costs saved by the avoidance of injuries or plant shutdowns or destruction of facilities are largely conjectural in nature and are viewed with skepticism by the doubting Thomases. On the other hand, for some there is no expenditure of assets (particularly money rather than time and effort) too large if it is made in the name of "safety." "After all, what is money compared to a person's life?"

I cannot unequivocally demonstrate that "x" amount of input will result in "y" bottom line improvement in a specified time frame, for not only can the association between "x" and "y" not be unequivocally established, but "x" and "y" cannot, themselves, be adequately established. This is at the micro level of detail. Although on a macro basis the task would appear easier, measurement problems remain. I will therefore not attempt to quantify an answer to the question of "Why Safety?"

However, I do not imply that for most employers there is no convincing evidence, however lacking in rigorousness.

The position of Du Pont on safety—"If we can't do it safely, we won't do it"—guided and sustained me, as a first-line supervisor, more than I ever care to have others know. When employee behavior was less than I expected I could almost always consider the problem in terms of safety. Because all the involved parties accepted that safety was inviolate, more appropriate behavior was normally forthcoming. Safety rules and standard operating procedures were the guideposts for normal operations. They were the authority when authority became necessary, as occasionally it did. My own confidence in my judgment—skill and knowledge—did not always suffice. My leadership skills did not always measure up to the task at hand. However, the concept that employees will not be put at risk did measure up. In this environment, where employee well-being was the first consideration to action, not only was excellence in safety achieved, but also mutual trust, cooperation and confidence was established. It comes as no surprise then that employees could then devote their entire energy, both physical and emotional, to getting the work done well, knowing that their management did not want production, cost, or quality results to be obtained at the expense of the employee's safety or health. We talked about "the only thing we want you to leave behind when you go home is your energy—no blood, no fingers, no eye-sight—just your energy which can be replenished while you are off." Without the solid rock of safety, I would not have been nearly as successful in establishing accepted leadership among a crew who knew more about the processes involved and how "the system works" than I did. I am confident that we produced more product, of higher quality, and at lower costs, than would have been the case in a less demanding safety environment.

A specific anecdote may be illustrative of this belief that safety is good business—that "safety pays, it does not cost." While assigned as an assistant plant manager, a research supervisor who had a high potential for advancement was assigned to me. The assignment was designed to give him manufacturing and some marketing exposure before moving up the ladder. In this assignment he was responsible for new process and product development, technical assistance to production and quality control—assuring customer satisfaction with our products. Several years later when I was a plant manager and he had become my boss he informed me that I was being reassigned as manager at another plant. He explained that my task was to "straighten out their safety." He said nothing about quality, production, costs, or employee relations.

This was in January. The plant to which I was being assigned had had a lost workday injury during the previous quarter. It was the first lost workday injury the plant had experienced, including start-up, some 14 years earlier. The plant population was about 800 employees. Aside from my reaction to yet another move, I was very pleased to see that he had learned the fundamentals—"get safety and you'll get the rest."

Four years later, we once again had demonstrated this truism—no lost workday injuries, substantially improved total recordable injuries, improved off-the-job lost workday incidence rates, higher plant productivity, improved quality and cost performance, and measurably significant improvement in employee relations. Management attention to the safety and health of employees yields improved results across the board, efficaciously.

On October 15, 1986, E. G. Jefferson, then recently retired as Chairman and Chief Executive Officer of Du Pont was awarded the Chemical Industry Medal of the American Section of the Society of the Chemical Industry. In his acceptance speech he chose to speak about safety—not about the myriad other aspects of the chemical industry in a global market. The *Chemical and Engineering News* printed an excerpt from this address on its editorial page in its November 17, 1986, issue. I have included this excerpt as Figure 1-1 as yet another testimonial from that body of believers that safety is good business.

This recognition that safety is good business—that attention to safety not only improves safety performance but other aspects of the business as well, continues to occur as Du Pont Safety Management Services clients become proficient in making the safety culture transplant work. In less than a year after working with a research organization, a director of research commented to me that "I really was not convinced that safety deserved more of my time and energy, but today safety is fun. I'm enjoying the effort I put into safety and my effectiveness with the organization has been increased enormously. I've become a fanatic on the subject. I've been working on "quality" for three years and I still don't know what I'm doing. Very frustrating." The connection between safety and employee well-being is perhaps more easily established than is the connection between employee well-being and quality. In the sense of Total Quality, doing a quality safety job is a part of doing a quality job, because safety is a part of the total job. In my consulting work, the safety area appears to jell more readily than the total quality concept. The specificity of safety perhaps accounts for this observed difference.

While hard data may not be available regarding why safety? some data on the impact of injuries and other manifestation of the failure of safety management are available. The National Safety Council's annual *Accident Facts* booklet provides a good summary of such statistics. Several pages from the 1989 Edition are shown in Figures 1-2 through 1-15. Data on nonwork-related injuries have been included because much of the costs of such injuries are, in fact, borne by employers. The costs shown in Figures 1-3 and 1-4 tend to be underestimated because they do not include all costs associated with the injury (see chapter footnotes).

The multiplicity of safety statistics can be confusing. Both the National Safety Council (NSC) and the Bureau of Labor Statistics (BLS) publish data; both acknowledge that the data are best estimates. The National Health Interview Survey conducted by the U.S. Public Health Service is yet another source of injury information. Probably the most accurate estimate of the cost per work-related disabling injury is obtained by dividing the NSC estimate of the total cost of work-related injuries ($48.5 billion in 1989) by the estimated number of work-related disabling injuries (1.7 million in 1989). This calculation yields $28,500, a number that is consistent with results obtained by independent analyses of work-related disabling injury experiences for individual companies. Applying this cost number to individual company and/or location data for

text continues on page 20

Safety is good business

Edward G. Jefferson retired earlier this year as chairman and chief executive officer of Du Pont. Last month in New York City he was awarded the Chemical Industry Medal of the American Section of the Society of the Chemical Industry. The following are excerpts from the prepared text of his acceptance speech.

Safety is good business in many ways. If you tour an operation that has demonstrated good, sustained safety performance, you will usually find the added benefits of good housekeeping, good product quality, and high morale. For the analysis and training that are essential to good safety bring also the benefits of superior operational control. The costs of injuries in terms of human suffering, the high costs of associated litigation, the costs of equipment damage and outage—all these can seriously threaten the health and reputation of the enterprise. Prevention is the only acceptable remedy.

As in all walks of life, very occasionally we can encounter the completely unexpected, as a result of limits in our knowledge or culpable human error. Yet these too are avoidable—they will yield to the adequacy of basic data, plant design, and operating systems, and to good training and wise human relations.

Safety provides us with a valuable corporate asset, one that brings much good will. Private-sector, multinational companies exist in the context of a social contract based on mutual benefit with the public and the governments in the countries in which they operate. To continue to manufacture in complex and potentially hazardous systems requires that we conduct ourselves in a manner that rewards the public's trust.

This is also the case when we work in other countries. Commitment to safety can enhance the image of American companies overseas. At Du Pont we make no concessions to culture when it comes to safety, and we have found that safety is fully transferable across cultures if you have the patience, tact, and will to insist on it. We have proof that it works: Last year, for the first time, our international operations surpassed our domestic operations in safety performance.

All these benefits are available to every company in every industry. But I believe it is essential that the chemical industry continue to obligate itself to the highest standard of safety possible. In a society increasingly suspicious of what we do, frequently misunderstanding why we do it, and often ignorant of who ultimately benefits, we have to communicate broadly the essential role of industrial chemistry in modern life. We must have an indisputable, positive message, and my years in this industry have convinced me that a good safety record is one of the most affirmative messages that chemical companies can convey to the world.

Today at Du Pont, no process is designed, no product manufactured, and no job performed without safety engineered into it. Safety is considered at the inception of everything we set out to do. And it is one of the chief factors determining whether or not we continue doing it.

[Du Pont's] basic philosophy [is] that every accident is preventable. And we will continue to view safety as good business and as fundamental to the continuing interaction among the company, its employees, customers, and the communities in which we operate.

Finally, as we look ahead at the new horizons for our industry, we all see many opportunities at home and abroad. I commend an unswerving attention to safety as an essential ingredient for the full realization of these opportunities, to help assure strong international competitiveness and to build a better public reputation. □

Figure 1–1

ALL ACCIDENTS, 1989

For the eighth consecutive year, accidental deaths were estimated to number less than 100,000 in 1989. The death total was 94,500, a decrease of 2,000 or 2 per cent from the 1988 total of 96,500. An increase in public deaths was offset by decreases in work and motor-vehicle. Home deaths were unchanged.

The death rate per 100,000 population, 38.1, was down 3 per cent from the rate of 39.3 in 1988. The population rate for 1989 work deaths is the lowest on record. The 1989 motor-vehicle death rate per 100 million miles (not shown below) was 2.25, also the lowest on record.

	Deaths	Change from 1988	Deaths per 100,000 Persons	Disabling Injuries[a]
All Classes[b]	**94,500**	**-2%**	**38.1**	**9,000,000**
Motor-vehicle	**46,900**	**-4%**	**18.9**	**1,700,000**
Public nonwork	42,800			1,500,000
Work	3,900			200,000
Home	200			([c])
Work	**10,400**	**-4%**	**4.2**	**1,700,000**
Nonmotor-vehicle	6,500			1,500,000
Motor-vehicle	3,900			200,000
Home	**22,500**	**0%**	**9.1**	**3,400,000**
Nonmotor-vehicle	22,300			3,400,000
Motor-vehicle	200			([c])
Public	**19,000**	**+3%**	**7.7**	**2,400,000**

Disabling Injuries[a] by Severity of Injury, 1989

Severity of Disabling Injury	TOTAL[b]	Motor-Vehicle	Work	Home	Public
All Disabling Injuries[a]	**9,000,000**	**1,700,000**	**1,700,000**	**3,400,000**	**2,400,000**
Permanent impairments	340,000	140,000	60,000	90,000	60,000
Temporary total disabilities	8,600,000	1,600,000	1,600,000	3,300,000	2,300,000

Source: National Safety Council estimates (rounded) based on data from the National Center for Health Statistics, state industrial commissions, state traffic authorities, state departments of health, insurance companies, industrial establishments and other sources. See glossary on page 105 for definitions.

[a]**Disabling beyond the day of accident.** Injuries are not reported on a national basis, so the totals shown are approximations based on ratios of disabling injuries to deaths developed from special studies. The totals are the best estimates for the current year; however, they should not be compared with totals shown in previous editions of *Accident Facts* to indicate year-to-year changes or trends.

[b]Deaths and injuries above for the four separate classes total more than national figures due to rounding and because some deaths and injuries are included in more than one class. For example, 3,900 work deaths involved motor vehicles and are in both the work and motor-vehicle totals; and 200 motor-vehicle deaths occurred on home premises and are in both home and motor-vehicle. The total of such duplication amounted to about 4,100 deaths and 200,000 injuries in 1989.

[c]Less than 10,000.

Figure 1-2

Costs of accidents in 1989

Accidents in which deaths or disabling injuries occurred, together with vehicle accidents and fires, cost the nation in 1989, at least

$148.5 billion

Motor-vehicle accidents . . . . **$72.2 billion**

This cost figure includes wage loss, medical expense, insurance administration cost, and insured property damage from moving motor-vehicle accidents. Not included are the cost of public agencies such as police and fire departments, courts, indirect losses to employers of off-the-job accidents to employees, the value of cargo losses in commercial vehicles, and damages awarded in excess of direct losses. Fire damage to parked motor-vehicles is not included here but is distributed to the other classes.

Work accidents . . . . **$48.5 billion**

This cost figure includes wage loss, medical expense, insurance administration cost, fire loss, and an estimate of indirect costs arising out of work accidents. Not included is the value of property damage other than fire loss, and indirect loss from fires.

Home accidents. . . . . **$18.2 billion**

This cost figure includes wage loss, medical expense, health insurance administration cost, and fire loss. Not included are the costs of property damage other than fire loss, and the indirect cost to employers of off-the-job accidents to employees.

Public accidents . . . . **$12.5 billion**

This cost figure includes wage loss, medical expense, health insurance administration cost, and fire loss. Not included are the costs of property damage other than fire loss, and the indirect cost to employers of off-the-job accidents to employees.

Certain Costs of Accidents by Class, 1989 ($ billions)

Cost	TOTAL[a]	Motor-Vehicle	Work	Home	Public Nonmotor-Vehicle
Total	**$148.5**	**$72.2**	**$48.5**	**$18.2**	**$12.5**
Wage loss	37.7	19.5	8.3	6.1	5.5
Medical expense	23.7	5.2	8.1	6.6	5.0
Insurance administration[b]	28.4	20.7	6.1	0.9	0.7
Fire loss	9.4	([c])	3.5	4.6	1.3
Motor-vehicle property damage	26.8	26.8	([c])	([c])	([c])
Indirect work loss	22.5	([c])	22.5	([c])	([c])

Source: National Safety Council estimates. Cost estimates are not comparable with those of previous years. As additional or more precise data become available, they are used from that year forward, but previously estimated figures are not revised.

[a]Duplications between work and motor-vehicle and home and motor-vehicle are eliminated in the totals.

[b]Home and public insurance administration costs may include costs of administering medical treatment claims for some motor-vehicle injuries filed through health insurance plans.

[c]Not included, see comments by class of accident above.

Figure 1-3

1989 accident cost components

TOTAL—ALL ACCIDENTS[a] .... $148.5 billion

These costs include:

Wage loss .... **$37.7 billion**

Since, theoretically, a worker's contribution to the wealth of the nation is measured in terms of wages, then the total of wages lost due to accidents provides a measure of this lost productivity. For nonfatal injuries, actual wage losses are used; for fatalities and permanent disabilities, the figure used is the present value of all future earnings lost.

Medical expense .... **$23.7 billion**

Doctor fees, hospital charges, the cost of medicines, ambulance and emergency medical services, and future medical costs incurred as the result of accidental injuries are included.

Insurance administration cost .... **$28.4 billion**

This is the difference between premiums paid to insurance companies and claims paid out by them; it is their cost of doing business and is a part of the accident cost total. Claims paid by insurance companies are not identified separately, as every claim is compensation for losses such as wages, medical expenses, property damage, etc., which are included in other categories above and below. *Not* included are administrative costs of health maintenance organizations and property damage claims in home and public accidents.

Property damage in motor-vehicle accidents .... **$26.8 billion**

Includes the value of insured property damage to vehicles from moving motor-vehicle accidents. The damage is valued at the cost to repair the vehicle or the market value of the vehicle when damage exceeds its market value. The cost of minor damage (such as scratches or dents incurred while parking) is considered part of the normal wear and tear to vehicles and is not included.

Fire loss .... **$ 9.4 billion**

Includes losses from building fires of $8.1 billion and from nonbuilding fires, of $1.3 billion. By class of accident these totals break down as follows: building—work $2.9 billion, home $4.4 billion, public $0.8 billion; nonbuilding—work $0.6 billion, home $0.2 billion, public $0.5 billion.

Indirect loss from work accidents .... **$22.5 billion**

This is the money value of time lost by noninjured workers. Includes time spent filling out accident reports, giving first aid to injured workers, and time lost due to production slowdowns. This loss is conservatively estimated as equal to the sum of lost wages, medical expenses, and insurance administration cost of work accidents.

See source and footnotes on page 2.

Figure 1–4

Trends in accidental death rates

(See pages 26 and 27 for death totals and crude rates.)

Between 1912 and 1989, accidental deaths per 100,000 population were reduced 54 per cent from 82 to 38. The 76 per cent reduction from 79 to 19 in the nonmotor-vehicle death rate was offset in part by the sixfold increase in the motor-vehicle death rate from 3 to 19. The reduction in the overall rate during a period when the nation's population more than doubled has resulted in 3,100,000 fewer people being killed accidentally than would have been killed if the rate had not been reduced.

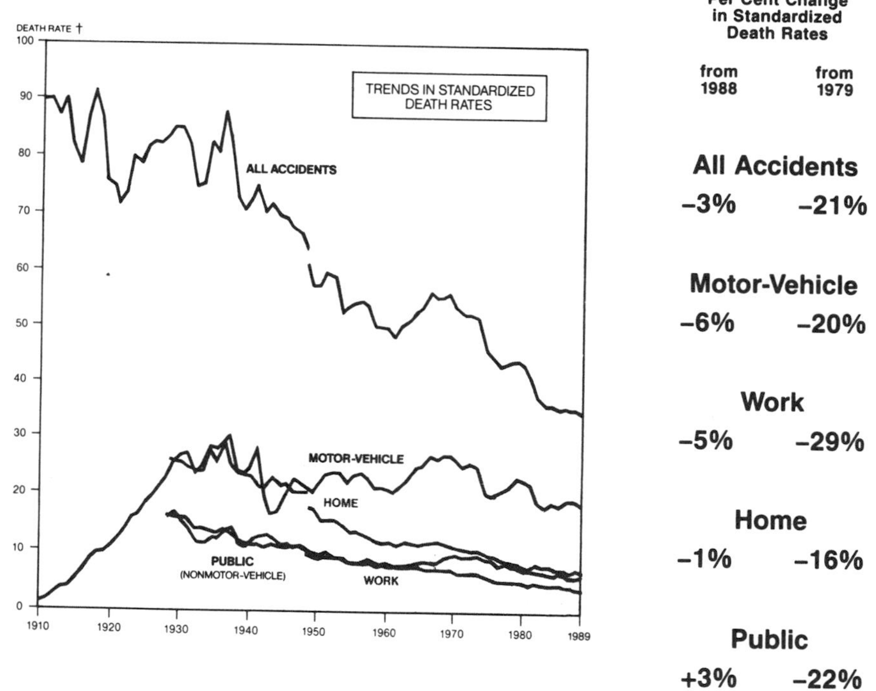

The age distribution of the population has changed greatly during this century, and these shifts can affect the accidental death rate. For example, if the proportion of the population aged 75 years and over increases, the overall accidental death rate will also tend to increase since the 75 and over age group has a much higher than average death rate. In order to eliminate the effects of population shifts over long periods of time, death rates can be standardized to the age distribution of the population in any one particular year (chosen as 1940). The 1989 standardized death rate of 34.7 per 100,000 population for all accidents was 3 per cent below the 1988 rate. The 1989 rates for motor-vehicle, work, and home showed decreases, while public showed an increase. Standardized death rates from 1910 to 1989 are shown in the chart above.

†Deaths per 100,000 population, adjusted to 1940 age distribution. The break at 1948 shows the estimated effect of classification changes.

Figure 1-5

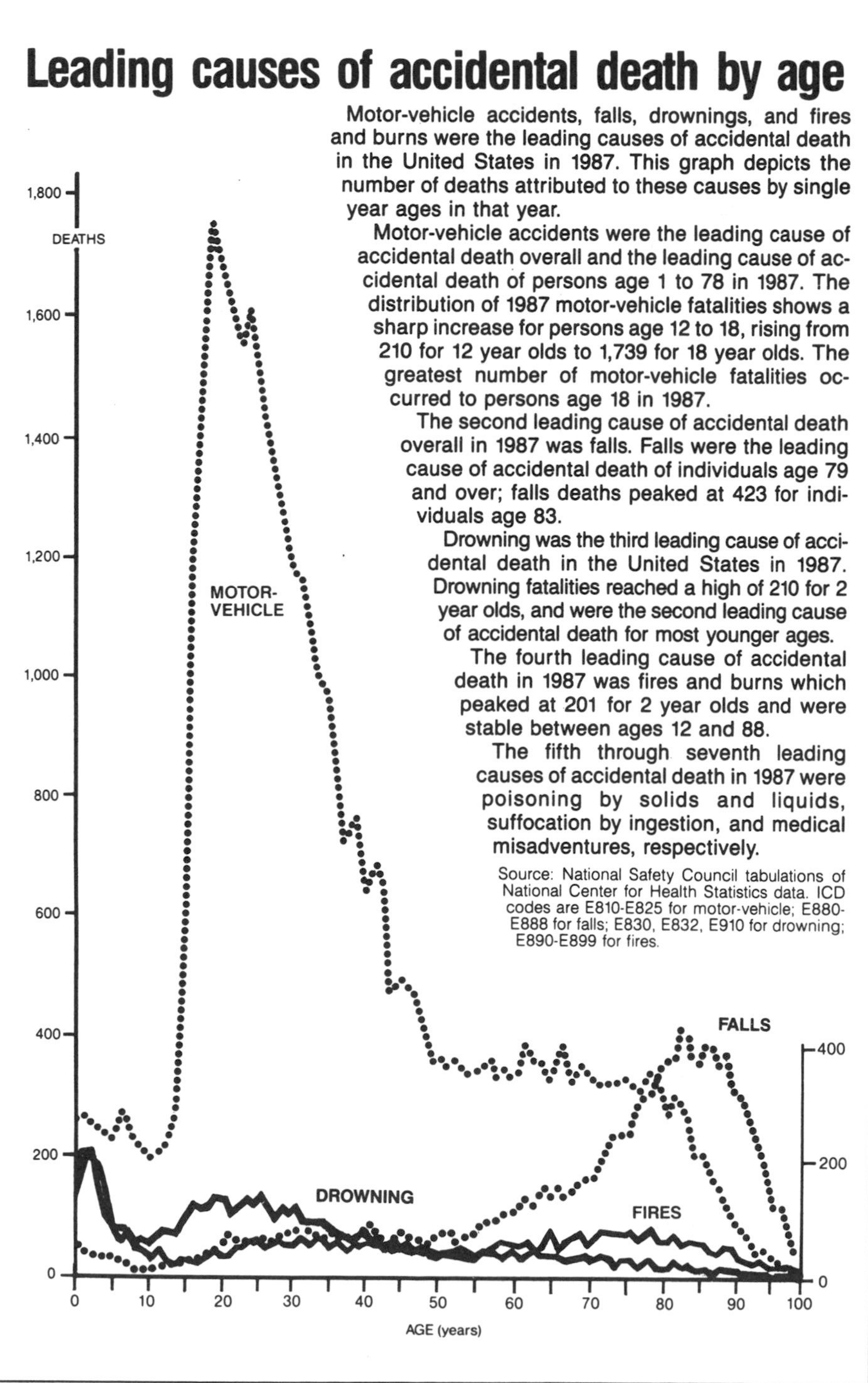
Leading causes of accidental death by age
Motor-vehicle accidents, falls, drownings, and fires and burns were the leading causes of accidental death in the United States in 1987. This graph depicts the number of deaths attributed to these causes by single year ages in that year.
Motor-vehicle accidents were the leading cause of accidental death overall and the leading cause of accidental death of persons age 1 to 78 in 1987. The distribution of 1987 motor-vehicle fatalities shows a sharp increase for persons age 12 to 18, rising from 210 for 12 year olds to 1,739 for 18 year olds. The greatest number of motor-vehicle fatalities occurred to persons age 18 in 1987.
The second leading cause of accidental death overall in 1987 was falls. Falls were the leading cause of accidental death of individuals age 79 and over; falls deaths peaked at 423 for individuals age 83.
Drowning was the third leading cause of accidental death in the United States in 1987. Drowning fatalities reached a high of 210 for 2 year olds, and were the second leading cause of accidental death for most younger ages.
The fourth leading cause of accidental death in 1987 was fires and burns which peaked at 201 for 2 year olds and were stable between ages 12 and 88.
The fifth through seventh leading causes of accidental death in 1987 were poisoning by solids and liquids, suffocation by ingestion, and medical misadventures, respectively.
Source: National Safety Council tabulations of National Center for Health Statistics data. ICD codes are E810-E825 for motor-vehicle; E880-E888 for falls; E830, E832, E910 for drowning; E890-E899 for fires.
DEATHS
1,800
1,600
1,400
1,200
1,000
800
600
400
200
0
MOTOR-
VEHICLE
FALLS
DROWNING
FIRES
400
200
0
0 10 20 30 40 50 60 70 80 90 100
AGE (years)

Figure 1-6

Work accident costs

The true cost to the nation, to employers, and to individuals of work related deaths and injuries is much greater than the cost of workers' compensation insurance alone. The figures presented below show the National Safety Council's estimates of the total costs of occupational deaths and injuries. Uninsured costs are estimated, conservatively, to be equal to insured costs. The Council recommends, however, that each organization establish its own ratio of uninsured to insured costs through a study of its own experience. Guidance for such a study is contained in the Council's *Accident Prevention Manual.*

TOTAL COST IN 1989 .... $48.5 billion

Includes wage losses of $8.3 billion, insurance administrative costs of $6.1 billion, and medical costs of $8.1 billion. Includes uninsured costs of $22.5 billion such as the money value of time lost by workers other than those with disabling injuries, who are directly or indirectly involved in accidents, and the cost of the time required to investigate accidents, write up accident reports, etc. Also includes fire losses of $3.5 billion, but excludes the cost of other property damage.

Cost per Worker $420

This figure indicates the value of goods or services each worker must produce to offset the cost of work injuries. It is *not* the average cost of a work injury.

Cost per Death $610,000

Cost per Disabling Injury $18,000

These figures include estimates of wage losses, medical expenses, insurance administration costs, and uninsured costs, and exclude any property damage costs.

Time lost because of work injuries

DAYS LOST

TOTAL TIME LOST IN 1989 75,000,000

Due to Accidents in 1989 35,000,000

Includes primarily the actual time lost during the year from disabling injuries, except that it does not include time lost on the day of the injury or time required for further medical treatment or checkup following the injured person's return to work.

Fatalities are included at an average loss of 150 days per case, and permanent impairments are included at actual days lost plus an allowance for lost efficiency resulting from the impairment.

Not included is time lost by persons with nondisabling injuries or other persons directly or indirectly involved in accidents.

Due to Accidents in Prior Years 40,000,000

This is an indicator of the productive time lost in 1989 due to permanently disabling injuries that occurred in prior years.

TIME LOSS IN FUTURE YEARS FROM 1989 ACCIDENTS 90,000,000

Includes time lost in future years due to on-the-job deaths and permanently disabling injuries that occurred in 1989.

Figure 1-7

Occupational fatality estimates

There are three commonly cited estimates of occupational fatalities. Each is quite different from the others not only in magnitude but also in scope and coverage. There are significant differences not only in what is counted, but also in the population covered, data sources, and methods. To use them properly, it is necessary to understand what they mean and how they were made.

National Safety Council[a]. The Council's estimate, 10,400 for 1989, covers unintentional injury deaths (ICD underlying cause of death codes E800–E949) of persons in the public and private civilian work force, age 14 and over, who were wage or salary workers (excluding private household workers), self-employed, or unpaid family workers. The non-motor-vehicle portion of the most recent (1987) National Center for Health Statistics (NCHS) death certificate tabulation by external cause and age group was apportioned into three major classes—work, home, and public—using factors determined from special studies. The work-motor-vehicle duplication was estimated from occupant deaths by type of vehicle, as reported by state traffic authorities, and added to the non-motor-vehicle work deaths to obtain the total. Because the NCHS tabulations were for 1987, state vital statistics and workers' compensation data were used to bring the estimates up to the current year using the link relative technique.

Bureau of Labor Statistics[b]. The BLS estimate, 3,300 for 1988, covers deaths due to injuries and illnesses that result from a work accident or from an exposure in the work environment in private sector employers with 11 or more employees (about two thirds of the total workforce). The estimate was obtained through an annual statistical survey of about 280,000 establishments stratified by industry and employment size category. The relative standard error of the fatality estimate is 7 per cent.

National Institute for Occupational Safety and Health[c]. The NIOSH estimate, about 6,400 in 1985, covers traumatic injuries (intentional and unintentional) of persons 16 years of age and older. It was made by counting death certificates obtained directly from the states using three criteria: (a) injury as an immediate, underlying or contributing cause of death (ICD codes E800–E999), (b) 16 years of age or older, and (c) a positive response to the "injury at work" item on the death certificate.

Discussion. Reconciliation of these three estimates involves adjusting for differences in definitions, coverage, sources, and methods. More fundamentally, however, all the estimates depend on the accuracy of the underlying record keeping systems. Considerable work is needed to improve these systems.

The Council and NIOSH estimates rely on the accuracy with which the death certificate is completed. It is well known that not all work-related fatalities can be identified with death certificates alone, or even in combination with workers' compensation reports[d]. The NIOSH estimate is probably understated because of death certificates with the "injury at work" item left blank or where the work association was missed by the certifier and the item was marked "no."

The BLS estimate relies on the accuracy of employers' records of work-related deaths and, especially in the case of occupational illnesses, the employer's ability to recognize the work relationship. Furthermore, "because fatalities are difficult to measure in an establishment survey, BLS believes the count significantly understates the work-related fatalities for the year."[b]

[a]National Safety Council Statistics Department. (1982). *Documentation of National Safety Council statistics department estimating procedures for motor-vehicle, work, home, and public deaths and death rates.* Chicago: Author.

[b]Bureau of Labor Statistics. (November 15, 1989). *BLS reports on survey of occupational injuries and illnesses in 1988.* (News Release USDL-89-548). Washington, DC: U.S. Department of Labor.

[c]National Institute for Occupational Safety and Health. (March 1989 Revised). *National traumatic occupational fatalities, 1980-1985.* Morgantown, W. V.: Author.

[d]Baker, S.P., Samkoff, J.S., Fisher, R.S., & Van Buren, C.B. (1982). Fatal occupational injuries. *The Journal of the American Medical Association, 248*(6), 692-697.

Figure 1-8

WORK ACCIDENTS, 1989

Between 1912 and 1989, accidental work deaths per 100,000 population were reduced 81 per cent, from 21 to 4. In 1912, an estimated 18,000 to 21,000 workers' lives were lost. In 1989, in a work force more than triple in size and producing 11 times the goods and services, there were only 10,400 work deaths.

	Workers[a] (000)	Deaths	Death Rates[b]	Disabling Injuries[a]
All Industries	**116,700**	**10,400**[c]	**9**	**1,700,000**
Agriculture[d]	**3,200**	**1,300**	**40**[e]	**120,000**
Mining, quarrying[d]	**700**	**300**	**43**	**30,000**
Construction	**6,500**	**2,100**	**32**	**190,000**
Manufacturing	**19,500**	**1,100**	**6**	**340,000**
Transportation and public utilities	**5,900**	**1,400**	**24**	**140,000**
Trade[d]	**27,400**	**1,100**	**4**	**340,000**
Services[d]	**36,200**	**1,500**	**4**	**300,000**
Government	**17,300**	**1,600**	**9**	**240,000**

Source: National Safety Council estimates (rounded) based on data from the National Center for Health Statistics, state vital statistics departments (see page 16), and state industrial commissions. Numbers of workers are based on Bureau of Labor Statistics data and include persons aged 14 and over.

[a]See definitions on page 105. [b]Deaths per 100,000 workers in each group.

[c]About 3,900 of the deaths and 200,000 of the injuries involved motor vehicles.

[d]Agriculture includes forestry and fishing; see also page 100. Mining and quarrying includes oil and gas extraction (preliminary MSHA reports indicate 115 deaths in coal, metal, and nonmetal mining in 1989). Trade includes wholesale and retail trade. Services includes finance, insurance and real estate.

[e]Agriculture rate excludes deaths of persons under 14 years of age. Rates for other industry divisions do not require this adjustment. Deaths of persons under 14 are included in the agriculture death total.

Workers, Deaths and Death Rates

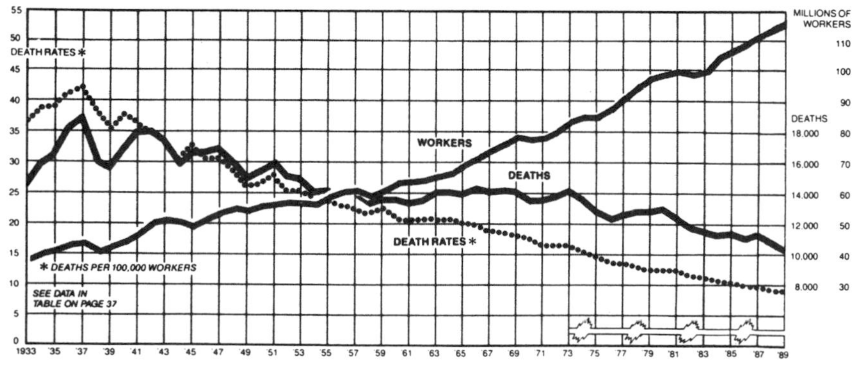

Figure 1-9

Worker deaths and injuries on and off the job

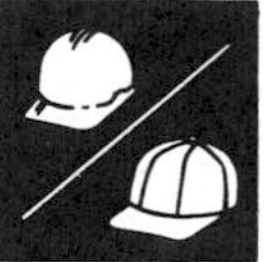

Three out of four deaths, and more than half of the injuries suffered by workers in 1989 occurred off the job. The ratios of off-the-job deaths and injuries to on-the-job were 3.5 to 1 and 1.6 to 1, respectively. Production time lost due to off-the-job accidents totaled about 60,000,000 days in 1989, compared with 35,000,000 days lost by workers injured on the job. Production time lost in future years due to off-the-job accidents in 1989 will total an estimated 280,000,000 days, more than three times the 90,000,000 days lost in future years from on-the-job accidents. Off-the-job accidents to workers cost the nation at least $45.8 billion in 1989.

Procedures for allocating the time spent on and off the job were revised for the 1990 edition. Death and injury rates in the table below are not comparable to rate estimates prior to this edition.

Place	Deaths		Disabling Injuries	1989 Rates[a]	
	1989	1988	1989	Deaths	Injuries
On and Off the Job	**47,300**	**47,800**	**4,500,000**	**.07**	**6.5**
On the Job	**10,400**	**10,800**	**1,700,000**	**.04**	**6.8**
Off the Job	**36,900**	**37,000**	**2,800,000**	**.08**	**6.3**
Motor-vehicle	23,300	24,100	900,000	.50	19.3
Public nonmotor-vehicle	6,800	6,400	900,000	.09	12.4
Home	6,800	6,500	1,000,000	.02	3.1

Source: National Safety Council estimates.

[a]Per 1,000,000 hours exposure, by place.

Part of body injured in work accidents

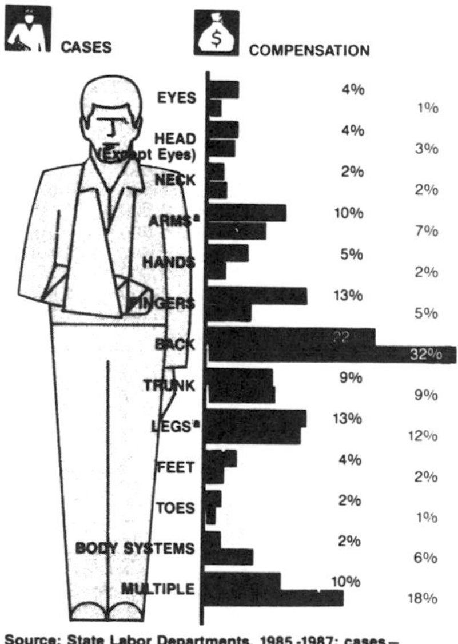

Source: State Labor Departments, 1985-1987; cases—21 States, compensation—12 States.
[a]Includes multiple or NEC extremity injuries amounting to about 1 per cent of the total cases and compensation.

Disabling work injuries in the entire nation totaled approximately 1,700,000 in 1989. Of these, about 10,400 were fatal and 60,000 resulted in some permanent impairment.

Injuries to the back occurred most frequently, followed by thumb and finger injuries and leg injuries, according to state labor department reports. See pages 35 and 43 for other compensation figures.

Eyes	**70,000**
Head (except eyes)	**70,000**
Neck	**30,000**
Arms[a]	**170,000**
Hands	**90,000**
Fingers	**220,000**
Back	**380,000**
Trunk	**150,000**
Legs[a]	**220,000**
Feet	**70,000**
Toes	**30,000**
Body Systems	**30,000**
Multiple	**170,000**

Figure 1–10

Workers' Compensation Cases

According to the Social Security Administration, an estimated $27,350 million was paid out under workers' compensation in 1987, an increase of 11 per cent from 1986. Of this total, $17,450 million was for income benefits and $9,940 million was for medical costs.

Both income benefits and medical payments increased in 1987. Black lung payments decreased by about 2.4 per cent. The 1987 total of approximately 88.4 million workers covered by workers' compensation increased by about 2.4 million from 1986. About 87 per cent of all wage and salary workers were covered in 1987.

The table below shows the trend in the number of compensated or reported cases in each reporting state or province. Due to the differences in population, industries, and coverage of compensation laws, comparison between states should not be made.

State or Province	Deaths[a]			Total Cases[a]			1987 Compensation Paid ($ 000)
	1989	1988	1987	1989	1988	1987	
Alabama	180	165	128	40,863	41,394	39,192	273,765
Alaska	32	36	45	31,742	25,990	24,123	139,367
Arizona	86	81	89	166,908	...	140,159	222,355
Arkansas	125	116	112	19,706	18,250	17,735	160,019
California	...	218	339	...	437,293	400,820	4,250,941
Connecticut	57	58	109	50,153	51,032	42,289	433,535
Florida	...	173	179	...	86,742	84,359	1,178,113
Georgia	228	226	297	293,744	306,663	295,752	510,062
Hawaii	...	46	45	...	50,101	43,108	137,028
Idaho	47	30	46	41,617	38,049	35,770	70,343
Indiana	93	105	114	87,249	74,341	70,674	201,532
Iowa	...	...	89	...	...	28,930	140,734
Kansas	69	96	88	72,674	69,933	67,386	174,953
Kentucky	...	104	136	...	41,119	39,463	274,434
Maryland[c]	...	103	74	...	18,716	16,528	373,756
Michigan	...	65	73	...	64,111	64,745	885,398
Minnesota	142	145	167	56,678	54,415	47,509	489,541
Mississippi	137	135	125	20,575	20,176	18,963	136,787
Missouri	168	148	130	193,188	185,570	182,628	320,379
Montana[c]	35	38	38	29,699	28,613	26,060	138,346
Nebraska	67	66	45	70,996	65,158	58,401	87,537
Nevada	46	34	29	99,348	94,482	73,415	180,204
New Hampshire	...	...	32	...	...	71,634	128,392
New York	...	829	858	...	553,484	548,329	1,206,565
North Carolina	139	180	168	75,810	73,020	68,107	271,990
Ohio	...	...	230	...	...	138,761	1,561,937
Oregon[b]	75	82	78	39,354	43,660	41,033	509,584
Pennsylvania	237	267	291	148,445	146,461	139,706	1,271,742
South Dakota	...	...	25	...	...	21,527	35,557
Virginia[b]	103	77	51	43,146	46,522	43,575	354,154
Wisconsin	123	130	135	77,391	76,917	68,369	368,910
Alberta[b]	...	119[d]	121	58,022[d]	59,735[d]	58,159	...
British Columbia[b]	...	212[d]	190	...	147,518[d]	126,479	...
Manitoba[b]	...	46[d]	50	...	40,307[d]	40,204	...
New Brunswick[b]	...	26[d]	29	...	33,474[d]	25,073	...
Newfoundland[b]	...	24[d]	24	21,646[d]	18,782[d]	17,377	...
Northwest Territories[b]	...	8[d]	7	...	3,413[d]	3,063	...
Nova Scotia[b]	...	53[d]	7	...	37,345[d]	26,688	...
Ontario[b]	...	502[d]	498	...	443,123[d]	431,249	...
Prince Edward Island[b]	...	1[d]	3	...	4,643[d]	3,860	...
Quebec[b]	...	119[d]	132	...	257,617[d]	263,889	...
Saskatchewan[b]	...	23[d]	27	...	33,319[d]	36,785	...
Yukon[b]	...	4[d]	2	...	2,000[d]	1,661	...

Source: Deaths and cases—State and provincial workers' compensation authorities for calendar or fiscal year. Costs—*Social Security Bulletin*, 1990, 53 (4), 2-11. States not listed did not respond to survey.
Definitions: *Reported cases*—a reported case may or may not be work-related and may not receive compensation. *Compensated cases*—a compensated case is one determined to be work-related and for which compensation was paid.
[a]Reported cases involving medical and indemnity benefits, unless otherwise noted.
[b]Closed or compensated cases. [c]Medical benefit cases only. [d]Preliminary.

Figure 1-11

OSHA occupational injuries and illnesses

The tables below and on pages 46 and 47 are from the 1988 survey of occupational injuries and illnesses conducted by the Bureau of Labor Statistics, U.S. Department of Labor. These figures are *not comparable* to the National Health Interview Survey data on page 13 due to differences in definitions nor to National Safety Council estimates on pages 1, 34, and 38 due to differences in definitions and employment coverage (OSHA excludes unpaid family workers, some self-employed, and farms with less than 11 employees).

OSHA incidence rates are based on cases or days per 100 full-time workers using 200,000 employee hours as the equivalent. Other definitions (see below) affect which cases are counted and how they are classified.

BLS Estimates of Occupational Injury and Illness Incidence Rates by Industry Division, 1987–1988

Industry Division	Incidence Rates[c]							
	Total Cases[d]		Lost Workday Cases		Nonfatal Cases Without Lost Workdays		Lost Workdays	
	1988	1987	1988	1987	1988	1987	1988	1987
Private Sector[c]	**8.6**	**8.3**	**4.0**	**3.8**	**4.6**	**4.4**	**76.1**	**69.9**
Agriculture, forestry, and fishing[e]	10.9	11.2	5.6	5.7	5.2	5.5	101.8	94.1
Mining	8.8	8.5	5.1	4.9	3.6	3.6	152.1	144.0
Construction	14.6	14.7	6.8	6.8	7.7	7.9	142.2	135.8
Manufacturing	13.1	11.9	5.7	5.3	7.3	6.7	107.4	95.5
Transportation and public utilities	8.9	8.4	5.1	4.9	3.8	3.5	118.6	108.1
Wholesale and retail trade	7.8	7.7	3.5	3.4	4.3	4.3	60.9	56.1
Finance, insurance, and real estate	2.0	2.0	0.9	0.9	1.1	1.1	17.2	14.3
Services	5.4	5.5	2.6	2.7	2.8	2.8	47.7	45.8

See source and footnotes below.

OSHA Definitions

(See BLS *Recordkeeping Guidelines for Occupational Injuries and Illnesses,* September 1986)

Occupational injury is any injury such as a cut, fracture, sprain, amputation, etc., which results from a work accident or from a single instantaneous exposure in the work environment.

Occupational illness is any abnormal condition or disorder, other than one resulting from an occupational injury, caused by exposure to environmental factors associated with employment. It includes acute and chronic illnesses or diseases which may be caused by inhalation, absorption, ingestion or direct contact.

Lost workdays are those days on which, because of occupational injury or illness, the employee was away from work or limited to restricted work activity. Lost workdays—away from work, are those days on which the employee would have worked but could not because of the occupational injury or illness. Lost workdays—restricted work activity, are those days on which: (1) the employee was assigned to a temporary job, or (2) the employee worked at a permanent job less than full-time, or (3) the employee worked at a permanently assigned job but could not perform all duties normally connected with it. The number of lost workdays (consecutive or not) should not include the day of injury or onset of illness.

Total cases include all work-related deaths and illnesses, and those work-related injuries that result in: loss of consciousness, restriction of work or motion, transfer to another job, or require medical treatment beyond first aid.

Nonfatal cases without lost workdays are cases that do not involve fatalities or lost workdays but result in: (1) medical treatment, other than first aid, or (2) loss of consciousness, or (3) transfer to another job, or (4) diagnosis of occupational illness.

Source and footnotes for table above and on pages 46 and 47.
Source: Bureau of Labor Statistics, U.S. Department of Labor, survey involving a nationwide sample of approximately 280,000 units.
[a]Industry division 2 and 3 digit SIC code totals include data for industries not shown separately.
[b]Standard Industrial Classification Manual. 1972 Edition, 1977 Supplement.
[c]Incidence Rate = $\frac{\text{(No. of injuries \& illnesses} \times \text{200,000) } \textbf{OR} \text{ (No. of lost workdays} \times \text{200,000)}}{\text{Total hours worked by all employees during period covered}}$
200,000 = base for 100 full-time equivalent workers (working 40 hours per week, 50 weeks per year).
[d]Includes fatalities. Because of rounding, the difference between the total and sum of the rates for lost workday cases and nonfatal cases without lost workdays may not reflect the fatality rate.
[e]Excludes farms with less than 11 employees.

Figure 1-12

BLS Estimates of Occupational Injury and Illness Incidence Rates for Selected Industries, 1988

Industry[a]	SIC Code[b]	Incidence Rates[c]			
		Total Cases[d]	Lost Workday Cases	Nonfatal Cases Without Lost Workdays	Lost Workdays
Private Sector[c]		**8.6**	**4.0**	**4.6**	**76.1**
Agriculture, forestry and fishing[c]		**10.9**	**5.6**	**5.2**	**101.8**
Agricultural production	01-02	12.2	6.2	6.0	110.6
Agricultural services	07	9.7	5.1	4.6	91.8
Forestry	08	12.4	6.5	5.8	138.3
Mining		**8.8**	**5.1**	**3.6**	**152.1**
Metal mining	10	8.7	4.9	3.7	150.5
Anthracite mining	11	10.0	8.1	1.8	199.8
Bituminous coal and lignite mining	12	12.0	8.6	3.4	241.9
Oil and gas extraction	13	8.3	4.3	3.8	141.6
Oil and gas field services	138	13.2	7.1	5.9	239.1
Nonmetallic minerals, except fuels	14	7.2	4.1	3.1	90.5
Construction		**14.6**	**6.8**	**7.7**	**142.2**
General building contractors	15	14.0	6.4	7.6	132.2
Heavy construction contractors	16	15.1	7.0	8.1	162.3
Special trade contractors	17	14.7	7.0	7.7	141.1
Manufacturing		**13.1**	**5.7**	**7.3**	**107.4**
Durable goods		*14.2*	*5.9*	*8.2*	*111.1*
Lumber and wood products	24	19.5	10.0	9.5	189.1
Logging camps and logging contractors	241	19.8	12.8	6.9	346.7
Sawmills and planing mills	242	19.9	10.2	9.6	192.1
Millwork, plywood and structural members	243	18.4	9.2	9.2	155.8
Furniture and fixtures	25	16.6	7.3	9.3	115.7
Household furniture	251	15.6	6.9	8.7	103.9
Stone, clay, and glass products	32	16.0	7.5	8.5	141.0
Concrete, gypsum, and plaster products	327	16.7	8.3	8.4	162.0
Miscellaneous nonmetallic mineral products	329	13.4	6.3	7.1	114.0
Primary metal industries	33	19.4	8.2	11.2	161.3
Blast furnace and basic steel products	331	16.8	6.5	10.4	159.5
Iron and steel foundries	332	27.4	11.8	15.6	185.7
Primary nonferrous metals	333	24.6	7.6	17.0	155.7
Nonferrous rolling and drawing	335	14.5	6.8	7.7	134.3
Fabricated metal products	34	18.8	8.0	10.8	138.8
Cutlery, hand tools, and hardware	342	13.5	5.9	7.6	112.1
Fabricated structural metal products	344	21.7	9.6	12.1	158.4
Metal forgings and stampings	346	23.7	8.9	14.8	162.9
Miscellaneous fabricated metal products	349	16.6	7.2	9.4	131.9
Machinery, except electrical	35	12.1	4.7	7.4	82.8
Farm and garden machinery	352	16.4	6.2	10.1	104.6
Construction and related machinery	353	16.5	6.6	9.9	112.1
Metalworking machinery	354	11.9	4.2	7.7	68.4
Special industry machinery	355	14.7	5.4	9.4	86.1
General industrial machinery	356	14.2	5.7	8.5	93.5
Office and computing machines	357	3.9	1.9	2.0	40.0
Refrigeration and service machinery	358	16.8	6.8	10.1	128.6
Miscellaneous machinery, except electrical	359	13.1	5.1	7.9	91.6
Electric and electronic equipment	36	8.0	3.3	4.6	64.6
Electric distributing equipment	361	10.3	4.3	6.0	82.5
Electric industrial apparatus	362	10.9	4.5	6.4	93.9
Household appliances	363	16.2	6.5	9.7	106.3
Electric lighting and wiring equipment	364	11.2	4.8	6.4	98.8
Communication equipment	366	4.2	1.8	2.4	39.9
Electronic components and accessories	367	6.1	2.6	3.5	44.7
Miscellaneous electrical equipment and supplies	369	12.1	5.0	7.2	105.7
Transportation equipment	37	17.7	6.6	11.1	134.2
Motor vehicles and equipment	371	23.3	8.4	14.8	168.7
Aircraft and parts	372	9.8	3.6	6.3	67.5
Ship and boat building and repairing	373	36.3	14.8	21.5	344.0
Railroad equipment	374	19.3	7.2	12.1	139.0
Guided missiles, space vehicles, parts	376	4.6	2.2	2.4	41.3
Instruments and related products	38	6.1	2.6	3.5	51.5
Measuring and controlling devices	382	6.1	2.6	3.5	57.5
Medical instruments and supplies	384	7.6	3.3	4.3	61.0
Photographic equipment and supplies	386	5.0	2.1	2.9	35.3
Miscellaneous manufacturing industries	39	11.3	5.1	6.1	91.0
Miscellaneous manufactures	399	13.1	5.9	7.2	98.9
Nondurable goods		*11.4*	*5.4*	*6.0*	*101.7*
Food and kindred products	20	18.5	9.2	9.4	169.7
Meat products	201	27.9	13.3	14.5	245.9
Dairy products	202	15.6	8.0	7.6	164.0
Preserved fruits and vegetables	203	17.2	7.9	9.3	128.8

See source and footnotes on page 45.

Figure 1-13

BLS Estimates of Occupational Injury and Illness Incidence Rates for Selected Industries, 1988, Cont.

Industry[a]	SIC Code[b]	Incidence Rates[c]			
		Total Cases[d]	Lost Workday Cases	Nonfatal Cases Without Lost Workdays	Lost Workdays
Grain mill products	204	13.1	6.4	6.6	114.1
Bakery products	205	13.0	7.2	5.8	156.9
Beverages	208	18.0	9.1	8.9	163.7
Miscellaneous foods and kindred products	209	15.3	7.9	7.5	139.4
Tobacco manufactures	21	9.3	2.9	6.3	53.0
Textile mill products	22	9.6	4.0	5.6	78.8
Knitting mills	225	8.6	4.1	4.5	79.9
Apparel and other textile products	23	8.1	3.5	4.6	68.2
Men's and boys' furnishings	232	10.5	4.8	5.7	103.3
Women's and misses' outerwear	233	5.0	2.0	3.0	41.4
Miscellaneous fabricated textile products	239	10.7	4.5	6.2	73.0
Paper and allied products	26	13.1	5.9	7.2	124.3
Paper mills, except building paper	262	12.9	5.2	7.7	132.6
Miscellaneous converted paper products	264	12.8	6.5	6.3	120.4
Paperboard containers and boxes	265	13.3	6.2	7.1	120.3
Printing and publishing	27	6.6	3.2	3.4	59.8
Newspapers	271	6.2	3.1	3.2	61.4
Commercial printing	275	7.9	3.7	4.3	65.6
Chemicals and allied products	28	7.0	3.3	3.8	59.0
Industrial inorganic chemicals	281	6.0	2.7	3.3	62.7
Plastics materials and synthetics	282	5.8	2.6	3.3	52.9
Drugs	283	5.3	2.5	2.8	43.7
Soap, cleaners, and toilet goods	284	8.5	4.1	4.4	67.2
Industrial organic chemicals	286	6.3	2.6	3.7	49.0
Agricultural chemicals	287	9.3	4.5	4.8	73.5
Petroleum and coal products	29	7.0	3.2	3.8	68.4
Petroleum refining	291	5.8	2.7	3.1	59.0
Rubber and miscellaneous plastics products	30	16.3	8.1	8.2	142.9
Miscellaneous plastics products	307	16.4	7.9	8.5	134.7
Leather and leather products	31	11.4	5.6	5.8	128.2
Transportation and public utilities		**8.9**	**5.1**	**3.8**	**118.6**
Railroad transportation	40	6.9	4.9	2.0	85.4
Local and interurban passenger transit	41	9.0	5.3	3.7	140.3
Local and suburban transportation	411	11.1	6.6	4.5	167.5
Trucking and warehousing	42	13.9	8.0	5.8	212.2
Trucking, local and long distance	421	13.9	8.1	5.8	218.6
Water transportation	44	12.2	7.5	4.7	294.9
Transportation by air	45	13.0	7.6	5.4	130.1
Transportation services	47	4.1	2.2	1.8	49.6
Communication	48	3.1	1.6	1.5	30.8
Electric, gas, and sanitary services	49	7.7	3.8	3.9	72.2
Electric services	491	6.2	2.8	3.5	52.1
Gas production and distribution	492	7.4	3.9	3.5	67.5
Wholesale and retail trade		**7.8**	**3.5**	**4.3**	**60.9**
Wholesale trade — durable goods	50	6.7	3.2	3.5	57.4
Wholesale trade — nondurable goods	51	9.1	4.8	4.3	86.7
Retail trade		*7.9*	*3.4*	*4.6*	*57.6*
Building materials and garden supplies	52	10.6	5.0	5.6	82.7
General merchandise stores	53	9.9	4.6	5.4	71.0
Food stores	54	11.3	4.7	6.5	91.2
Automotive dealers and service stations	55	6.7	2.7	4.0	46.5
Apparel and accessory stores	56	2.5	1.1	1.4	26.2
Furniture and home furnishing stores	57	4.9	2.3	2.6	43.4
Eating and drinking places	58	8.8	3.5	5.3	54.1
Miscellaneous retail	59	4.0	1.8	2.2	33.9
Finance, insurance, and real estate		**2.0**	**0.9**	**1.1**	**17.2**
Banking	60	1.5	0.6	0.9	10.4
Insurance carriers	63	1.7	0.8	1.0	14.0
Real estate	65	4.7	2.4	2.3	43.7
Services		**5.4**	**2.6**	**2.8**	**47.7**
Hotels and other lodging places	70	10.4	4.6	5.8	80.6
Personal services	72	3.3	1.7	1.6	29.9
Business services	73	4.3	2.1	2.3	39.8
Auto repair, services, and garages	75	6.6	3.2	3.4	61.2
Miscellaneous repair services	76	8.1	4.0	4.1	82.9
Motion pictures	78	2.8	1.0	1.8	24.4
Amusement and recreation services	79	8.7	3.9	4.8	59.2
Health services	80	7.3	3.7	3.6	69.6
Legal services	81	0.6	0.3	0.3	4.9
Educational services	82	3.8	1.6	2.1	26.9
Social services	83	5.2	2.6	2.6	44.7
Museums, botanical, zoological gardens	84	6.9	3.1	3.8	44.4
Miscellaneous services	89	1.7	0.7	0.9	15.1

See source and footnotes on page 45.

Figure 1-13 (*continued*)

Occupational Injury and Illness Incidence Rates by Industry, 1988, Reporters to the National Safety Council

(Note: The 1989 rates were not available at press time, and may be found in *Work Injury and Illness Rates, 1990.*)

Industry	SIC Code[b]	Incidence Rates per 100 Full-Time Employees[a]					
		Total Cases	Lost Workday Cases	Cases Involving Days Away From Work & Deaths	Nonfatal Cases Without Lost Workdays	Lost Workdays[c]	Days Away From Work
All Industries[d]		**8.78**	**3.58**	**2.17**	**5.20**	**72**	**49**
Agriculture, forestry, & fishing		**10.59**	**4.22**	**3.50**	**6.35**	**82**	**56**
Agricultural production, crops	01	15.40	5.27	3.60	10.14	91	35
Forestry	08	4.02	1.06	0.85	2.92	53	46
Mining		**5.37**	**1.43**	**1.06**	**3.93**	**46**	**36**
Metal mining	10	10.36	2.03	1.85	8.33	77	65
Bituminous coal & lignite mining	12	9.51	1.75	1.46	7.74	51	30
Oil & gas extraction	13	2.58	1.07	0.74	1.49	34	26
Nonmetallic minerals, except fuels	14	6.86	1.74	1.03	5.12	50	38
Construction		**10.97**	**4.28**	**3.32**	**6.68**	**93**	**77**
General building contractors	15	13.13	4.88	3.81	8.25	117	101
Heavy construction contractors	16	10.09	4.10	3.13	5.98	86	70
Special trade contractors	17	16.66	4.59	4.54	12.07	96	95
Manufacturing		**9.69**	**3.56**	**1.84**	**6.13**	**68**	**42**
Durable goods		*12.31*	*4.42*	*2.29*	*7.88*	*82*	*50*
Lumber and wood products	24	10.75	4.47	3.32	6.27	126	100
Sawmills and planing mills	242	13.26	5.36	4.19	7.90	130	104
Millwork, plywood, and structural members	243	9.46	4.39	2.95	5.06	144	114
Furniture and fixtures	25	17.47	6.76	1.63	10.71	132	27
Household furniture	251	9.03	2.51	1.59	6.51	38	31
Stone, clay, and glass products	32	12.70	4.99	2.91	7.71	101	68
Cement, hydraulic	324	7.99	2.27	1.66	5.68	61	44
Concrete, gypsum, and plaster products	327	7.93	2.81	2.44	5.12	72	62
Miscellaneous nonmetallic mineral products	329	8.89	4.12	3.05	4.77	81	63
Primary metal industries	33	15.57	4.89	2.27	10.67	104	63
Blast furnace and basic steel products	331	11.99	3.97	2.30	8.01	107	77
Iron and steel foundries	332	29.90	8.08	3.30	21.80	137	72
Primary nonferrous metals	333	16.05	5.64	2.78	10.40	121	71
Nonferrous rolling and drawing	335	12.20	4.07	1.40	8.13	76	36
Fabricated metal products	34	12.38	4.41	2.21	7.96	73	47
Metal cans and shipping containers	341	14.38	4.44	1.62	9.94	74	39
Cutlery, hand tools, and hardware	342	10.71	4.07	3.08	6.64	88	46
Fabricated structural metal products	344	5.54	1.96	1.52	3.58	45	38
Metal forgings and stampings	346	27.10	9.47	2.92	17.63	126	65
Miscellaneous fabricated metal products	349	11.12	3.16	2.47	7.95	64	54
Machinery, except electrical	35	9.38	3.38	1.95	6.00	63	36
Farm and garden machinery	352	10.41	3.55	0.64	6.86	52	12
Construction and related machinery	353	11.67	4.25	2.57	7.41	88	52
Metalworking machinery	354	13.17	5.02	3.56	8.15	80	64
Special industry machinery	355	9.40	3.18	2.51	6.22	44	38
General industrial machinery	356	8.09	3.19	2.40	4.89	54	39
Office and computing machines	357	2.23	1.24	0.67	0.99	26	9
Refrigeration and service machinery	358	17.12	4.86	3.34	12.26	89	60
Miscellaneous machinery, except electrical	359	7.73	3.61	1.29	4.11	71	29
Electric and electronic equipment	36	4.38	1.76	1.12	2.62	35	21
Electric distributing equipment	361	11.39	4.85	2.50	6.54	104	50
Electric industrial apparatus	362	6.92	2.55	1.53	4.37	39	23
Household appliances	363	9.50	2.33	1.81	7.17	44	21
Electric lighting and wiring equipment	364	9.96	3.35	1.87	6.61	78	46
Communication equipment	366	2.19	0.90	0.63	1.30	18	10
Electronic components and accessories	367	3.79	1.30	0.94	2.49	24	16
Miscellaneous electrical equipment and supplies	369	7.63	3.95	2.94	3.68	78	57
Transportation equipment	37	18.34	6.57	3.27	11.77	109	69
Motor vehicles and equipment	371	32.47	11.50	5.62	20.97	188	118
Aircraft and parts	372	7.43	2.60	1.65	4.82	53	39
Ship and boat building and repair	373	13.63	5.23	1.94	8.40	58	38
Railroad equipment	374	17.28	5.28	4.88	11.97	123	116
Guided missiles, space vehicles, and parts	376	3.49	1.28	0.32	2.21	20	6
Instruments and related products	38	5.52	2.43	1.11	3.09	44	24
Measuring and controlling devices	382	7.34	3.09	1.87	4.25	53	25
Medical instruments and supplies	384	5.82	2.36	1.04	3.46	42	22
Miscellaneous manufacturing industries	39	9.74	4.74	3.74	5.01	78	62
Nondurable goods		*7.00*	*2.68*	*1.37*	*4.32*	*54*	*33*
Food and kindred products	20	15.27	5.52	3.10	9.75	107	66
Meat products	201	27.04	10.27	4.38	16.76	163	88
Dairy products	202	9.06	3.42	2.46	5.63	70	52
Preserved fruits and vegetables	203	23.14	6.26	3.20	16.87	132	74

See source and footnotes on page 49.

Figure 1-14

Occupational Injury and Illness Incidence Rates by Industry, 1988, Reporters to the National Safety Council, Cont.

Industry	SIC Code[b]	Incidence Rates per 100 Full-Time Employees[a]					
		Total Cases	Lost Workday Cases	Cases Involving Days Away From Work & Deaths	Nonfatal Cases Without Lost Workdays	Lost Work-days[c]	Days Away From Work
Grain mill products	204	9.29	2.57	2.08	6.72	77	64
Bakery products	205	13.61	5.30	2.89	8.30	120	73
Beverages	208	10.19	3.38	2.40	6.81	83	59
Miscellaneous foods and kindred products	209	6.28	2.96	1.73	3.31	75	57
Textile mill products	22	6.17	2.17	0.52	3.99	38	17
Weaving mills, cotton	221	6.13	1.83	0.35	4.29	33	14
Knitting mills	225	7.89	3.34	0.94	4.55	38	14
Apparel and other textile products	23	7.01	4.02	1.18	2.99	68	35
Miscellaneous fabricated textile products	239	6.45	2.61	0.86	3.85	58	44
Paper and allied products	26	10.65	3.66	2.42	6.98	90	67
Paper mills, except building paper	262	12.29	3.68	2.28	8.61	91	65
Miscellaneous converted paper products	264	7.47	3.45	2.21	4.02	77	56
Paperboard containers and boxes	265	11.01	5.10	3.56	5.90	122	99
Printing and publishing	27	8.32	3.69	2.66	4.62	58	44
Newspapers	271	5.00	2.78	2.27	2.20	46	38
Commercial printing	275	10.99	4.60	3.03	6.38	70	53
Chemicals and allied products	28	3.59	1.42	0.59	2.16	27	14
Industrial inorganic chemicals	281	5.21	1.99	1.06	3.21	44	29
Plastics materials and synthetics	282	3.32	1.16	0.43	2.15	26	12
Drugs	283	2.92	1.30	0.69	1.62	21	13
Soap, cleaners, and toilet goods	284	4.12	2.38	1.41	1.72	47	29
Paints and allied products	285	4.72	2.40	0.83	2.32	36	20
Industrial organic chemicals	286	3.62	1.31	0.36	2.31	24	10
Agricultural chemicals	287	2.59	0.90	0.38	1.68	22	13
Miscellaneous chemical products	289	4.34	1.84	0.98	2.50	38	22
Petroleum and coal products	29	4.45	1.77	0.92	2.67	41	23
Petroleum refining	291	4.10	1.64	0.71	2.44	38	20
Paving and roofing materials	295	6.64	2.83	2.35	3.81	78	60
Rubber and miscellaneous plastics products	30	8.91	4.29	2.58	4.62	86	55
Miscellaneous plastics products	307	10.18	4.41	2.35	5.76	103	62
Leather and leather products	31	9.14	4.68	1.57	4.46	78	34
Transportation & public utilities		**6.61**	**3.76**	**2.75**	**2.85**	**83**	**63**
Railroad transportation	40	7.32	5.72	5.04	1.59	205	188
Local and interurban passenger transit	41	15.87	10.59	10.54	5.28	203	202
Local and suburban transportation	411	16.90	11.25	11.25	5.66	214	213
Trucking and warehousing	42	22.67	15.81	15.62	6.85	278	276
Trucking, local and long distance	421[c]	23.64	16.56	16.55	7.06	293	292
Water transportation	44	6.77	3.74	3.72	3.00	156	155
Transportation by air	45	6.52	3.46	2.78	3.06	54	42
Pipelines, except natural gas	46	4.01	1.51	1.30	2.51	40	30
Communication	48	1.89	0.86	0.68	1.03	23	13
Electric, gas, and sanitary services	49	5.74	2.84	1.55	2.89	54	31
Electric services	491	5.04	2.39	1.01	2.65	49	23
Gas production and distribution	492	6.57	3.38	2.42	3.18	55	36
Water supply	494	12.36	6.30	5.94	6.06	138	119
Wholesale & retail trade		**6.62**	**3.46**	**2.16**	**3.16**	**64**	**46**
Wholesale trade—durable goods	50	9.70	5.03	3.12	4.66	101	72
Wholesale trade—nondurable goods	51	4.75	2.57	1.92	2.15	45	36
Retail trade		**3.35**	**1.72**	**0.87**	**1.63**	**23**	**15**
Automotive dealers and service stations	55	2.58	1.13	0.52	1.45	22	15
Services		**4.99**	**2.34**	**2.22**	**2.64**	**35**	**28**
Business services	73	1.40	0.66	0.53	0.74	11	7
Hospitals	806	7.75	3.71	3.55	4.04	53	44
Educational services	82	4.33	2.26	2.21	2.07	48	43
Social services	83	10.87	4.10	4.10	6.77	64	49
Public administration (government)		**11.85**	**5.10**	**4.67**	**6.75**	**106**	**96**
Executive, legislative, and general	91	18.74	6.75	5.91	11.98	127	115
Police protection	9221	9.45	2.69	2.64	6.76	74	47
Fire protection	9224	11.29	3.53	3.18	7.76	140	127
State departments of transportation		9.64	5.07	5.10	4.53	144	144
Offices		2.28	1.09	0.81	1.18	17	13
Research and development or laboratory		2.61	0.91	0.53	1.70	13	7

Source: Based on reports of National Safety Council members participating in the *Occupational Safety/Health Award Program.* These rates should not be interpreted as representative of the industries listed or of Council member companies. A more complete list of industries may be found in *Work Injury and Illness Rates, 1989.*

[a] Based on OSHA definitions, see page 45. 200,000 employee hours used as the equivalent of 100 full-time employees.

[b] *Standard Industrial Classification (SIC) Manual,* 1972 Edition.

[c] Lost workdays include both days away from work and days of restricted work activity.

[d] Totals for division and 2 and 3 digit SIC codes include data for 4 digit codes not shown separately. Rates for each industry may not be comparable to the previous year due to changes in numbers of reporters.

[e] Excludes refuse collection without disposal.

Figure 1–15

continued from page 3

disabling injuries provides cost numbers that are usually a surprise to many managements. (A disabling injury is defined as one that results in death or some degree of permanent impairment, or that renders the injured person unable to effectively perform his or her regular duties or activities for a full day beyond the day of injury.)

Further comparison of these costs with bottom line net income also provides some startling information for many managements. I have known cases in which the single easiest action a management can take to improve bottom line performance is to reduce injury costs. Unfortunately, many managers simply regard injury costs as an inherent cost of doing business, about which they really have "no control given the 'liberality of workers' compensation laws' and the 'recalcitrance of unions.'" This is indeed an excuse. While admittedly an exceptional example, I know of one location that reduced its incidence (and the associated costs) of workers' compensation cases by 90% within six months of the time that management decided that injury performance was a performance criterion subject to management influence. The numbers are significant. This was a large facility with a large problem. The problem was significantly reduced, without labor strife. Clients of Du Pont's Safety Management Services routinely achieve a 50% reduction in lost workday incident rate in the first two years following a Du Pont consultancy.

Although these results take management time and effort, they translate directly to the bottom line. The remainder of this book is devoted to developing an understanding of how management can productively apply its time and effort in leading their employees to continually improved levels of safety performance—to the benefit of all.

Another perspective on the impact of the cost of injuries in a company's financial performance is to examine the level of sales required to support these costs. If 5% is used as the median value of profits as a percentage of sales for the top U.S. industrial companies in the 1989 Fortune 500, sales of $570,000 are required to support the $28,500 cost of each disabling injury. In the competitive environment in which most companies operate, taken together with the level of injury performance of most companies, reducing injuries by one is an easier route to increased profitability than by increasing sales by $0.6 million. Although the use of this type of analysis can be questioned, the message is the same—SAFETY PAYS.

INDUSTRY RESPONSIBILITY

Figure 1-16 is a *Wall Street Journal* (4-20-90) article related to the Phillips Petroleum Company plant explosion in Pasadena, Texas, on October 23, 1989. The proposed OSHA fines are a small part of the cost of this explosion to Phillips. In December 1989, an Exxon refinery in Baton Rouge, Louisiana, exploded. Prior to this a Shell Oil Company facility at Norco, Louisiana, exploded. The Exxon *Valdez* grounding in Prince William Sound is another example of failed safety. The Bhopal, India, release of toxic gases by a Union Carbide Company facility has forever changed Union Carbide as a company. Industrial mishaps can be endlessly cited. Private companies

OSHA Seeks to Fine Phillips Petroleum $5.7 Million Over Texas Plant Explosions

The Labor Department moved to fine **Phillips Petroleum** Co. $5.7 million, accusing the company of willful safety violations in connection with the explosions at a chemical plant near Houston in October.

Phillips said it would contest many of the citations. "We really take issue with the word 'willful' because we don't think we compromised the safety of our workers," a spokesman said.

This article was prepared by Albert R. Karr in Washington and David D. Medina and Caleb Solomon in Houston.

The alleged violations are viewed by many as part of an industry-wide pattern of safety hazards that has led to numerous explosions and fires at oil and chemical plants in the past two years. Many experts blame these accidents on operations at or above practical capacity. Some unions, consultants and industry executives say companies don't want to stop production and do needed maintenance, and this, they say, has compromised safety.

The department's Occupational Safety and Health Administration said it has uncovered internal Phillips documents "that called for corrective action but which were largely ignored." And in a report on chemical-industry safety problems that will go to the White House soon, a study commissioned by the Labor Department will note other instances of chemical companies that "refused to be responsive to" internal audit reports that warned of safety hazards, said Alan McMillan, an OSHA official. Those instances won't show the same "scope" as the Phillips documents, however, he said.

Work on that report has been pushed along by the Phillips catastrophe.

The explosions and an accompanying fire killed 23 workers and injured more than 130 at Phillips's Pasadena, Texas, petrochemical plant. The $5.7 million fine is the second-largest the agency has ever proposed against a single company.

OSHA also proposed penalties of $730,000 against **Fish Engineering & Construction** Inc., a Houston-area contractor on the chemical plant's site. Fish said it would contest the citations.

OSHA accused Phillips of 566 willful violations, involving failure to protect 566 workers from fire and explosion dangers, and of other "serious violations." The citations included failure to prevent the uncontrolled release of flammable vapors, use of inappropriate valves and inadequate fire protection. Fish was cited for 181 willful violations, including failure to protect its workers from fire and explosion.

Labor Secretary Elizabeth Dole said there was "clear evidence that this explosion was avoidable had recognized safety procedures been followed." OSHA officials wouldn't discuss the Phillips documents.

The fire and explosions, one of America's biggest postwar industrial accidents, shook downtown Houston a dozen miles away and resulted in the most fatalities of any accident at an oil refinery or petrochemical plant in recent years.

Some industry officials said a vastly reduced work force and the oil industry's increasing dependence on outside contractors have contributed to heightened danger at plants.

Fish has been the almost-exclusive maintenance contractor at the Pasadena site for about 17 years and has performed a similar role at other Phillips plants, OSHA said. Four of the workers killed and 52 of those injured worked for Fish.

"Phillips is not a renegade," said Richard Leonard, director of special projects for the Oil, Chemical and Atomic Workers Union. "There is very little difference between them and other companies around the country," he said.

Figure 1–16

OSHA Seeks to Fine Phillips Petroleum

Glen Williamson, an OSHA deputy regional director, said yesterday's action "sends a very clear signal that the agency is going to take a very strong enforcement position." OSHA has come under fire from safety experts for what they consider innocuous fines, sometimes only hundreds of dollars, for violations at many plants, but it has been taking a stronger tack since Gerard Scannell took over as head of the agency last year.

Even so, Rep. Tom Lantos (D., Calif.), chairman of the House Government Operations Subcommittee on Employment and Housing, said the Phillips explosion showed "the cop was not on the beat." He noted that two months before the October explosions, an accident at the same plant killed one worker and seriously injured two others, but OSHA didn't do a complete inspection. The last full sweep was in 1974.

After hearing news reports of the August incident, OSHA investigators did show up, ultimately determining that during routine maintenance, gases escaped to an area where welding torches touched off a flash fire and explosion. OSHA fined Phillips $720.

OSHA said its inspections of Phillips plants in a four-state region showed 18 deaths and many hospitalizations prior to October.

Mr. Scannell said the primary cause of the fire and explosions in October was the release, during maintenance work, of four highly flammable process gases from an open valve between a reactor vessel and a chemical-settling leg. Most of the gas escaped quickly because of high pressure, and a huge vapor cloud sped through the plant and exploded when it came in contact with an ignition source, OSHA said. Other explosions followed.

Contrary to Phillips procedures and industry practice, there was no backup protection against valve failure or untimely valve opening, OSHA said.

Phillips's own investigation asserted that the valve should have been closed but wasn't because of "human error," a spokesman said.

The Phillips explosions seemed to frighten the oil industry into tightening up its maintenance procedures. Unlike the situation in 1988 and 1989, when many companies postponed maintenance and ran their plants full out, this year they have closed down equipment to perform necessary housekeeping. Plants are running around 80% to 85% of capacity, and the number of fires and explosions appears to have been reduced markedly. But in December, part of a huge Exxon Corp. refinery in Baton Rouge, La., exploded, killing two workers.

Phillips and Fish have 15 days to contest the citations before the independent Occupational Safety and Health Review Commission.

Figure 1-16 (*continued*)

do not have an inalienable right to operate. They operate at the pleasure of and under circumstances proscribed by the public.

Why Safety? If not for employees, if not for the stockholders, if not for the public, then for survival.

SAFE PLACE CONCEPT—OCCUPATIONAL SAFETY AND HEALTH ACT OF 1970

However large these industrial catastrophies and the absolute necessity for industry to do a better job loom in our minds, we would all do well to look at the data in Figure

1-2. One half of the total costs to the U.S. economy in 1989 are ascribed to motor vehicle accidents. One half of all fatal accidents in the United States during 1989 were motor vehicle deaths. Work-related costs accounted for just under one third of the nation's total accident costs. In terms of fatality—the ultimate injury—work-related deaths accounted for only 11% of the total; of these, 41% were motor vehicle related. The *place* where Americans are being killed is the country's highways. It would seem that a disproportionate effort is being placed on workplace safety rather than on highway safety.

I believe this disproportion may stem from the mistaken notion that employers can provide a safe place for workers to work. The Occupational Safety and Health Act of 1970 (OSHA) specifies that among several of its purposes are: "(1) . . . encouraging employers and employees in their effort to reduce the number of occupational safety and health hazards at their places of employment . . . . " Under Section 5, entitled Duties, "Each Employer (1) shall furnish to each of his employees employment and a *place of employment*[1] which are free from recognized hazards that are causing or are likely to cause death or serious physical harm to his employees . . . . "

Under Section 8(a), Inspection, Investigations, and Recordkeeping, "In order to carry out the purposes of this Act, the Secretary . . . is authorized—(1) to enter . . . ; and (2) to inspect and investigate . . . , any place of employment and all pertinent conditions, structures, machines, apparatus, devices, equipment, and materials therein."

Although the Act (Section 5.(a)(2) b) requires that "Each employee shall comply with occupational safety and health standards and all rules, regulations, and orders issued pursuant to this Act which are applicable to his own actions and conduct," the emphasis on inspections, standards, and fines has been placed upon the employer to provide a *safe place.* As discussed in the Preface, *places* do not have the attribute of safety. It is people who behave safely or unsafely. *Places* can be configured so as to make it easier for people to behave safely but *places* cannot be made safe. Going up and down steps is a hazardous undertaking. Falling down steps is a common every day occurrence. The reason for handrails on steps is to make it easier for transit to be made without injury.[2] I wonder if our congressional offices are equipped with doors free from recognized hazards (pinch-points)? Of course not.

Management cannot provide a safe *place* in which to work, it can provide an environment in which employees work safely.

In Figure 1-17 is an op-ed article from *The Wall Street Journal* which addresses the issue of measuring "workplace safety" and OSHA effectiveness. The last sentence ends with "and a commitment to policy experiments that would give it a fighting chance to find out what works." What works is leadership. And as the author Peter Drucker, puts it (see Chapter 2), "It is mundane, unromantic and boring." It is hard work, demanding emotional commitment. It was not my experience to find it boring, however.

The article in Figure 1-17 points out the difficulty of analyzing safety statistics. To make a point that is not made by Mendeloff, the graph in Figure 1-9 shows a rather steady (constant slope) decline in worker death rates starting about 1951. There appears to be no increase in the rate of decline subsequent to enactment of the OSHA Act in 1970.

More recently, OSHA has begun to demonstrate an improved understanding of safety. Some regulations—for example, 29CFR 1910.1450, titled "Occupational

The Hazards of Rating Workplace Safety

By John Mendeloff

In controversial policy areas, statistics are powerful and easily manipulated weapons. In few places is that more true than in the area of occupational safety, where supporters and critics of the Reagan administration's enforcement policies clash on the meaning of injury data.

Using the Bureau of Labor Statistics' annual Survey of Occupational Injuries and Illnesses, officials of the Occupational Safety and Health Administration claim credit for a major reduction in the injury rate over the past 13 years. Critics, mainly in organized labor, use the same statistics to bolster their complaints about the administration's "nice guy" approach to enforcing regulations. They note that improvements halted in the early '80s and call for a return to earlier policies.

Before assessing the claims about the impact of the administration's enforcement policies, it's necessary to understand what the injury data really represent. As the accompanying table shows, the total injury rate has declined sharply since the early 1970s. As the table also shows, the drop was due solely to a sharp decrease in one of its components, the rate of injuries that didn't result in lost workdays. While that rate dropped by more than 40%, the rate of injuries that resulted in one or more lost workdays rose more than 30%. Which of the two rates—if either—tells the "truth" about changes in workplace risk?

Analysts at the Bureau of Labor Statistics acknowledge that the big drop in the rate of injuries that don't result in lost workdays wasn't due to any change in workplace risk, but instead was primarily, if not wholly, due to changes in employers' understanding of reporting requirements. In other words, this rate is not a valid indicator of risk trends and cannot be used to support claims about the impact of changes in enforcement.

The rate for injuries that result in lost workdays also is seriously flawed as a measure of risk levels. Recent research shows that the increases in the 1970s were strongly influenced by an improvement in workers' compensation benefits. Higher benefits increased the incentive for workers to report injuries to insurers and, ultimately, to the Bureau of Labor Statistics. More-liberal benefits may also help explain the increase in the number of lost workdays per worker. This rate has gone up even more sharply than the rate of injuries that result in lost workdays, indicating that the average injury leads to more lost time than it once did. Interpretations of the injury data should acknowledge the impact of compensation programs.

Studies also agree that the rate of injuries that result in lost workdays has a strong cyclical component. The rate tends to go down when business is slow and to rise when hiring picks up. This reflects the higher accident rate of inexperienced workers. Interpretations of the injury data should also take this factor into account.

Countering the critics' claim that safety hazards are growing is a striking decline in the fatality rate. Some of the improvement may reflect better medical treatment for accident victims. There also is evidence that the higher insurance premiums caused by more-liberal benefits have prodded employers to improve their safety performance.

Critics of OSHA argue that the decline in the fatality rate reflects the shift in employment from more-hazardous sectors such as construction and manufacturing to white-collar and service jobs. While there is some merit to that argument, it ignores the steep declines in the fatality rates within the manufacturing and construction sectors. While the fatality rate for the private sector as a whole dropped 28% between 1978 and 1986, the rate for manufacturing fell 26% and for construction, 42%. As with the injury rates, it's not clear what influence—if any—the Reagan administration's policies have had.

What are the changes in OSHA's enforcement policy during the Reagan years that have caused so much contention?

The sharpest change is OSHA's slash in the average penalty per violation by more than 50%.

Second is a policy that curtails physical inspections in the manufacturing sector. This means that when an OSHA inspector turns up at a work site, he begins his inspection with a "records check" (except when an inspection is triggered by a worker complaint or an accident). Only if the records show an injury rate higher than the manufacturing average does he

Figure 1–17

perform a physical inspection.

The third big change is the shrinkage of OSHA's inspection force. The number of annual inspections remains unchanged, however, mainly because many more are targeted on the construction industry, where inspections require fewer manhours than they do in manufacturing. Today, construction-sector inspections account for about 60% of all inspections, compared with less than 30% in the 1970s.

It's impossible to interpret the true impact of these changes. One reason is that studies of OSHA show that OSHA policies have at best a small effect—up to 10%—on the rate of injuries and fatalities. Another reason is that none of the studies control for all of the variables described above.

The studies of OSHA do agree, however, that the number of OSHA inspections is a more important factor in preventing injuries than the size of its penalties. For this reason, the impact of the penalty reductions shouldn't be large.

Supporters of the records-check policy argue that it allows OSHA to focus on the bad actors; critics warn that it encourages employers to underreport injuries. A National Academy of Sciences panel reported last year, however, that it could find no evidence that the records-check policy has had any impact on underreporting.

As for the shift in inspections from manufacturing to construction, no studies exist on where inspections do the most good. It is intriguing that the decline in the manufacturing death rate halted in the early '80s. There may be a causal connection, but we also need to assess whether the shift accelerated the drop in the construction death rate.

The difficulties in developing accurate statistics on workplace injuries and in assessing OSHA's impact are disconcerting. Simplistic claims about the effects—good or bad—of OSHA policy changes should be viewed with skepticism. While it is possible that the changes under the Reagan administration have had an effect—negative or positive—on safety, the available evidence hardly forces us to either conclusion. Not only does the validity of the data as indicators of workplace risk remain uncertain, but there are no studies that control for the important variables.

When OSHA was established in 1970, the big concern was that many less-serious injuries were not being counted and so the Bureau of Labor Statistics surveys have emphasized getting a complete count. Despite all the political interest in counting workplace injuries, the most glaring intelligence failure for policy purposes is the absence of any serious effort to analyze the causes of workplace injuries and the efficacy of countermeasures. Although greater accuracy is desirable, OSHA's greater needs are better data on the causes of accidents and a commitment to policy experiments that would give it a fighting chance to find out what works.

Mr. Mendeloff's most recent book is "The Dilemma of Toxic Substance Regulation" (MIT, 1988). He served last year on a National Academy of Sciences panel on occupational safety and health statistics.

Occupational Injury And Fatality Rates

	Injuries[1]				Fatalities[2]		
Year	Total Cases	Cases with Lost Workdays	Cases without Lost Workdays	Number of Lost Workdays	Total	Manufacturing	Construction
1973	10.6	3.3	7.3	51.2	—	—	—
1974	10.0	3.4	6.6	53.1	9.8	—	—
1975	8.8	3.2	5.6	54.6	9.4	—	—
1976	8.9	3.4	5.5	57.8	7.9	—	—
1977	9.0	3.7	5.3	60.0	9.1	—	—
1978	9.2	4.0	5.2	62.1	8.2	5.9	30.6
1979	9.2	4.2	5.0	66.2	8.6	5.4	30.6
1980	8.5	3.9	4.6	63.7	7.7	5.5	26.4
1981	8.1	3.7	4.4	60.4	7.6	5.1	26.8
1982	7.6	3.4	4.1	57.5	7.4	4.2	25.2
1983	7.5	3.4	4.1	57.2	5.6	4.1	22.3
1984	7.8	3.6	4.2	61.8	6.4	4.3	20.2
1985	7.7	3.6	4.2	63.3	6.2	4.1	27.2
1986	7.7	3.6	4.2	63.9	5.9	4.2	17.9

[1]Per 100 full-time workers [2]Per 100,000 workers; figures for earlier years not comparable

Source: Bureau of Labor Statistics

Figure 1–17 (*continued*)

Exposure to Hazardous Chemicals in Laboratories"—are reflecting this improved understanding.

The above not withstanding, the Act exists. It is part of the realities of life with which employers must grapple. The task is to recognize the appropriateness of adopting management practices that drive employee performance toward the goal of injury-free behavior. The Act should be made redundant. Management motivation must not be based on the legalism of the Act. This is a prescription for failure.

Leadership is needed for success. Employees will not perceive management as providing leadership when they see management being motivated because of government regulations. They will see a reluctant management trying to comply with the law, i.e., a management trying to *follow* the law, not lead. They will see their management trying to provide a *safe place* in which workers can perform their tasks—a mirage, an unattainable goal. They will see that their management does not understand the fundamentals of safety. They will see their management trying "cookbook" solutions to safety. Injuries do not just happen; they are caused by the actions of people. It is to this central feature of safety that successful managers will devote their time, money, and energies. Concern for employees, customers, the public, the environment, and the well being of stockholders is the proper foundation for success in safety. This book discusses what managers who want to lead can do to establish themselves as leaders.

Fortunately, this standard, 29CFR 1910.1450, reflects much of what is contained in "Prudent Practices for Handling Hazardous Chemicals in Laboratories" (National Academy Press, 1981). Unfortunately, much of the wisdom contained in this publication has now been codified into "law" and cannot be changed except by a change of the "law," a slow process. In the meantime, new, improved procedures may not be adopted because of fear of being found guilty of "willful violation" of an OSHA regulation and the ensuing fines and adverse publicity associated with such fines or proposed fines. In addition, at the time of this writing, strong proposals were being made to Congress to criminalize findings of "willful violation." All of these actions rob both OSHA and management of the opportunity to demonstrate the leadership without which legislation will be ineffective—unfortunate and misguided.

In 29CFR 1910.147, titled "Control of Hazardous Energy Sources," OSHA has specified procedures for locking or tagging which, in the main, represent desirable practices. They reflect much of what has been found to be successful in industrial practice. Beyond the fact that codification of such practices is undesirable, it is interesting that those sectors of the U.S. economy that have the highest accidental death rates have been exempted from the regulation, namely Agriculture, Construction, Electric Utilities, and Mining (regulated by separate regulations under the Mine Safety Health Act—1977). The data in Figure 1-9 show the estimated death rates for these and other sectors for the United States. One wonders why those activities that have the highest death rates, and hence pose the greatest risk for individual workers are exempt from a "good thing."

On April 26, 1990, Elizabeth H. Dole, Secretary of Labor, reported to President Bush on OSHA's stewardship regarding the Phillips Petroleum Company explosion. She wrote that "OSHA, the Federal agency charged with the responsibility for assuring a safe and healthful workplace, arrived at the Phillips site within an hour of the accident." She also reported that "OSHA's comprehensive investigation of the accident was initiated immediately." She attached an Executive Summary of that report. The report places considerable emphasis on increased OSHA rule making as a preventive action. The last sentence of this summary states, "OSHA's role, however, is not that of a supervisory body for the industry or for the individual plant; as specified in OSHA Act, the responsibility for the safe operation of any workplace always remains with the employer." Why is OSHA issuing rules of conduct and administering punishment (fines), i.e., supervising?

As mentioned earlier, the new OSHA-*mandated* regulations (29CFR 1910.147) regarding lock-out procedures clearly specify how lock-outs shall be made. It does not seem sound policy that one organization makes the rules (OSHA) but another organization (the employer) is responsible for the results. Of course, employers should be the responsible party; they should also have responsibility for how results are obtained. Society, through government, cannot logically have it both ways. If real progress is to be achieved, this logical inconsistency needs resolution.

SUMMARY

The safety and health of employees, the public, and the environment is mandated by a large and proliferating body of legislation. This legislation has been established largely as a result of real or perceived short-comings in the results being obtained by employers.

Independent of the appropriateness of specific portions of such legislation, conducting operations in a way that employees, the public, and the environment are not adversely affected has been demonstrated to be "good business." The long-term interest of stockholders is maximized by doing so. Safety efforts are not, in a true sense, expenses that represent a burden on a business. They represent expenditures designed to lower the overall cost of operations. When wisely spent, such expenditures, in fact, do reduce operating cost. Safety has been demonstrated to be good business.

NOTES

1. Italics added.
2. Are employers and architects guilty of willfully providing an unsafe place (OSHA terminology) by installing marble steps 10 feet wide? Is the center of these steps a recognized hazard? By not providing a handrail?

CHAPTER 2

MOTIVATION OF TOP MANAGEMENT

THE NEED FOR EMOTIONAL COMMITMENT

In order to succeed at leading the organization for which it is responsible toward achieving excellence in safety, top management must have a source of motivation that transcends intellectual recognition of the need to improve. There must be an emotional source of drive toward excellence which carries on when purely rational analysis suggests that enough has been done; there must be an emotional source of motivation that stimulates and drives top management to believe that *all* injuries can be prevented and to take action that will propel the organization toward this goal.

The cost of injuries may provide the needed emotional drive for some managers. These costs—which were outlined in Chapter 1—are significant. They are not "just the cost of doing business." They are avoidable costs, not fixed overhead costs as they are frequently considered by many organizations. These are costs for which management is responsible and can profitably control. It should be expected to do so! If this expectation does not provide the necessary motivation, direct personal involvement can often provide an effective supplement.

Direct personal involvement is the best way, perhaps the only way, to inject an emotional aspect into the leadership process. This is what the American public was expressing intuitively by their negative reaction to a decision by Exxon's chairman not to go to the scene of the Valdez oil spill. Four case histories further illustrate this point.

Case I

An employee had lost his foot as a result of an on-the-job injury.[1] At the suggestion of a Du Pont safety management consultant, the CEO of the corporation—not just the plant manager or division director—took the company plane and visited the injured employee in the hospital in which he was recuperating. The conversation went approximately like this:

CEO: "John, I'm Bill Smith, head of the company. I've flown out here today to express my sympathy to you. I'm so sorry this has occurred."
John: "So am I. But it is my foot that is gone, not yours! Why did you let this happen?"
CEO: "John, I don't know. Do you hold me personally responsible for the loss of your foot?"
John: "Yes!"
CEO: "John, tell me what happened."
John: John gives a thorough report on how the injury occurred.
CEO: "But, don't we have rules against doing that?'
John: "Yes, but I broke the rules."
CEO: "Why?"
John: "Because you and your supervision don't enforce the rules. They don't make us follow the rules."

Employees understand that management is fully responsible for what occurs at the workplace, particularly if what occurs is undesirable. In this case, John acknowledged breaking the rules, but quickly shifted the burden of responsibility from himself to supervision. This is normal employee behavior, particularly in an atmosphere in which management (supervision) has recognized that hazards exist and has accomplished the intellectual task of writing rules, but has failed in its responsibility as supervisors to require compliance. The task of requiring compliance has become so distasteful to many supervisors that they simply ignore violations. In this environment employees and society will be quick to point out management's failure and therefore its culpability for the resulting injury. Supervision simply "must care enough" to do whatever is required to achieve the end result that employees do not engage in unsafe behavior. And that is what this book addresses.

Case II

Let me tell you about an experience of my own. A powerhouse organization was *pneumatically* testing a refrigeration machine.[2] Several machines had recently been successfully tested under the overall supervision of the previous powerhouse supervisor, who had died of a heart attack the previous week. The new powerhouse supervisor was not familiar with the design details of the various refrigeration machines. The machine under test was of a different design from those previously tested with success, under the direct supervision of the powerhouse first-line supervisor. The building housing the refrigeration machines had been barricaded at a distance of approximately 50 feet as a requirement established by top management (site manager) during a safety review of the testing procedure. In place was instrumentation for remote readings of test pressures which had been installed and used in three previous tests.

During the test procedure, the first-line supervisor and a powerhouse operator violated the barricade and proceeded to a window in the powerhouse wall to observe a pressure gauge on the refrigeration machine under test to verify the accuracy of the remote instrumentation. This act clearly demonstrated a failure in the safety morale of the supervisor and his operator, as well as others who were present but not "in charge"; a safety barricade was being violated and no one did anything effective in getting the supervisor and the operator back outside the barricade. (Binoculars could have been used to read the pressure gauge remotely.) Unfortunately, the event that had been anticipated for by the barricade occurred. The machine erupted. A large elbow was separated at a flange connection after the bolts by which it had been attached were stressed beyond their yield-point.

Unfortunately, the elbow was blown into the window through which the two employees were observing gauge readings. Fortunately, a portion of the energy transmitted to the elbow was absorbed by a structural building column. Both employees sustained cuts to their faces and neck areas and some damage to their ear drums. Safety glasses had provided substantial protection to their eyes.

Both men were taken to the hospital, their wives were informed, and arrangements were made for the services of a plastic surgeon. When one of the wives saw me (local top management should be at the hospital when an employee has been injured sufficiently to be taken to a hospital for possible hospitalization), her greeting was "What have you done to my beautiful husband?" Yes, "What have *you* done to my beautiful husband?" My own reaction was, of course, "What has your beautiful husband done to himself and to my safety performance?" However, the wife was correct and I hoped my face did not reveal what my first thoughts were. My second thought was that, indeed, I had failed to create the necessary understanding and discipline that would have prevented the unsafe behavior. I had presumed that Du Pont employees would have exercised the required discipline, but I was wrong. The wife's reaction is normal for spouses or close relatives of injured employees and reflects their correct understanding of management's responsibility for the prevention of injuries to employees.

Upper management had required the barricade, but had not sufficiently inculcated in the work force the safety discipline necessary to achieve an injury-free workplace.

Needless to say, this wife's words made a lasting impression—and a constructive impression—on me. As a direct result, upper management took a series of operational steps that successfully demonstrated to employees their need to work safely, without injury.

Because the words "operational steps" are not likely to convey much that is helpful to the reader, I will be more specific. Although the operator involved in the above incident was in no way reprimanded, the first-line supervisor was not so spared. This distinction reflects the fact that supervision held the primary responsibility. The operator had received injuries; the decision was that these were adequate to change his future behavior, which should be the purpose of discipline. The first-line supervisor had also been injured, at least as severely. But it was believed, because of his greater responsibility and because of his direct involvement in disregarding the barricade and his responsibilities to the operator, disciplinary measures should be taken. They were.

The new powerhouse supervisor was not disciplined. His behavior was considered reasonable under the circumstances; that is, other machines had been successfully tested, and procedures had been reviewed and approved by upper management and were being implemented by an experienced, well-esteemed first-line supervisor.

The superintendent to whom the powerhouse supervisor reported also escaped disciplinary measures, not because they were not justified, but because it was expected that he would soon retire and no justifiable purpose would be served. His continued employment was to be so short that he would not have benefited as a supervisor from the disciplinary experience and our "culture" would not have supported visible discipline from which others may have learned.

Several visible and less punitive steps were also taken: (1) A one-day visit was made by all "upper management"—the site manager and all superintendents reporting to him—to a large Du Pont facility that had established a superior safety record. All employees for whom the site manager was directly responsible knew of this visit, as it was widely publicized. (2) An increase in the frequency and intensity of the management safety audit program for the organization was initiated. (3) A more vigorously supported and active participation in the process hazards review process by upper management was established. (4) Other actions were initiated that were less obvious but equally as significant because of their persistent presence in the day-to-day management of the organization's activities. The safety aspects of virtually all activities were carefully scrutinized by the site manager at every opportunity. I believe there was no remaining doubt regarding the need to avoid another "unfortunate" safety episode.

Following this injury experience and the preventive measures undertaken, the organization achieved more than ten years of injury-free performance[3]—a total of 17.5 million exposure hours (13.5 million if the injury cited in the footnote is used as reference point).

Case III

A third case history provides an additional example of what management "can do" to support a successful safety program. The involved manufacturing site had a long-standing, well-recognized safety rule that stated "no equipment shall be operated from which an installed guard has been removed, without prior approval of the area supervisor or superintendent."

During the 12 midnight to 8:00 A.M. shift, a quality problem had become recognized. Vibration of a drive motor was thought to be a possible source of the problem. The shift mechanic (who was a part of the engineering and maintenance organization and therefore did not report through the manufacturing organization), together with the manufacturing first-line supervisor responsible for the operation, decided to check the vibration of the equipment using a stroboscope. (A stroboscope is a lamp that provides the ability to change the frequency of the emitted light. This enables rotating equipment to be "stopped" to the eye, and thus facilitates detection of vibrations of a different frequency.)

During the next regular morning "production" meeting at which events of the previous 24 hours were reviewed and plans for the future determined, the quality question arose. It was reported that the vibration analysis had been done on the 12 to 8 shift. The superintendent raised the question of how this could have been accomplished without removal of the guard. An examination of the equipment suggested that, indeed, an adequate analysis could not have been accomplished without removal of the guard. The test was repeated, with the superintendent's permission to do so with the guard removed. The results confirmed those reported by the 12 to 8 team of the mechanic and the shift supervisor. The superintendent then called the shift supervisor at home to determine if the observations that he and the mechanic had reported were obtained while the guard had been removed. The supervisor confirmed that the guard had been removed in violation of the safety rules. Maintenance supervision called the mechanic and received the same report. After a discussion with upper management, the following disciplinary steps were taken:

The mechanic was reassigned to the day shift for additional training and was required to work as a "helper" to a mechanic who was well known for his thoroughness regarding safety. The mechanic's classification as mechanic was not changed; only his work assignment was changed. The purpose of this reassignment was to re-establish his ability to work unsupervised at night. The thought was that he had been on shifts too long and needed some additional exposure to "daytime" standards. Although no change in job classification was involved, the change from "shifts" to "days" reduced this mechanic's pay by approximately 10%. He was also not allowed to work overtime without supervision. After approximately six months, he was allowed to exercise his seniority and he returned to shift work.

The supervisor involved was not allowed to return to work on his next scheduled shift; that is, another member of supervision was required to "cover" for him. The man in question was an experienced and effective supervisor with 30+ years of service. He was told to think about whether he could continue to be an effective member of supervision, and if he concluded that he could he should prepare a written paper in which he presented his "case" for retention. He was also instructed to give particular attention to the matter of his trustworthiness to operate without supervision and as a responsible member of management. It was suggested that he take about one week to accomplish this re-evaluation. He did. He also presented a convincing argument for his retention as a supervisor. He was returned to his supervisory position. Both the union and much of supervision presumed that the supervisor was not paid during his "time off." Whether he was or not has never been revealed. A good case can be made for either treatment.

Needless to say, the actions became well known throughout the plant, of which this particular operation was but a small part. The decision needed to be able to withstand union challenge. It did! The challenge was that surely the rule had been violated in the past without management's taking so severe an action. Upper management had done its homework. At the time of the decision to reassign the mechanic, a survey of supervision (approximately 140 people) was quickly made to determine if any of them could recall an instance in which this rule had been violated. None surfaced, and none was subsequently revealed by the union. This finding also supported the action taken regarding the supervisor. A direct, overt, conscious decision has been made to ignore a well-established and understood safety rule. There were no mitigating circumstances. The superintendent was at home and available by telephone. The responsibility was unambiguous. The mechanic should have refused participation in this rule violation and the supervisor should not have initiated or participated in the unsafe action, even though he had good intentions.

It was the unsafe behavior, not an injury, that precipitated the disciplinary action. This distinction is important. Management must vigorously support established rules on a continuous, uninterrupted basis—not just when an injury occurs.

Case IV

A fourth anecdote provides yet another view of a vigorousgly supported safety program and management's responsibility to it. I was demonstrating the process of conducting management safety audits to a client. We were watching a young electrician work on a control circuit. We observed that he was doing some things well but also that he was working without safety glasses and without gloves, neither of which was required by the client's work rules. We wondered if the electrical circuit had been tagged out as was required by the client's work rules. I introduced myself to the electrician as being from Du Pont and explained that I was showing some of his supervision what we in Du Pont call a management safety audit. He responded immediately that "he was in trouble." I explained that it was not our purpose to get him in trouble, but rather to tell him some of the good things we had seen him do, and then see if he could recognize some actions he could change that would improve the safety of his work. "Well," he responded, "I would have been fired three times if this were a Du Pont facility." I was taken aback—in fact, I was embarrassed—because I had been stressing with the client that demonstrated management interest, not harsh discipline, was the main tool in achieving safety—although discipline has its place.

I asked the young man if he had actually worked for Du Pont and he said, "Yes." I asked, "Where?" He replied, "In Corpus Christi, Texas. It was on the chlorine project." His answer established his credibility. I then suggested that he tell us about the three items he had on his mind. He said, "I don't have safety glasses on, but they are not required here. I don't have gloves on, but they are not required here. And I don't have my personal lock on this circuit."

This employee could immediately relate his present circumstances to those he recognized as a Du Pont requirement. There was no hesitation. He responded immediately upon hearing I was from Du Pont. I asked him if he had ever known anyone to have been fired from Du Pont for the reasons he mentioned. He answered, "No, because when you work for Du Pont you follow the rules. Everyone understands this. They follow the rules and, therefore, no one gets fired. But you will if you break the rules!" Sometime, somehow, Du Pont had established a clear understanding of the need to follow the rules. This employee's testimony may have been an exaggeration, but it was spontaneous—and credible.

I then asked the electrician if those rules were good rules. He said, "Yes." I queried, "If they are good rules, why don't you follow the rules even if you are not at Du Pont?" He responded by saying they were not required. I persisted, "But if they are good rules, wouldn't it make sense to follow them even if they are not required?" He said, "Yes, but you know how it is—most of us won't do the right thing just because it's right. Supervision has to make us do it. We don't want to take the time. We don't think anything is going to happen to us." I then asked, "In view of the strict discipline you mentioned at Du Pont, did you enjoy working there? Would you work for Du Pont again?" He said, "I'd go back tomorrow if I had the chance." I asked, "Why?" He answered, "Because I know I will be able to go home every night. They even required us to wear life jackets when we worked on the pier out in the water, and were they hot! But it was a good idea."

I then returned to the work situation and asked the employee if the circuit on which he was working was de-energized. He said, "Yes, by one of these tags they use here." I asked if he would feel more comfortable using his own personal lock. He responded, "Yes." We thanked this employee for his contribution and moved on. He had taught my client more than I ever could.

ESTABLISHING AND MAINTAINING CREDIBILITY

It is management responsibility to establish working conditions, and to see that they remain established. Management is responsible for the results that are obtained. It is not a responsibility that can be delegated solely to the individual employee. Employees should be expected to behave "properly" but it is management's task to define what is "proper"—and "proper" is whatever it takes to remain injury-free if that is one of management's goals.

These four case histories illustrate the absolute necessity for management to establish its credibility regarding its interest in and dedication to employee safety. Credibility is not easily established, and once established it is easily lost.

Peters and Waterman put this fact this way in *In Search of Excellence*:[4]

> Hands-on systems of leadership and instilling values thrive only to the extent that they are *totally* credible to those down the line. Credibility is built up almost entirely "because I was there." Without emotional commitment, without understanding of the product, there will be no suspension of disbelief.

Drucker addresses the issue of leadership similarly in the editorial from *The Wall Street Journal* shown as Figure 2-1.

The article by Vermont Royster (Figure 2-2), captures one man's way of "being there" as well as how he instilled trust. There is nothing new about managing by walking around. Those who have done so successfully also found useful things to do while walking around. The interested manager, I hope, will find in this book many useful things to do while "walking around." Chapters 7 and 8 on Management Safety Audits emphasize this point.

The four vignettes may suggest that discipline has a major role to play in achieving excellence in safety. There is a place for discipline in achieving excellence in safety, and working safely should be a condition of employment. As Drucker states, "Effec-

Leadership: More Doing Than Dash

By Peter F. Drucker

Leadership is all the rage just now. "We'd want you to run a seminar for us on how one acquires charisma," the human-resources VP of a big bank said to me on the telephone—in dead earnest. Books, articles and conferences on leadership and on the "qualities" of the leader abound. Every CEO, it seems, has to be made to look like a dashing Confederate cavalry general or a board-room Elvis Presley.

Leadership does matter, of course. But, alas, it is something different from what is now touted under this label. It has little to do with "leadership qualities" and even less to do with "charisma." It is mundane, unromantic and boring. Its essence is performance.

In the first place, leadership is not by itself good or desirable. Leadership is a means. Leadership to what end is thus the crucial question. History knows no more charismatic leaders than this century's triad of Stalin, Hitler and Mao—the misleaders who inflicted as much evil and suffering on humanity as have ever been recorded.

The Undoing of Leaders

But effective leadership doesn't depend on charisma. Dwight Eisenhower, George Marshall and Harry Truman were singularly effective leaders yet none possessed any more charisma than a dead mackerel. Nor did Konrad Adenauer, the chancellor who rebuilt West Germany after World War II. No less charismatic personality could be imagined than Abe Lincoln of Illinois, the raw-boned, uncouth backwoodsman of 1860. And there was amazingly little charisma to the bitter, defeated, almost broken Churchill of the inter-war years; what mattered was that he turned out in the end to have been right.

Indeed, charisma becomes the undoing of leaders. It makes them inflexible, convinced of their own infallibility, unable to change. This is what happened to Stalin, Hitler and Mao, and it is a commonplace in the study of ancient history that only Alexander the Great's early death saved him from becoming an ineffectual failure.

Indeed, charisma does not by itself guarantee effectiveness as a leader. John F. Kennedy may have been the most charismatic person ever to occupy the White House. Yet few presidents got as little done.

Nor are there any such things as "leadership qualities" or a "leadership personality." Franklin D. Roosevelt, Winston Churchill, George Marshall, Dwight Eisenhower, Bernard Montgomery and Douglas MacArthur, were all highly effective—and highly visible—leaders during World War II. No two of them shared any "personality traits" or any "qualities."

What then is leadership if it is not charisma and not a set of personality traits? The first thing to say about it is that it is work—something stressed again and again by the most charismatic leaders: Julius Caesar, for instance, or Gen. MacArthur and Field Marshal Montgomery, or, to use an example from business, Alfred Sloan, the man who built and led General Motors from 1920 to 1955.

The foundation of effective leadership is thinking through the organization's mission, defining it and establishing it, clearly and visibly. The leader sets the goals, sets

Drucker on Management

Effective leadership doesn't depend on charisma. Eisenhower, George Marshall and Truman were singularly effective leaders yet none possessed any more charisma than a dead mackerel.

Figure 2–1

the priorities, and sets and maintains the standards. He makes compromises, of course; indeed, effective leaders are painfully aware that they are not in control of the universe. (Only misleaders—the Stalins, Hitlers, Maos—suffer from that delusion.) But before accepting a compromise, the effective leader has thought through what is right and desirable. The leader's first task is to be the trumpet that sounds a clear sound.

What distinguishes the leader from the misleader are his goals. Whether the compromise he makes with the constraints of reality—which may involve political, economic, financial or people problems—are compatible with his mission and goals or lead away from them determines whether he is an effective leader. And whether he holds fast to a few basic standards (exemplifying them in his own conduct) or whether "standards" for him are what he can get away with, determines whether the leader has followers or only hypocritical time-servers.

The second requirement is that the leader see leadership as responsibility rather than as rank and privilege. Effective leaders are rarely "permissive." But when things go wrong—and they always do—they do not blame others. If Winston Churchill is an example of leadership through clearly defining mission and goals, Gen. George Marshall, America's chief of staff in World War II, is an example of leadership through responsibility. Harry Truman's folksy "The buck stops here" is still as good a definition as any.

But precisely because an effective leader knows that he, and no one else, is ultimately responsible, he is not afraid of strength in associates and subordinates. Misleaders are; they always go in for purges. But an effective leader wants strong associates; he encourages them, pushes them, indeed glories in them. Because he holds himself ultimately responsible for the mistakes of his associates and subordinates, he also sees the triumphs of his associates and subordinates as his triumphs, rather than as threats. A leader may be personally vain—as Gen. MacArthur was to an almost pathological degree. Or he may be personally humble—both Lincoln and Truman were so almost to the point of having inferiority complexes. But all three wanted able, independent, self-assured people around them; they encouraged their associates and subordinates, praising and promoting them. So did a very different person: Ike Eisenhower, when supreme commander in Europe.

An effective leader knows, of course, that there is a risk: Able people tend to be ambitious. But he realizes that it is a much smaller risk than to be served by mediocrity. He also knows that the gravest indictment of a leader is for the organization to collapse as soon as he leaves or dies, as happened in Russia the moment Stalin died and as happens all too often in companies. An effective leader knows that the ultimate task of leadership is to create human energies and human vision.

Earning Trust Is a Must

The final requirement of effective leadership is to earn trust. Otherwise there won't be any followers—and the only definition of a leader is someone who has followers. To trust a leader, it is not necessary to like him. Nor is it necessary to agree with him. Trust is the conviction that the leader means what he says. It is a belief in something very old-fashioned, called "integrity." A leader's actions and a leader's professed beliefs must be congruent, or at least compatible. Effective leadership—and again this is very old wisdom—is not based on being clever; it is based primarily on being consistent.

After I had said these things on the telephone to the bank's human-resources VP, there was a long silence. Finally she said: "But that's no different at all from what we have known for years are the requirements for being an effective manager."

Precisely.

Mr. Drucker is Clarke professor of social sciences at the Claremont Graduate School.

Figure 2-1 (*continued*)

Manager's Journal

By Vermont Royster

It can be interesting to read how academics and others who have never managed anything think chief executives should manage their enterprises, just as it can be to read commentators say how a U.S. president should run the Oval Office.

But to me the more interesting of these Journal features are those that tell how actual managers manage. And reading these accounts always brings to mind memories of the late Bernard Kilgore, one-time chief executive of Dow Jones and architect of the modern Wall Street Journal. His was a very personal style rarely seen.

Barney was barely 35 in 1943 when he became *de facto* chief executive due to the long illness of his predecessor (he would shortly gain the formal title). His previous managerial experience was limited; he had been chief of the Journal's Washington bureau and, briefly, managing editor.

Perhaps his youth had something to do with his style, for though he was supremely confident of what he wanted to do with the newspaper and the company, he had to deal with subordinates who were much older. In any event he hardly ever called any department head to his office. Instead, he made a daily practice of going to see them.

After the morning's paper work, he would start from his eyrie on the top floor and walk down through the building, floor by floor. On the way he would stop off at the office of the advertising director, the circulation manager, the comptroller, the editor, managing editor and other key people. If they were busy, he might wave and pass on. If not, he would stop and ask them what was going on in their area, what plans they had and so forth. If he had questions, he asked. If he had thoughts, he would express them, more often phrased as suggestions rather than orders.

Along the way he also would stop to chat with secretaries, clerks or copyboys. These journeys would end in the basement where the printing presses were located. There, too, he would talk not only with the production manager but also with linotype operators and pressmen, many of whom he knew and all of whom knew him. Only the newest employee ever called him Mr. Kilgore. To everyone else he was Barney.

It was all informal and seemingly unstructured. But by day's end he would have a clearer idea of the company's affairs than he would ever get from memos or reports. Very little escaped him.

His method was the same with other company offices. He would often drop in unannounced in San Francisco or Dallas and follow the same routine as in New York. This gave everyone the feeling "attention was being paid" to whatever he was doing.

Dow Jones did, it's true, have something called a management committee on which the department heads were nominally members, but it rarely met more than once a year. That was, supposedly, to finalize the budget. But in fact Barney already had the figures and had approved them, so the business was quickly concluded.

For the Journal itself, for which he already had visions as a national newspaper, his method was equally unorthodox. Every morning he gathered with key editorial people in what became known around the shop as the "kaffee klatsch." Sometimes these gatherings were post-mortems on the morning paper, which Barney had read thoroughly and about which he would have comments of both praise and criticism. At other times there would be seemingly desultory conversation about the state of the world and what developments might be worth future stories.

Everybody was expected to join in, and anybody who disagreed with Barney was expected to say so. I have a vivid memory of once saying one of his ideas was "stupid" and then gulping at using the word to my boss, stammering an apology. He merely chuckled, shrugged his shoulders and said, "Not to worry. I'm the one person around the shop who can't afford to get mad."

Nonetheless, there was never any doubt about who was the boss. When he said something had to be done, it was best done quickly. When he said "no" to a project, that was it. But such direct orders were rare. He always preferred persuasion.

Even as the newspaper grew and the company expanded into new activities, Barney retained his personal style, even though the time inevitably came when he couldn't have the same personal contact with everyone on the much larger staff. "Creeping bureaucracy" was his phrase, always uttered with a touch of sadness. But he never ceased trying for the personal touch. When we moved into larger (and more sumptuous) quarters, his office door remained open to passersby. To see Barney you didn't need an appointment.

His method of choosing key people was equally personal. To a large extent, especially in the beginning, he had to choose from among people already on the staff, and that was always his preference. When he needed a new managing editor or editor, he would choose, in part, by past performance—but also in part by his intuitive feeling of whether the person could deal with larger responsibilities. In that way he was remarkably successful.

His immediate successor, William F. Kerby, had been with the paper for many years as a managing editor, executive editor and as a corporate vice president. I remember when Dow Jones bought the Chicago Journal of Commerce, Barney did all the preliminary negotiations and then sent Bill Kerby to Chicago to complete the deal while he himself went off on vacation. That was his way of showing trust in and putting a challenge to Kerby. When that challenge was met, Kerby was thereafter marked to be the next chief executive.

I'm well aware that this style wouldn't suit every chief executive and every organization. Barney's personal style grew out of the kind of man he was, a visionary who was too shy to go about barking orders. Anyway, I leave the business of giving managerial advice to MBA professors and others who know better than I how organizations should be run.

But wouldn't it be refreshing someday to see even a president of the United States who got out of the Oval Office now and then, instead of letting someone else choose his visitors? Who simply wandered around the Executive Office chatting with secretaries and popping in unannounced on subordinates in the White House basement?

That might at least keep him from being surprised at what some of his people are up to.

Mr. Royster is editor emeritus of the Journal.

Figure 2-2 "Life With Barney at The Wall Street Journal"

tive leaders are rarely 'permissive.'" However, management *leadership* in safety is the primary means and the practices discussed in this book can provide management with the tools to demonstrate leadership. Rarely is discipline necessary when adequate management leadership has been demonstrated.

As well established as is Du Pont's dedication to safety, employees are constantly sensitive to any signs of diminution of this dedication. In most companies, managers have not established the needed level of trust and belief within their subordinates. Suspicions run deep that management's interest in safety may flag or is only a facade. Because the average employee has seldom seen the needed dedication to excellence in *any* endeavor (why do we all remember Vince Lombardi's credo that "winning is not the most important thing; it's the only thing?"), many tend to be cynical about management safety efforts. They are quick to perceive any management action that might indicate "back sliding" on the part of any member of the management team at any level.

In the early spring of 1986, Du Pont published its first corporate "mission statement." This statement included many of the normal items contained in such documents, including a strong safety statement that was physically positioned last—not first, where the majority of Du Pont employees had expected it. This mission statement also emphasized the need to take prudent business risks.

The placement of the safety statement was interpreted by many employees—including some site managers, marketing managers, and other actively visible management personnel who are encountered by the great bulk of employees on a day-to-day basis—as a de-emphasis of the historic role of safety within Du Pont. Responding to this interpretation, and a deterioration in the company's safety performance in 1986 and 1987, the chairman of the board, the CEO, and the president of the company made a videotape with the message that Du Pont had not pulled back from its historic commitment to employee safety. The message was that the company had a number of "missions" and that safety was an integral part of each of them and that placement of the safety statement at the end was meant to emphasize this fact, not diminish it. Employees heard the words, believed that their top management meant what it said, but still asked, "Why don't they just move the safety statement to the top of the page? That would remove lingering doubts." Communicating is tough, isn't it?

The chairman took full responsibility for the two-year deterioration in performance (leadership!). He acknowledged that he had expected that Du Pont's safety culture was sufficiently well established that its momentum would suffice as the company undertook major reorganization steps. He acknowledged that the lesson that safety must be sought continuously—day after day—had to be learned once again. He expressed the view that his job performance in safety for the past two years had to be judged as unsatisfactory and that it was his intention to correct this performance before he turned over the responsibilities of chairmanship to his successor two years hence. Among other actions, he took the top thirty or so of his subordinates to the Pocono mountains in Pennsylvania for a full day (Saturday) meeting of soul-searching regarding their failed safety performance.

In 1988, performance improved; the Lost Workday case frequency rate was 0.03. Performance improved again in 1989, virtually matching the best performance records in the company's history of 0.02 established in 1982 and 1985. There were no fatalities in 1989, in comparison to two fatalities in 1982 and two in 1985. Leadership gets results.

In addition, the interpretation of the classification rules regarding back injuries were altered slightly during this time period (although this was denied by OSHA), making some back cases recordable which were not previously recordable. Back injuries remain a significant source of injuries[5]; when the numbers in absolute terms get small, each case becomes significant. A frequency rate of 0.024 for Lost Workday Cases for Du Pont in 1989 represented twenty-seven cases, world-wide. Employment averaged 110,000.

SUMMARY

Management needs a continuing source of motivation to instill an adequate sense of safety discipline within the organization, if the drive toward excellence is to be ongoing and sustainable. For some managers, recognition of the true costs of injuries and acceptance that these are controllable costs may be sufficient. For many, direct personal involvement with the injured and his or her family will be necessary. Others may become adequately motivated simply by the need to make improvements, or to be better than the competition. Whatever the source, the needed ingredient is that quality known as LEADERSHIP.

NOTES

1. I have attempted to avoid the use of the word "accident." Its meaning is ambiguous. An accident may or may not result in an injury. Also some dictionaries cite as a definition "due to chance" or "the result of an unforeseen or uncontrollable event." The concept of an uncontrollable act is inconsistent with the concept that all injuries can be prevented, which is the central truth upon which successful safety management is founded.

2. Pneumatic testing is an example of an entire family of hazardous circumstances in which "stored energy" is involved. Others are: compressed springs, compressed gases, and objects at elevated heights. These are all hazardous because of the possibility that the stored energy may be released in an uncontrolled manner with possible uncontrolled results. The concept of "stored energy" can be the basis of a particularly useful safety education program.

3. This statistic omits an injury that was thought by some to have arisen out of "normal activity of daily living" and a pre-existing personal condition. The injury was, however, officially classified as work-related.

4. T. J. Peters and R. H. Waterman, Jr., *In Search of Excellence,* Harper & Row, Publishers, Inc. New York, 1982, p. 293.

5. See Figure 1-10, Chapter 1, page 13.

CHAPTER 3

SAFETY POLICY

In this chapter we begin the process of examining those organizational arrangements—concepts and activities—through which the actions of managers can lead to demonstrated leadership in safety.

Although virtually all executives profess to be interested in "safety" and most probably have some sort of safety statement "on the books," they frequently lack the dedication to establish the safety leadership necessary for achieving excellence in their organizations. Many managers really do have a desire for their organizations to seek safety excellence, but simply do not understand the subject well enough to provide the requisite leadership. Lacking understanding at the top, the organization fails to develop the tools and skills needed to achieve long-term excellence.

THE CONTINUOUS SAFETY MANAGEMENT PROCESS

A myriad of arrangements and activities are available to managers who strive for effective ways to demonstrate their concern for employees, the public, and the environment, as shown in Figure 4-1. These arrangements and activities appear in circular form—an integrated whole that provides for continuous measurement, evaluation, and renewal. The process is markedly similar to that of Statistical Quality Control (SQC), although it has developed in a different way. Shewhart developed SQC as an almost "full blown" body of applied science.[1] He was dealing with product measurements—that is, numbers. Shewhart presented his analysis and a pragmatic scheme for continually improving the quality of manufactured product through well-structured, rigorously applied statistical procedures.

The development of the Central Safety Committee concept and its ancillary activities (see Figure 4-2) occurred about the same time—1928. It was in 1928 that Du Pont first recognized, through empirical data, that injuries arise from the unsafe acts of people and therefore *all injuries can be prevented.* Because management, ultimately, is responsible for the behavior of employees, beginning in 1928 Du Pont management has been held fully responsible for the prevention of injuries. The arrangements and activities illustrated in Figures 4-1 and 4-2 were not developed "full blown." They are the current distillation of trial and error—pragmatic testing of what works in the reality of the day-to-day environment in which employees work. This testing continues, and new arrangements and activities will surely be forthcoming as both leaders and followers seek improvement.

The raw material of Statistical Quality Control is things; the raw material for safety is people, not things. Many have found numerous similarities between SQC and the Central Safety Committee (CSC) concept.[2] These disciplines have in common the fundamental concept of measurement, evaluation, and feedback to the system for taking improvement steps. Their differences reflect the differences between things and people—the inanimate versus the animate. Individually, things do not change from day-to-day, whereas people seem to be, individually as well as collectively, in a perpetual state of change. Thus, different mechanisms for success have been developed. The emerging concept of Total Quality has attempted to expand the concept of Statistical Quality Control to every activity. In this sense, the Central Safety Committee and its ramifications can be thought of as a subset of Total Quality.

The arrangements and activities depicted in Figure 4-1 are managed through the Central Safety, Health, and Environment Committee, the chairman of which is the leader, or would be leader, of the involved organization. This management structure is outlined in Figure 4-2. It is through the operation of the CSC that the "head" of the organization places his or her safety imprimatur on the organization. It is through the CSC that effective implementation of the organization's safety policy takes place. The operation of the CSC is examined in detail in Chapter 4.

DEVELOPING A SAFETY POLICY

In Figures 3-1 through 3-6 are shown a variety of safety policy statements reflecting a wide variety of styles and to a lesser degree content. Good internal safety policy statements provide two messages:

1. A declaration of management's commitment to the well being of employees, the public, and the environment.
2. A set of principles, or philosophies, by which management is guided in putting the commitment statement into practice. A well thought out safety policy provides the anchor to which members of the organization can turn for guidance in the day-to-day execution of their work in an ever-changing environment. When well prepared, a Safety Policy establishes the basic "ground rules" or points of operational philosophy upon which all employees can (must) agree. These serve as the foundation for the specific actions that may be taken in the future. These points are not normally obvious to everyone.

text continues on page 48

SAFETY ORGANIZATION AND ADMINISTRATION

The Du Pont Company's safety philosophy was aptly put by Mr. Walter S. Carpenter, Jr., when he was Chairman of the Board (1948-1962).

"We in the Du Pont Company long ago concluded that the safety of employees is of the greatest interest to management, ranking in importance with production, quality of product, and costs. We have found that maintenance of safe operating procedures in our plants is of benefit far beyond any resulting dollar savings, the human values involved being of greater importance to both employer and community. Also, the acceptance and practice of fundamental safety principles by management and men, with the reduction of personal injuries to a minimum, inject an element of team play which does much to foster a spirit of friendly cooperation throughout our Company."

Du Pont Safety Philosophy

The success of the Company's safety effort depends upon a thorough understanding and acceptance of the principles upon which this effort is based:

1. **ALL INJURIES CAN BE PREVENTED.** The key word here is "ALL." This is a realistic goal and not just a theoretical objective! A supervisor with the responsibility for the well-being of employees cannot be effective without fully accepting this principle.
2. **MANAGEMENT, WHICH INCLUDES ALL LEVELS THROUGH THE FOREMAN, HAS THE RESPONSIBILITY FOR PREVENTING PERSONAL INJURIES.** Since line organization has the responsibility for every operational activity of the Company, each supervisor must accept his share of the responsibility for the safety of the employees.
3. **IT IS REASONABLY POSSIBLE TO SAFEGUARD ALL OPERATING EXPOSURES WHICH MAY RESULT IN INJURIES.** It is preferable, of course, to eliminate the sources of danger. However, where this is not reasonable or practical, supervision must resort to such measures as the use of guards, safety devices, and protective clothing. No matter what the exposure, an effective safeguard can be provided.
4. **IT IS NECESSARY TO TRAIN ALL EMPLOYEES TO WORK SAFELY AND TO UNDERSTAND THAT IT IS TO THEIR ADVANTAGE, AS WELL AS THE COMPANY'S, TO WORK SAFELY AND THAT THEY HAVE A DEFINITE RESPONSIBILITY TO DO SO.** Adequate training of the employee is a responsibility of supervision. Each individual, however, must be convinced that he has a responsibility for working safely and that to do so not only benefits the Company but indeed is a very real personal benefit.
5. **IT IS GOOD BUSINESS FROM THE STANDPOINT OF BOTH EFFICIENCY AND ECONOMY TO PREVENT PERSONAL INJURIES ON THE JOB AND OFF THE JOB.** In addition to the humanitarian aspects, injuries cost money and reduce efficiency.

Safety Responsibilities

Safety, an integral part of every job, is a line organization responsibility. To whatever extent each individual is responsible for operations, to that same extent he is responsible also for the safety of such operations. The manager is responsible for the safety of all plant employees. When a foreman, a supervisor, or a superintendent is given the job of running an operation, responsibility for the safety of the employees working in that operation goes with it. Finally, the individual employee in accepting his job assumes the responsibility for working safely. When these divisions of responsibility for plant personnel are systematically united for safety as they are united for operations, the result is a safe working organization identical with the operating organization.

Figure 3-1

SAFETY & HEALTH PHILOSOPHY AND POLICY

The DuPont Company has always operated on the basis that the safety and health of employees are of the greatest importance, ranking along with quality, production, employee relations, and costs. Safe operating procedures and practices are of benefit far beyond any dollar savings, the human values involved being much greater to employer, employee, and community. Success of the ABC organization effort depends upon a thorough understanding and acceptance of the following principles.

1. All injuries or any damage to health can be prevented.
2. The prevention of bodily injury and the safeguarding of an individual's health must be the first consideration in all actions and are the responsibility of each employee.
3. Rules and procedures to minimize the possibility of bodily injury or damage to health are essential parts of the company safety and health program. All individuals are responsible for knowing and following the safety and health rules and procedures applicable to their assignments. In addition to strict adherence to these rules, **each individual is responsible for using sound judgment on each assignment and for being aware of potential hazards to himself/herself or others before taking action.**
4. Supervision is responsible for correcting work conditions and employee actions that may cause bodily injury or damage to health, property and environment and to inform employees of known potential hazards encountered in the workplace.
5. Supervision is responsible for training individuals and making equipment and appropriate job procedures available so that each assignment can be completed without bodily injury or damage to health, property, or environment.
6. Orderliness and cleanliness (housekeeping) of the work environment are integral parts of the prevention of injuries and damage to health.
7. Off the job, the conduct of each employee should be such that disabling injuries or illnesses are avoided. Supervision will provide all reasonable means of educating employees toward this goal.

Figure 3-2

Policy Guidelines on Health, Safety and Environmental Conservation

This statement, a revision of an earlier one, sets out to guide individual ABC companies on health, safety and environmental conservation matters. It has been endorsed by the Steering Committee for Safety and Environmental Conservation and by the Committee of the Managing Directors.

Policy guidelines

It is the policy of ABC companies to conduct their activities in such a way as to take foremost account of the health and safety of their employees and of other persons, and to give proper regard to the conservation of the environment. In implementing this policy ABC companies not only comply with the requirements of the relevant legislation but promote in an appropriate manner measures for the protection of health, safety and the environment for all who may be affected directly or indirectly by their activities.

In following this policy they:

- Recognize the importance of the on-going involvement and commitment of management and other employees and the necessity of ensuring that they have the required skills and support;
- Seek to conduct all their activities in such a way as to avoid harm to the health of, or injury to, employees and others and damage to property;
- Work on the principle that all injuries should be prevented, and promote actively amongst all those associated with their activities the high standards of safety consciousness and discipline that this principle demands:
- Use their best endeavours to provide products, together with practical advice on their application, which will not cause injury to health or undue impact on the environment when they are used in accordance with this advice;
- Apply the best practicable means to preserve air, water, soil and plant and animal life from adverse effects of their operations and to minimize any nuisance that may arise;
- Use their best endeavours to ensure that contractors working on their behalf apply health, safety and environmental standards fully compatible with their own;
- Keep their employees, contractors, and the relevant authorities appropriately informed of known potential hazards that might affect them; and make them aware of what is being done to minimize the risks and to improve the quality and safety of the working environment;
- Establish and maintain contingency procedures to minimize harm from accidents that may nevertheless occur, and work with the relevant authorities and emergency services in an appropriate manner in the development and application of these contingency procedures;
- Include an assessment of health, safety and environmental matters in the factors to be taken into consideration before entering into new ventures or activities or acquiring companies;
- Work with governments, local authorities, industry, academic and professional bodies and employees or their representatives as appropriate and take the initiative, where necessary, to promote workable and improved codes of practice and timely and practical regulations which relate to the above matters;
- Conduct or support research directed towards the improvement of safety and health at work, towards ensuring the safety of their products and towards the conservation of the environment;
- Facilitate the transfer to others, freely or on a commercial basis, of know-how ABC Companies develop in these fields;
- Include expected future requirements and anticipated developments in all the above areas in their long-term planning.

Figure 3-3

Sample Safety Policy I

This site safety policy is established to support the XYZ corporate safety policy and to provide an on-site safety policy to guide plant employees in attaining an injury-free environment in which to work. It is a statement of management's attitude toward safety; all employees are expected to share this attitude and philosophy.

The plant believes it is management's responsibility to provide a safe working environment—this includes both a safe physical environment and employees who perform their work in a safe, injury-free manner.

We believe:

1. All injuries can be prevented.
2. Safety is an integral and equal part of all business considerations: production, cost, quality, profit, and employee relations.
3. Prevention of both on- and off-the-job injuries is good business practice.
4. All operating exposures can be safeguarded, and it is the responsibility of management to ensure that this is accomplished.
5. Safety is a condition of employment.

It is management's responsibility to:

1. Train all employees in safe work practices.
2. Conduct frequent in-the-plant safety audits to ensure employee participation in the ongoing safety efforts of the plant, to ensure the use of safe work practices, and to take corrective action as necessary.
3. Require every employee to use safe work practices in the performance of job duties.

It is the responsibility of all employees to:

1. Adhere strictly to site safety principles.
2. Integrate safety into each job function and live by this philosophy in the performance of job duties.
3. Understand that this policy is designed to protect the well-being of employees and to avoid loss of plant property and equipment.
4. Understand and accept the safety attitude and philosophy reflected in this site safety policy.
5. Understand and accept that safety is a condition of employment.

Figure 3–4

Sample Safety Policy II

Employee safety and health are of prime importance to the company and its management. We are corporately committed to the well-being of every employee.

Supporting Principles

All injuries, occupational illnesses, and damage to the environment can be prevented.

Each supervisor is responsible for administering the accident prevention program and will be evaluated accordingly.

Safety is the responsibility of every employee and every employee must follow safe working practices.

Training is an essential element for a safe working environment.

Safety performance reviews must be a continuing process.

All injuries, all unsafe practices and all incidents with injury potential will be investigated.

The prevention of accidents, illnesses, and damage to the environment is good business.

Figure 3-5

DU PONT SAFETY POLICY

We will not make, handle, use, sell, transport, or dispose of a product unless we can do so safely and in an environmentally sound manner.

Figure 3-6

continued from page 42

The preparation of a safety policy is not a trivial undertaking. To be useful, the policy statement must be effectively communicated. To accomplish effective communication management must *understand* the policy and its implications for the organization. This understanding is not likely to exist if a safety policy is prepared by others. The policy should be homemade—developed by the top management of the organization to which it applies. Although corporate policy statements may be necessary for guidance of mid-level supervision, communication with the rank-and-file—the people who most frequently are injured—is best accomplished by local site managers. Plant or site managers, regional marketing managers, and group business managers are the "top" managers of the organizations to which most employees feel they belong. These are the managers whom most employees consider their expected leaders. These are the managers whom employees view as the most important in directing "their" organization. For this reason, every manufacturing site or operational organization should prepare its own personalized safety policy. If the site is a large one in which its many pieces have little or nothing in common, each piece should prepare its own safety policy, reflecting the commitment, beliefs, and principles of the management of the individual pieces. The need here is to avoid the absentee landlord syndrome from which sterile policies are likely to emerge.

The preparation of such policy statements is time and energy consuming. They require management thought. They are best hammered out at the top. For maximum educational value as well as for the quality of the resulting statement, the "top" should include all management personnel reporting directly to the "top." By proceeding in this fashion, each member of the "top's" staff (each direct subordinate) must participate and as a consequence is more likely to become a strong, understanding supporter of the final document. It is essential that commitment be fully developed at this level. The quote from *In Search of Excellence* cited in Chapter 2 applies here.

Such a procedure—utilizing the top manager and his or her staff to develop an organizational safety policy—does not usually include the organization's safety professional. This is not an oversight; it is by design. Safety is a line management responsibility. By formulating a safety policy in this fashion, management demonstrates its understanding of this central truth. By management's behavior, members of the organizatiion will get the message that safety is a line management responsibility that cannot be delegated to the safety professional. This does not preclude seeking the safety professional's reaction to an interim draft, but responsibility must be retained by top management.

Developing the policy in this fashion should result in extensive discussions among the top management team. This method is desirable. During these discussions, the participants raise many questions, pose challenging arguments to each other, and ultimately provide themselves with answers—explanations of why the words and ideas that have been incorporated into the policy statement have been used and others have been discarded.

Many organizations have found it useful for these "questions" and their "answers" to be recorded for future use. The management team should not be reluctant to record evidence of controversy or "struggle." This will increase the credibility of the final result; it will provide additional evidence of the seriousness with which the policy was developed and management's commitment to getting it "right."

COMMUNICATING A SAFETY POLICY

After a local safety policy statement is developed, it must be communicated appropriately throughout the organization. A local policy statement provides the guidelines needed *within* the organization; that is, it guides the behavior and decision making of persons in the organization. The local safety policy is an internal message, not an external one. The local safety policy statement is not *designed* for external audiences. It can, of course, be used with selected external audiences to communicate internal policy. Policy statements designed for external audiences do not convey the message needed *within* the organization. External audiences are heterogeneous in their needs and capacities to understand; policy statements *designed* for external audiences lack the focus needed to be truly effective in the workplace. Recognition of this distinction leads to internal and external policy statements best suited to their respective audiences. Of course, internal and external policy statements must be consistent with one another, but effective external communications are usually short statements that are not accompanied by elaborating text. The examples included here contain examples of both. The reader may find it useful to examine these and to make a judgment regarding their purpose and effectiveness.

The communication of a new or revised local safety policy should not be accomplished simply by its publication. It should not be posted on bulletin boards, or appear as an article in the local "house organ" or newspaper or as part of a safety bulletin. The point here is that it is not a document for which a casual reading suffices. It must be thoroughly explained why a new policy has been prepared and how individuals may be affected by it. This is best accomplished by having each member of the top management team that developed the policy explain the policy statement to his or her immediate subordinates in separate meetings called for this purpose. The Q & A (questions and answers) "package" developed during the policy formulation meetings should be discussed during these meetings. New questions may arise. Better answers may be developed. Before further down-the-line communication takes place, answers to these new questions together with enhancements to the answers in the original Q & A package should be developed. Indeed, these second tier meetings may develop a need to alter the policy statement somewhat. A review at the second level can result in improvement in both content and "flavor" before down-the-line communications continue. One iteration is usually sufficient, if it is done well.

A policy statement developed at the top and confirmed or validated at the next level is normally ready to be communicated through each level of the organization, using each level of line management to communicate to employees for which it is responsible. Having participated in a similar discussion with his or her immediate supervisor, and assisted by the prepared Q & A package, every first-line supervisor should also expect to conduct an instructional meeting with subordinates. New questions that arise during these discussions, together with any answers supplied by supervision, should be fed up the line for answers or for evaluation as to the appropriateness of answers supplied by first-line supervisors. The object is to achieve a thorough understanding of policy by all employees. Having accomplished this, the policy should be incorporated as the first item in the Safety Manual. (The role of the Safety Manual is discussed in Chapters 5 and 6, *"Standards of Performance."*) As part of a permanent record, it will be available as a reference to guide future decisions and to use in connection with new employee orientation.

The safety policy is a commitment and principles document. It should not contain rules or procedures. The safety policy should not normally require much change; rules and procedures are subject to continual change as technology and processes change, as lessons are learned through incident and injury investigations, and as new, perhaps more diverse, employees are brought into the work force.

The development of a new or revised safety policy that reflects the concepts of safety expounded in this book will test management's commitment to the safety and well-being of employees. It will take understanding and perseverance on the part of top management.

I have a client who became irritated with me when I suggested that three months be allocated to the development of a safety policy. One month was thought adequate. Six months later, after much hard work, an excellent policy was developed. This was an unusually long time frame. The organization did not have a clear "top manager" on-site. The organization was guided by a group of managers, ostensibly of equal rank. This method required a large measure of cooperative goodwill as a consensus was reached. However, the resulting document was one that this group of managers was confident they could give their full support.

WHAT SHOULD BE IN A SAFETY POLICY?

What are the principles that have been found useful in undergirding successful safety management? Six principles are in general use throughout Du Pont, as adapted to the needs of the local organization. I have found these both necessary and sufficient for all organizations with which I have consulted. They have withstood the test of time and wide application throughout the world, in widely differing social cultures, work arrangements, and economic circumstances. I urge their wide adoption without diminishment by additions or omissions.

1. All injuries Can Be Prevented. This statement normally evokes disagreement. Many people simply do not believe, upon initial reading, that the statement is correct. I recall a conversation with a shift supervisor in a powerhouse. After listening to him for some time describe the operation to me, I turned the conversation to the hazards it involved. I ventured the comment that, in spite of the many hazards present in the workplace, all injuries could be prevented. He objected strenuously, adding the observation that "when it is time for the Lord to call me, He will. I will have no control of this event." This reaction is not unique, nor is it of much value to debate the issue on religious grounds.

I then asked the supervisor if any of his employees had ever been injured. He responded, "Yes, and every one of them could have been prevented if the operator had been paying better attention to what he was doing." I assured him that this is what I was talking about—that every injury could have been prevented, by someone. The statement does not say that all injuries *should* be prevented. You will note that this word *should* is used in example safety policy #3. With the use of the word *should*, a value judgment has been injected that renders the statement arguable and largely useless. I can easily envision circumstances in which the possibility of injury is preferable to an alternative. For example, if injuries from automobile usage *should* be avoidable, then automobiles should not be used, because we know that their use is, in fact, going to result in injuries to people—injuries that, upon investigation, could have been avoided by someone, without foregoing the use of automobiles. The point is not that injuries will not occur, but simply that they can be (could have been) prevented.

Similarly, a statement that "all injuries *must* be prevented" is essentially useless. This dictum will not be fulfilled unless there are no people available for injury. The facts are that people are imperfect in their behavior and knowledge and that therefore injuries will continue to occur. However, retrospectively, every injury with which I have become familiar could have been prevented.

Safety policy statements that include the concept—the belief—the fact—that all injuries can be prevented makes it clear that management does not accept the concept that injuries are the results of accidents.[3] **Accidents do not "just happen"; they are caused—by people.** By explicitly recognizing this characteristic of injuries, management has established the fundamental concept upon which all effective safety efforts are based. If injuries arose out of the capriciousness of nature, there would be little sense to efforts to gain understanding of their cause and the development of actions to diminish their occurrence. Too often, both individuals and their supervision have accepted injuries as "just one of those things that happen." This reaction to an injury avoids the need to do anything. Everyone accepts the status quo; injuries continue to occur, but no change in behavior is required. There is a misdirected self-interest, however, in this attitude; responsibility has been avoided. This attitude regarding injuries is still very much in existence, in spite of denials to the contrary. Thus, it is important that a policy statement include an unambiguous statement that ALL injuries are preventable. Such a statement simply rejects the notion that injuries cannot be prevented, and thus motivates an organization to find what can be done to prevent those injuries that do occur.

In fact, to increase the explicitness of management's safety commitment, the statement should be enlarged. The word "injury" normally connotes traumatic damage to an individual. Illness connotes damage to an individual which has developed over time. Because, today, we better recognize the damage being inflicted on our environment, and hence on people, as a result of man's economic activities, a safety policy should include "damage to the environment" as well. Thus, the policy statement can read: "All injuries, and damage to health or the environment can be prevented."

By stating the policy in this fashion, the question of "how" arises. This provides the spark from which corrective action can be generated.

2. Management Is Responsible for the Prevention of Injuries. This statement establishes both the burden for safety of employees on supervision and the supervisory authority over the steps required to achieve the desired results. This statement of managerial responsibility is a corollary to the idea that safety is an integral part of every job assignment. And whoever is responsible for the job should expect to be responsible for the safety aspects of the job. This, of course, includes the individual doing the work. Establishing management responsibility for employee safety in no way relieves individual employees of their responsibility for working safely. Both are fully responsible. Clearly establishing management responsibility for employee safety also establishes the principle that responsibility for safety cannot be delegated. It is a mutual *additive* responsibility, not a *shared* responsibility. Management cannot "wash its hands" of safety responsibilities by exhorting employees to "work safely."

Many organizations whose policy statement clearly specifies management responsibility undermine this policy both in practice and organizationally. It is accomplished through a number of devices, but primarily as a result of delegating line management responsibilities to the safety staff or other staff activities.

Several examples from actual safety manuals follow:

a. "They (the Safety and Health Department) have a responsibility to establish, promote, and present programs within the Division to maintain safe working and health conditions, . . . also to ensure compliance with standards and regulations." It is not sound policy to allow or require staff organizations to establish programs for line organizations. This is a line management responsibility that should not be delegated. If the staff department has responsibility to ensure compliance, then it must have authority to require compliance; such authority places it in a line management role and is inappropriate.
b. Some organizations have formed safety inspection teams to inspect and report their findings. These teams are normally composed of line management personnel and have been created to assist line personnel see the motes in their eyes. If this were all, there would be no confounding of responsibility. However, when "It is the responsibility of the inspection team to decide on necessary corrective measures or courses of action to be taken and assign personnel to follow up to ensure agreed-upon work is initiated," the question arises as to who is running the place—the inspection team or the line management that is involved. Such arrangements diminish line management responsibility and the efficacy of expended resources.
c. "All managers . . . are responsible for applying this policy to all facilities, activities, products and services to which they are assigned, thereby ensuring that effective practices for employee health and safety are implemented." Management has been made responsible. Good. But then, "The Manager-Occupational Safety and Health will establish procedures or programs to comply with Government safety and health standards, and to provide a sound safety program." This sentence transfers responsibility to

the safety officer, thereby letting line managers off the hook. Line managers and their employees are the appropriate persons to establish procedures and programs as required in order *to avoid injury*, not in order to comply with government safety and health standards. Assigning this task to the safety officer has at least two serious defects:

i. It transfers responsibility away from line managers.
ii. It places the safety officer as an adversary in the "compliance" or "policeman" business, rather than in a partnership relationship with line managers.

Safety personnel should function as a resource to assist line management. This is not to suggest that safety personnel should not foster an increased recognition by line management of its responsibility. They should, and thereby they will create a need for their advice and guidance. By doing so, safety personnel will become increasingly welcomed in the work force as a resource to help employees and their supervision in their quest for an injury-free environment. Safety personnel need not be perceived as a well-meaning but sometimes disruptive force that interferes with "getting the job done."

Policy statements designed for employee guidance—that is, for internal use—should be based on concern for employees, the public, and the environment, not on government regulations. By doing so, the policy is more useful in educating employees, and in conveying to them management's concern for their well-being, than merely complying with third-party directives. The less said about third-party involvement, the more creditable is management's demonstration of concern. In addition, management can then do what is "right," because it is "right," not because it is required. This premise also causes management to more fully seek what is "right" rather than be tempted to believe its task is done when statutory requirements have been fulfilled. Nonetheless, management should, of course, quietly determine that its actions meet legal requirements.

This "need" to reflect regulatory requirements in safety policies is demonstrated in the following statement: "It is the policy . . . to meet its moral, social, and legal responsibilities to provide a safe place to undertake (work), free from recognizable hazards that might cause serious harm, and in compliance at all times with applicable laws and regulations." This wording should be compared with the wording of the Occupation Health and Safety Act of 1970.[4]

3. All Hazards Can be Safeguarded. According to this statement, while hazards are known to exist in the workplace (all known hazards cannot be removed from the workplace), employees, the public, and the environment can be safeguarded in regard to these hazards. This principle is a commitment to the idea that work activity can be organized to function in a fail-safe manner. It makes possible the concept that employees should not take risks while still getting things done. Hazards *can* be safeguarded—rendered free of risk by physical safeguards or through operating procedures that, when followed, will avoid injury. The statement is a *can be* statement, not a *must be* or *should be* statement.

Because of the greater certainty of being "in place," physical safeguarding is generally to be preferred over reliance on operating rules and procedures. However, accomplishing physical safeguarding is not always technically possible or economically justified. On the other hand, if process variables are not well understood or are hard to effectively control, physical safeguards must be utilized. If this is not possible, an operation must be shut down because it cannot be safely run. Many examples of providing physical safeguards to supplement operating procedures can be cited, for example, blow-out panels, barricaded explosion-proof test cells that are remotely operated, pressure relief valves, and chemical fume hoods. Remoteness of location is a form of physical safeguarding, as for ammunition storage depots. However accomplished, the principle remains that hazards can be safeguarded. The challenge is to do so by recognizing the hazard and providing an appropriate safeguard, one that works.

Making judgments between physical safeguards or administrative (rules and procedures) safeguards and/or the degree of dependence on some mix of safeguards demands a high order of management skill, knowledge, and understanding if both effectiveness and economy are to be achieved. Some redundancy is frequently appropriate as well. Experience gained through management safety audits, injury investigations, process hazard reviews, and reviews of rules and procedures will improve the operating results obtained and provide effective, lowest cost solutions.

My experience suggests that organizations that are technically strong in the engineering disciplines excessively rely on physical safeguards. They try to create a safe *place*, a place in which an idiot can go unharmed. Resources are wasted, for employees are not idiots. Low technology operations frequently suffer the other extreme. They fail to see opportunities in which a technical solution to a hazard would be effective and accomplished at lower cost because an operating procedure would be significantly simplified and, as a consequence, result in a labor cost savings.

A couple of examples come to mind. Rotating equipment and the nip points such equipment presents have been a significant source of finger and hand injuries. For operational reasons such hazards are frequently difficult to physically guard. I know of one operation in which considerable design money was spent trying to develop a braking mechanism for such a machine. The rotating rolls were rubber-covered steel rolls 10 to 12 feet long and approximately 12 inches in diameter which rotated at "high" speed. The forces that were involved were enormous, particularly when, to be effective in protecting an arm (nothing could be done for a finger), the deceleration would have to be accomplished within a revolution or so. Extricating an arm would be virtually impossible because of weight and positioning of the rolls. The idea of physically braking these rolls was abandoned. Administrative controls established that the involved rolls must never be touched, for any reason, without the drive-train being shut down and physically locked-out by the person who was to touch the rolls (Lock, Tag, and Try Procedure; see Chapter 6). Years passed uneventfully until an experienced operator doing a nonstandard activity (one with no job procedure) allowed the tip of the scissors in which he had his hand engaged to touch the rubber-covered roll. His hand was dragged into the nip point and received serious injury. The failure here was not only the unsafe act by the employee of allowing an extension of his body to touch the roll, but also the failure to preclude this particular nonstandard operation by installation of a simple exclusionary rail to prevent any attempt to perform the nonstandard operation. The better solution was some modest physical safeguarding coupled with adequate operating procedures and associated discipline (compliance).[5] A repeat incident has not occurred for many years.

The second example also involves a pinch-point, but a much more simple pinch-point. An employee experienced an injury when a door was closed while he had his fingers between the door and the door jam at the hinged area of the door. The investigation determined that this pinch-point could be safeguarded by installation of a vertical flexible grommet that would preclude anyone from putting his or her hand in the pinch-point. After several trial installations and cost assessments, the conclusion was reached that this was an example of trying to solve problems solely through engineering design changes. The effort was abandoned as misplaced emphasis. The hinged area was painted yellow as an alternative. More than 25 years have elapsed and I know of no further injuries from this source in this organization. *Safety awareness* appears to have been an adequate solution.

You will note the similarity between "safeguards can be" and "all injuries can be." Neither statement says "will be." The "can be" statement affirms the reality of the situation and *suggests* that ways *should* be found to safeguard all hazards. This is a suggestion only, and may not always be viewed as appropriate. For example, substantial safeguards for a police officer can, and often are, provided. However, there are times when the officer is expected to put his or her personal well-being at unavoidable risk in the course of duty. Society has recognized that armed fugitives need to be apprehended and apprehended in a timely manner. This risk to the police officer in no way invalidates the concept that all injuries can be prevented. In the case of the police officer, the decision has been made to "get the job done"; in the case of normal commercial business activity, it virtually always makes sense, both morally and economically, to avoid injury to employees and others who may be affected by the activity involved. Society expects this and levies sanctions against commercial organizations that fail to do so.

I have done consulting work with municipal police and fire organizations. Lest the public interest be used by such organizations as an excuse for high injury rates, I note that for one fire department some 70 percent of its injuries occurred in the fire house, not on fire sites. In addition, many of the injuries experienced on the fire sites had nothing to do with expeditious fire fighting or rescue operations. Many fire site injuries were the result of poor work practices, which, with adequate recognition and subsequent training, can be avoided with no adverse effect on efficiency. In fact, efficiency may well be improved because of the resulting increase in personnel availability.

Likewise, in police work, alternatives to force and the attendant potential for injuries are increasingly being developed. Modern day handling of prison riots is particularly instructive in this regard. Conversely, the use of force in handling the MOVE problem in Philadelphia in May 1985 is generally recognized to have enlarged rather than diminished the problem.

4. Training Is Essential. The basic principle involved here is that an employee new to an operation—whether a situation of being a new employee, a reassigned employee, or an employee confronting new or revised equipment or procedures—cannot be expected to be capable of working safely without being trained about the hazards of the new tasks and about the rules and procedures created to avoid injuries from the hazards. The existence of administrative means (rules and procedures) for avoiding injuries, coupled with management responsibility for injury prevention, places responsibility for training on management—not the training department.

Training is the means by which management inculcates the skills and knowledge required to accomplish the work of the organization, including accomplishing it without injury. Including the necessity for training in a safety policy statement establishes both management's commitment to employee training, and also, and equally important, management's expectations that employees have a responsibility for both learning and skill development. Training and its relationship to safety are discussed more fully in Chapter 5.

5. Safety Is Good Business. In Chapters 2 and 3, the concept that safety makes money has been thoroughly explored. I will not belabor this fact here except to note that it is important that this economic aspect of an organization's safety policy be clearly stated. Thus, the idea that safety is a good thing "if we can afford it" is not a correct one. Safety is not a luxury to be encouraged only when there is spare cash. Good safety will generate the "spare cash." Safety is not an indulgence to be "enjoyed" during "good times." Failure to recognize this aspect of success in safety actions is illustrated when safety budgets are reduced during economic downturns or adverse earnings reports. Indeed, it is when earnings are low that improved safety can provide a viable route toward significantly improved earnings.

6. Working Safely Is a Condition of Employment. This key element of a sound safety policy simply makes known the fact that management will not continue to let an employee who has demonstrated an unwillingness and/or inability to accomplish assigned tasks safely continue to put himself or herself and fellow employees and others at risk. After all else has failed, management has the obligation to remove such employees from workplace hazards. With diligence, this separation should occur before injuries or damage to health or the environment takes place. If this principle has been clearly established and understood by employees, it is seldom necessary to exercise its provision. It must, however, be part of the tools available in the workplace if a workplace environment is to be created in which employees work safely. The last good thing a supervisor can do for an employee who cannot or will not work safely is to separate the employee from the hazard—the work. Whether such action is viewed as an act of compassion or as a disciplinary action depends, I am sure, upon who is making the judgment. I believe that both views are correct.

If the situation is a "cannot" one, perhaps an alternative assignment can be arranged which the employee can safely accomplish and which would be an appropriate solution short of separating the employee from the business unit. In situations in which an employee "will not" work safely, solutions other than discharge are not likely to prove successful and thus should be avoided whenever possible.

The above solutions all sound reasonable and straightforward. In practice, however, supervision frequently has trouble arriving at the "cannot or will not" decision. The path toward arriving at this decision is filled with opportunities for misstepping. Discipline, as a part of a well-rounded safety program, is discussed in Chapter 12. Although disciplinary tools, including discharge, must be part of the safety tools available in the workplace, I cannot remember a discharge case for safety in which I was personally involved. I do know of discharge cases for safety on a second-hand basis.

Employees who are otherwise perfectly desirable employees seldom persist in unsafe behavior. If they are satisfactory in other aspects of job performance, their safety performance is, or will shortly become, satisfactory when appropriate, progressively more stringent disciplinary action is instituted.

I have gone to some length in item 6 of this discussion to avoid the use of the word "injury" in connection with working safely. Injury is normally clear evidence of unsafe work by someone. If only injury is relied on as a measure of safety, most of the unsafe action will be missed. Emphasis must be placed on avoidance of all unsafe acts, not only those that have resulted in injuries.

The appropriateness of an emphasis on unsafe acts rather than just injuries also applies to companies. Figure 1-16 is a newspaper article reporting, among other things, that OSHA proposes to fine Phillips Petroleum Co. $5.7 million for willful violation of OSHA rules in connection with the explosion of its polyethylene plant. Does anyone think that this fine will return the dead, heal and/or restore the wounded, resurrect the plant, restore the jobs and prospective earnings of the operation, or erase the nightmares of the survivors? Will this fine increase the dedication of Phillips' employees and their contractor to work more safely? I think not. The lessons to be learned will be learned, if they are learned, independent of this fine. The fine serves no useful purpose insofar as Phillips Petroleum Co. and its employees are concerned. In fact, the fine serves no useful function for any company or its employees. The loss of life, of physical facilities, and of sales is much more eloquent in establishing the need for better performance than is a fine that is small compared to the experienced loss. Assessing a fine on an employer who has had a mishap, even a serious mishap, is analogous to chastising an employee who has been injured. It is largely unproductive activity. It alienates people and companies and makes enemies, not friends. It is frequently counterproductive because defensive mechanisms set in which get in the way of constructive change. Change is resisted because to acknowledge that change is necessary is seen as an admission of guilt for which additional chastisement will be forthcoming. As with supervisors who mete out criticism or punishment to subordinates who are injured because of some mistake they have made, governments mete out fines to satisfy "higher-ups" or to fulfill some political expectation (pressure groups), or to satisfy their own need to remind themselves of their power and the need for justification for their continued existence, or out of a misguided understanding of how to achieve improved results.

This is not to say that discipline should never be utilized. In the Phillips case, OSHA has determined (as reported) that the Pasadena plant was guilty of numerous violations, including the company's own procedures. How many other company locations are equally guilty of similar violations? Surely, the Pasadena plant was not the only guilty operator in the country. Why is OSHA not applying fines left and right? Why must OSHA wait until twenty-three deaths have occurred? The answer is that the *system* is defective—fatally so. OSHA cannot police the U.S. workplace. If OSHA believes the Phillips Pasadena plant is typical of other Phillips' plants, and they have no reason to believe that Pasadena plant is unique, it seems logical that OSHA require Phillips to shut down all Phillips plants. That would get attention; that would be an effective message to Phillips and all employees; that is what is meant by "if you can't operate it safely, don't operate it." This, of course, would be a politically impossible action. It would also be a dumb action. How would it ever be determined that it was "safe" for Phillips to start up again? Under such a scenario, all U.S. industry would be in the same pitiful status as our nuclear power industry is today. Real progress will not be made by levying fines, but through education, cooperation, recognition of outstanding—if not perfect—performance, and effective persuasion. Real progress will not be achieved through adversarial regulatory procedures.

One of the best, that is, most effective, safety supervisors with whom I have worked was a gentle, kind, pleasant, moral, up-from-the-ranks gentleman who inspired, motivated, guided, and assisted employees at all levels, including plant managers, in the organization to more fully recognize their individual importance in achieving an injury-free workplace. Never did I know of his use of threats or intimidation. He "caught more flies with honey than others catch with vinegar." I believe OSHA would be more successful in improving the safety performance of U.S. industry by emulating some of the strategies and tactics used by this successful safety supervisor.

FAULTY SAFETY POLICY STATEMENTS

Clearly recognizing the preventability of all injuries will avoid the shortcomings of many well-intentioned, but defective, safety policy statements. I have seen policy statements that read: "It is the policy of XYZ company/location to make the XYZ operation the safest possible place to work." I presume this declaration means "as safe as we can make it." If so, it implies that there are some unsafe things, conditions, or actions that are acceptable or cannot be changed. This is not a concept consistent with a commitment to excellence. This accepts the notion that some injuries are just not preventable. This is simply untrue, and cannot be a part of a successful safety effort.

Another declaration that can be found in policy statements is: "It is the policy . . . to limit exposure to high risk or hazardous situations." This statement implies that some exposure to high risk or hazardous situations is satisfactory. The object of achieving excellence in safety is not limiting, but *always* conducting work in a manner that precludes injury or exposure—not an easy task. The focus of a sound safety policy should be on people, not on things. The task is not to minimize situational risks; the task is to lead employees so that their behavior does not adversely affect their safety or health. The task is to establish as operational fact: "if it cannot be done safely, don't do it."

A focus on people (human) values accomplishes at least two advantages:

1. There is increased employee support for measures taken to avoid personal injuries.
2. There is a decreased likelihood that supervision will try to equate a specific cost with a specific safety hazard or risk. A policy that includes the concept of "safest possible" provides the opportunity to fall into this trap—the trap that a situation is viewed to be "as safe as possible—under the circumstances." From this premise follows chance taking, short-cuts, expediency, and injuries.

Another sentence that is frequently found in safety policy statements is "we are committed to reducing risk to an acceptable level." This suggests that risk assessment is quantifiable and that management and employees are willing to undertake an activity that is thought to result in injury at a specified frequency. The issue of risk reduction is better framed by developing the "all injuries can be prevented" concept. In keeping with this concept, no activity need be undertaken until management and employees believe the activity can be accomplished free of injury. Although certain probabilistic calculations can be made to assist in decision making, employee behavior is of such an overriding importance in determining the injury propensity of an operation that "as operated" risk calculations are of dubious value.

Many employees simply do not adequately understand the concept of risk and their relationship to it. The following statements may be of help in understanding hazards and their relationship to risk:

- Hazards are present in all work activity.
- Employees should not take risks relative to hazards.
- Employees should take appropriate action relative to hazards so as to avoid injury to themselves and/or to others.

Some other faulty ideas are commonly found in policy statements. For example, "We will devote the necessary resources to achieve this objective. Personal safety will not be sacrificed because of economic incentives for productivity in operations or maintenance." This idea implies that with expenditure of enough resources, personnel safety can be achieved. This is a dead-on-arrival idea. Increasing the level of expenditures on safety—for professional safety staff, design of equipment, or reduced risk measurement levels—seldom enhances long-term performance; increasing direct management involvement and responsibility usually does. The level of resources that is used is relatively unimportant compared to the degree and effectiveness of management effort that is applied.

Another commonly expressed idea is that XYZ company "has assigned highest priority to safety considerations." Although desirable and commendable, this statement is an assertion; it is not a policy statement.

A common failing of many policy statements is that they "make promises" that cannot, will not, be kept. The "promises" nature of some of the above mentioned policy statements is apparent. When an injury occurs, or when fewer resources are used than someone thinks appropriate, the "promise" has been broken. Policy statements should avoid establishing petards. They should proclaim:

1. Management commitment to establishing an environment in which work gets done without injury to employees or the public and without damage to the health of employees, the public, or the environment.
2. A set of principles upon which this commitment becomes operational.

SUMMARY

Every organization that is a distinct operational entity needs to clearly establish for its employees the principles that will guide management in its efforts to carry out its safety, health, and environmental responsibilities. The safety policy statement provides these principles.

To be effective, these principles must not be platitudes. They must be operating principles—statements that individuals in the organization actually can use in determining their actions. They must be statements that individuals, particulary supervisors, can cite as the basis for the action they are taking.

The following statements provide the basis for such policy statements.

1. All injuries and damage to health and the environment can be prevented.
2. Management is responsible for the prevention of injuries and damage to health and the environment.
3. All hazards can be safeguarded.
4. Training is essential.
5. Safety is good business.
6. Working safely is a condition of employment.

Safety policy statements should establish:

SAFETY IS SOMETHING THAT EMPLOYEES ACHIEVE—IT IS NOT SOMETHING THAT IS PROVIDED BY THE EMPLOYER

NOTES

1. W.A. Shewhart, *Economic Control of Quality of Manufactured Product*, D. Van Nostrand Company, Inc., New York, 1931.

2. For convenience, the full title of this committee will usually be shortened to this form in this book.

3. See footnote 1, Chapter 2, page 40.

4. See Chapter 1, in which a quote from Section 5 of the Act is provided (page 23), as well as a discussion regarding safe *places* (pages 23-26ff).

5. This injury would not have occurred had the employee not violated a general plant rule requiring knives and scissors to be sheathed when not actually in use.

Chapter 4

ORGANIZATION FOR SAFETY: THE CENTRAL SAFETY COMMITTEE AND ITS SUBCOMMITTEES

Providing a structured, systematic process through which employees can participate and management can demonstrate leadership has been the basis for achieving excellence in safety. The elements for such an organization for safety are shown in Figures 4-1 and 4-2.

Figure 4-1 depicts the continuous nature and interrelationships of a successful safety management process. It depicts the centrality of the Central Safety Committee and the supporting activities that have been found useful in establishing successful safety leadership. Figure 4-2 shows how these activities are led and managed.

THE CENTRAL SAFETY COMMITTEE

The centerpiece of an organization for safety is the Central Safety Committee (CSC)[1]. This is the group that provides the central leadership role within the organization. This is the group that provides the organization that Drucker believes leaders should provide. In the previously cited *Wall Street Journal* article, he indicates "leadership involves more work than charisma and more doing than dash."[2] The CSC provides the organizational structure through which to make this work both effective and efficient.

Drucker mentions " . . . mission, defining it and establishing it, clearly and visibly. The leader sets the goals, sets the priorities, and sets and maintains the standards." The CSC is the operational vehicle through which the organization's leader makes these things happen. Drucker continues, "what distinguishes a leader from the misleader are his goals." A leader is able to "hold fast to a few basic standards; a misleader is willing to compromise those standards, if he can get away with it." High standards

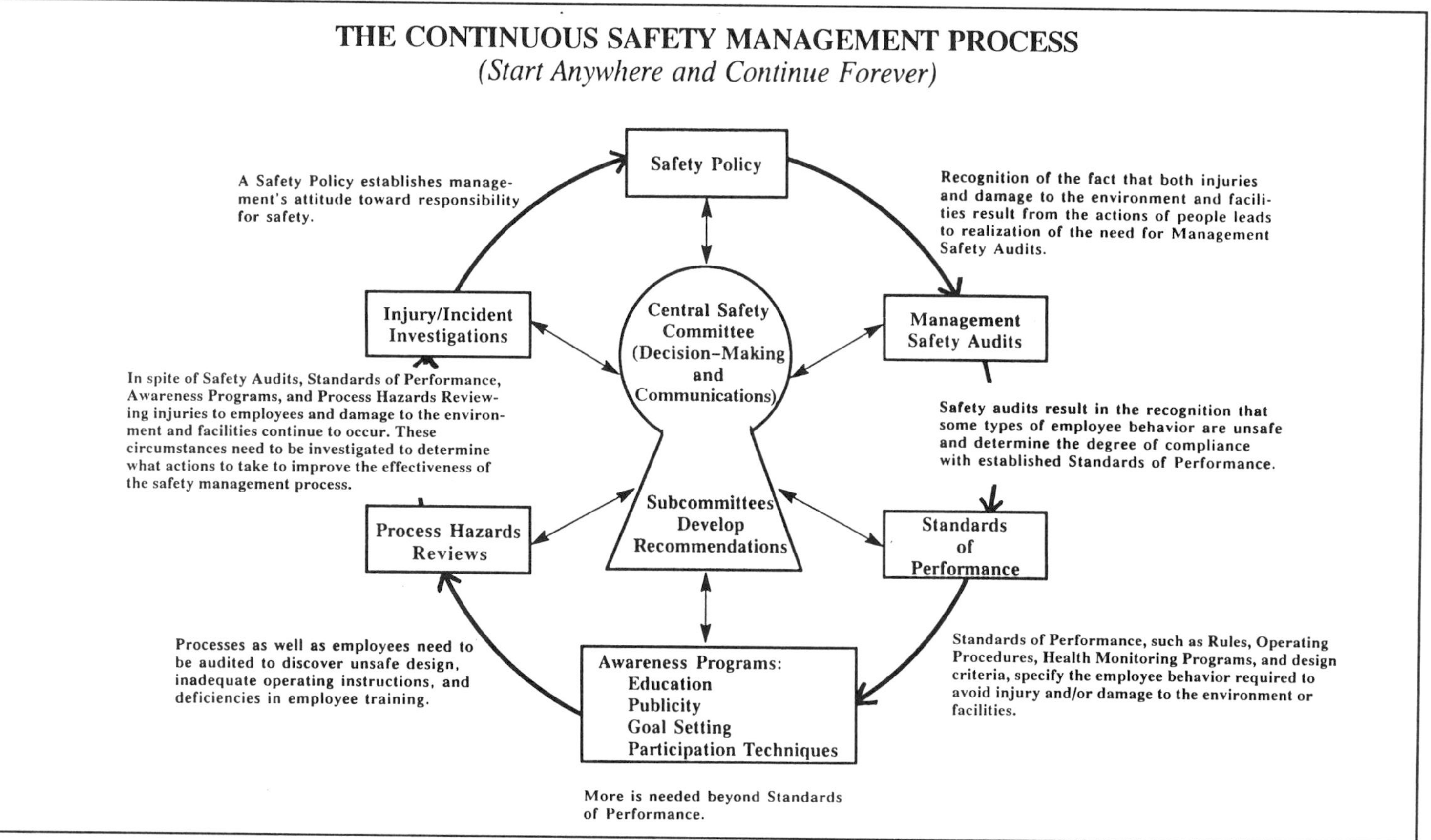
THE CONTINUOUS SAFETY MANAGEMENT PROCESS
(Start Anywhere and Continue Forever)
Safety Policy
A Safety Policy establishes management's attitude toward responsibility for safety.
Recognition of the fact that both injuries and damage to the environment and facilities result from the actions of people leads to realization of the need for Management Safety Audits.
Injury/Incident Investigations
Central Safety Committee (Decision–Making and Communications)
Management Safety Audits
In spite of Safety Audits, Standards of Performance, Awareness Programs, and Process Hazards Reviewing injuries to employees and damage to the environment and facilities continue to occur. These circumstances need to be investigated to determine what actions to take to improve the effectiveness of the safety management process.
Safety audits result in the recognition that some types of employee behavior are unsafe and determine the degree of compliance with established Standards of Performance.
Subcommittees Develop Recommendations
Process Hazards Reviews
Standards of Performance
Processes as well as employees need to be audited to discover unsafe design, inadequate operating instructions, and deficiencies in employee training.
Awareness Programs:
Education
Publicity
Goal Setting
Participation Techniques
Standards of Performance, such as Rules, Operating Procedures, Health Monitoring Programs, and design criteria, specify the employee behavior required to avoid injury and/or damage to the environment or facilities.
More is needed beyond Standards of Performance.

Figure 4-1

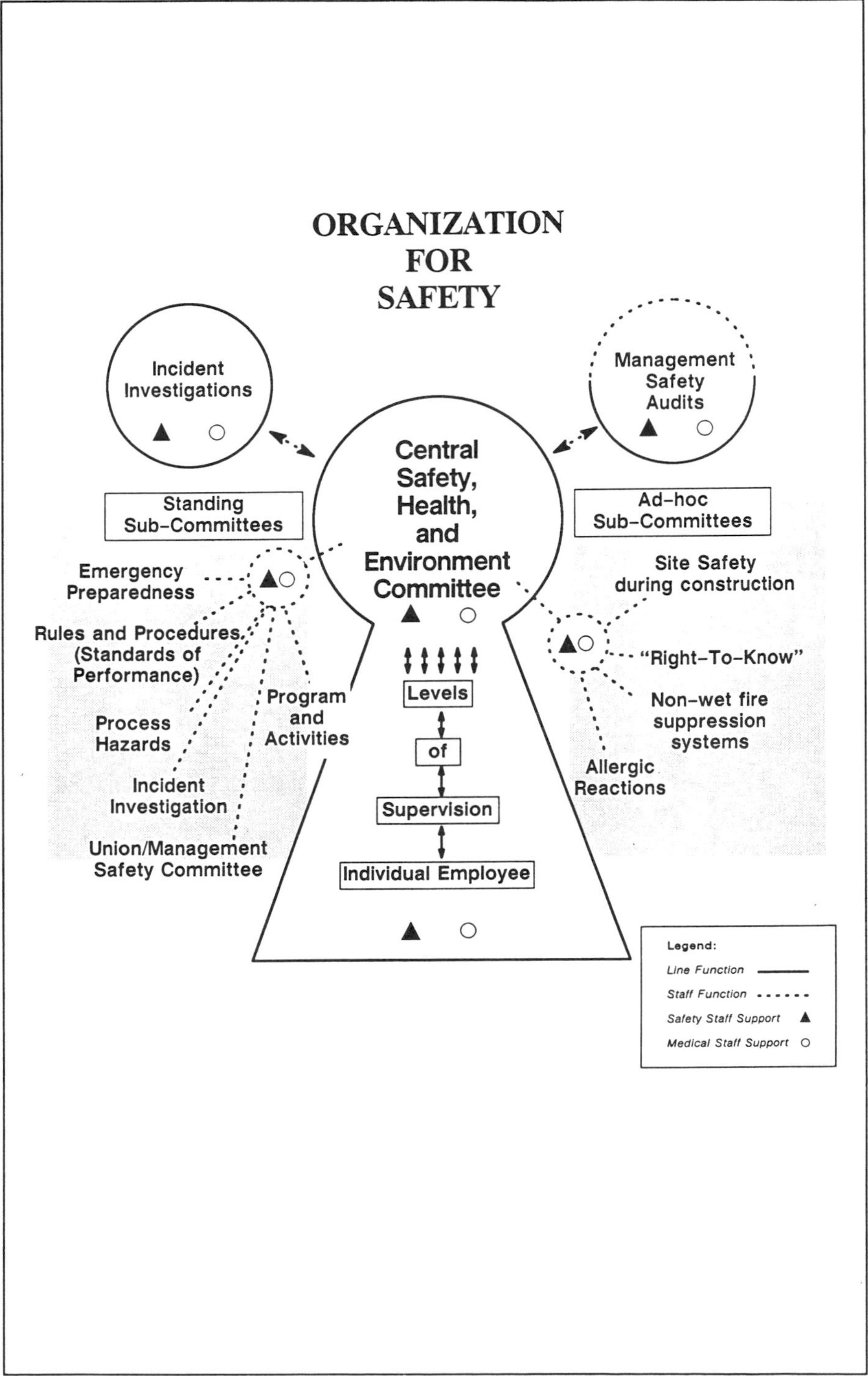

ORGANIZATION
FOR
SAFETY
Incident
Investigations
Management
Safety
Audits
Central
Safety,
Health,
and
Environment
Committee
Standing
Sub-Committees
Ad-hoc
Sub-Committees
Emergency
Preparedness
Rules and Procedures
(Standards of
Performance)
Process
Hazards
Incident
Investigation
Union/Management
Safety Committee
Program
and
Activities
Levels
of
Supervision
Individual Employee
Site Safety
during construction
"Right-To-Know"
Non-wet fire
suppression
systems
Allergic
Reactions
Legend:
Line Function
Staff Function
Safety Staff Support
Medical Staff Support

Figure 4-2

of acceptable behavior are essential. The CSC is the central means through which "missions," "goals," and "standards" are established and maintained.

An additional requirement for achieving excellence in safety "is that the leader see leadership as a responsibility rather than rank and privilege. Effective leaders are rarely permissive. But when things go wrong—and they always do—they do not blame others." This facet of safety leadership is reflected in good injury investigations, which recognize that when something has gone wrong and an injury has occurred, something in the safety management process has gone wrong. The resulting investigation then focuses on determining what action management can take to "fix" the process and prevent reoccurrence.

Drucker points out that an effective leader will want strong associates, pushing them, encouraging them, praising them, and promoting them. The CSC subcommittee structure provides the avenue through which strong associates can make an impact on the organization and be recognized for having done so.

According to Drucker "the final requirement of effective leadership is to earn trust. . . . Trust is the conviction that the leader means what he says." Perhaps more than any other management activity, safety provides the leader a route through which to establish employee trust.

The "mission" of safety is protection of the employee, the facilities through which employees earn their livelihood, the public, and the environment. Standards can be established which need not be compromised (alternate strategies for accomplishing tasks—yes, but compromise on basic standards—no). The absence of permissiveness in safety allows the message "I mean what I say" to come through loudly and clearly. Training and ultimately disciplinary action reinforce the "no permissiveness" aspect of safety. If disciplinary action becomes necessary to reinforce the concept of "I mean what I say," the effective leader will not shrink from this responsibility. Because evidence for the need for safety disciplinary measures normally becomes apparent in the workplace—through failure to work safely—the first-line supervisor becomes the key figure, the leader, in disciplinary procedures. Immediate and individual action is required. (See Chapter 12, "Discipline.")

Mission, goals, standards, responsibility, establishment of trust—all of these ingredients are essential to leadership and the quest for excellence. The CSC and its subcommittees provide management a proved organizational structure through which to accomplish these ends.

A question immediately arises as to what constitutes an "organization." This is not a trivial question; it goes to the heart of the organizational arrangements within the enterprise. The concept is that an organization for safety, a safety unit, is a group of employees who have an overriding common interest in the safety of all employees who share the common physical environment or a common managerial "umbrella." Thus, a plant site may be populated primarily by manufacturing employees, but also perhaps by technical or research employees as well as marketing support personnel. These groups differ functionally, but are employed at the same site. Therefore, in spite of their functional differences, they have much in common. In this example, the site would be the organization for which a CSC would exist. A freestanding marketing or research group occupying separate facilities would have its own CSC. A large site on which distinctly separate large organizations exist may well find it useful to establish a site CSC as well as CSCs for each of these distinct large organizations. The site CSC would address only those safety items that are site-wide in nature, leaving the primarily independent larger organizations to establish their individual CSCs. The fundamental requirement is that each employee be a part of safety unit for reasons he or she understands, and that he or she recognizes the existence of a CSC for this safety unit.

The Central Safety Committee is normally composed of the head of the safety unit organization and each of his or her immediate subordinates—for example, the plant manager and all the superintendents reporting to this manager. Variations of this arrangement are appropriate when organizational arrangements are more complex or less clearly hierarchial. I have a research client in which five organizations exist on a single site, sharing facilities. The heads of each of these organizations nominally are equals; four of the "heads" report to the same superior who spends one day a week at the site. The fifth "head" reports to a different superior. It was concluded that what "made sense" was that a single safety unit be established for all five organizations. They use the same cafeteria, the same storerooms, the same semi-works facilities. They share a common central analytical organization, and personnel are moved from one group to the other as needs arise. A sense of community exists; however, no single "head" exists. The solution was to establish a single CSC for the combined group composed of the five group heads. The chairmanship of the committee rotates among the five group heads.

Some organizations believe that the CSC should be larger, incorporating the manager, his or her immediate subordinates, and their subordinates (area supervisors). Their argument is that this system provides more direct participation in the CSC by lower levels of management and therefore provides less opportunity for the superintendents to act as filters between the manager and the management representatives closer to the operation. I have participated in this type of arrangement. Although it can be made to work, I believe this arrangement is more difficult to manage well and is less effective. It tends to by-pass a level of management that has something to contribute. The group is too large for open, controversial discussions to take place with a high level of confidence that what should remain confidential does in fact remain so. This large group frequently results in a babble of voices, lacking coherency and accountability. The group meeting can become a stage in which one or more members put on their "show." Subordinates frequently use an enlarged group as a means of determining which of their superiors has the most influence or clout. These are all extraneous activities in regard to safety.

Central Safety Committees, because they are composed of line managers who may view themselves as both decision makers and problem solvers, are prone to become discussion groups devoted to problem solving. This is a mistake. As we shall see, the CSC should not allow itself to become a problem-solving body. It should be a decision-making body only.

A headquarter's organization might well have a single CSC that covers the entire headquarters organization—that is, all functional groups—provided that individual employees recognize and believe that this grouping "makes sense." The headquarter's

CSC would *not* also be a super-CSC under whose umbrella the various plants, sales offices, and research facilities would operate. The CSC functions only for the immediate safety unit for which it exists and in which employees can participate.

Figure 4-2 shows three major activities attached to the central keyhole, the CSC. Injury and Incident Investigation is discussed in Chapters 9 and 10; Management Safety Audits is discussed in Chapter 7 and 8. This chapter will describe the workings of the CSC and its subcommittees. The small triangles shown in Figure 4-2 indicate the existence of a safety staff. This "staff" may be a single person or a portion of a person for relatively small organizations; several persons may be appropriate for larger organizations. The complexity of the operations, the injury frequency rate, and the degree of responsibility, in fact, discharged by line management, all affect the appropriate ratio of the number of safety staff to total employees. A starting point might be one safety staff per thousand employees. This ratio may be low. Increased governmental regulations, government mandated programs, increased attention to hygiene and its attendant air monitoring, and activities such as community outreach, all drive the needed ratio higher. The risk is that, with line management perceived as already having its hands full, and in its zeal to improve safety, the safety staff will be enlarged sufficiently that, with the concurrence of some members of management, it will begin trying to do things that should be done by line management—for example, making decisions! Safety staff should offer analyses, facts, alternative schemes, and suggestions, but never make operational decisions.

The responsibility for the safety and health of employees is clearly the responsibility of their direct supervision. This is not a responsibility that can be delegated to a staff organization. To assist management in the successful discharge of this responsibility, Du Pont has, through a continuous trial and error process over many years and many types of operations, evolved a staff support system that includes the safety staff, but goes well beyond the safety staff. This staff support system has two main components: (1) the "safety staff," and (2) the subcommittees of the CSC.

THE SAFETY STAFF SUPPORT SYSTEM

Within Du Pont, the normal organizational arrangement is that the "safety office" is headed up by the site safety supervisor. Depending upon the size of the operation, this may be a full-time assignment with several assistants in a large plant, or may be a part-time assignment in a small operation. In any event, it is an identifiable assignment that appears on normal organizational charts. The assignment has a specific job description and job classification. Safety supervisors have not usually had specific safety experience prior to assignment to the safety staff. Most safety supervisors have had operational experience as line supervisors. Many are "up from the ranks" personnel.

It is not unusual for college graduates, mostly engineers, who have had first-line supervisory experience, to take assignments as site safety supervisors. Some of these find a career in safety work. Others return to direct line operating assignments or move on to other assignments not directly associated with safety. For the duration of the assignment as safety supervisor, the safety supervisor is the safety professional for the organization. All of these arrangements are straightforward and similar to the "safety office" arrangements in many companies.

THE SUBCOMMITTEE STAFF SUPPORT SYSTEM

The second staff support system—the subcommittees of the CSC—are much more extensive in terms of size and composition. These subcommittees are normally chaired by a member of the CSC. Thus, a chairperson of a subcommittee is a line manager reporting to the site manager. Similarly, the members of a subcommittee are line personnel in the various functional groups within the total organization. Typically, few if any of the subcommittee members are persons who are in the line organization of the chairperson of the subcommittee.

Although the subcommittees are composed of line managers, their functions are staff functions. They study, gather facts, and assess understanding and attitudes. They also review operating procedures, incident investigations, and process hazards reviews. They develop programs designed to publicize, to educate, to train, and to improve procedures. Finally, the subcommittees make recommendations to the CSC for decision making. This task returns responsibility to line management, which constitutes the CSC. Assignments to subcommittees are ad hoc assignments, almost always supplemental to the regular line responsibilities of the persons who are assigned. This scheme of staff support provided by members of the line organizations has a number of virtues:

1. Recommendations are more likely to be based on a better understanding of the basic work situation than if they were developed by the "safety office." Efficiency is improved because of the direct involvement of knowledgeable and affected line personnel.
2. Recommendations are more likely to be "realistic" than if they were developed only by the safety office.
3. Recommendations developed by a subcommittee and accepted by the CSC are more likely to be enthusiastically endorsed and supported because there exists a body of employees (subcommittee members and other employees with whom subcommittee members have had discussions) who understand the issues involved and support the actions being taken. This group of employees will assist in "selling" the decision thus made; selling is not left only to the line management function.
4. Recommendations are more likely to be "new" or "innovative" because the subcommittee is not in a decision-making mode, and thus unlikely to be overly inhibited or conservative. Members have more freedom to think innovatively. The study, planning, and development work is separated from the decision and implementation work. It is, however, being done by line managers, not staff persons.
5. The work of the subcommittee can be "constructively guided" in an indirect manner by the CSC chairperson, while he or she still retains the responsibility for actual decision making for the CSC, including the final and decisive vote. This arrangement provides the opportunity to "try" ideas that may or may not survive close scrutiny without ascribing authorship to ideas that subsequently appear defective.

These can have arisen anonymously within the subcommittee. Those ideas that appear to have merit, and get approved by CSC, can be credited to their authors.

Because few, if any, of its members are restrained by the presence of a supervisor in their management line, the subcommittee will frequently develop ideas and action plans that are subsequently approved and adopted by the CSC—plans that either would never have been brought forth or would have died at birth or soon thereafter within the direct line organization. Subcommittees are "sanctuaries" in which ideas can be nurtured and developed, and yet still be directly communicated to the CSC chairperson—through the subcommittee chairperson.

6. The subcommittee chair can also "lobby" for as well as test the acceptability of ideas arising in the subcommittee among his or her peers on the CSC prior to having the subcommittee formally present its recommendations.

7. While not purely a safety issue, line management participation in subcommittee activities gives employees who are normally functioning in a line activity the opportunity to "see the world" as a person in a staff assignment sees it. That is, they are expected to get something done, but with little or no authority or resources to do so. Membership on subcommittees of CSC also increases the opportunity for upper level management to observe more directly the performance of people not in their own direct organization.

These subcommittees, while staff organizations, can substantially assist line management to more effectively discharge its responsibilities for the safety of personnel for whom it is responsible.

To repeat, line management is responsible for safety. The safety office and the subcommittees of the CSC are important staff organizations that are available and are expected to provide assistance to the line organization.

8. Although largely composed of line managers (supervisors), personnel in all management functions serve on these subcommittees. Thus, Engineering, Personnel (Human Resources), Security, Training, and other areas are expected to bring their perspectives to subcommittee deliberations.

THE CENTRAL SAFETY COMMITTEE MEETING

In Figure 4-3 is shown a typical Central Safety Committee meeting agenda. This agenda is issued by the safety supervisor, who along with the medical director or nurse, or contract doctor or nurse (whoever is the "top" of the medical services), are ex officio members of CSC. They contribute when asked, as they should be, but are not free to "vote." Their roles are purely advisory.

As can be seen, the format is essentially a reporting one. Subordinates are reporting to their boss relative to their safety stewardship of the areas of operation to which they have been assigned responsibility. These reports are made in the presence of other of the boss's subordinates, their ostensible peers, the medical representative, and the safety supervisor. Thus, this audience not only learns what is going on, but also enhances the likelihood that these reports are factual and unbiased. A physical arrangement of the meeting which places the safety supervisor and medical representative farthest from the chairperson can also facilitate the latter objectives. The

Sample Agenda

CENTRAL SAFETY COMMITTEE MEETING

July 16, 1989

Item	Responsible
I. Report on Injuries/Incidents Occupational Illnesses	Each Manager/Superintendent
II. Disability Report	Each Manager/Superintendent
III. Serious Incident/Injury Status Reports #1-89 #2-89	Responsible Manager/ Superintendent
IV. Audit Reports and Comments	Each Manager/Superintendent
V. Subcommittee Reports and Discussion	Chairman, Subcommittees
VI. Medical Report a. General plant health b. Major illness cases warranting discussion	Plant Physician/Nurse
VII. Safety and Fire Report a. Overall safety statistics, trends, analyses b. Number of fires—highlights of same c. Workers' Compensation Cases, Status Report/Action needed/ approval needed d. Significant safety items from other sites and corporate headquarters	Safety Representative
VIII. Wrap-up and Communication Plan	Chairman, CSC

Figure 4-3

table should not be round (oval is acceptable) or square. The chairperson should be able to assess the reactions of these two staff persons, while other members of the committee should not be able to conveniently do so while they are reporting to the chairperson. Under these circumstances, committee members will find it useful to have discussed any areas of controversy with the appropriate staff person prior to the meeting. Differences of opinion or understanding may still exist, but by prior consultation on controversial items the committee member can make known these differences and thereby demonstrate a full understanding and position, be it not a "professional's" position. This procedure minimizes the likelihood that "surprises" will complicate the chairperson's task of effectively resolving differences.

The *first* order of business is that each line manager reports on the injuries his or her organization has incurred since the last meeting. This report should include classification of any injuries that have occurred during the previous month (or other report period), including medical treatment, restricted workday, lost time, and first-aid cases with significant potential for more serious injury.

First-aid cases without potential for more serious injury should not be reported at this meeting. I do not imply that first-aid cases should not be reported at all by the injured. Indeed, as is discussed in Chapters 5 and 6, a cardinal safety rule is: "All injuries or suspected injuries, regardless of how slight, must be reported to supervision and medical immediately." Although every injury represents an opportunity to learn something, relatively insignificant injuries without significant potential for more serious injury are simply not worth the time of line management to keep track of and report. Beyond this aspect, attaching undue significance to such small injuries encourages nonreporting. Nonreporting should be considered a serious infraction of safety rules and should be dealt with as a serious act of misconduct. Small injuries can easily be hidden from supervision, at least until the end of the day at which time they can be described as having occurred off-site. This is clearly a degenerative sequence of events. Keeping a low profile on first-aid cases with no significant potential for more serious injury avoids providing employees a temptation for misconduct.

As each CSC member reports the numbers, the chairperson should expect elaboration regarding the status of the injury investigation and /or report (see Chapters 9 and 10). If the report has already been published, the chairperson may wish to review the major recommendations of the report and inquire about reactions of other CSC members to the recommendations. By demonstrating specific interest in injury reports, the chairperson can create an atmosphere that supports thorough and effective injury investigations. The emphasis must be on analysis and corrective action steps to be taken by management personnel.

The *second* agenda item is a disability report from each CSC member. These reports should include the number of employees who have not been at work since the last meeting for medical reasons and the total number of days of work missed by these employees. The medical representative should be expected to keep a graph showing the percent disability (absent hours/total hours) for the organization on a monthly basis as well as on a year-to-date basis.

In addition, some organizations have found it useful to establish a "screen" or criterion by which individual employees who may need some special attention are highlighted. For example, any employee who has been absent more than eight days total or more than four times during the past twelve months may be a candidate for special attention. Each of these cases must be examined and judged on its own merit. A thirty-year employee who has had a heart attack and has been absent only on this one occasion does not represent a "problem" needing special attention even though the person is absent for more than the eight-day criterion. On the other hand, an employee who has missed work on five occasions in the past twelve months for a total of only six days may well be a "problem" needing attention. A multiplicity of one- or two-day medical absences is suggestive that a "problem" exists that needs to be recognized and corrected. Supervisory consideration of appropriate action is warranted. It is here that first-line supervisory knowledge of employees is critical. Upper supervision should provide the stimulus, as needed, for attention to those employees with attendance records indicating problems.

By reviewing attendance statistics and discussing the actions to be taken regarding "problem" employees, the CSC meeting will serve to improve the consistency with which employees are dealt by supervision. This, in turn, will increase the success of applying the needed attention as well as raise the standards of the organization.

The medical representative can make valuable contributions to these discussions by providing line management with direct and knowledgeable medical information regarding diagnosis and prognosis of employee medical conditions. This information, of course, should not violate good medical ethics regarding employees' right to privacy. Simple explanations of the implications of certain medical procedures give supervision confidence that they can successfully handle employee reactions. Further discussion of this subject appears in Chapter 13.

The *third* agenda item is the reports by committee members on the serious incidents (including near misses) that may have occurred in their respective organizations since the last meeting. These reports reflect incidents "since the last meeting." Each report requires a CSC member (or someone in his/her organization) to keep track of the data personally rather than to rely on published monthly data. The objective in these reports is that the CSC members themselves report their safety stewardship and be subjected to queries about these events and about steps to prevent reoccurrence.

Adopting a "since last meeting" criterion avoids the temptation to simply refer to published monthly report data without discussion. The objective is to require personal involvement. The numbers are not the only important element; it is the attention of top management that is also important.

Serious incidents are events in which employees have or could have been seriously injured or in which significant financial costs or environmental damage were or could reasonably have been expected to have been incurred. This definition includes the occurrence of injuries more serious than first-aid cases. Thus, during this portion of the meeting devoted to serious incidents, those events discussed during injury reporting are not repeated. Some organizations may want to drop the word Serious. Outsiders—for example, newspaper reporters—may find the word Serious titillating in the event that a copy of a report finds its way into their hands. (Incident Investigation, Chapter 9, comments on this aspect of reporting the results of injury investigations.) Again, discussion of these reports provides an opportunity to commend good performance and to encourage better performance when necessary.

The above definition leaves considerable room for judgment regarding what is or is not a serious incident. The freedom of judgment provides the opportunity for management to lower the degree of significance required as the organization improves its performance. It is desirable, in the absence of actual injuries, to have a mechanism to keep the full potential for injuries clearly in the minds of employees. The recognition of the threat (possibility) of becoming injured should be ever present. Serious incidents can provide a means for accomplishing this result. Organizations should adopt a "floating" concept of what is serious in order to generate some serious incidents each month, if possible. In this context, serious incidents become good things, not bad things. That is, events are being recognized and acted upon, rather than being overlooked or ignored.

The *fourth* item on the CSC meeting agenda is the Management Safety Audit System reports (see Chapters 7 and 8). During this part of the meeting the results of the management safety audits conducted in the previous report period are presented. The method of presenting these reports varies, depending upon the particular audit scheme in use and, perhaps, the preferences of the CSC members. One arrangement is to expect the safety professional to have analyzed all individual team reports and to have summarized the findings into two or three major categories on which the CSC can focus its attention. Another arrangement is to have each CSC member report an analysis of the audits conducted in the member's area of responsibility. Another is to delegate the analysis responsibility to some member of supervision on a rotational basis, in lieu of the safety professional, and to have this person make the report. When the number of audits is relatively small, still another reporting arrangement is to have the chairperson of each audit team make the team's report.

From these reports the upper management of the organization can assess the kinds of unsafe acts employees are committing, whether the frequency of such acts is increasing or decreasing, whether the proportion that constitutes explicit violation of established rules in comparison to exercise of poor safety judgment is changing, and lastly the suggested areas that need specific management attention. If additional management attention is deemed appropriate, the committee can make use of its existing subcommittee structure or establish an ad hoc committee to study the problem and report back to the CSC its findings and recommendations. The CSC can then act. Decisions made in this fashion will capture many of the advantages that were outlined earlier in this chapter.

The first four reports are performance reports: Injuries, Incidents, Disabilities, and Unsafe Acts. The *fifth* item on the CSC agenda is reports from the chairs of the subcommittees (both standing and ad hoc). Most of the reports from standing subcommittees do not normally require CSC action. They merely let the CSC know what the subcommittee is studying, as well as perhaps indicate what the committee is finding and what direction their recommendations may be taking. Thus, the CSC is "prepared" for the forthcoming report; it also gives CSC members an opportunity to steer the subcommittee into a somewhat different direction, or, at least, to give the subcommittee alternatives it should consider before coming forth with specific recommendations.

Standing subcommittees are not normally expected to present recommendations at every meeting of the CSC. On the other hand, ad hoc subcommittees should be expected to get their work done and develop their recommendations in a reasonably short time period—usually one to two months. Unusually complex issues assigned to an ad hoc subcommittee may take longer. To avoid this development, a reassessment of the subcommittee charge may be in order. Ad hoc subcommittees seem to work best when their work is intensive, but only for a short time period. The idea is that a specific problem exists that needs to be solved and that a solution is needed quickly.

An ad hoc subcommittee of the CSC should usually be chaired by a member of the CSC. Occasionally, it will be prudent to depart from this arrangement. An ad hoc subcommittee may be formed to study and make recommendations on an issue on which specific detailed technical knowledge is required. Perhaps there exists in the organization a knowledgeable senior manager or technical person, possessed of unusually good judgment and respect. Such a person might well be asked to chair an ad hoc subcommittee. Such assignments can be successful in their own right and they lessen the burden on the upper management group. Such assignments should not be made for this reason, of course, but it is a side benefit.

The *sixth* report, the Medical Report made by the medical department representative, should contain anything about which this representative wants the CSC to be informed. New procedures for routine employee medical examinations, difficulties in obtaining employees for routine examinations, steps taken to keep private physicians better attuned to the site "back-to-work" program, new governmental regulations, and new medical capabilities—for example better treatment facilities, seasonal medical advice, and vaccines—would all be appropriate information for the Medical Report.

The *seventh* agenda item is the report of the safety supervisor. This report should include:

1. a summary injury report for the total organization
2. report of fires not otherwise reported
3. safety supervisor's safety audit report (report of his or her observations)
4. new governmental regulations
5. report of any safety inspections by governmental agencies
6. report of safety-related investigative reports from other company units or noncompany reports that may be of significance
7. any other activity or problems about which the CSC should be informed

The *eighth* item on the agenda is that a member of the CSC "read back" those items needing to be communicated down through line management together with an indication of how far down. All usual communication emanating from a CSC meeting should be done by word-of-mouth. This method requires each level of supervision to become personally involved. It requires that supervision "say the words" and "answer the questions." Thus, time will be spent on safety and management will be viewed as demonstrating its interest in safety. Such communication will not be accomplished by use of minutes that are passed out to be read when convenient. Verbal communication provides an opportunity for supervision to amplify and emphasize certain points of particular interest to them as individuals—perhaps citing examples to which subordinates can more easily relate.

This verbal communication should be accomplished at a speed of one organization level per half day. For example, in a four-layer management structure—site manager, superintendent, area supervisor, first-line supervisor—nonsupervisory personnel should be informed by the end of the day after a morning meeting of the CSC meeting.

The CSC meets, let us say, on the second Thursday morning of each month. The superintendents then meet with their respective area supervisors or equivalents Thursday afternoon. The area supervisors meet with their first-line supervisors on Friday morning and the first-line supervisors meet with their nonsupervisory employees on Friday afternoon. The following Monday, while "walking their spaces," the manager and superintendents can ask employees if they have any questions regarding the items that came out of the CSC meeting. They can also use this opportunity to evaluate the thoroughness and faithfulness with which the communications have been executed. It also provides upper management an opportunity to directly amplify or correct the CSC messages as well as any other items that may arise during the contact. Again, this activity gives management a vehicle through which to demonstrate its interest in employee safety.

Normally, CSC "messages" should not be more than two or three items. Employees simply will not try to relate to and understand more than this number. Subjects should be picked carefully and communicated thoroughly and clearly for the purpose of gaining employee understanding, not just to prove "we told them."

THE SUBCOMMITTEES OF THE CENTRAL SAFETY COMMITTEE

Central Safety Committee subcommittees are of two general functional classes: (1) those that actually generate activity or initiate direct work (always retaining CSC approval), and (2) those that review the work of others. Some may be hybrid. Subcommittees are also classified by the time horizon of their work (see Figure 4-2).

Standing Subcommittees

Areas of safety that are expected to be ongoing areas of interest normally have a standing subcommittee created to give attention to this continuing interest. Examples of subcommittees devoted to such ongoing interests are shown in Figure 4-2.

Subcommittees are normally chaired, as indicated earlier, by a member of the CSC. The other members of the committee come from all levels of the management organization. This makeup results in a committee that brings a full cross-section of points-of-view and interests to the committee. The committee members are expected to bring their own views and understanding to subcommittee deliberations, but they are also expected to bring the views of their peer group as well as those of their subordinates. Thus, the subcommittee is provided the opportunity to be aware of and to consider a full range of perspectives from top to bottom and across functional groups.

Membership on a subcommittee should be established as part of an employee's assignment. As this will take both time and energy, contributions to the work of the subcommittee must be recognized by supervisors as part of an employee's job performance (contribution).

Rules and Procedures Subcommittee

The rules and procedures subcommittee has two areas of interest: (1) site-wide rules and procedures, and (2) the rules and procedures of subsections or divisions of the site organization. The subcommittee is directly responsible for the development and maintenance of site-wide rules and procedures in an up-to-date and understandable condition. For those rules and procedures applicable to subsections or divisions within the site, responsibilities of the Rules and Procedures subcommittee are restricted to a review of the subdivision rules, concentrating on adequacy, appropriateness, consistency, clarity, and enforceability. Its objectives are to recognize problems in these areas, develop suggested solutions, and alert the responsible line manager of their interest in the rules and procedures in a way that encourages the responsible line manager to react favorably to their suggestions. The subcommittee should not take responsibility for preparing the subsection rules and procedures. This is a responsibility of the specific subsection line manager.

When first establishing a CSC and the subcommittee structure, the Rules and Procedures subcommittee will have a heavy workload during the transition from the existing circumstances to the CSC system. Its first task might well be to examine the existing Safety Manual or other repository regarding the AACCE criterion: Adequacy, Appropriateness, Consistency, Clarity, and Enforceability. A major consideration regarding appropriateness is the rules or procedures that require approval by the safety supervisor prior to line management action. For example, provisions requiring "safety" approval of a piece of equipment or process before the facility can be put in service are inappropriate. This is a line management responsibility that should not be delegated to the safety office. A rule specifying that line management must consult with the safety office prior to putting a facility into service is appropriate. This rule keeps with line management the decision making and hence the responsibility for results and yet provides that line management obtain input from the safety office prior to acting.

The Rules and Procedures committee may well discover that the subdivisions each have rules pertaining to a given subject, for example, eye protection. These subdivision rules may have been written completely independently of each other and as a consequence use different wording with different implications when none was intended. They may be different by intent, but not consistent as viewed by employees. These rules are good subjects for establishing site-wide rules with only one set of words. If there is no need for a site-wide rule because the applicability of the rule is restricted to a few employees in different subdivisions, the need still exists for consistency among the subdivisions. Adoption of an identical rule by each of the line management involved will accomplish this and can be one way the Rules and Procedures committee can contribute.

The concepts of clarity and enforceability are closely connected. If rules and procedures are not absolutely clear by their wording, employees will not be sure what is expected of them. Rules and Procedures that are not clear to employees become the subject of conflict and are hard to enforce. Enforcement becomes lax, and general respect for safety deteriorates. For example, a rule might state that steel-toed safety shoes are required in the warehouse areas. There is a passageway through which both pedestrians and forklifts pass. The passageway provides access from the warehouse lunchroom and the supervisor's office to the front office. Question? Does the mail clerk need to wear safety shoes when in this passageway? The clerk probably does not think of the trip to the supervisor's office as being one in the warehouse. The forklift truck operator surely considers this space part of the warehouse; he moves products through the passageway just as he does through any other passageway in the warehouse. If it is the intent that the mail clerk must wear safety shoes, the rule is clear. However, as many organizations will find it difficult to require the mail clerk to wear safety shoes in this situation, the rule becomes unclear and will not, in practice, be enforced. The rule is defectively written. Figure 4-4 lists some thoughts about those instances when a rule is not a rule. The Rules and Procedures subcommittee can help the safety effort by discovering some of the circumstances in which a rule is not a rule and make recommendations to the responsible line managers or to the CSC.

Standard Operating Procedures (SOPs) of the various departments (subdivisions) are also a fruitful area of activity for the Rules and Procedures subcommittee. Again, the task of the committee is a review of these, preferably on a sample basis, to assess their quality and to express the subcommittee's judgment to the responsible line manager and to the CSC as well. The topic of Standard Operating Procedures is discussed in Chapters 5 and 6.

A list of rule-making responsibilities of the Rules and Procedures subcommittee might include such areas as:

1. Development of a list of general site safety rules applicable to all employees:

   - All injuries or suspected injuries, regardless of how slight, must be reported to supervision and medical immediately.
   - Smoking is permitted only in specific smoking areas.
   - Running, except in emergencies, is not permitted on the site.
   - "Strike-anywhere" matches are not permitted on the site.
   - Possession or use of illegal drugs or alcohol is not permitted on site.
   - All off-the-job injuries that have the potential to be aggravated by work-related activity must be reported to supervision upon return to work following the injury.
   - All employees must comply with the safety rules of the areas of the site that they enter. An employee is responsible for knowing these area rules as they apply to him or her.
   - Employees must wear vehicle restraints (seat belts) while on the site, and while off the site if on company business.

WHEN IS A RULE NOT A RULE?

1. WHEN IT IS NOT IN WRITING, IN A LANGUAGE EMPLOYEES CAN READ.

A rule which has been established by verbal edicts soon gets forgotten, gets misconstrued as to what was really said, and permits variation in content by various interpreters of the rule. As a result, the rule becomes a source on confusion, becomes unenforceable and a negative factor in the safety effort. By requiring that all rules be written, rules will become better formulated and refined as to meaning.

2. WHEN IT IS NOT THOROUGHLY COMMUNICATED TO ALL EMPLOYEES WHO MAY NEED TO KNOW.

Burying a rule in some written note to supervision meets the test of being "in writing" but will not accomplish the task of influencing employee behavior- the purpose of a rule.

3. WHEN IT IS NOT THOROUGHLY UNDERSTOOD BY ALL EMPLOYEES WHO MAY NEED TO KNOW.

Rules need to be understood in order to be effective in influencing employee behavior. This means they need to be written in language which is comprehensible by the employee whose behavior they intend to guide. Short, one subject, one verb, sentences make the best rules. The scope of applicability must be well specified. Employee understanding of rules needs to be established and routinely verified.

4. WHEN IT IS NOT FOLLOWED.

Even the best of rules become non-rules if they are not followed. A rule that is not followed, not enforced, quickly becomes ignored by more and more employees. When this happens, the rule is no longer a guide to employee behavior. By failing to enforce a rule, the rule becomes ineffective.

5. WHEN IT BECOMES OBSOLETE, BUT STILL EXISTS.

Circumstances change; rules need to be changed to reflect the realities of these changed circumstances. Out-of-date rules are particularly detrimental to achieving excellence in safety. They may actually be hazardous, if followed. They generate contempt for safety rules. They "advertise" loudly and clearly that safety rules are not important enough to be kept up-to-date.

Figure 4-4

- Incidents that have potential for serious injury, serious health effects, significant property damage, and/or adverse impact on the environment must be reported to supervision immediately.

2. Development of a list of site-wide procedures:

   - Injury reporting and investigating
   - Procedure for inspection of new or altered equipment
   - Vessel entry requirements and permit
   - Locking, tagging, and trying
   - Sources of radiation energy
   - Waste handling
   - Emergency response
   - Spills
   - Notification of governmental agencies
   - Handling of governmental visits
   - Pressure vessel inspections
   - Adverse weather precautions

In preparing procedures, the Rules and Procedures subcommittee need not try to prepare all these procedures without help. Many of these procedures require technical and procedural requirements beyond the capabilities of the subcommittee membership. This requisite does not relieve it of its responsibilities. The subcommittee needs to find a way to bring the requisite knowledge to the task of procedure writing. The formation of task force groups, enlisting the contributions of those employees who do have the requisite knowledge under the guidance of one or more of the subcommittee members, is one scheme that has been found useful. An alternative is the formation of an ad hoc subcommittee of the CSC to deal with a specific rule or procedure question. This method, however, should be used sparingly. It is likely to bog down the CSC by placing too many activities under its direct supervision.

Because rules and procedures have been found essential to achieving excellence in safety, the Rules and Procedures subcommittee is of vital importance to the effective functioning of the Organization for Safety.

The Incident/Injury Investigation Subcommittee

Like the Rules and Procedures subcommittee, which prepares rules and procedures for organization-wide applicability and monitors those established by smaller subdivisions within the organization, the Incident/Injury Investigation subcommittee[5] is a hybrid subcommittee in that it both reviews and participates in incident investigations. However, the Incident/Injury Investigation subcommittee is also responsible for maintaining that part of the Safety Manual related to incident investigations. In organizations that have adequate procedures for investigating incidents, this function of maintaining the Safety Manual should represent only a small part of its work. In organizations in which procedures for investigating and reporting incidents are not well established, the Safety Manual part of the subcommittee's work should represent an early and major part of its work. Chapter 9 provides the basics for developing specific procedures for investigating and reporting incidents.

After establishing investigative and reporting procedures, the major work of the subcommittee is to monitor and contribute to line management investigations of incidents. This is accomplished in two parallel ways: (1) the entire subcommittee reviews completed investigations, on a sampling basis, and (2) a member of the subcommittee is present at incident investigations and participates when asked to do so by the chairperson of the investigation committee. It is important that this representative of the Incident/Injury subcommittee, and the safety supervisor as well, not become the authority figure during management's investigation. They are present to assist, not lead or dominate. Therefore, the presence of neither of these two "outsiders" should be made a requirement for proceeding with an incident investigation. By monitoring incident investigations, members of the Incident/Injury Investigation subcommittee gain an increased understanding of the skill and knowledge of line management in conducting investigations, as well as develop a better sense of the techniques that seem to work and those that do not. They can then discuss these observations at subcommittee meetings and use them as the basis for recommendations to the CSC for changes in investigation procedures and/or recommendations regarding training needed by line management. The presence of a representative of the Incident/Injury Investigation subcommittee also encourages the full disclosure of all facts related to the incident under investigation as well as the development of a full range of management actions designed to avoid reoccurrence.

As with other subcommittees of the CSC, the Incident/Injury Investigation subcommittee should make periodic reports and recommendations to the CSC for its consideration and action. In the interest of efficiency, these reports should usually be verbal reports that can be written up if desired by the CSC. Where strong management communication skills exist, verbal reports frequently suffice and may occasionally be preferable to written reports.

Any changes in investigation and/or reporting procedures recommended to the CSC should, of course, be presented in writing. This formality allows members of the CSC to see and consider the specific recommendations. If action by the CSC is expected at the meeting at which the recommendations are to be presented, prior distribution of the recommendations should be made in order that CSC members have an opportunity to think about the recommendations and perhaps discuss them with their subordinates. The CSC should not be expected to act on recommendations at the same meeting in which the recommendations are presented unless they have had prior opportunity to consider the recommendations. The CSC should not allow itself to be "pressured" into a premature decision. Actions by the CSC are the actions of the "head" of the organization and they need to be consistently credible and trustworthy.

Safety Program and Activities Subcommittee

The Safety Program and Activities subcommittee contributes to the total safety effort by developing and encouraging others to develop training and motivational activities that effectively promote maintenance of and improvement in employee safety behavior. Employee behavior is fundamental to avoiding injuries and damage to facilities and the environment. And, although each employee is responsible for his or her own behavior, management is responsible for results and therefore has both the "right" as well as the responsibility for ensuring that employee behavior is continuously appropriate and without relapses. This challenging task, of course, is never completed. The task continues as long as there are employees. Establishment of standards of appropriate behavior is essential to this task. Employees deserve to know what management considers appropriate. Rules and procedures establish these standards. However, rules and procedures can be overly relied upon. That is, when overdone, rules and procedures become so dominant a factor in the workplace that employees no longer expect to have to think about what they are doing. Beyond this point, an excess of rules results in conflicting instructions to employees because circumstances are seldom exactly those anticipated by the rule or procedure writer. Thinking continues to be required if employees are to avoid injury.

Thus, the activities of the Program and Activities subcommittee are designed to improve employee knowledge of and adherence to established rules and procedures and to THINK SAFETY.

Innovative committee members will find new means to these ends. Inclusion of non-exempt personnel on this committee can frequently enhance the appeal of the subcommittee's efforts to the non-exempt employee group. Although this subcommittee fundamentally is a publicity organization, most subcommittees have found that their effectiveness increases as the direct participation of employees in its activities increases.

Outlined below is a sample of activities of the Program and Activities subcommittee that have proved useful.

1. *Organization of a series of "safety topics for the month."* This can be published in the form of a calendar on which the topic for each month is printed, along with some ideas and resource materials for use at monthly safety meetings.

2. *Safety contests.* I recall one in which four-line jingles were written, each of which was related to one of eighteen Master Safety Rules. The participant was required to write out the rule that he or she thought best fit each rhyme. By drawing from among the correct answers submitted by members of each work group, a winner for that work group was selected. From the winners of each work group, a site winner was drawn by chance. The names and pictures of winners at the work-group level were shown on easels throughout the site; the site winner was presented a gift of relatively small value—for example, a fire extinguisher, smoke alarm, or life jacket. A new rhyme was posted each week until all Master Safety Rules were covered. A grand prize winner was selected by random drawing from among all entrants who had successfully identified each Master Safety Rule. The rhymes were designed to require employees to think about the rules; the association was not obvious. As a result, relatively few employees submitted the eighteen correct answers. From those who did, first, second, and third prize winners were selected by draw. Grand prizes were only slightly more valuable than weekly prizes. The names of employees who had all eighteen entries correct were posted widely throughout the plant.

Supervision encouraged participation and second-level supervision kept themselves informed regarding degree of non-exempt employee participation. The program generated an excellent response from employees and clearly reinforced employee awareness of the safety rules involved.

Another safety contest that achieved measurable results was based on off-the-job lost workday cases (LWCs). It incorporated two concepts that have merit in safety contests. First, chance was not a factor in "winning" or not—there was no drawing to determine a winner. And, secondly, the contest was based on group performance, thereby creating peer pressure as a motivating factor.

The plant was divided into teams of approximately twenty employees, maintaining work group identity to the maximum extent possible. To encourage peer pressure and facilitate the creation of team identity, it was thought important that all members of a team should know each other at the onset of the program. Each team was assigned the number of days which the team was required to be injury free off the job (no injuries so serious that an employee missed a day at work) in order for the team to win. Smaller teams had more days, larger teams had fewer days. The goals were the same for every team in terms of total exposure days. The goal was set to represent a significant improvement over the then current performance level. If a team experienced a lost workday case either on the job or off the job, it was disqualified. The challenge was not open ended. On-the-job LWCs virtually never occurred and were not a factor during the life of the program. The prize was a small cake (worth about $3.00 at the time) that was awarded to employees by their first-line supervisor as they exited the plant gate. This timing got the prize home, and, in turn, stimulated discussions of family safety when the family was most likely to be together. The program was repeated several times before it lost its stimulating punch and was abandoned. It sounds corny, but it worked. Off-the-job lost workday cases were significantly reduced.

Another safety program judged to have been very effective involved having full-day meetings of employees to hear well-prepared talks on safety followed by small group discussions to "Assess Our Own State of Safety." Each employee was asked to answer a series of questions regarding safety which were designed to help the employee classify himself or herself into one of these categories: a doubting Thomas; a real, but passive believer; or an active missionary. The results were anonymously tabulated and each employee's responses were put in an envelope and sealed by the employee. During the ensuing year, the plant-wide safety program was built around the subjects upon which the questions had been formulated. At the end of the year, during a regular safety meeting, employees were again asked to respond privately to the set of questions and to classify themselves into one of the three categories. The year's program was judged to have been particularly effective because a significant number of employees rated themselves higher on the scale. Subsequent safety meetings were devoted to discussions of why people do not become safety missionaries. What impediments does management erect that discourage development toward missionary status? What are the differences in personal experiences that caused some employees to "progress" to missionaries and others not to do so? Both management and nonmanagement employees learned a lot about themselves and the impediments, real and perceptual, that exist in making continuous safety progress.

Yet another program of a different sort comes to mind. Many manufacturing or processing plants and research laboratories have had good success with a safety open house. This involves opening a facility or parts of it to employees and their families. Displays and demonstrations of some of the hazards of both home and work environments are set up together with the proper steps to be taken to avoid injury. Examples of safety rules, and operating procedures can be illustrated. Half masks, full-face masks, and self-contained on demand breathing apparatus can be demonstrated. Air sampling devices can be used to measure the reduction in oxygen in exhaled air as well as the increase in carbon dioxide. The hazards of under-the-sink cleaners, if used improperly, can be illustrated. The effectiveness of automobile seat belts can be demonstrated even at low speeds by use of inclined slides, sometimes referred to as "convincers," that provide for instantaneous stops at, say, five miles an hour. An imaginative Program and Activities subcommittee can think of many interesting and effective ways to convey the safety message.

Four specific programs have been outlined above. Commercial companies can provide program materials as well. For example, safety bingo cards, or playing cards on which employee-contributed safety slogans can be printed, are readily available. My own experience is that "home-grown" programs that have been well planned get the best results. Direct involvement in all phases of such programs by non-exempt personnel contributes immensely to their success and in the process increases the participants' personal commitment to safety.

Process Hazards Review Subcommittee

The fourth "standard" CSC subcommittee is the Process Hazards Review subcommittee. This subcommittee also has a dual function: (1) creating and maintaining the procedures for process hazards reviews, and (2) monitoring the results of process hazards reviews conducted by line management. As with incident/injury investigations, participation in process hazards reviews by a member of the Process Hazards Review subcommittee can significantly contribute to the effectiveness of these reviews and to management's understanding of the effectiveness of such reviews. As a group, this subcommittee is expected to review, on a sampling basis, the effectiveness of process hazards reviews conducted by the responsible line-management. The subcommittee should report its findings, conclusions, and recommendations to the CSC as requested or as the subcommittee finds appropriate, as well as to line management who have been responsible for conducting process hazards reviews.

A process hazards review is a detailed analysis of a specific operation which is designed to uncover any pre-construction or existing deficiencies in "as installed" equipment design, materials of construction, operating procedures, employee selection and training procedures, emergency plans, and so forth. The objective of a process hazards review is to discover or recognize any situation that can not be safely controlled by the means actually available in the workplace.

The review team needs:

1. to examine piping and instrumentation diagrams for adequacy during normal operation
2. to verify that these diagrams reflect "as-built" conditions
3. to consider "what if" situations such as power failure, equipment and/or instrumentation failure, variations in both supply and composition of raw materials that are being introduced to the process, inappropriate operator response to changing situations, and other perturbations that may be introduced to the process from external sources
4. to examine standard operating procedures and judge their adequacy, particularly in regard to the safety aspects of each step
5. to determine, by actual observation and testing of employees, if appropriate employee training has been accomplished
6. to examine log books and "process sheets" for evidence of inadequate operational control or lack of conformity with standard operating procedures
7. where possible, to exercise safety devices to determine if they operate properly; and where not possible, to examine test results logs for conformity of results and timeliness of tests
8. to use any other measures designed to gain assurance that the process will be operated safely, without injury to personnel, or damage to property or to the environment

This list is a tall order that will take the time of knowledgeable people. The membership of the subcommittee will need to bring a wide variety of skills and knowledge to the task. However, because these subcommittee reviews usually establish the standards that will be used by normal line management process hazards reviews, it is of the utmost importance that they be done well. In this respect, subcommittee reviews both check on the quality of process hazards reviews already done by line management as well as provide the basis for recommendations to the CSC regarding efficacy of the process hazards review process.

These reviews are expensive when the process is both complicated and hazardous. But it is precisely these conditions that warrant the expense. The adverse consequences of the failure of such processes have been well established. Bhopal, the Narco, Louisiana, refinery explosion, the pollution of the Rhine from Switzerland to the sea as a consequence of the toxic spillage, the explosion of a potassium nitrate ship at Texas City, Texas, the unconfined vapor-cloud explosion of the Flixborough Works in England, as well as the more recent explosion of the Phillips Petroleum Company polyethylene plant, the neoprene plant explosion in Louisville, Kentucky, the oil tanker spillages off the coast of France and in the Prince William Sound in Alaska—the list goes on and on. None of these events and their resulting loss of life, property, and jobs were necessary. They were the result of human failures—failures of individuals, but primarily failures in management. Process hazards reviews are one technique through which management can exert its influence and credibly communicate to employees its dedication to their safety, to stockholders its concern for their financial investments, and to the public its concern for their safety, the environment, and jobs.

Some organizations have Process Safety Review committees that are appointed by upper management. These committees are charged with "providing rigorous process and equipment safety checks" and are frequently authorized to grant or withhold approval of start-ups. This authority significantly distinguished such Process Safety Review committees from the Process Hazards Review subcommittee of the Central Safety Committee. Process Hazards Review subcommittees have no vested authority. They can be very persuasive because of their stature within the organization, but authority remains with line management.

Not all process hazards reviews need be major undertakings. "Cut the cloth to fit the client." Simple processes or operations presenting few hazards of low significance may be accomplished with not much more than the answering of a few simple and straightforward questions. Other reviews take a team of several people and several weeks. Very large, complicated processes may be more effectively handled by considering individual unit operations within the overall process that are reviewed as separate, but related processes.

There are three well-known and commonly used analytical techniques for conducting process hazards reviews:

1. "What If" Analysis
2. Failure Mode and Effect Analysis
3. Fault Tree Analysis

In the "what if" approach to examining process hazards, the review team "simply" asks itself "what if" questions and then determines the process consequences of these questions in the actual situational circumstances in which the process is being operated. Some examples follow:

1. What if valve "A" begins to leak? Will it become known? How? What consequences? How corrected? Corrective procedures written and available? Do operators know these procedures? Do they practice them?
2. What if power fails? What happens without operator intervention? How could this system fail? What is proper operator intervention? Procedures written and available? Status of emergency lighting? Emergency power sources? Operator action required for proper restart?
3. What if solenoid "X" fails? What happens?
4. What if line A is ruptured between points "X" and "Y"?

The "what if" questions can go on and on for complex operations. For this reason, process hazards reviews are usually more productively pursued by looking at each identifiable portion of an operation, a unit operation, separately so as to keep the questioning focused on an area in which the review team has knowledge and can get a sense of accomplishment for a finite piece of work. Such unit operation analyses must also, however, ask questions that relate the particular operation to those that precede and follow it—for example, provision must be made for considering the interrelationship of various operations.

The other two methods are more sophisticated techniques requiring specialized training in the techniques themselves. The Failure Mode and Effect Analysis technique starts with a specified hypothesized failure and traces the effects such a failure or combination of failures is expected to produce. Fault Tree Analysis starts with the selection of a specified undesirable event and systematically analyzes the possible sources of the cause of the event. The "what if" procedure suffices for most analyses and is the technique most commonly used.

Proficiency in conducting process hazards reviews is achieved by means of technical competence and practice in an environment in which management supports the time and effort required to conduct reviews. This book, I hope, will make a contribution in establishing management recognition of the need for process hazards reviews and a system for continually monitoring their efficacy. The former objective will have to be sought elsewhere.

Other Subcommittees

Emergency Preparedness
Hazardous Materials
Union/Management Safety Committee
Contractor Safety
Ad hoc subcommittees, as needed

Other subcommittees—both standing and ad hoc—can be effective in assisting the CSC establish safety leadership and an effective safety management process (Figure 4-2). The subcommittee structure is the same for all subcommittees. First, the subcommittee should be chaired by a responsible senior member of management, preferably someone who reports directly to the "head" of the organization; then the subcommittee should be populated with a cross-section of employees from various functional groups and position levels having an interest or potential interest and knowledge of the subject the subcommittee is charged to study.

The reports of these subcommittees, injury reports, the Management Safety Audit reports, and the Serious Incident/Injury Investigation reports, the disability reports, and the reports from the Safety Supervisor and Medical department representatives constitute the standing agenda for the CSC. These are the management processes through which top management demonstrates dedication to safety and enlists the contributions of employees at all levels within the organization to achieve their common goals: no injuries—no damage to health—no damage to facilities—no damage to the environment.

SUMMARY: THE CENTRAL SAFETY COMMITTEE AND ITS SUBCOMMITTEES

The responsibility for the safety and health of employees clearly lies with their direct supervision.[6] This is not a responsibility that can be delegated to a staff organization. To assist line management in better understanding this responsibility, Du Pont has, through a continuous trial-and-error process over many years and many types of operations, evolved a staff support system. This staff support system has two main components: (1) the "safety office," and (2) subcommittees of the Central Safety Committee (CSC).

The normal organizational arrangement is that the safety office is headed by the site safety supervisor or manager—safety, health, and environment. Depending upon the size of the operation, this may be a full-time assignment with several assistants in a large plant, or a part-time assignment in a small operation. In any event, it is an identifiable assignment that is shown on normal organization charts. The assignment has a specific job description and job classification.

Du Pont safety supervisors may or may not have had specific safety training, other than that obtained as a result of prior Du Pont work experience. Most safety supervisors have had operating experience as line supervisors. Many are "up-from-the-ranks" personnel. It is not unusual for college graduate engineers, who have first-line supervisory experience, to take assignments as site safety supervisors. Some of these find a career in safety work; others move back into direct line operating assignments or move on to other assignments not directly associated with safety except as the responsibilities of their new assignments may require. For the duration of this assignment, the safety supervisor is the safety professional for the organization. All of these arrangements are very straightforward and similar to the safety office arrangements in many companies.

The second staff support system—subcommittees of the CSC—can be the source of some confusion. These subcommittees are normally chaired by a member of the CSC. Thus, a chairperson of a subcommittee is a line manager reporting to the site manager. Similarly, the members of a subcommittee are line personnel in the various functional groups within the total organization. Typically, few, if any, of the subcommittee members are in the line organization of the chairperson of the subcommittee.

The subcommittees have staff functions. The members gather facts, study them, and assess understanding and attitudes. The subcommittees also review procedures and investigations; they develop programs designed to publicize, to educate, to train, and to improve procedures. Finally, the subcommittees make recommendations to the CSC for decision making. This arrangement keeps responsibility in line management, which comprises the membership of the CSC. Assignments to subcommittees are ad hoc, almost always supplemental to the regular line responsibilities of the assigned persons.

The scheme provides several virtues to members of the line organization. Some of these are:

1. Recommendations are more likely to be based on a better understanding of the basic work situation than if they are developed by the safety office. Efficiency is improved because of the direct involvement of knowledgeable and affected line personnel.
2. Recommendations are more likely to be realistic than if they are developed only by the safety office.
3. Recommendations developed by a subcommittee and accepted by the CSC are more likely to be enthusiastically endorsed and supported because there exists a body of employees (subcommittee members and other employees with whom subcommittee members have had discussions) who understand the issues and support the actions being taken. The employee group assists

in "selling" the decision because "selling" is not left only to the line management function.

4. Recommendations are more likely to be new or innovative. The subcommittee will not have been overly restrictive or conservative because it is not a decision-making body. The study, planning, and development work is separated from decision-making and implementation work.
5. The work of the subcommittee can be constructively guided in an indirect manner by the CSC chairperson to the extent he or she desires, while still allowing the CSC to retain the responsibility for actual decision making. This arrangement provides the opportunity to try ideas that may or may not survive close scrutiny, without ascribing authorship to those ideas that subsequently appear defective. These ideas can have arisen "anonymously" within the subcommittee. Ideas that have merit and receive approval by the CSC can be credited to their authors.

   The subcommittee members are seldom restricted by the presence of a supervisor in their management line. Therefore, they frequently develop ideas and action plans that are subsequently adopted by the CSC, that either would never have been brought forth or would have died quickly within the direct line organization. Subcommittees are "sanctuaries" in which ideas can be nurtured and developed, yet they are still within direct communication with the CSC through the subcommittee chairperson.
6. The subcommittee chair can also lobby for, as well as test, the acceptability of ideas arising in the subcommittee among his or her CSC peers prior to formally presenting its recommendations to the CSC.
7. Although not purely a safety issue, line management participation in subcommittee activities gives employees who are normally functioning in a line activity the opportunity to "see the world" as a person in a staff assignment sees things—being responsible for getting something done, but having little or no authority or resources to do so. This experience can teach line managers how to more effectively manage their relationships with staff personnel. Membership on CSC subcommittees also increases the opportunity for upper-level management to observe the performance of people not in their own direct line organization.

These subcommittees, although staff organizations, can substantially assist line management to discharge its responsibilities more effectively for the safety of personnel for whom it is responsible.

To repeat, line management is responsible for safety. The safety office and CSC subcommittees are important staff organizations that are available to provide assistance to the line organization.

SUMMARY

Good intentions and hard work regarding safety will not achieve safety excellence. Leadership and the operational organizations through which to demonstrate leadership while securing the contribution and support of "followers" is the ingredient that can lead to safety excellence. The Central Safety Committee and its subcommittees provide management the operational tools through which to demonstrate the required leadership.

NOTES

1. Most organizations currently utilizing this organizational structure are using the title "Central Safety, Health, and Environment Committee." The shorter "Central Safety Committee" will usually be used in the remainder of this text. No separate meaning should be attached to this shorter term.
2. Peter F. Drucker, "Leadership is More Doing than Dash," *The Wall Street Journal*, January 6, 1988, p. 36.
3. Drucker, *ibid.*
4. This is the normal arrangement. Organizational complexities necessitate different CSC structures, but the CSC and its members are the top line management personnel on the site and act together in matters pertaining to the safety of personnel for whom they are responsible and who have a common, shared responsibility for the organization.
5. This subcommittee is frequently called simply the Incident Investigation subcommittee. Incidents then include events that did not lead to personal injury or significant property damage as well as events that did result in injuries and property damage.
6. This summary is provided to facilitate communication. It is designed to be reproduced and used as an educational vehicle.

Chapter 5

STANDARDS OF PERFORMANCE: PRINCIPLES

As Drucker has reminded us, setting of standards is a requisite of leadership.[1] Standards establish what is expected of followers—if followers they would indeed be. This requirement is confirmed if one examines organizations that have established excellence in safety performance. These organizations rely heavily on the existence and continued development of standards as a means to assist in the task of securing the behavior of individuals necessary to avoid injury.

THE PROCESS OF SAFEGUARDING

In Chapter 3, one of the key principles of successful safety leadership was identified as "all operating hazards can be safeguarded." The process of safeguarding can be accomplished by installing physical safeguards or by establishing rules, work procedures, standard operating procedures, and engineering design standards that, when followed, provide the requisite safeguards. Taken together, these written instructions provide the safety standards of performance for an organization. In practice, physical safeguards as well as good work procedures are required. This chapter concerns safety standards of performance.

SAFETY RULES AND PROCEDURES

Rules and Procedures are the written general instructions regarding personal behavior for which it has been thought appropriate to specify standards. By personal behavior I do not mean only moral behavior. Rules and procedures include written instructions on how to accomplish tasks. Safety rules and procedures are the instructions on how to accomplish tasks *safely*. Rules are specific instructions to do or not to do clearly specified actions. Safety procedures are instructions on what is required from a safety viewpoint in regard to specific, but generic tasks. Standard Operating Procedures apply to specific tasks. They are not, basically, safety documents, but should contain safety-related material including any specific safety rules or procedures that must be followed.

In practice, Standard Operating Procedures may contain safety instructions but safety procedures should have no operating instructions. Thus, a maintenance operating instruction regarding general purpose use of a grinding machine may give instruction for the type of grinding wheel to use for various metals, but may also include specifications that safety glasses and a face shield must be worn at all times when a grinding wheel is used. The eye and face protection rule has been included within the procedures for grinding. These same requirements may also exist as a rule that specifies that "safety glasses and face shield shall be worn when operating a grinder." The distinction is a significant one. The significance of rules and procedures is that they must not be thought of as optional—that is, *they must be followed.* If written material is prepared to *assist* or provide *guidelines* for safe behavior, this material cannot be thought of as rules or procedures. If material is designed to be optional in use, it should be identified as "guidelines" or "description of process." Operating Manuals (OM) are frequently prepared to describe a process and its operation. General technical guidance for actual operation of the facilities is frequently included. A casual review of some operating manuals may lead one to believe that, indeed, the manual is a set of operating procedures. Unless the provisions of the manual explicitly must be followed, such manuals are useful documents but they are not operating procedures. Operating procedures must specify precisely what is to be done and under what circumstances it is to be done. The content of operating procedures is not an overall guideline to action; it is specific instructions that *must* be followed, without options.

To prepare good rules and procedures is not an easy task. They must be realistic in their requirements. They must be capable of enforcement without ambiguity. They must be understood by the employees to whom they apply. They must be thorough but not so thorough as to constitute a body of written material that, because of its volume, cannot be clearly communicated to all who need to know.

If safety shoes are specified for a work area, there should be no unwritten understanding that the rule means "for those actually doing work," and therefore, first-line supervision or perhaps upper supervision is somehow exempt from the requirement. The rule, if the intention is to exempt supervision except first-line supervision, should read "safety shoes are required in this area for all hourly role and first-line supervisory personnel." This distinction would, of course, be bad practice. Leaders should lead by example. Privilege is not an attribute of a real leader.[2] If there is no need for safety shoes in a protected aisle that serves as an access route to a supervisor's office in an otherwise safety shoe area, the aisle should be exempted from the safety shoe requirement. To do so may make mail delivery easier, make doing business with internal customers easier, and so forth, with no diminishment in attention to safety. The rule can still be strictly followed and enforced.

If clothing, including underclothing, must meet certain standards regarding composition (to avoid static electrical charges in a possibly explosive atmosphere such as one in which solvents are poured), then all persons who enter the work area in question must meet these standards. Rule writing is not easy!

I recall visiting a plant in which the plant traffic rules for vehicles were "compliance with governmental traffic regulation." One of these governmental regulations specified that seat belts "shall be worn by all front-seat occupants." This, then, was the plant rule. I suppose because the rule was a "derived" rule—rather than an explicitly stated rule established by plant personnel and therefore a rule in which some "ownership" had been established—there was little commitment to compliance. In fact, a superintendent (he reported to the plant manager) with whom I was about to ride from the office building out to the plant area had to be cajoled into fastening his seat belt prior to proceeding to the plant area. His reasoning was that while technically there existed a safety rule requiring use of seat belts, the rule was based on over-the-road driving conditions, not driving conditions such as those prevailing on site, with a controlled population and low speed limits. It was clear that he used his seat belt only because of my presence. This was a safety rule that, in practice, had informally been allowed to be ignored. Management had allowed deviation from the rule to be acceptable and routine.

Several years later, two supervisors were killed as a result of a minor vehicular collision at low speed on this site. Each was driving a company vehicle while on duty in the plant on the early 4 P.M. to 12 P.M. shift. The weather conditions were described as very light snow fall. The collision occurred at an intersection of plant roads. No other unusual circumstances existed. Based on the very minimal damage to the vehicles, speed was judged to be quite slow. One supervisor was killed immediately, presumably because his head was thrown forward striking the post supporting the roof of the vehicle. The second supervisor died several days later from complications associated with crushed ribs, presumably from striking the steering wheel. Neither was wearing a seat belt. Had the plant established strict compliance with the safety rule requiring the use of seat belts on company property, I believe these two deaths would have been prevented. More importantly, the plant work force was reported to have held this belief also. The employees involved were "good" employees. They were working in an environment that did not require conformity to established safety rules!

In spite of the fact that "good judgment" appears to be continually in short supply, good judgment must still be relied upon. Rules and procedures can substantially supplement but not replace the use of "good judgment." In fact, rules and procedures are nothing more than a codification of "good judgment." Good rules and procedures represent the "wisdom" that has been learned through experience. Their value lies in not only the fact that their content is sound, but also that they have been written, communicated, learned, accepted, and followed. There is no need for each employee to learn by his or her own direct experience. In fact, in some instances this is impossible. Only those who survive catastrophic events have the opportunity to learn and profit from the experience. Rules and procedures are codifications, but because experience should be an open-ended phenomenon through which wisdom is continuously being developed so should rules and procedures be continuously under development and subject to change by those who are responsible for results.

SAFETY MANUALS

The depository for safety rules and procedures is the Safety Manual. This is the location where employees can discover the written safety instructions that they must follow in carrying out specified general tasks. This is the location of the wisdom that the organization has decided to reduce to writing and perpetuate through training and use. A good safety manual is logically organized and has a thorough table of contents and a well-developed index, as prospective users are likely to need assistance. In computer terms, it should be "user friendly." Indexing should include task-related headings, as well as requirement-related headings. A prospective user who is going to do some welding should be able to find "welding" as well as "flame permits" in the index. The safety manual is more than a depository; it is a working document. Yet, I have seen safety manuals, usually prepared by safety professionals, which are pedantic, "preachy," full of virtuous suggestions and guidelines, and so poorly indexed, if indexed at all, that readers could more efficiently find material by thumbing the pages rather than by using the index. Figure 5-1 shows the table of contents for a three-section safety manual. Figure 5-2 reprints the index for this same manual, which is one for a chemical research facility. By examining Figure 5-1, readers quickly grasp the overall organization of the manual. By examining the index readers are given assurance that they will be able to find readily what they want. The information in the manual becomes available. Samples of the actual contents of this manual are included in Chapter 6. Figure 5-3 shows the table of contents of a safety manual for a manufacturing site; Figure 5-4 is its index.

These safety manuals differ; they meet the needs of the local organization for which and by which they have been developed. Their contents have been determined by line management in cooperation with employees to be of value to their organizations. They have not been prepared by the safety staff.

In spite of the obvious differences between these two manuals, they have much in common.

Common Elements of Safety Manuals

1. Both of the manuals illustrated here are divided into three identifiably different sections. The *first* section is devoted to **general items** that apply to all employees, independent from their particular assignment. The *second* section is devoted to particular, identifiable distinct **tasks**. The *third* section is devoted to particular, identifiable, distinct **hazards**, mostly chemical hazards, for which rules and procedures have been developed to safeguard against these hazards wherever they may be encountered.

2. Both manuals provide a system for identifying individual rules and procedures as well as groups of rules and procedures. Examples of this are evident in Figures 5-1 and 5-3. Where letters and numbers are used, letters provide differentiation among major categories of rules and procedures as in Figure 5-3. The only point to be made here is that the safety manual is *organized* and organized in a manner consistent with the needs of prospective users.

3. Both manuals specify how changes in the manual shall be made. As discussed in Chapter 4, the Rules and Procedures subcommittee of the Central Safety Committee formulates those rules and procedures that are applicable to all employees independent from their particular job assignments—all those that appear in Section I as shown in the sample tables of contents. The subcommittee then proposes these new or modified rules and procedures in writing to the Central Safety Committee for approval. The CSC may wish to seek comments regarding a proposal from others within the organization before they act upon the proposal. If the proposal is approved, the safety supervisor is then authorized to issue the new rule or procedure for incorporation into the safety manual by each holder of a safety manual.

The safety supervisor (coordinator) is the custodian of the safety manual; that is, he or she is responsible for such needs as:

1. issuing new or revised pages
2. having copies available for new users
3. collecting copies no longer needed—to ensure that out-of-date manuals do not exist
4. bringing to the attention of appropriate people the need for changes in content
5. assuring that new materials meet the desired editorial standards
6. avoiding conflicting material and\or undesirable repetition of the same material

It is the sites' safety manual, but the safety supervisor is the one person who has administrative responsibility for its quality. The safety supervisor does not control its content. This is the responsibility of line management, functioning through the Central Safety Committee and its subcommittees.

Safety manuals should be widely disseminated throughout the organization in order to make the manual readily available to each and every employee. By readily available, I mean close at hand so that it becomes, in fact, a usable reference. For example, every workshop, laboratory module, manufacturing operation and research office, marketing office, and so forth should be provided a copy. No one should have an excuse for not using the safety manual.

Changes to the *second* portion of the safety manual are normally the responsibility of the line supervisor who is responsible for a specific operation and are approved by the "head" of that operation. Thus, maintenance rules and procedures are approved by the maintenance supervisor, operating rules and procedures by the supervisor of the operating area, and powerhouse rules and procedures by the powerhouse supervisor. Of course, if these supervisors are thought to be "too close" to the situation, their supervisor should be the authorizing authority. One example of this can be seen in the samples of powerhouse procedures shown in Chapter 6. These have been prepared by hourly roll personnel and their immediate first line supervisor and authorized by the utilities and waste management superintendent. The CSC does not

text continues on page 115

SECTION I

BASIC SAFETY AND HEALTH

TABLE OF CONTENTS

Figure 5-1

SECTION II

General Safety Procedures
(Also see Chemical/Laboratory Safety Procedures)

TABLE OF CONTENTS

Figure 5-1 (*continued*)

132 Working with Asbestos and Refractory Ceramic Fibers (RCF's) (4/1/87)
134 Safety Rules and Practices Governing On-Site Contractors (3/30/89)
136 Maintenance and Inspection of Hydraulic and Geared Lifting Equipment (excluding Chain Hoists) (3/15/88)
138 Pressure Vessel Procedure (1/30/89)
139 Pressure Relief Device Procedure (1/30/89)
140 Barricade Procedure (9/15/90)
142 Compressed Gas Cylinders, Regulators and Piping (3/30/89, 3 and 4—9/15/90)
144 Safety Rules and Practices for Laboratory Fume Hood Use (1/30/89)
146 Local Exhaust Ventilation Guidelines (9/30/89)
150 Safe Use of Pressure Gauges (9/30/89)
154 Prevention of Contamination of Laboratory Services (9/15/90)

Revised 12/28/90

Figure 5-1 (*continued*)

SECTION III

Chemical/Laboratory Safety Procedures (Also see General Safety Procedures)

TABLE OF CONTENTS

Figure 5-1 *(continued)*

INDEX

A

Figure 5-2

Figure 5-2 (*continued*)

Figure 5-2 (*continued*)

Figure 5-2 (*continued*)

R

S

Figure 5-2 (*continued*)

Figure 5-2 (*continued*)

SAFETY MANUAL

ABC PLANT

Contents
Volume I
PLANT RULES & REGULATIONS

Figure 5-3

Contents
Volume II
PLANT RULES AND REGULATIONS

Figure 5-3 (*continued*)

SAFETY MANUAL

ABC PLANT

Contents
Volume III
Chemical Rules & Regulations

Figure 5-3 (*continued*)

"SAFETY HOW" - ALPHABETICAL INDEX

Figure 5-4

C

D

E

Figure 5-4 (*continued*)

Figure 5-4 (*continued*)

H

Halls	A-1-1
Hand Rails	A-1-1
Handling, Chemical	C
Handling, Compressed Gas Cylinder	A-11-1
Hard Hats	A-1-1
Heavy Objects	A-2-1
Hoists	A-9-2
Horns, Car & Truck	A-1-3
Horseplay	A-1-1
Hose	A-1-3
Hose, Gas	B-6-4
Hot & Corrosive Material Procedures	B-3-1
Housekeeping	A-4-1, A-4-2

I

Injury Cause Codes	B-1-4
Injury Classification	B-1-4
Injury Procedures	A-1-1, B-1-1, B-1-2
Injuries, Investigating	B-1-3
Injuries, Off-the job	B-1-6
Inspection Chart, Equipment	A-9-2, A-9-3
Inspections Color Code	A-1-1
Inspections, Periodic	A-9-1

K

Kelite	B-3-5, B-3-7, B-3-9
Knives	A-1-3, B-10-1

L

L. P. Cylinders	B-10-1
Ladders, Extension	A-10-2
Ladder Rules	A-10-1,A-2-1
Ladders, Step	A-10-2
License Examination Check Lists	
Tractors	B-9-5
Load Lugger	B-9-6
Rider Type Lawn Mower	B-9-7
DMT & Stores Fork Trucks	B-9-8
Electric Fork Truck	B-9-9
Austin Western Crane	B-9-10
Licensing, Mobile Equipment	B-9-1
Lifting	A-1-3
Liquids, Flammable, Procedures	B-11
Locker Room	A-3-1

Figure 5-4 (*continued*)

7-1-66

Figure 5-4 (*continued*)

Figure 5-4 (*continued*)

Figure 5-4 (*continued*)

T

U

V

W

Y

Z

Figure 5-4 (*continued*)

continued from page 93

get involved in the creation or approval of these more specialized rules and procedures. The CSC does not, however, ignore them. The Rules and Procedures subcommittee of the CSC is charged with periodically reviewing these specialized procedures, perhaps on a sampling basis, and recommending changes to responsible line supervision as they believe appropriate. The subcommittee can bring unresolved differences about which it feels strongly to the CSC for adjudication. In a well-functioning organization this step should rarely be necessary; nevertheless, the "system" provides for this resolution as part of the procedure for making changes to the safety manual. Again, the safety supervisor, as custodian of the manual, actually issues the new or revised rule or procedure to all safety manual holders.

The *third* portion of the manual is normally prepared by the Hazardous Materials subcommittee of the Central Safety Committee. In this capacity it functions in the same way the Rules and Procedures subcommittee functions relative to the General Rules, normally found in the first portion of the manual.

There can be some "farming out" of responsibility for various areas of the safety manual. For example, while the Rules and Procedures subcommittee is fundamentally responsible for section one of the manual, the Emergency Response subcommittee should prepare the rules and procedures dealing with emergencies. The Incident Investigation subcommittee is expected to keep the procedures for investigating injuries and incidents up-to-date with their thinking. Needs that appear to be best met by the creation of a special ad hoc committee of the CSC can be handled in this fashion; the subcommittee is abandoned when the CSC has approved its recommendations. All of these subcommittees should be chaired by a high level member of management, preferably one of the site manager's immediate subordinates, and its membership selected from throughout the organization. The question frequently arises regarding hourly roll employee membership on subcommittees. A number of factors influence this decision. In small organizations, the answer, I believe, should universally be "yes." There simply is not enough management personnel available. In larger organizations this question probably depends on the "style" of the organization. Historically, hourly personnel may have been asked to evaluate or react to a recommendation of a subcommittee—a testing of the waters—prior to its formal submission to the CSC, but they would not usually serve on the subcommittee as members. As the benefits of successfully managing a more participatory work environment are being better recognized, hourly roll personnel can make a contribution by direct membership on a subcommittee. The question is not how an employee is paid, but whether means can be found to maximize the total energies and commitment of the entire work force toward creating an environment in which employees work safely. In work situations in which a high degree of "worker" participation is already established, "worker" membership on a subcommittee will be the natural practice. In work situations in which there is a desire to increase participation, membership on a safety-related subcommittee has been found an ideal vehicle for doing so. These subcommittees are not "bargaining" committees and should not be allowed to become forums for bargaining. In the presence of union representation, this aspect and union views must be carefully considered and managed if members of the bargaining unit are to be constructive participants. In this regard, it has been found constructive to have a Union/Management safety committee function as a subcommittee of the CSC (see Figure 4-2, page 63). This provides the opportunity for constructive union participation in the safety effort. Where it is deemed desirable to include union-represented employees on other subcommittees, they should be selected as individuals, not because they are union officers or stewards.

4. Both manuals have been written by users, not by the safety staff. The safety manual should not be a compendium of advice from safety professionals. It should be a record of the rules and procedures that the line organization has created for its own use in its pursuit of an injury-free work environment. They are self-imposed rules and procedures.

5. Both manuals provide written evidence of the date of the latest *revision* of each rule or procedure. Although not shown on these examples, the date of the last *review* of each rule and procedure is kept by the safety supervisor. Rules and Procedures must be regularly reviewed on not less than a specified frequency.

6. Both manuals exclude Operating Procedures. The safety manual should contain only safety related rules and procedures. However, the safety manual is not the only place safety-related rules and procedures should be maintained. Standard Operating Procedures are detailed, step-by-step descriptions of how to accomplish specific tasks. These should include not only safety-related material, both rules and procedures, but also general advice or guidance regarding the hazards associated with the operation.

STANDARD OPERATING PROCEDURES

We can see the distinction between rules and procedures and Standard Operating Procedures (SOPs) if we refer to Chapter 6, Figures 6-2 and 6-4 and compare these with Figures 6-13 and 6-14. Operating procedures virtually always refer to a specific operation that is not sitewide in applicability, that is, an operation that is the responsibility of a manager of part—not the whole—of a site or operation. Therefore, as with section two of a safety manual, the responsibility for operating instructions rests with this manager. He or she may be required by organizational arrangements to adopt operating instructions based upon stringent requirements of a technical or process engineering group; but, in the end, operating instructions should be line management instructions to employees for whom they are responsible. In practice, these operating instruction can frequently be actually written by the employees for whose use they are intended. Again, the emphasis is that these documents can be readily understood by and be useful to the anticipated user.

In order that understandability and usefulness are achieved, operating procedures should be written in language that the user readily comprehends. This goal suggests that technical exquisiteness is not an objective. Sentences should normally be short, with clearly established subjects and verbs. Words should be words of the workplace, not those of the research laboratory or engineering design groups. User-written and-tested procedures will make achieving this goal more likely. Standard operating procedures need to be approved and authorized by line management. To ensure technical correctness, some organizations have found it a useful practice to obtain engineering or research comments or guidance, as well. Authorization, however, should always remain with line management.

As we can see in Figures 6–12 through 6–18 (pages 166–88) a useful way to keep safety requirements clearly in mind is to specify (1) the equipment that will be necessary to accomplish the task (no improvising), (2) the personal protective equipment needed, and (3) any applicable safety rules or procedures. These appear at the beginning of the write-up. In the body of the write-up, the right-hand side of the page is reserved for safety notations immediately opposite the procedural steps. Copies of such procedures in clear plastic covers can then be made immediately available to employees in the workplace in which the work is to be accomplished.

If the written operating procedures are actually used when tasks are performed, these procedures can easily be kept up-to-date. However, for simple procedures that are well known by operating personnel Standard Operating Procedures are not likely to be routinely used when tasks are performed. In these situations, provision must be made for timely review of SOPs so as to avoid the development of differences between practice and procedure. Circumstances change with time; SOPs need to be changed with time as well.

A primary source of information concerning operation of equipment is the manufacturer's equipment manual. As with process operating manuals, manufacturers' manuals should be used as a resource, not as the finished product. Operating procedures are specific instructions, not general guidelines. Only direct line management can effectively issue instructions, and they should prepare these in a standardized format so as to avoid any ambiguity regarding their meaning or applicability. Manufacturers' manuals can not meet this test.

EMPLOYEE SAFETY HANDBOOKS

Many organizations have chosen to publish a small handbook (approximately 4"x6") that contains the major safety rules and procedures. These are bound or stapled booklets that employees find convenient to keep in their pockets or toolboxes. They have the virtue of ease of accessibility. Unfortunately, they also normally represent a condensation or even an alternate version of the rules and procedures that are in the safety manual. Even when disclaimer statements in the handbook acknowledge that the handbook is a secondary document, and the safety manual the prime one, safety handbooks tend to take on a life of their own because they become a major reference source. In addition to these negatives, such handbooks are virtually always out-of-date. Revision of parts of a safety manual is a continuous process. Just as organizations are changed and equipment is updated, word changes should take place to better reflect current thinking on some subjects. All of these changes must be reflected in the safety manual; that is, such changes can not be effective until published in the safety manual.

In order to accommodate for these changes, the hard copy of the safety manual should take the form of looseleafs in a binder that makes replacement of pages easy. Because such changes cannot be made in the typical bound employee handbook, there is always some concern that the handbook may not have the latest word on some issue. Hence, the safety manual must ultimately be used. Some organizations have tried to solve this problem by issuing the handbook in looseleaf form with a binder. The bulkiness of the resultant handbook normally precludes its being carried in an employee's pocket. For these reasons, employee handbooks should generally be avoided in favor of real safety manuals that are very accessible to every employee. Using these, employees become more familiar with the "real thing," as well as avoid the problem of having source documents that may be inconsistent.

CONTRACTOR SAFETY MANAGEMENT

Organizations around the world are increasingly concluding that the use of outside contractors to perform selected work represents a cost-effective way of operating. Examples of such practices cover a wide range of activities. Mechanical and electrical work on major overhauls of facilities, routine maintenance work that takes place on a daily basis, janitorial work, computer programming, food service operations, secretarial services, medical and health maintenance services, power house operations, and stores and inventory warehousing are typical activities being contracted to outside vendors who do the work within the "fence" of the landlord organization. Today virtually all parts of an organization's operation are subject to consideration for outside contracting. This practice can have a dramatic effect on the safety environment of a workplace. Contractors are no longer working within a barricaded area at the side of a facility. They are working hand-in-glove with the regular employees. The behavior of all employees, regardless of their employment status, now determines the safety environment in which work gets done. And, although each employer is responsible for its employees, the landlord employer must be responsible not only for its own employees but also for the way contracted employees discharge their safety responsibilities. The coordination and safety management task has become far more complex than in the past. Organizations have attempted to cope with this task in a variety of ways.

1. Reviewing the safety performance of prospective contract organizations prior to putting the organization on the bidder's list.
2. Establishing contractor safety handbooks that are a part of the contract agreement and with which, therefore, all contract personnel must conform. The rules and procedures may be slightly different from those for their "own employees."
3. Providing in the contract language that site safety rules, procedures, and standard operating procedures will be the standards by which the contractor will conduct its work—that is, no separate contractor rules or procedures.
4. Establishing evaluation procedures to assure that contract personnel have the requisite skill and knowledge.
5. Establishing clear contractual terms regarding the need to work safely as a contractual necessity and specifying the consequences of failing to do so.
6. Establishing performance monitoring procedures.
7. Including contractor personnel in the organization's safety program by including contractor personnel on the Central Safety Committee and its subcommittees, Management Audit Teams, Injury/Incident investigations, and "crew" safety meetings.

The article shown in Figure 1-16 (page 21) emphasizes the importance of contractor safety. My own experience, with both Du Pont and non-Du Pont clients, confirms a desperate need for increased emphasis on contractor safety. It may be time for some organizations to re-evaluate the long-term cost effectiveness of extensive use of contractor personnel to accomplish tasks that are potentially hazardous and to which contractor personnel bring no specialized competency. The cost of adequately training constantly changing contractor personnel may simply price such contractor work out of the market. Conversely, contractor personnel who have become part of the permanent work force may legitimately ask who is their employer—the organization that issues their checks, or the organization that supervises their day-to-day activities?

Contracting is not going away; it is increasing. It deserves more management attention than I have seen it usually get. There are exceptions. I know of one large petrochemical company that uses the safety performance of both "own employees" and "contractor employees" as measures of management performance. Other organizations have begun to measure and publicize contractor safety performance. Some have built in contractor remuneration rewards or penalties based on safety performance as a means of encouraging improved performance and evidence of management interest in safety. Even so, performance by contractors is normally considerably poorer than that of the contracting organization. This is evidence that there is much to be done in the area of contractor safety.

SUMMARY

Leadership requires clearly establishing the goals of an organization as well as providing the direction needed to achieve these goals. In safety, rules and procedures that, when followed, are expected to result in the avoidance of injury are an integral part of this needed direction. They are the standards of performance that are essential ingredients of the recipe for achieving excellence in protecting the safety and health of employees, the public, and the environment.

NOTES

1. See Figure 1, Chapter 2, page 36
2. Ibid.

Chapter 6

STANDARDS OF PERFORMANCE: EXAMPLES

GENERAL SAFETY RULES

As pointed out in Chapter 5, some safety rules apply to all persons in an organization or safety unit. Figures 6-1 to 6-4 show examples of general safety rules which have been obtained from actual operating organizations. As we can see by examining these samples, organizations have different needs. These differences in needs have been reflected in these general safety rules. Differences in needs arise out of differences in the type of activities in which the organizations are involved as well as in the injury history of the organization.

Some organizations have chosen to have two levels of master or basic safety rules (Figures 6-3 and 6-4). The distinction being the degree of injury likely to result from failure to adhere to the rule. One site defines this distinction as follows:

Safety Rules

The objective of Safety Rules is to prevent serious injuries. If we think that a serious injury could occur, the rule must be as follows:

A. Must be a positive statement.
B. Allow no latitude for judgment or interpretation.
C. Imply a penalty for anything but unqualified compliance.

Safe Practice

Items that we do not feel could cause a serious injury or items that cannot meet the above stipulations should be considered a safe practice.

Not all successful organizations have chosen to make this distinction; they have found no need to do so given their types of work, injury history, and work "climate." Making this distinction does not resolve all problems in rule writing. Figures 6-3 and 6-4 both provide for safe practices; master safety rule #2 requiring *reporting of injuries* in Figure 6-3 is item #1, *safe practice*, in Figure 6-4. *C'est la vie.*

I have included four samples of general safety rules not only to demonstrate their differences but also to provide the opportunity to recognize their many similarities—those general rules that commonly appear in the safety manuals of organizations that have excelled in safety.

The requirement to report all injuries is a common one. The currently preferred wording is "All injuries or suspected injuries, regardless of how slight, must be reported to supervision and medical immediately." Supervision needs to know in order to investigate and develop actions to prevent reoccurrence and to provide for the employee's absence from the workplace, if necessary. Medical needs to know to assure appropriate treatment whether it is provided on site or off site. In addition, the site safety supervisor needs to know reasonably soon so that the injury can be properly classified and entered on the OSHA log. The current U.S. regulatory requirement for entering on the log is six days from the date of diagnosis. If treatment is to take place off site, it is important that supervision and medical personnel be involved in the activity to assure first-rate treatment for the employee and positive, constructive contacts with employee family members. (This aspect of "managing the injury" is discussed in Chapters 10 and 11.)

The important point is that, as a matter of principle, all injuries or suspected injuries must be reported. You should note that suspected injuries are included. In practice, these are frequently back cases. Again, the fundamental reasons for early reporting is to encourage prompt corrective actions to prevent reoccurrence or aggravation and to assure timely and appropriate medical attention. An additional reason exists. Failure to report suspected injuries creates an environment of distrust and irritation when suspected injuries are not reported until it is clear that an injury exists. Delayed reports raise the question of whether or not an injury, in fact, occurred at work. Strong emphasis on early reporting can create an atmosphere in which the negative aspects of delayed reporting can be avoided and an opportunity for early corrective steps can be provided where these are indicated.

Another common aspect of these rules and practices is their emphasis on personal protective equipment—gloves, safety shoes, safety glasses. Personal protective equipment has been a major factor in reducing injuries and damage to health. I believe this is true not only because this equipment provides the wearer a physical safeguard, but also because it provides the wearer a psychological safeguard. It conveys the message that an activity of increased hazard is being embarked upon which requires not only physical protection but mental alertness as well. The manufacturing sites represented in Figures 6-2 to 6-4 require safety shoes (toe protection) and safety glasses, just for a person to *enter* the nonoffice areas of the plant. Experience has demonstrated that, even though substantial

text continues on page 133

Introduction

This SAFETY AND FIRE PROTECTION MANUAL is published to help you perform your job safely. The rules and procedures included in the Manual have evolved from many years of working experience and represent, therefore, the contributions of many employees over a long period of safety-oriented work. Because of the wide variety and uniqueness of much of the work performed at this site by highly skilled personnel, much of our safety program is based on suggestions or recommendations and procedures rather than on a large number of Safety Rules. However, specific Safety Rules have proved effective in injury reduction and are, therefore, an important and significant part of our safety program.

Additions and revisions are distributed periodically. It is most important that old sheets be removed and replaced with the new ones upon receipt so that the Manual is always up to date.

RULES AND PROCEDURES:

Safety rules and procedures are designed to help employees avoid injury and prevent damaging incidents. The Basic Safety Rules listed below apply to all employees. They should be known thoroughly and followed carefully.

Procedures have been prepared to cover specific areas and portions of the work at this site. Some of those included in this manual apply to all employees while others pertain only to those engaged in work related to the procedures. In addition to the General and Chemical/Laboratory procedures included in this manual, departments, divisions and sections may have other specific ones for their personnel.

Employees are subject to disciplinary action or dismissal for disregard of safety rules and procedures.

BASIC SAFETY RULES

1. ALL INJURIES, or suspected injuries, regardless of how slight, must be reported promptly to the Medical Section and supervision.
2. INCIDENTS with potential for serious injury must be reported promptly to supervision.
3. EYE PROTECTION is required where chemicals are stored or handled or where mechanical work is being done.
4. SMOKING is not permitted outside buildings, in elevators, automobiles or other places designated as "No Smoking" areas.
5. ELECTRICAL WORK must be done only by authorized personnel.
6. HORSEPLAY and other acts of carelessness which might endanger the safety of employees are prohibited.
7. USE OF ILLEGAL DRUGS or intoxicants, or persons under the influence of illegal drugs or intoxicants, are prohibited at the site.
8. RUNNING is not permitted on site grounds, except in an emergency.
9. GOOD HOUSEKEEPING must be practiced at all times.

Figure 6-1

Safety How*

MASTER SAFETY RULES

R-1A-1

SAFETY RULES:

1. All injuries and foreign bodies in the eye, no matter how slight, must be reported to supervision and Medical immediately.
2. If splashed or sprayed with any hazardous liquid, immediately wash the affected body area with large quantities of water and then report to Medical. If the eyes are involved, continue applying a steady stream of water until first aid assistance arrives.
3. "Strike anywhere" and other wooden matches are prohibited in the plant. Safety matches (book type), lighters, and smoking are permitted in designated areas only.
4. Exits, stairways, corridors, passageways, switch panels, and emergency equipment must be adequately lighted and kept clear of obstructions at all times.
5. Equipment must not be operated unless all guards are in place, except as specifically authorized by supervision. When guards are removed, SAFETY HOW R-2 must be observed.
6. Safety shoes must be worn by all employees except plant office personnel who do not routinely go into work areas. (Such employees are required to wear safety shoes when entering plant areas.) Where electrically conductive footwear is required, appropriate signs shall be posted.
7. Minimum eye protection (industrial safety lenses in safety frames without sideshields) shall be worn in all areas of the Plant except as outlined below.
   - A. Areas and assignments where more stringent eye protection requirements exist (monogoggle areas, safety glasses with side-shields, welding hoods, etc.)
   - B. AREAS WHERE NO EYE Protection IS REQUIRED
     - (1) Administration Building and vicinity (as defined on attached map).
     - (2) All other plant offices and restrooms.
     - (3) Safety glass cleaning stations.
8. Compressed air must never be applied to any part of the body or clothing. Monogoggles must be worn by everyone within 10 feet when compressed air or steam is discharged to the atmosphere. When used for cleaning purposes, compressed air must be reduced to 30 PSI and have a spring operated control valve at the nozzle.

* An Alternative name for Safety Manual

Figure 6-2

9. Rings, wristwatches and bracelets shall not be worn outside the Administration Building or plant offices. Loose clothing shall not be worn within three (3) feet of moving machinery.
10. Firearms, ammunition and fireworks are prohibited within the plant unless specifically authorized by the Plant Manager or his designate.
11. One hand should be kept free for use on the handrail on stairways unless specifically authorized by supervision.
12. Each employee servicing equipment, entering tanks or placing himself in a position to come in contact with moving machinery, corrosive liquids or electrical circuits must use Lock, Tag, and Think procedure as specified in Safety How R-2A.
13. Service (air, water, brine, steam, etc.) and/or process (acid, caustic solvents, viscose, etc.) commodities may be interconnected only with prior written approval of Power Supervisor, Safety Supervisor and Area Superintendent of area concerned.
14. When operating any electrical disconnect (220 V or greater) the person operating the switch shall wear side shield eye protection and leather gloves, stand to the hinged side of the receptacle and face away from the switch.
15. Safety equipment (shoes, eye protection, tools, etc.) shall not be altered or modified without prior approval of area supervision and the Safety Supervisor.
16. Horseplay and engaging in fighting or instigation of fighting is forbidden.
17. Running and jumping (except under extreme emergencies) and hazardous throwing of objects are prohibited.
18. Climbing on equipment, machinery, pipe lines, ducts, tank tops, etc. is prohibited unless specifically authorized by supervision.
19. Posted speed limits and traffic regulations must be observed.
20. Dangerous or unsafe conditions and defective equipment must be reported to supervision and promptly corrected or removed from service.
21. Employees must know the location of the main power disconnect and emergency stop before operating equipment.
22. Keep all chair legs on the floor.
23. Hair protection is required for employees working on or around moving machinery when it is felt by supervision that a safety hazard exists.
24. Suspected occupational health hazards, especially hazardous vapor conditions, must be reported to supervision.

Revised xx/xx/xx **Reviewed** xx/xx/xx

Figure 6-2 (*continued*)

Safety How

PLANT MASTER SAFETY RULES

1. EMPLOYEES SHALL KNOW AND OBSERVE PLANT SAFETY RULES APPLICABLE TO THEIR WORK. COMPLIANCE WITH ALL SAFETY RULES IS REQUIRED OF EACH EMPLOYEE, AND IS A REQUISITE FOR CONTINUED EMPLOYMENT.
2. ALL PLANT INJURIES, NO MATTER HOW SLIGHT, MUST BE REPORTED TO SUPERVISION AND THE MEDICAL SECTION IMMEDIATELY.
3. THE FOLLOWING ARE PROHIBITED:
   a. HORSEPLAY OR FIGHTING.
   b. RUNNING OR JUMPING, EXCEPT IN EXTREME EMERGENCIES.
   c. INTOXICANTS, OR PERSONS UNDER INFLUENCE OF INTOXICANTS.
   d. FIREARMS.
   e. SMOKING OUTSIDE OF DESIGNATED AREAS.
   f. TAMPERING WITH EQUIPMENT.
4. NO EQUIPMENT SHALL BE OPERATED UNLESS ALL GUARDS ARE IN PLACE, EXCEPT BY SPECIAL PERMISSION OF THE MAINTENANCE SUPERVISOR, OR ON WEEKENDS, THE SHIFT PRODUCTION SUPERVISOR.
5. NON-SAFETY GLASSES, FINGER RINGS, WRIST WATCHES, UNTUCKED NECKTIES, LOOSE CLOTHING OR LOOSE RAGS SHALL NOT BE WORN OUTSIDE OF OFFICES, CORRIDORS, OR CAFETERIAS.
6. DANGER ZONES ARE DESIGNATED BY "SOLID YELLOW BARRICADES" AND/OR "BLACK AND YELLOW ROPES". ONLY AUTHORIZED PERSONNEL ARE ALLOWED WITHIN THESE AREAS.
7. THE LOCKOUT PROCEDURE MUST BE FOLLOWED AT ALL TIMES. (R-6)
8. SAFETY INTERLOCKS SHALL NOT BE BYPASSED, EXCEPT BY WRITTEN PERMISSION OF SUPERVISION. (SEE RULES AND PRACTICES G-25-_)
9. ALL NAILS PROTRUDING FROM ANY TYPE OF MATERIAL SHALL BE REMOVED OR TURNED DOWN IMMEDIATELY.

Revised: xx/xx/xx - Change in Rule No. 8

Figure 6-3

10. "STRIKE ANYWHERE" MATCHES ARE NOT PERMITTED ON THE PLANT.
11. FLAMMABLE OR CORROSIVE LIQUIDS MUST BE STORED AND TRANSPORTED IN "APPROVED" CONTAINERS.
12. GLOVES AND GOGGLES OR APPROVED CONTAINERS SHALL BE USED WHEN TRANSPORTING GLASSWARE.
13. ALL CONTAINERS SHALL BE LABELED WITH THE NAME OF THE CONTENTS. IF THE SUBSTANCE IS POISON OR IS CORROSIVE, THE CONTAINERS SHALL BEAR AN APPROPRIATE LABEL.
14. EMERGENCY EQUIPMENT SHALL BE KEPT PLAINLY MARKED AND FREE FROM ANY INTERFERING OBSTACLES THAT COULD DELAY THEIR USE IN CASE OF NEED.
15. SAFETY SHOWERS AND EYEWASH FOUNTAINS SHALL NOT BE BLOCKED.
16. NO PERSON SHALL WALK OR STAND ON THE TOP OF TANKS OR DUCTS WHERE WALKWAYS ARE NOT PROVIDED, EXCEPT BY APPROVAL OF THE SAFETY SECTION.
17. ALL SHARP OBJECTS SUCH AS GLASS, RAZOR BLADES OR KNIVES WHICH ARE TO BE DISPOSED OF SHALL BE PUT IN SPECIAL CONTAINERS FOR REMOVAL TO DISPOSAL AREA.
18. TOE PROTECTION, WITH SUITABLE SHOES, IS REQUIRED OUTSIDE OF OFFICES, CORRIDORS OR CAFETERIAS EXCEPT AS NOTED IN R-2.
19. NOTHING SHALL BE PLACED OR STORED ON TOP OF ELECTRICAL EQUIPMENT SUCH AS SWITCHES, STARTERS, JUNCTION BOXES AND MOTOR CONTROL CENTERS.
20. DO NOT TOUCH PRINCIPLE

    I WILL NOT TOUCH MOVING PRODUCT OR EQUIPMENT WITH ANY PART OF THE BODY OR A HAND-HELD TOOL UNLESS AUTHORIZED BY AN EXCEPTION. AN OPERATING PROCEDURE OR SAFETY RULE MUST BE IN PLACE AND FOLLOWED FOR EACH EXCEPTION. SEE INFORMATION 4 FOR "DO NOT TOUCH" EXCEPTION LIST.

Revised: xx/xx/xx - Added Rule No. 20

Figure 6-3 (*continued*)

PLANT MASTER SAFETY PRACTICES

1. Good housekeeping practices and standards shall be maintained at all times.
2. Promptly correct all unsafe practices and conditions when practicable and report all such items to supervision at the first opportunity.
3. Incidents that may have weakened or damaged equipment must be reported to supervision at once.
4. Non-work injuries, which could become aggravated on the job, shall be reported to supervision within the first half hour of starting work.
5. Any person present in or passing through an area shall observe the rules of that area.
6. Only authorized persons shall operate plant equipment.
7. Footwear that has become weakened or damaged should be reported to supervision at once. This type of footwear should be removed from service as soon as possible. (See R-2)
8. Exit and Safety Shower lights shall be lit at all times.
9. The plant policy is to dispose of, or replace, glass items wherever possible in the workplace.
10. All glass containers are banned from locker rooms and shower areas. Thermos bottles are not considered glass containers.
11. Skin contact with organic liquids is to be avoided.
12. When seated keep all 4 legs of a chair or stool on the floor, and at least one foot must remain in contact with the floor, unless table or desk is equipped with a foot rest.

Revised: xx/xx/xx - Addition of Practice 12.

Figure 6-3 (*continued*)

Item 300

General Plant Safety Rules

1. Equipment turned over to service groups will be locked, tagged, cleared and tried by the Owner Area before work starts.
   —Before working on the equipment each individual will insure that equipment has been locked out by the Owner Area and will perform an individual L.T.C.T., or, if working under Supervisory Lockout, will lock and tag the Supervisory Lockout Box. Refer to Plant Safety Manual Item 1040 for detailed procedure.
2. Each safety lock will have only one key and, while in use, it will be kept on the user.
3. Approved safety shoes and glasses will be worn as minimum protection in all areas where manufacturing, craft, or laboratory work is performed, and in other areas when exposed to like hazards.
4. Running and horseplay are prohibited.
5. Guards must be in place before any power equipment can be operated, unless authorized by owner area supervision.
6. Before entering a barricaded area, permission must be obtained from employees assigned to work within the barricade or line supervision involved.
7. Keep all parts of the body from under a suspended load.
8. The chain or gate at the top of a ladder entrance to platforms or a pit entrance will be closed except when entering or leaving.
9. Compressed gas cylinders will be secured upright except Freon cylinders while being emptied and 2,000-pound chlorine cylinders.
10. Possession of firearms or ammunition within plant security fence requires approval from the Site Security Officer.
11. Rings, wrist watches, bracelets or any dangling jewelry will not be worn on any operating job or craft assignment.

Effective: xx/xx/xx

Figure 6-4

Item 305-a

General Plant Safe Practices

1. All plant injuries, non-work injuries and serious incidents must be reported to supervision immediately.
2. Only employees with proper knowledge and training will operate or adjust equipment.
3. Material Safety Data Sheets (MSDS) are required for all chemicals used On-Plant.
4. Before use, new or altered equipment and/or buildings must have a safety inspection.
5. Knives and scissors will be separately sheathed when not attended or in use.
6. An individual's clothes, hairstyle and jewelry should not present a hazard by:
   —impairing vision or safe movement
   —exposing skin to potential burns
   —entanglement in equipment or yarn
7. Barricades are required to protect employees from exposure to:
   —asbestos repair/removal
   —x-ray
   —pressure testing
   —equipment lifts involving suspended loads
   —major overhead work
   —hazardous or flammable chemicals
   —floor excavations
   —energized exposed electrical equipment
   —restricted areas for contractor work
   —high potential hazards (leaks, spills, defective equipment) or obvious dangers (open manholes, floor opening)
   —unusual work in high traffic locations.
8. Safety cones are required to alert employees to lower potential hazards than those listed in Safe Practice #7. In addition flags will be used in the main plant corridor.
9. Stepping over or stooping under barricades is prohibited.
10. Nothing shall be left on unattended ladder.
11. Hand rails should be used when going up or down steps whenever practical.
12. All roll-up doors should be pinned, with pedestrian or truck loading doors in the full up or down position.
13. All cabinets and bookcases 3 feet or higher must be anchored per anchoring standards. Sliding doors and drawers will be closed when not in use and will have stops.

Effective Date: xx/xx/xx
ITEM 305-A (1)

Figure 6-4 (*continued*)

14. Storage cabinets for flammable solvents and oils must be grounded to building steel or water pipes.
15. The contents of all containers will be identified. All chemicals will be labeled and stored either in safety cans with tight fitting caps and anti-flash screens or other approved containers. If glass containers larger than one (1) quart are used, they will be taped.
    (EXCEPTION: Chemical Labs.)
16. Smoking shall be permitted only in designated areas and lighted tobacco items must not be left unattended. Ash trays shall be emptied into approved containers.
17. Fire and safety equipment, and emergency exits shall not be blocked.
18. With hands positioned inside disc guards where provided, yarn buggies and waste tubs will be pushed by one person, may be pulled to get into a position to push.
19. Fifteen (15) feet shall be maintained between all manually assisted traffic moving in the same direction, and the vehicle must be on the downhill side of the individual handling it.
20. All electrical breakers, switches or push buttons shall be properly identified when their functions are not obvious.
21. When operating handle type electrical switches the operator shall stand to one side, turn his head away and operate the switch in a quick complete movement with one hand or an approved assist tool. When operating double-throw switches, a pause in the center "off" position is required.
    EXCEPTION: Batch Polymer, Fourth Floor, Rowan Oil Immersed Switches for portable blender power supply.
22. Check safety showers and eye wash stations each shift when work is being performed.
23. Use a safety shower immediately if sprayed or splashed with a hazardous material. Conventional washing may be used if the exposure is minor.
24. No-mars will not be used on the facial area.
25. Material should be placed so that it is not likely to fall.
26. Air used for cleaning purposes will be limited to 30 PSI.
27. Remove staples from paper with a staple remover.
28. When working on a roof within fifteen (15) horizontal feet of a vent or relief stack, a Roof Permit (No. 75.7) is required.

Effective Date: xx/xx/xx

Figure 6-4 (*continued*)

ITEM 305-A (2)

29. While seated both feet shall never be placed on a desk, table or any other object of similar height.
30. Anyone exposed to noise levels in excess of 85 dBA will be required to wear properly fitted and approved hearing protectors, except as noted in paragraph 5 of Item 426.1.
31. Climbing or standing on anything not designated for that purpose requires approval of supervision for each instance, unless covered by a specific job procedure.
32. Material used for containment of combustible or flammable liquids, must be disposed of daily and protected from sources of ignition.
33. Splashproof goggles must be unattached from hard hats when being worn as eye protection.
34. Leather gloves shall be worn when connecting or disconnecting 220 or 440 volt electric plugs.
35. Compressed air shall never be directed toward a person's body.
36. Nothing shall be tied off to conduit.
37. A Plant trained employee equipped with identical equipment will attend any person working with a Scott Air Pak.
38. Any object more than six feet in length shall be carried horizontally and shall be supported or escorted at each end, unless activity is in fabrication or erection area or in actual use at an established manufacturing process.

Effective: xx/xx/xx

Figure 6–4 (*continued*)

continued from page 122

efforts are made to control events, these will not be 100% successful; thus, personal protective equipment has been found useful.

AREA OR SUBDIVISION SAFETY RULES[1]

Because of the known hazards of particular operations in specific areas of a facility, rules of conduct to safeguard these hazards are needed. Figures 6-5 to 6-8 are samples of such area rules. Again, the emphasis on adequate personal protective equipment is evident, particularly when opening process piping in which hazardous materials has been present.

RULES FOR SPECIAL PIECES OF EQUIPMENT

Some hazards are related only to the use of specific pieces of equipment. Figure 6-7 contains examples of the rules that have been found appropriate for some of these.

A close examination of these rules might suggest that these were not prepared and edited by English majors. They were prepared by operating personnel, and in particular those employees most directly affected by them. This "bottoms-up" approach does not relieve management of the leadership role of setting standards. Although employees "on the floor" have experiences that can provide insight to the injury potential of various types of activity (not all injury prevention rules need be written in blood), they should not be relied upon exclusively to develop these rules. Such employees normally have not developed the necessary conviction that *all injuries can be prevented.* They too easily accept the concept that an injury or event was just "one of those things," or "it would not have happened if I had taken more care" without defining what "more care" means. Many employees view rules and procedures as an undesired abridgement of their freedom of action and therefore will not recommend adequate rules and procedures to guide their behavior. The fact remains that rules and procedures, when well prepared, understood, and followed by the work force, make a significant contribution to employee safety and health, to protection of the public and the environment, and to continuity of operation.

SAFETY PROCEDURES

Figures 6-1 to 6-7 contain rules pertaining to specific areas or pieces of equipment. Figures 6-8 to 6-11 provide examples of safety procedures. Safety procedures are written instructions regarding a generic activity—for example, glove selection, locking and tagging, by-passing process interlocks, and welding permits.[2]

text continues on page 165

Casting Area Safety Rules

A. GENERAL

The General Plant Safety Rules apply in addition to the following area rules. (See Section A-1)

1. Safety pins on hoists must be in place before lifting any load.
2. Standing on film that is subjected to a driving force, or moving, is prohibited.
3. Do not touch with any part of the body, or extension of the body, any film or equipment that is exposed to a driving force other than human, except those noted in the subsequent rules.
4. Make vertical lifts only. Do not subject hoists to "drifting" or other non-vertical pulls.
5. Observe hoists drums for proper cable alignment before and during hoist operation.
6. All floor buffers used in the Casting area must have rubber balls mounted on the electrical cord 18″ apart with a sleeve-type spacer in between.
7. No wrist watches, rings, jewelry of any type, or loose clothing will be worn when working in the Casting area. Long ties must be tucked in shirts.
8. Toe protection, and long sleeve shirts buttoned at the wrists, must be worn when working in the Casting area.
9. Side shield safety glasses must be worn at all times within the areas designated by yellow lines and in the Cast and Windup Pits.
10. Leather gloves must be worn when working in the Casting area, except for:
    a. Handling and scissor cutting of 50 through 200 gage film samples.
    b. Washing equipment
    c. Taping rolls and cores, or removing tape
    d. Recording data
    e. Making panel board adjustments
    f. Operating gage measuring devices
    g. Performing work where the use of leather gloves is unsafe or impractical.
11. Holes or slits in gloves will be permitted.
12. Hard hats must be worn in the posted areas and when entering a waste wagon.
13. Ear protection in Casting is required as follows:
    a. Chipper room when exposure is to be more than 10 minutes
    b. Windup pit
    c. Line 4 Cast pit when shredder is running
    d. Anyone working in close proximity to steam cleaning operations
    e. ECR in Sub station 2, 3, & 12 over L-3
14. Smoking is permitted only in designated areas.

Figure 6-5

15. When operating manual Dow valves or high pressure steam, a face shield and heat resistant gloves must be worn.
16. Hoists with a suspended load must never be left unattended.
17. Steel measuring tapes are not to be used around moving rolls or machinery.
18. Maximum number of mill roll cores on "A" frames along side of bins will be: 14″ diameter cores 9 per "A" frame
    10″ diameter cores 18 per "A" frame
    6″ diameter cores 36 per "A" frame

    Mill roll cores and tidland shafts will not be stored on the floor.

B. DITCH STATION

1. To inspect a ditch station through the slide gate, gloves and nitrometer mask must be worn.
2. Two people are required for ditching. All hot material except polymer requires one operator to be fully clothed in a heat resistant suit. The stand-by operator, after the initial bleed is established, can reduce his protection to heat resistant pants, and rubber boots, with hood, coat and gloves available.
    a. When establishing a polymer bleed, ditching or moving degraded polymer, a complete heat resistant suit must be worn. After a clear bleed of polymer is established, hot suit equipment can be reduced to pants, boots or spats, gloves, and face shield.
3. When transporting hot materials, a guide operator must precede the way for the operator transporting the material.
4. When inspecting or performing maintenance work at a ditch station which requires opening of the ditch station doors, full heat resistant suit (also called "Hot Suit") must be used. NOTE: A full suit consists of hood, jacket, pants, spats or boots, and gloves.
5. Ditch cans must have the ground wire attached before being placed in the ditch station.
6. Ditch cans are to be filled no more than 3/4 full.

Revised xx/xx/xx

Figure 6-5 (*continued*)

Polymer Area Safety Rules

A. GENERAL:

The General Plant Safety Rules apply in addition to the following area rules. (See Section A-1)

1. A continuous N_2 purge must be maintained on any vessels or system being opened which contain hot flammable material. N_2 purge must be maintained on the vessels or systems during the time it is open until the flammable liquid is gone.
2. No more than one opening is allowed in any hot process vessel or systems at the same time.
3. A full rubber suit must be worn when working around or underneath filter element wash tanks or within chained off area under acid-kelite mix tank, unless tanks have been drained and thoroughly flushed with water and locked out.
4. A full rubber suit must be worn when breaking any lines or opening any vessel which has contained acid or kelite; such as the neutralizing tank, bulk acid tank or bulk kelite tank or any associated lines.
5. Electric Hoist Operation:
   a. Only one person shall stand in front of open gate.
   b. Operator must wear safety belt provided when chains are down.
   c. Ground area below must be clear and unobstructed.
   d. The guard chains must be in place on the ground floor.
   e. Operator must be outside the chained off area.
   f. Guide rope must be used when raising or lowering the 4th floor hoist. Guide rope is not necessary when using the 2nd floor hoist if hoist cage is used.
6. Toe protection and long sleeves, down and buttoned, are required for anyone doing work in the area, except control room operator may have sleeves rolled up while inside only.
7. No rings or loose clothing are to be worn by anyone doing work in the area. Neckties must be tucked in.
8. A fire extinguisher must be readily available when opening equipment or lines which have or had flammable or hot material in them.
9. Racked polymer filter elements shall not be left unsupported in an upright position.
10. Following is a list of jobs and the minimum safety equipment required:

	Job	Equipment
a.	Probing inside melter	Hot suit hood & gloves
b.	Cleaning filter bodies	Face shield, hot suit coat & gloves

Figure 6-6

c. Observing open vent cans	Face shield
d. Operating Polymer filter block drain valves when hot material is in filter or line	Full hot suit

11. When ditching hot liquids, the ditch can must be properly filled (2/3s full), covered, posted with a "HOT" sign stating time, date, type of material and be left to cool in the designated area.
12. When ditching, moving or handling hot material, a full hot suit is required. This includes rubber boots.
13. When ditching polymer, a full hot suit must be worn until a clear bleed is established. Then the protective equipment may be reduced to hot suit pants or long coat, boots or spats, and hot suit gloves.
14. When bleeding a polymer filter and a ditch can cover is being used, protective equipment may be reduced to hot suit, gloves, face shield and long sleeves. If the ditch can cover is not used, the normal protective equipment as stated in rule 13 plus a face shield or hot suit hood must be worn.
15. When moving cans of hot polymer, hot suit pants or long coat, and rubber boots or spats must be worn.
16. Approved flake goggles must be worn when working of flake bins, lines, plugs or handling bags of flake.
17. Roll-away doors must be opened to height of 6′6″ and chains locked with pins.
18. Face shields must be worn when operating liquid Dow valves which have not been operated since newly installed or since being repacked.

B. TANK FARM:

1. Tank cars must be grounded before connecting loading lines.
2. The protective seal cover must be in place before loading Methanol.
3. The area must be constantly patrolled when pumping Methanol.
4. When climbing onto or off of cars, the ladders, handrails and the catwalks provided must be used.
5. Before starting to work on a car the derail switch must be placed on the applicable track and locked and the sign placed east of it.
6. A tank car must not be left connected over night to unloading stations.
7. The tank farm is a restricted fire area. Matches, lighters, torches, portable electrical tools or any spark and flame-producing device are not permitted in this area unless approved by both the area supervision and the safety supervisor.
8. Walking on rails is prohibited.

Figure 6-6 (*continued*)

9. Do not load or unload tank cars during a thunderstorm.
10. Carwheels must be chocked and brakes set before any work is done on the car.
11. Identification tags must be used on the derail signs and wheel chocks. The last person to remove his lock and tag must also remove the safety devices.
12. A distance of 10 feet must be maintained from the cars when they are being switched by the railroad.
13. When moving a car with the capstan, one man must be stationed at the car brake. Do no apply wheel chocks or remove wheel chocks while capstan rope is attached to car.
14. Do not use car incher bar unless you have been properly instructed.
15. Walking between cars is prohibited unless there is a clearance of 10 feet or more between cars.

Figure 6-6 (*continued*)

Maintenance Safety Rules

A. GENERAL

The General Plant Safety Rules apply in addition to the following area rules.

1. Maintenance personnel must observe the Safety Rules of the area in which they are working as well as their own Maintenance Safety Rules.
2. Only authorized personnel listed on "Qualified Operators List" will operate equipment in the maintenance shop.
3. Equipment must be properly locked out in accordance with "Lock-Out" Procedure before any work is started.
4. All work on a process containing hot or hazardous material will be done according to "Safety How" Section B-3.
5. Work of any nature on or near any radioactive source must be personally authorized by the plant radiation officer or his designate in case of his absence.
6. Flame permits must be obtained prior to use of open flames and welding equipment in any area outside of maintenance shops.
7. Control maintenance supervision's approval must be obtained prior to drilling or cutting holes in walls or floors to determine location, if any, of hidden electrical wiring.
8. Only properly authorized or licensed personnel will operate powered mobile equipment such as tractor, fork lift truck, etc. Maintenance foreman can authorize a mechanic to operate any mobile equipment, without a license during the time equipment is being check or repaired by maintenance.
9. Adjustments and repairs on moving machinery must have special permission of maintenance foreman for each occurrence.
10. Entry into any tank, boiler, vaporizer, closed vessel, sewers, manholes, pits or open tanks over five feet deep requires a "Tank Entry Permit" according to Safety How, Section B-5.
11. Maintenance personnel will not operate equipment and/or valves on any production or power area equipment unless authorized to do so by supervision.
12. Floor or roof loading must be checked before transporting heavy equipment.
13. Power tools and shop equipment must not be left unattended when in operation.
14. Side shield safety glasses must be worn when in the maintenance shops, specified operating area and at all times when working with tools and equipment.

Figure 6-7

15. No rings or watches are to be worn by any member of maintenance doing maintenance work.
16. Mechanics will wear long sleeve shirts or arm protection in accordance with area safety rules governing the area in which they are working. Short sleeves or long sleeves rolled to the elbow are permissible in maintenance shops and area whose safety rules do not require long sleeves.
17. All jobs that have potential hazards to other people not involved with the job will be roped off in accordance with the plant "Rope-Off Procedure" according to Safety How, Section A-5.
18. Jumping from any level is not permitted.
19. Sharp edge tools (without guards), glass or other fragile material must not be carried in pockets.
20. Use "hot" signs to warn others of hot surfaces in your work areas.
21. Approach operators of all power driven equipment from the front or side only to obtain their attention. Do not walk up behind operator and touch him to gain his attention.
22. A vise or clamp should be used for holding small objects on which work is being performed with sharp edge tools.

B. RULES FOR ELECTRICAL WORK

1. The General Plant Safety Rules, Section A-1, apply in addition to the following area rules.
2. All electrical equipment and circuits shall be considered energized until each portion is proven to be de-energized.
3. No switch, breaker, pushbutton, etc., shall be operated by maintenance personnel without permission of operating supervision.
4. Switches in motor control centers must not be operated with the enclosure door open.
5. A physical break must be accomplished between the incoming power and MCC, starter, or switch, before any work is done on a motor control center, starter, or switch.
   1) *Old Design MCC:* Remove "shorting Plug" and install "Insulation Plug."
   2) *New Design MCC:* Rack out self-contained unit until hole in support arm matches hole in self contained unit frame, insert "Ball-Lok" pin into holes. Pins are maintained in foreman's desk in substation.
      EXCEPTION: Physical break from incoming power not required when replacing fuses and/or resetting overloads.
6. No connections or disconnections shall be made to energized electrical circuits which contain voltages over 50 rms, A.C. or 100 volts D.C. without

Figure 6-7 (*continued*)

specific instructions from and in the presence of the maintenance supervisor and with approval of the Plant Manager.

EXCEPTION: Cartridge type fuses in open clips may be removed or replaced in energized circuits after approval and specific instructions from control supervision, but in no case in circuits above 125 volts A.C.

7. When measuring circuits other than low current electronic circuits, of 500 volts or more, leather gloves over high voltage rubber gloves shall be worn.
8. All electrical lines and equipment to which 500 volts or more are applied, except low current electronic equipment, shall be grounded before any maintenance work is performed. The grounded cable shall be touched to each conductor by use of a hot stick before securing the cables to conductor.
9. All splices and joints and free ends of conductors must be covered with an insulation equivalent to that of the conductor, or with an insulating device suitable for the purpose.
10. Metal rules, metal fish tapes, cloth or synthetic tapes with metal strands will not be used where there is a possibility of contacting energized electrical circuits.
11. In hazardous areas, never change lamps or perform work which may cause an arc from energized circuits.
12. The oil reservoir of an oil immersed starter must not be removed unless the safety insulating plug is installed in the safety jack.
13. At least two men shall be employed on all work being done adjacent to energized circuits. This includes motor starters and switch gear any time the insulation plug is not installed, also on Reliance equipment or relay cabinets, etc., when doing any work other than visual checks and pot adjustments.
14. No temporary connections or installations, exclusive of approved extension cords, should be made without specific instructions from control supervision. Temporary installations are only to be made for special jobs of short duration where it is impractical to install permanent wiring.
15. A fuse gap shall never be bridged with metal except the grounded neutral or grounded phase portion.
16. No energized electrical equipment shall be operated or tested by manually operating relays.

    EXCEPTION: After evaluating to determine what relays must be latched or unlatched on the towveyor system to restore proper relay sequence, an insulated tool may be used to operate relays controlling the *Towveyor System only.*
17. Holes shall not be drilled, cut or punched in junction boxes or switch enclosures, etc., without first de-energizing the circuit, removing covers and checking for adequate clearance. If the circuits cannot be locked out, the job will only be done with approval of control maintenance supervision after precautions have been taken to insure that the job can be done safely.

Figure 6-7 (*continued*)

18. Wire shall not be pulled into motor control centers, cabinets, junction boxes, etc., where there is a possibility of contacting energized electrical circuits, until proper precautions have been taken, and approved by control supervision.
19. Thermocouples shall be installed in thermowells. Any exception to this must first have the approval of both maintenance and operations area supervision and be equipped with a locking device making it impossible to remove the thermocouple. The same also applies to other types of elements.
    An entry must be made in the maintenance tickler file to insure the removal of any temporary thermocouple installation.

C. BATTERY CHARGING AREA

1. Smoking or open flames will not be permitted in battery charging area.
2. Goggles approved for acid work and rubber gloves must be worn when handling acid or electrolyte and when removing battery cell caps.
3. Glass carboys must never be used without wooden crates.
4. Metal tools must never be used for cleaning top of cells nor shall metal objects be placed on top of batteries.
5. Repair work requiring the use of an open flame shall not be attempted unless:
   a. Battery has been idle for at least two hours with cell caps removed to permit the escape of gas.
   b. All caps must be replaced and the entire battery covered with the exception of the cell being repaired.
6. Do not attach or remove charging leads while charger is running. Be sure the charge switch is in "off" position.
7. Electrolyte shall be stored only in plainly marked approved containers.
8. Areas shall be designated with <u>Blue</u> tape on the floor.
9. In areas where eye protection is not a normal requirement, battery charging areas will also be designated with yellow tape on the floor.

Figure 6-7 (continued)

D. PORTABLE POWER TOOLS

1. Disconnect motor on all portable tools before changing or adjusting any part of the tool.
2. Do not use 110 volt electrical or extension cord tool from crib that does not have the current inspection tape attached. All tools must be checked on the portable tool tester for proper operation each time they are checked out.
3. Portable grinders, saws and buffers must not be used as fixed tools in a vise or fastened by other means.
4. Face shield must be worn when using the paint scaler, portable grinder, skill saw, or when drilling overhead.
5. Place portable power tools in a safe position before connecting to power.
6. Portable drill motors shall have drills removed from chucks during transportation or when left unattended.
7. All rotating portable equipment shall be allowed to come to a complete stop before laying tool aside.
8. Portable power tools shall be disconnected when left unattended.

E. BENCH AND PEDESTAL GRINDER

1. Full face shield must be worn (over side shield glasses) while operating grinder or dressing grinding wheels.
2. Gloves must not be worn when grinding small pieces that require hands to be within 3″ of the grinding wheel.
3. Gloves must be worn at all times when using wire brush for cleaning.
4. Never grind on side of wheel, except when using a wheel designed for the purpose.
5. Grinder must be used by only one person at a time.
6. Work rests must be adjusted to within 1/16″ of wheel surface before each grinding operation.
7. Do not raise wheel guard until grinder is up to speed.
8. Push stop button and close wheel guard before leaving grinder.
9. Do not grind sheet metal 16 gage (1/16″) or thinner.
10. Run a new wheel one full minute with guard closed before grinding.
11. Lock out main disconnect, or if 110 volt motor, disconnect grinder from outlet box and lock plug-in end of electrical cord in lockout box, when making any repairs or adjusting tool rest, adjusting wheel, or changing wheel.
12. Material too small to be held securely by hand, with fingers behind tool rest, will be held with vise grips. (precision grinding such as tool bits may require holding by hand even though small in size.)

Figure 6-7 (*continued*)

13. Grinding wheels will be inspected and dressed if necessary before each grinding operation.
14. Work rest must be adjusted to where it just clears end of wire brush before starting wire brush cleaning operation.
15. Open only one guard at a time.
16. Do not grind non-ferrous metals or other soft materials. When this type grinding is necessary, it will be done under special supervision on special wheels.

F. CUT OFF BAND SAW

1. Gloves must be worn at all times while operating this saw.
2. Check blade tension before starting.
3. Do not force saw into material by hand.
4. Lock out main breaker at panel when:
   A. Repairing any part of power saw.
   B. When changing blades.
   C. When changing speeds.
   D. When cleaning saw, coolant sump and brushes.
5. Saw to be used for cutting metal only.
6. Secure material in vise before starting cut, and support material being cut off.
7. Keep saw guides as close to work as possible.
8. Do not lift material being cut off until cut is finished.

G. ENGINE LATHE

1. Do not measure work while it is turning.
2. Do not attempt to stop rotating chuck or work piece with the hands.
3. Do not start or stop spindle with tool bit contacting work.
4. Shut off motor when chucking or removing work.
5. Do not hold file, abrasive cloth or paper by hand, in contact with rotating work piece in lathe.
6. Always remove chuck wrench after making chuck adjustments.
7. Work, cutting tools, and auxiliary equipment must be held securely before starting Lathe.
8. Stop Lathe immediately at any sign of loose work, excessive vibration, or noise. (If reason is not apparent, notify foreman.)
9. Lock out main disconnect when:
   a. Changing chucks or face plate.
   b. Changing change gears.
   c. Repairing any part of lathe.
   d. When any guard is removed.

Figure 6-7 (*continued*)

10. No loose clothing will be worn while operating engine lathe. Wear gloves only when handling material and equipment.
11. Do not store work or tools on machine.
12. Move tool away from work area before chucking or removing work.
13. Apply pressure away from tool bit when tightening or loosening tool or work.
14. Do not change gears while spindle is in motion.
15. Keep change gear door closed while lathe is running.
16. Engine lathe and area will be cleaned up of turnings and chips as needed during each job.

H. WELDING BOOTHS & EQUIPMENT

Arc Welding

1. Any one assisting on a welding operation will wear the *same protective clothing* as the person doing the welding except the *welding hood.*
2. Long gauntlet leather gloves and arm protection must be worn on T.I.G. or M.I.C. welding jobs.
3. Insulated welding gloves will be worn on all coated electrode arc welding jobs.
4. Side shield glasses will be worn under welding hoods.
5. Flame retardant overalls and coat will be worn when T.I.G. or welding overhead of any body position. Leather coat and flame retardant overalls are required when welding with stick electrode overhead of any body position.
6. Welding equipment must be checked, before any job is started, for safe and operable condition.
7. Welding screens must be used to separate more than one welding job in any one welding booth.
8. Shoes & gloves must be dry during welding and dry underfoot conditions maintained.
9. Flowrator regulator valve must be shut off when not in use and/or changing cylinders.
10. Arc welding hood with #9, #10, or #12 lenses required on all arc welding jobs.
11. Spats are to be worn when wearing anything less than 8 inch shoes.
12. Cylinders containing oxygen, acetylene or any inert gas are not to be brought into the shop welding booths and hooked up for use unless special permission is obtained from supervision.

Figure 6-7 (*continued*)

SAFETY PROCEDURE	PROCEDURE NO. 117
	ISSUED 11/2/81
	REVISED March 17, 1986

GLOVE SELECTION AND USE

INTRODUCTION

Over one half of the injuries to Site employees traditionally occur to the fingers and hands. Wearing gloves for all chemical, mechanical, and materials handling work, unless their use would present a greater hazard, should reduce the number of these injuries. This procedure gives information and guidance for the selection and use of gloves of various kinds to provide a margin of safety for chemical as well as mechanical uses.

SELECTION

Since no single glove material is effective for all uses, it is important to analyze a job carefully before starting so that the best type or types can be chosen. Butyl, Neoprene, natural rubber, nitrile, knit Kevlar®, polyvinyl chloride, polyethylene, leather, fiberglass and cotton gloves are available on the Site through Chemical Stores.

Chemical Use

In choosing a glove for chemical use, several factors must be considered:

- Chemical and physical properties of the chemical
- Nature and severity of the potential exposure
- Duration of protection
- Physical performance required
- Length of glove needed

Table I provides a summary of the types of gloves that have demonstrated the best protection from specific chemicals based on performance tests. The information in this table has been taken largely from Haskell Laboratory's guide, "Chemical Resistance of Protective Clothing", available in the Safety Office and in many reading rooms on the Site. More detailed information can be obtained in that guide or by contacting the Site Industrial Hygienist.

For operations in which chemicals may run off the gloves onto the forearm or upper arm, long gloves with the edges turned back to form a cuff should be worn.

Proper removal of contaminated gloves is important. The first glove can be removed easily and in the conventional manner. To remove the second glove, carefully reach inside the edge on the palm side of the contaminated glove and firmly grasp the material. Then carefully remove the glove by turning it inside out over the hand as the hand is withdrawn. Contaminated gloves should be discarded.

Mechanical & Materials Handling Uses

Mechanical and materials handling uses cover a wide range of activities, such as using hand tools, carrying or working with pieces of metal, plastic, glass or wood, or handling glassware. Factors to consider when choosing a glove for these uses are:

- Physical properties of the material to be handled. Are there sharp or rough edges? Are splinters possible?
- Length of glove needed. Will wrists or forearms be exposed?
- Temperature of material being handled. Are the materials very cold or hot?
- Dexterity required. Can the necessary manipulations be made with the proper tools?

Glassware handling requires special thought. It is usually performed in conjunction with the use of chemicals, and for most cases, such as washing of glassware and simple manipulations, the recommendations for gloves for chemical use can be followed.

However, when attaching tubing to glassware or applying force to glass fittings, the glass may break, leaving razor-sharp edges. Most chemical-use gloves will not provide proper protection against lacerations from these edges. If at all possible Kevlar® gloves should be worn, although their knitted or woven construction will allow chemicals to penetrate through to the hands. In these cases, two pairs of gloves should be considered, with the Kevlar® glove on the inside, next to the hand, and the chemical resistant glove on the outside.

Table II provides a summary of gloves for mechanical and materials handling activities and should be consulted for proper glove selection.

ANIMAL HANDLING

When handling animals, protective gloves should be considered consistent with:

- the risk of the species being handled
- the task to be performed
- whether protection is required for bites/scratches or allergic sensitivity

This means choosing between Kevlar®, leather, or a lightweight latex glove. For protection from bites/scratches, the choice should be Kevlar® or leather. Latex or similar glove should be worn only for protection from animal allergens.

Figure 6-8

117-2
Revised 3/17/86

Long leather gloves must be worn when handling non-human primates. Kevlar® or leather gloves must be worn when working with agitated animals. In many cases, it may be necessary to wear both latex and Kevlar® gloves for proper protection.

CARE OF GLOVES

Before putting on a glove, it should be examined for punctures, tears, or worn through areas. If a defect is found, the glove must be discarded. Periodically, chemical-use gloves should be tested for leaks by inflating with air and immersing in water. Bubbles will indicate leakage. (Do not use this test for polyvinyl alcohol gloves as they are water soluble.) An alternate test involves spinning the gloves by holding the cuff between the hands and, when full of air, twisting the cuff to seal. Loss of pressure will indicate leakage.

Gloves which are impervious to water should be thoroughly washed with water after each use, before they are removed. If you suspect that the gloves are contaminated and that the contamination will not wash off or has weakened or permeated the glove material, remove them as outlined on Page 1, column 1 of this procedure and discard. Gloves should always be stored in a clean, accessible area. Do not store contaminated gloves. Polyvinyl alcohol gloves should be stored in a plastic bag.

Occasionally a person may develop dermatitis on the hands or forearms from wearing impermeable gloves. Needed protection can normally be provided by taking one or more of these precautions:

- Changing gloves more frequently
- Washing gloves out and drying thoroughly
- Wearing a pair of light cotton gloves as a liner
- Dusting the hands with talcum powder or corn starch before wearing the gloves.

TABLE I

Glove Selection Summary

	Recommended	**Not Recommended**
Acetic Acid (Glacial)	Neoprene	
Acetone	Neoprene, Natural Rubber	
Acrylonitrile	Butyl, Neoprene	
Ammonium Hydroxide	Neoprene	
Aniline	Neoprene, Natural Rubber	
Benzene	PVA, Nitrile	PVC
Bromine[1]	Viton	
n-Butanol	Nitrile, Neoprene	
Butyl Acetate	Nitrile, Neoprene	PVC
Carbon Tetrachloride	Nitrile, PVA,[2]	PVC
Chloroform	PVA, Neoprene,[2]	PVC
Chloroprene	PVA	
m-Cresol	Natural Rubber, Nitrile, Neoprene, PE	
Cyclohexane	Nitrile, Neoprene	
Dichloroethane	Viton[2]	
1,4-Dichloro-2-butene	PVA, Nitrile, Neoprene	
Dimethylacetamide	Butyl, Natural Rubber	
Dimethylformamide	Butyl, Neoprene	PVA
Dimethylsulfoxide	Nitrile, Natural Rubber, PE	
Dioctyl Phthalate	Natural Rubber, Neoprene, Nitrile	
Dioxane	Neoprene, Nitrile	PVA
Epichlorohydrin	Butyl	PVA
Ethanol	Nitrile, Neoprene, Natural Rubber, PE	
Ethylene Dichloride	PVA, Neoprene	PVC
Ethylene Glycol	Natural Rubber, Nitrile, Neoprene, PE, PVC	
Ethylenimine	Butyl	
Formaldehyde	Nitrile, PVC, Neoprene	
Formic Acid (90%)	Neoprene, PVC	
Freon TF	Nitrile, Neoprene	

Figure 6-8 (*continued*)

117-3
Revised 7/23/84

	Recommended	**Not Recommended**
Hexamethylphosphoramide	Butyl, Natural Rubber, Nitrile, Neoprene	
Hexane	Nitrile, Neoprene, PVA	
Hydrazine (65%)	Natural Rubber, Nitrile, Neoprene, PVC	
Hydrochloric Acid (37%)	Natural Rubber, Nitrile, Neoprene, PVC	
Hydrogen Fluoride	Neoprene	
Hydrogen Peroxide (30%)	Natural Rubber, Nitrile, Neoprene, PVC	
Hydroquinone	Natural Rubber, Nitrile, Neoprene, PVC	
Maleic Acid	Natural Rubber, Nitrile, Neoprene, PVC	
Methanol	Neoprene, Nitrile, PE	PVC
Methyl Ethyl Ketone	Butyl, Nitrile, Neoprene	
Methyl Iodide	Neoprene	
Methyl Methacrylate	Butyl, PVA	
Methylene Chloride	Butyl, Neoprene	PE, PVC
Naphtha VM&P	Nitrile, PVA	
Nitric Acid (70%)	Neoprene, PVC	
Nitrobenzene	PVA	
Oxalic Acid	Natural Rubber, Nitrile, Neoprene, PVC	
Pentane	Nitrile, Neoprene	PVC
Perchloric Acid (60%)	Natural Rubber, Nitrile, Neoprene, PVC	
Perchloroethylene	Nitrile, PVA	
Phenol	Natural Rubber, Nitrile, Neoprene	
Phosphoric Acid	Natural Rubber, Nitrile, Neoprene, PVC	
Polychlorinated Biphenyls (PCB's)	Butyl, Nitrile, Neoprene	
Potassium Hydroxide	Natural Rubber, Nitrile, Neoprene, PVC	
Propanol	Nitrile, Neoprene	
Pyridine	Neoprene, PE	
Silver Nitrate	Neoprene[3]	
Sodium Hydroxide (50%)	Natural Rubber, Nitrile, Neoprene, PVC	
Sulfuric Acid	Neoprene	
Tetrachloroethane	Neoprene,[2]	PVC
Tetrahydrofuran	Neoprene	
Toluene	Butyl, Nitrile	PVC
Toluene Diisocyanate	PVA, Natural Rubber	
Trichloroethane	Viton[2]	
Trichloroethylene	Butyl, PVA	
Xylene	Butyl, Nitrile	

PVA = polyvinyl alcohol
PE = polyethylene
PVC = polyvinyl chloride
NITRILE = acrylonitrile/butadiene rubber, sometimes referred to as NBR

[1] Information from
[2] Recommendations for Viton taken from NIOSH Report LA-8572-MS, "Permeation of Protective Garment Material by Liquid Halogenated Ethanes and a Polychlorinated Biphenyl.", Feb., 1981.
[3] Recommended by P&EP personnel.

Figure 6-8 (*continued*)

117-4
Revised x/xx/xx

TABLE II

Gloves for Typical Mechanical & Materials Handling Uses

Activity	**Recommended Gloves**
Animal Handling	Kevlar®, Leather, PVC
Carrying Equipment, Cartons	Leather, Kevlar®
Cold Work	Fiberglas, Nomex®
Cutting with Knives, Razor Blades	Kevlar®
Furniture Moving	Leather, Kevlar®
Glassware Handling:	
— attaching tubing	Kevlar®
— picking up broken pieces	Kevlar®
— releasing stuck stopcocks	Kevlar®
— washing	Neoprene
Hand Tool Use	Leather
Hand Truck Use	Leather
Hot (Thermal) Work	Fiberglas, Nomex®
Milling, Hot Plastic or Elastomer	Cotton with wristband removed and back slit
Sheet Metal Work	Leather, Kevlar®, Metal-reinforced fiber
Welding	Leather, various lengths

Figure 6–8 (*continued*)

Safety Procedure

Procedure No. 118-1
Issued 1977
Revised 9/15/90

LOCK, TAG, CLEAR AND TRY PROCEDURE

I. SCOPE

This procedure is designed to prevent injury by the operation of power equipment (electric, steam, gasoline, diesel, hydraulic, pneumatic, etc.), opening of valves in pipelines containing hazardous materials (acids, caustics, steam, compressed air), and energizing electrical circuits.

II. DESCRIPTION OF TERMS

A. LOCKS Padlocks are used to immobilize an electrical switch, electrical plug or valve. The key must be in the possession of the person applying the lock(s). Locks shall be of substantial construction and shall not be provided with master or duplicate keys. Several locks keyed to one key may be used by an individual employee. Locks used to protect personnel must always be identified with a "Lockout tag" (Exhibit A).

Each resident department and Site Administration is responsible for establishing and controlling the purchase and issuance of safety locks in their respective group. Multiple lock adapters are available from the Storeroom for group locking.

B. LOCK OUT TAGS/MAGNETIC SIGNS The Lockout Tag (Exhibit A) shall be used for identifying locks per IIA above for the lockout of all valves, switches, and other equipment in accordance with this procedure. THIS TAG SHALL NOT BE USED FOR ANY OTHER PURPOSE. Only one name shall be printed on each "Lockout Tag". These tags may be obtained from Stationery and Forms 3770.

Normally, Lockout Tags shall be used only in conjunction with locks. However, lockout tags may be used alone when locks cannot be applied. Supervision must be consulted for these situations. Lockout Tags used alone must be secured with nylon tie-wraps or equivalent strength material. The tag shall be reviewed daily while work is in progress.

If wires have been disconnected from a switch for safety purposes while work is being done on that circuit, a Lockout Tag (Exhibit A [hard copy only], Stationery and Forms (3770) shall be attached to the wires (and "Locked Out" Tape (3772) placed over the switch handle).

All Lockout Tags and "Do Not Operate Without Approval of" Tags (Exhibit C) on equipment must be reviewed every six

Figure 6-9

months to determine the status of the hazard or work. If the condition is unchanged, the tag(s) shall be updated.

Whenever a circuit in an electrical panel is locked out, a magnetic "DANGER" sign (Exhibit B, 3771) shall be placed on the panel cover to alert employees who may need to enter the panel.

C. CLEAR Before trying an electrical start button or switch, an employee must be sure that all other personnel are CLEAR of equipment so that any switch malfunction will not result in an injury.

D. TRY All personnel participating in locking out power-driven equipment or electrical circuits shall TRY the control button or switch after locking and/or tagging the main disconnect device to insure proper deactivation. Witnessing the TRY portion of this procedure meets the intent of procedure. Recognize that systems with interlocks will normally require additional effort to assure an effective try test.

III. BASIC LOCKOUT PROCEDURE

A. EMPLOYEES WORKING ON EQUIPMENT THAT IS THEIR RESPONSIBILITY Each person working on equipment which is shut down for repairs, modification, test evaluation, product changes, operational adjustments or cleaning and who may be exposed to injury through operation of the equipment must LOCK, TAG, CLEAR & TRY, to be certain that the equipment cannot be started, energized or activated. For example: An operator cleaning a process mill, must lock out the main disconnect switch, attach a signed and dated lockout tag, clear the mill of any other employees and try the start switch before starting work.

B. PROCEDURE FOR TURNING EQUIPMENT OVER TO OTHERS TO WORK ON The operating (proprietor) area is responsible for insuring that piping is clean, vessels or tanks are safe from entry and the equipment to be released for service is properly deactivated, locked and/or tagged, cleared and tried. The operating (proprietor) supervisor or his assignee shall LOCK and TAG all necessary valves and electrical switches, make sure equipment is CLEAR; then for power-driven equipment or electrical circuits, TRY the start button or start switch. Personnel shall be particularly alert to interlocked equipment to make sure that the equipment is, in fact, locked and not inoperative temporarily because of an interlock, timer, etc. The proprietor's lock and tag shall be applied first and removed only after the work is completed and the equipment is safe to operate.

All personnel who are to work on the equipment shall then add their LOCKS and TAGS, CLEAR the equipment of personnel and

Figure 6-9 (*continued*)

TRY the control button or switch (or witness the TRY). Employees subsequently assigned to work on locked-out equipment shall also follow this procedure. Where work extends beyond the shift on which it was started, and is to be continued by the oncoming shift, employees on the oncoming shift shall install their locks and tags. The employees on the outgoing shift must remove their locks when their work is complete and lockout responsibility has been assumed by the oncoming shift. If work is incomplete and the equipment must remain out of service, lock(s) and tag(s) shall remain on the equipment until the job is finished or the work has been reassigned.

COMMON EQUIPMENT PROPRIETORSHIP:
Site personnel involved in maintenance work on general facilities and service equipment listed below are considered the proprietor and shall be solely responsible for locking, tagging, clearing and trying before starting work:

—Hood exhaust fans
  Note: The hood shall be tagged stating
  "DO NOT USE, MECHANICS REPAIRING HOOD EXHAUST SYSTEM"
—Space heaters
—Service lines
—Room and building air handling equipment
—Lighting and distribution breaker panels

For portable equipment (for example, plug and cord connected lab instruments) the proprietor is defined to be the person having possession of the equipment.

EXCEPTIONS TO PARAGRAPH III: When it is necessary to turn equipment on and off frequently for checkout or troubleshooting, the proprietor may pass LOCK-TAG-CLEAR and TRY responsibility to the servicing group. The assignment of lockout responsibility may be accomplished by the proprietor signing and dating a "DO NOT OPERATE WITHOUT APPROVAL OF ________" tag (Exhibit C). The word "MECHANIC" shall be written in the blank and the statement "RELEASED FOR TROUBLESHOOTING" added to the tag. This tag shall be signed by the proprietor and then hung on the normal lockout position.

C. PROCEDURE FOR TURNING EQUIPMENT OVER AFTER WORK HAS BEEN COMPLETED After work has been completed on locked and/or tagged equipment, the person or persons placing the locks (servicing group) and/or tags must notify area personnel

Figure 6-9 (*continued*)

(proprietors) that the work has been completed and that energy has been reapplied to the equipment prior to their return to the work location, in those exceptions where locks and/or tags have not been applied by the proprietor.

IV. POWER-DRIVEN EQUIPMENT—OTHER THAN ELECTRICAL

Equipment powered by other than electricity shall be made inoperative by a means at least as secure as the electrical lockout.

A. Gasoline—Remove battery cables or leads to spark plugs and affix a lockout tag.
B. Hydraulic, pneumatic—Block lines as required, lock out
C. Steam and Air—Close, lock and tag block valve

CAUTION: Components under pressure may require depressurizing before working on them to prevent movement while work is in progress.

V. PROCESS LINES

All process line valves that safeguard employees shall be locked and tagged by the proprietor first. If a valve does not hold, the line must be disconnected and blanked. Two valves in a series may be used to improve the probability of holding. The proprietor shall release the pressure and bleed the materials, the lines must be disconnected and capped or blanked before repair work is allowed to proceed. Each person who will work on the lines or equipment shall also lock and tag before starting work.

It may not be possible to lock out small valves using a chain. In these cases, a can, cable or similar device with lock and tags shall be used.

VI. FIRE LINES

Fire lines shall not be locked. The Fire Chief or his delegate shall close the valve, tag it, and drain the lines. All mechanics who will work on the open line, their supervisor and the Fire Chief shall review and sign the procedure work sheet prior to starting work. The Fire Chief or designate shall inform all mechanics involved prior to reopening the valve.

VII. VESSEL/CONFINED SPACE ENTRY

All lines carrying corrosive, toxic, flammable or hot process materials to vessels that are to be entered must be isolated by two valves in series and drained, or disconnected and blanked. See Safety & Fire Protection Manual, Procedure 122.

VIII. GROUP LOCKOUT

Group locking may be used when a large number of people and/or many lockout points are involved. The supervisor or designate of the equipment must LOCK, TAG, CLEAR & TRY, place his/her key or keys for the locks in a box, then lock and tag the box and retain possession of that key. All persons involved in the work

Figure 6-9 (*continued*)

shall then lock and tag the box. A complete list of all lockout points shall be prepared for complex lockouts so that no valve or switch is overlooked. Persons involved in group lockout shall assure themselves that the equipment is deactivated.

IX. GENERAL

A. LOCKS AND TAGS SHALL BE REMOVED BY THE PERSON WHO PLACED THEM ON THE EQUIPMENT. An exception may be made when the person is not available, i.e. not on the Site, and whereabouts unknown. In such cases, the person's supervisor may remove them AFTER CAREFUL investigation to determine that they may be removed safely. The supervisor must return the removed lock and/or tag to the person who placed it on the equipment. This shall be done upon his/her return to the Site and before returning to the work area.

B. PLUG-IN ELECTRICAL EQUIPMENT shall be unplugged from the power source when repairing, cleaning or altering if exposure to hazardous motor-driven parts or open electrical circuits is possible. A lockable device shall be applied to the cap and locked and tagged to prevent its being plugged in when the cord cap (plug) is not under positive control of the individual working on the equipment.

C. CONTRACTOR employees shall follow the Site lockout procedure. The Site Contract Administrator responsible for arranging the contract work on site equipment shall also lock, tag, clear and try before work starts and shall remove same after work is complete and all personnel are clear and the equipment has been determined safe to return to service. Contract Administrators may be exempted from locking out for administrative purposes on *routine contracts* by authorization of their second-level Supervisors.

D. For some equipment, removing the source of power may not be adequate. Where components can move dangerously due to STORED ENERGY, as with large flywheels, springs, residual pressure, etc., specific additional steps shall be used, e.g., physical restraints, removing belts, etc.

E. During installation of NEW EQUIPMENT, piping and electrical services, the supervisor of the craft group doing the work (or Contract Administrator) shall be responsible for initiating locking and tagging when appropriate. Each mechanic involved shall lock and tag to prevent exposure.

F. PANEL BREAKER SWITCHES all new panel installations (lighting and distribution) shall have provision for lockout prior to being placed into service "Locked Out" tape (3772) shall be placed over the switch handle on all locked out circuits in electrical panels and a

Figure 6-9 (*continued*)

Danger Sign (Exhibit D, Stat & Forms 3771) shall be displayed in addition to the use of lock and Lockout Tag. Where provision for lockout does not exist, conditions shall be reviewed and tags updated daily.

On lighting panel breaker switches that have not yet been equipped with provision for lockout, the wires shall be lifted from the breaker and a Lockout Tag attached to the wires.

On distribution panel breaker switches (which are only operated and locked out by craft personnel) not yet equipped with provision for lockout, the switches shall be taped open and tagged by all who could be exposed to open wiring or operation of equipment.

G. When it is impractical to lock out GLASS LABORATORY EQUIPMENT setups or other specialized laboratory equipment, piping and electrical apparatus should be disconnected and a lockout tag applied.

H. It may be essential to LUBRICATE and MAKE ADJUSTMENTS repairs to equipment which cannot be shut down, or to operate equipment intermittently while adjustments are in progress. In such cases, where it is not practical to lock and tag the equipment, the work may proceed after adequate precautions are taken. Such actions may include the use of certain tools to avoid hand contact with equipment, rubber blankets over energized contacts, consultation with supervision, or other appropriate precautions. The equipment shall not be left unattended while moveable parts are exposed.

X. EXCEPTIONS

It is recognized that there may be cases where it is impractical to apply the procedure and exceptions may need to be made. SUCH EXCEPTIONS MUST BE KEPT TO A MINIMUM AND WILL BE MADE ONLY WITH WRITTEN APPROVAL OF THE SECOND LINE OPERATING AND/OR CRAFT SUPERVISION DIRECTLY INVOLVED WITH THE WORK.

The decision for allowing exceptions to this Procedure as outlined above shall be made individually for specific cases or operations by each department.

XI. OSHA REGULATIONS

A. GENERAL OSHA Standard 1910.147, Control of Hazardous Energy (Lockout/Tagout Procedures) imposes specific requirements regarding a lockout procedure as well as training, auditing, and enforcement requirements.

This Lock, Tag, Clear, and Try procedure meets the procedural requirements of Standard 1910.147.

Figure 6-9 (*continued*)

B. TRAINING, AUDITING FREQUENCY AND ENFORCEMENT

OSHA Standard 1910.147 requires all employees who are authorized to install or place locks and/or tags must receive training initially and whenever there is a change in their job assignments, a change in machines, equipment or processes that present a new hazard, or when there is a change in the lock and tag procedures. In addition, this stipulation applies to other employees whose work operations are, or may be, in an area where lock and tag (energy control) procedures may be used.

All training must be documented as to the date, names and subject matter covered. All retraining must also be documented in the same manner. The Safety Office maintains appropriate training material, but each S & OH Coordinator is responsible for maintaining the training records for his/her department or Service Division unit.

In Safety audits, OSHA mandates that special attention must be given to lock and/or tag outs of equipment, with respect to interviewing authorized employees as to their understanding of the procedure and their responsibilities. This information must be recorded in the audit report as well as all deficiencies noted and corrected.

Unauthorized removal or tampering with lockout locks, tags, tapes or signs is prohibited.

Violations of this procedure shall be handled in accordance with all other violations of the company's safety procedures and the company's safety management philosophy.

C. WORDING ON LOCKOUT TAG The warning of disciplinary action in this procedure and on the lockout tag is required by 1910.147. Employees are reminded that disciplinary action up to and including dismissal may result from disregard of *any* safety rule or procedure, not just those that may have specific warnings to this effect.

Figure 6-9 (*continued*)

Exhibit A

DANGER
LOCKOUT TAG
DO NOT OPERATE
THIS TAG MUST NOT BE REMOVED BY ANYONE EXCEPT THE PERSON WHO SIGNED AND ATTACHED IT
SAFETY FIRST
Signed by ____
Date ____

DANGER
LOCKOUT TAG
DO NOT OPERATE
THIS TAG MUST NOT BE REMOVED BY ANYONE EXCEPT THE PERSON WHO SIGNED AND ATTACHED IT
SEE OTHER SIDE

DANGER
LOCKOUT TAG
DO NOT OPERATE
THIS TAG TO BE REMOVED ONLY BY THE PERSON WHO ATTACHED IT
THIS LOCKOUT IS PROTECTING A LIFE
VIOLATION OF THIS LOCKOUT WILL RESULT IN DISCIPLINARY ACTION
SEE OTHER SIDE
3770

DANGER
LOCKOUT TAG
DO NOT OPERATE
CIRCUIT #
PHONE #
RADIO #
NAME ____
DATE ____
SEE OTHER SIDE

Exhibit B

CAUTION
DO NOT REMOVE THIS TAG
Signed by ____
Date ____
25

CAUTION
DO NOT REMOVE THIS TAG
REMARKS ____
SEE OTHER SIDE.
READY MADE SIGN CO., INC.
LONG ISLAND CITY, N.Y. 11101

Figure 6–9 (*continued*)

Exhibit C

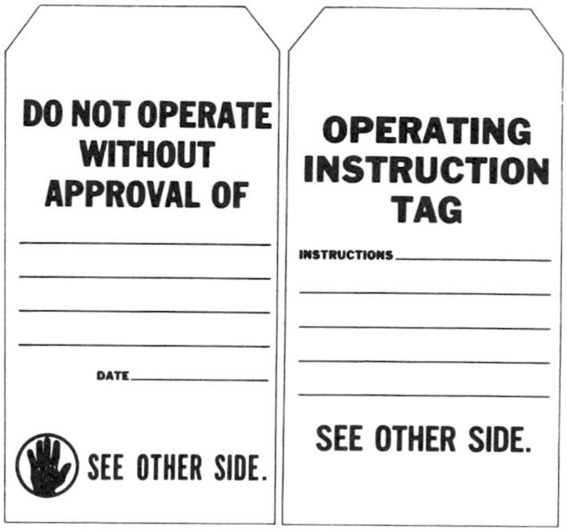

DO NOT OPERATE
WITHOUT
APPROVAL OF
DATE
SEE OTHER SIDE.
OPERATING
INSTRUCTION
TAG
INSTRUCTIONS
SEE OTHER SIDE.

Exhibit D

DANGER
DO NOT OPERATE
LOCKED OUT BREAKERS

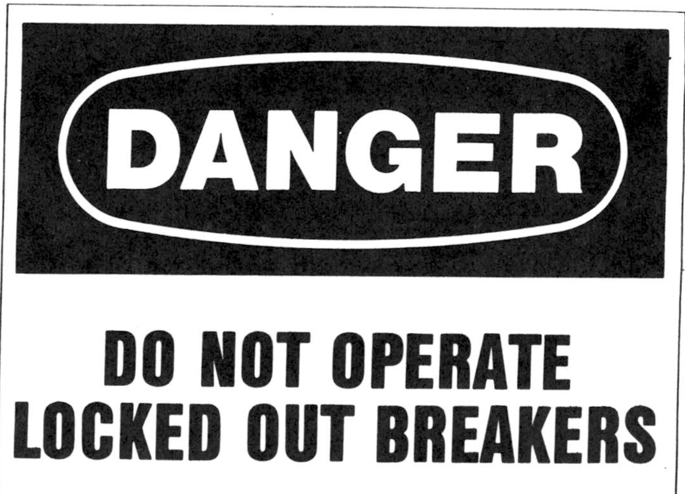

Figure 6-9 (*continued*)

SAFETY PROCEDURE	PROCEDURE NO. 122 ISSUED 1977 REVISED November 7, 1986

ENTERING VESSELS AND UNDERGROUND MANHOLES

APPLICATION

This procedure must be followed when entering confined spaces such as manholes, boilers, ductwork, vessels, etc. Its intent is to protect entering personnel against such hazards as oxygen deficiency, hazardous gases, contamination, high temperature, fire, difficulty in escaping, etc.

Vessels and confined spaces may be closed on all sides, top and bottom, with entry provided through restricted openings, or may be open completely on one side, top or bottom. Entry is defined as breaking the plane of the vessel or confined space with any part of the body other than the arms.

The procedure does not apply to contractors who have suitable safety procedures as determined by the company management authorizing their contract work, or to vessel and ductwork being fabricated provided the entire top or one end of the vessel is open. However, escape must be planned and respirable air must be maintained.

PROCEDURE

1. Prior to entering any vessel, manhole, or ductwork the following minimum requirements must be observed.
   - 1.1 No person may enter any vessel, manhole, or ductwork without the specific approval of his supervisor or contract administrator (with the appropriate contractor supervision), and then only after the entry permit (see Exhibit "A") has been authorized.
   - 1.2 At least one standby person is required, equipped with a reliable means of summoning additional assistance e.g. horn, two-way radio, etc.
   - 1.3 A barricade must be placed around the opening whenever the opening is left unattended. If a manhole cover is left off overnight, a substantial barricade (wooden standards, snow fence, etc.) with flashing lights, must be erected around the opening.
   - 1.4 A test for combustible gas and oxygen concentration (19.5% minimum) must be made using a combination oxygen-explosimeter, which has been calibrated by the person using the instrument, immediately prior to the test. The contract administrator and contract supervision will conduct the test for the contractor personnel.
     - 1.4.1 A combination oxygen-explosimeter is available in Pipe Shop and E&I Shop.
     - 1.4.2 If the oxygen concentration test indicates an oxygen deficiency (less than 19.5%), forced ventilation shall be provided. No entry shall be permitted until subsequent tests indicate that the atmosphere is safe.
     - 1.4.3 If the flammability (combustible gas) test indicates explosive concentrations of gas, forced ventilation shall be provided. No entry shall be permitted until subsequent tests indicate that the atmosphere is safe.
     - 1.4.4 Whenever toxic vapors or gases may be present, a concentration determination must be made. Consult the Site Safety, Industrial Hygiene and Fire Protection Section for recommendations. No entry shall be made until tests indicate the atmosphere is safe.
   - 1.5 Reanalysis of the atmosphere inside vessels, manholes, and ductwork must be made after every work break but no longer than every four hours.
     - 1.5.1 A continuous monitor, with alarm, is an acceptable substitute for reanalysis.

2. In addition to the minimum requirements (above) the following procedures must be observed before entering or working in any vessel, ductwork, or manhole greater than five feet deep. (NOTE: For telephone, computer, or electric manholes, the additional requirements are not mandatory but should be considered by appropriate supervision and/or the Contract Administrator for application in those situations.)
   - 2.1 Equipment required at the job site:
     - Two thirty-minute pressure-demand self-contained breathing equipment.
     - Wrist harnesses—one for each person in the vessel or manhole plus one for the standby person.
     - Full support life harnesses—one for each person in the vessel, ductwork, or manhole plus one for the standby person.
     - Audible signal (horn, radio, etc.)
     - Ground fault circuit interrupter—required with power tools and lights.
     - Life lines—one for each person in the vessel, ductwork, or manhole plus one for the standby person.
     - Mechanical lift—if top entry.
     - Flashlight or extension light.
     - Thermometer
     - Fire extinguisher—if required by flame permit.

Figure 6-10

122-2
Revised 11/7/86

2.1.1 The following equipment is contained on specially designed carts which are maintained by Central Shops for company personnel use. The carts are locked when not in use. Keys are available in Pipe Shop, E&I Shop, and at the Main Gate for after-hour service.

- Two thirty-minute pressure-demand self-contained breathing equipment.
- Three wrist harnesses
- Three full support life harnesses
- Three life lines
- Audible signal - horn
- Mechanical lift
- Water fire extinguisher

2.2 A mechanical lift device shall be in place before any person enters a manhole, ductwork, or vessel with a top entry.

2.3 When using a portable ladder, it must extend at least three feet above the entry point.

2.4 A full support life harness (wrist harness for tight openings) shall be worn at all times in the vessel, ductwork, or manhole. A life line shall be attached to the harness and secured outside to prevent the entire lifeline from being pulled into the vessel, ductwork, or manhole. When it is impractical to attach lifelines because of the configuration of the vessel or manhole, or because of the large number of people involved, the Supervisor or Contract Administrator may waive the lifeline attachment requirement. In such instances, however, the lifeline must be ready at the entry point for use in the event of an emergency.

2.5 Sufficient manpower shall be available outside a vessel, ductwork, or manhole in the event rescue becomes necessary. At least one person wearing equipment identical to the person inside is required at the entry point. A second person must be within sight and hailing distance, or in contact via two-way radio and be aware of his/her duties and responsibilities.

2.6 Hard hats must be worn while in the vessel, ductwork, or manhole.

2.7 All personnel assigned to the job shall be trained to use all appropriate equipment such as: mechnical life, analyzer, self-contained breathing equipment, two-way radio, etc.

2.8 Pipelines attached to vessels shall be disconnected and blanked or capped. Disconnection or blanking is sufficient for lines carrying nonhazardous materials such as air or water at low pressures. Blanks shall be of sufficient strength to withstand operating pressures normally maintained in the pipeline and shall be fabricated of metals which are compatible with the material contained in the pipeline. Valves in pipelines must be locked out per safety procedure—Lock, Tag, Clear and Try Procedure

2.9 Sections of steam or condensate lines in manholes which require alterations, repairs or additions shall be shut off, locked out, and drained before work procedes. When impractical, the Supervisor or Contract Administrator shall decide if work may proceed safely and what additional safeguards are necessary, e.g. blankets, face masks, special gloves, etc.

2.10 When the air temperature in vessels, ductwork, or manholes in which work must be done exceeds 95F, time limits for remaining inside shall be set to minimize the adverse effects of heat and humidity. The Safety, Industrial Hygiene, and Fire Protection Section shall be consulted in these cases.

2.11 Sanitary and process sewer manholes and boilers are considered special cases. In addition to following the preceding steps, entry must be approved by the appropriate 2nd level Service Division Supervisor. Entry into such manholes could be very hazardous from both the toxicity and explosive vapors standpoints and in some cases, it may be advisable to stop the inflow to some sewers completely.

2.12 When welding is to be performed, surface coatings such as preservatives or corrosion-resistant finishes must be removed for a distance at least 4 inches from the point of welding or burning, or sufficient distance to prevent the evolution of fumes. Forced ventilation must be used.

2.13 Gas cylinders and welding machines shall remain outside vessels or manholes.

2.14 Gas hoses must be tight and removed from vessel, ductwork, or manhole when not in use.

2.15 Persons inside must wear fire retardant clothing when welding, burning, or heating with flame.

Figure 6-10 (*continued*)

122-3
Revised 11/7/86

EXHIBIT A

Entry Permit
For Working in Vessels, Underground Manholes, and Ductwork

Bldg.__________ Location______________________________ Date____________________

Vessel/Manhole______________________________ Time Period Authorized________________
(Number or Description)

The Contract Administrator and/or the supervisor of the person(s) entering the vessel, manhole, or ductwork will cross out all items that do not apply and approve the permit when the "does apply" items have been completed. Review safety procedure 122 "Entering Vessels and Underground Manholes" before proceeding.

______ • Forced ventilation operating.

______ • Lock, Tag, Clear and Try Procedure complied with.

______ • Shutoff of Building Services Permit obtained.

______ • Welding, Open Flame, and Sparking Equipment Permit obtained.

______ • Contaminated and Hazardous Equipment Release obtained.

______ • Barricades and User's Identification Tag in place before opening vessel or manhole.

______ • Cart inventory complete.

______ • Area around hole clear of tripping hazards and items that might roll or fall in.

______ • Calibrate combination oxygen analyzer-explosimeter in fresh air. Check flammability reading against a known flammable gas.

______ • Test for flammability before entry. Reading ______________________________

______ • Test for oxygen concentration before entry. (Must be at least 19.5%.) Reading________________

______ • Test for toxicity, when applicable, before entry.

______ • Schedule frequency of retesting:

Oxygen	Flammability	Toxicity

______ • Measure temperature and set working time limits.

______ • Lighting adequate.

Figure 6-10 (*continued*)

122-4
Revised 11/7/86

_______ • Mechanical lift in place and operable.

_______ • Electrical items for use inside connected through ground fault interrupter.

_______ • Full support life harness (or wrist harness for tight openings) worn by each person inside, with life line (unless waived by Supervisor or Contract Administrator) fastened to the harness and the other end fastened outside.

_______ • At least one person wearing equipment identical to the person in the vessel, manhole, or ductwork assigned to be at the entrance at all times people are inside.

_______ • Self-contained breathing equipment cylinders indicate full.

_______ • Audible signal working.

_______ • A third person assigned to be within audible distance or in contact via two-way radio.

_______ • All persons involved trained to operate all required equipment.

WELDING

_______ • Gas cylinders and welding machines outside.

_______ • Gas lines tested for leaks.

_______ • Equipment to be welded, burned or heated free of coating which could evolve fumes.

_______ • Persons inside wearing fire retardant clothing.

_______ • Water fire extinguisher on hand.

	Persons Assigned to Job:
______________________ Contract Administrator (if applicable)	______________________
______________________ 2nd Line Supervisor (if applicable)	______________________
______________________	______________________
______________________ Supervisor(s) of Person(s) Assigned	______________________

Figure 6–10 (*continued*)

SAFETY PROCEDURE	PROCEDURE NO. 212 ISSUED 1977 REVISED November 7, 1986

HYDROGEN CYANIDE PROCEDURE

INTRODUCTION

This procedure was developed to cover practices for the safe use of HCN and related compounds (e.g. cyanogen and cyanogen halides) which may release cyanide ion or cyanogen or generate HCN when acidified (e.g. sodium or potassium cyanide). The use of the term HCN in this procedure is intended to be specific for hydrogen cyanide and to indicate general applicability to related compounds.

I. ORIENTATION OF USERS

All users of HCN shall receive an orientation on HCN procedures before starting to work with this material. The orientation must be repeated annually. These orientations will be given by the Medical Section at the employee's request and with the approval of the employee's supervisor. Orientation of non-technical employees will be approved by supervision of the technical employee.

II. PROPERTIES OF HCN AND THE HAZARDS INVOLVED

A. PHYSICAL PROPERTIES

HCN is a colorless, poisonous, flammable liquid with a molecular weight of 27.03, melting at -14°C. and boiling at 26°C. It has a flash point of -18°C. and forms explosive mixtures in air at concentrations ranging from 5.6% to 40% by volume. It is readily soluble in many liquids including water, alcohols and ether. See also "Detection," Section VIII.

B. HAZARDS FROM FIRE, EXPLOSION AND UNCONTROLLED POLYMERIZATION

Because of its low flash point and wide range of explosive mixtures, hydrogen cyanide presents a serious fire and explosion hazard (See Section IIA, Physical Properties). Another often overlooked hazard is that of spontaneous polymerization. These detonations result from the attack of the CN^- ion upon HCN. The reaction is unpredictable and may occur in pure unstabilized HCN if in the presence of a base. Amines, hydroxides and cyanide salts which are capable of producing the CN^- ion should not be added to liquid HCN without suitable precaution.

These polymerization reactions have been characterized by a preliminary period of slow reaction; the rate being dependent upon the initial temperature, pressure, and the concentration of the alkaline reactant. The dark brown substance which initially forms remains in solution and may catalyze the polymerization. This is followed by a much shorter period of violent reaction during which the pressure and temperature rise rapidly. The presence of sulfuric acid or copper and sulfuric acid decreases the intensity of the reaction. In general, if liquid HCN is heated above 115°C. in a sealed vessel, a violent exothermic reaction will occur.

Commercial HCN is normally stabilized by phosphoric acid although sulfuric acid or sulfur dioxide may be used also. Either acid may be removed readily by distillation while it is extremely difficult to remove sulfur dioxide. Distilled HCN constitutes a greater explosion hazard than stabilized HCN and should be used only by those experienced in the art.

C. TOXICOLOGY

HCN in one of the most toxic and rapidly acting substances encountered in industry. It enters the body readily by inhalation, by absorption of vapor or liquid through the intact skin and by ingestion. It acts by interrupting cellular respiration. The lethal dose for a person is in the range of 0.5 to 1.5 mg per kg of body weight.

The limiting non-fatal concentration is determined by the time of exposure, the concentration and the physical condition of the individual. The following table indicates the expected effects from various concentrations of gas in the atmosphere.:

10 ppm:	maximum safe limit for prolonged exposure.
20-40 ppm:	slight symptoms after several hours of exposure.
50-60 ppm:	maximum that can be tolerated for 1 hour without serious poisoning.
100-240 ppm:	dangerous for exposures of 30 to 60 minutes.
300 ppm:	may be fatal after a few minutes of exposure.
3000 ppm:	rapidly fatal.

Concentrations in the range of 20 ppm to 300 ppm can usually be detected by odor and produce such symptoms as: dizziness, confusion, marked weakness, severe headaches, sweating, nausea and vomiting. If exposure continues, loss of consciousness results.

Exposures to concentrations above 300 ppm results in rapid loss of consciousness and at higher levels collapse and death may be instantaneous.

Figure 6-11

212-2
Revised 3/17/86

HCN can be absorbed readily through the unbroken skin as well as through cuts and small scratches. No definite recommendations can be made concerning the degree of poisoning by various concentrations of HCN in contact with the skin but it is known that dangerous amounts may be absorbed through the skin in vapor concentrations over 100 ppm.

III. EMERGENCY FIRST AID

Antidotes are available for cyanide poisoning. Since methemoglobin in the blood forms very stable complex with free cyanide, cyanomethemoglobin, amyl nitrite, and sodium nitrite solution, for intravenous injections, produce additional methemoglobin to trap cyanide in the blood stream. The administration of oxygen along with nitrite produces a protective effect against cyanide poisoning, as well as increases the effectiveness of the antidote. Therefore, in first aid treatment, if the patient is breathing, it is important to give amyl nitrite and oxygen. If the patient is not breathing, artificial resusitation should be started immediately and continued until breathing starts.

These emergency first aid procedures are to be followed in case of cyanide exposure:

1. Remove patient from contaminated area.
2. Remove any contaminated clothing and deluge affected area with water—keep patient warm.
3. Hold amyl nitrite pearl in front of patient's nose and mouth for 15 seconds and repeat at 15-second intervals. Give oxygen for the 15 seconds between the amyl nitrite intervals. Use a fresh pearl every 5 minutes until 3 or 4 pearls have been administered.
4. If patient is not breathing, give artificial resuscitation. When breathing starts, give amyl nitrite and oxygen.
5. Call Medical (Ext.   ) or after normal working hours, the Main Gate (Ext.   ) for professional assistance.

IV. FIRST AID EQUIPMENT

An HCN first aid kit including an oxygen cylinder with face piece and amyl nitrite pearls should be located in the Safety Station of any floor of a building when work with cyanides is in progress. In special cases, first aid kits and oxygen cylinders may be located nearer the work area but NOT IN THE SAME ROOM. It is the responsibility of the chemist working with HCN to check this oxygen cylinder daily and to replace it with a new one when the pressure falls below 1500 p.s.i. If more than one person in the area is using HCN, a definite agreement may be reached as to who is responsible for checking the cylinder. Alternatively, all HCN users in the area should check the cylinder. The main cylinder valve must be kept closed and pressure kept off the gauge except when the cylinder is being used or checked. A tag should be attached to the cylinder indicating that it is reserved for emergency HCN first aid.

VI. HANDLING PRECAUTIONS

All work with HCN must be carried out in a well-ventilated area. In laboratories, all work with HCN must be confined to fume hoods which should have a minimum face velocity of 60 ft./minute. Work with HCN in semiworks areas requires equally stringent precautions to prevent escape of HCN vapors or liquid. Strong local exhaust ventilation in conjunction with good general ventilation is a necessity.

Care must be exercised to prevent contact of liquid HCN or its vapors with the skin, particularly if there are any cuts or breaks in the skin. Neoprene or butyl gloves should be worn at all times when working with HCN. Shoulder length gloves or gloves and separate sleeves should be worn when working under conditions where an HCN concentration greater than 100 ppm is possible, such as may occur in a hood under certain conditions.

Whenever work with HCN or related compounds is being carried out in a laboratory or semiworks there must be at least TWO PEOPLE PRESENT IN THE AREA AT ALL TIMES, both of whom must have received an HCN orientation within the past year. The person in direct charge of the work should not leave the laboratory at any time during the course of a run involving HCN.

No reaction containing HCN may be run UNDER PRESSURE in other than a high pressure laboratory or semiworks area until it has been reviewed with supervision and the Safety & Fire Protection Section to insure adequate precautions are taken.

Signs warning of the use the HCN should be posted at each entrance to the laboratory or semiworks area whenever work is being done with HCN. "Warning" or "No Admittance" signs should be posted on the doors to fan lofts and roofs whenever cyanides are being used or stored in hoods.

All reaction equipment in which cyanides are used or produced should be set in or over shallow pans so that spills or leaks will be contained. In the event of spills of HCN or cyanide solutions, the contaminated area should be evacuated promptly and it should be determined immediately if any personnel have been exposed to cyanide vapors or liquid splash. Consideration should be given to the need for evacuating other parts of the building or notifying other occupants of the spill. In general, it is usually best not to attempt to dilute or absorb such spills if they occur in well ventilated areas. If a hazardous situation exists, the Safety Section should be notified.

Sodium cyanide and acids should not be stored or transported together. An open bottle of NaCN can generate HCN in high humidity conditions and HCN may be liberated from NaCN solution spills.

VI. DISPENSING

When HCN is dispensed or withdrawn from cylinders in a laboratory or semiworks area, the cylinders must be stored in a fume hood or a special cylinder cabinet with exhaust ventilation. Signs warning of the presence of cylinders of HCN must be placed at each entrance to an area where cylinders are stored or are in use. In dispensing liquid HCN from a cylinder it is recommended that the cylinder be pressurized to not more than 10 p.s.i. with dry nitrogen or dry air (house air or nitrogen should not be used for this purpose) when the pressure in the cylinder falls below that necessary to maintain a steady flow of liquid. In general, cylinders should not be

Figure 6–11 (*continued*)

continued from page 133

STANDARD OPERATING PROCEDURES

Safety rules and procedures relate exclusively to the safety aspects of work. Under normal circumstances doing work safely enhances both the quality of the work and the productivity of the effort because the work is more likely to be done "as it should be done." However, doing work safely does not ensure that quality of workmanship will necessarily follow. Therefore, Standard Operating Procedures (SOPs), are and should be in common use. The SOPs provide an excellent vehicle through which to give additional support to the safety effort.

Figures 6-12 to 6-18 provide examples of SOPs illustrating how safety rules and procedures can be directly incorporated into the specifications for accomplishing specific tasks. Again, these should be prepared by the prospective user with the assistance of supervision, as needed, and should be approved/authorized at an appropriate higher managerial level.

ENGINEERING DESIGN STANDARDS

Engineering design standards are yet another source of information regarding desired behavior. In this case, it is the behavior of design personnel that is the focal point. Design standards emanate from a variety of sources—corporate design standards, professional associations such as the American Society of Mechanical Engineers (ASME), the National Fire Protection Association (NFPA), local building codes, and various other governmental agencies such as OSHA. The key point about these standards and a coherent safety program is that these sources should be considered guidelines, not standards of performance, until an organization formally adopts such external standards as internal standards of performance for members of the organization. Figures 6-19 and 6-20 show examples of engineering design standards from Du Pont. The OSHA requirements are identified here in shaded or grey print; they appear in red in the original.

Several features of these design standards are worthy of note. In reference to Figure 6-20, the words "subcommittee No. 28" appear at the lower left-hand corner. These words identify the subcommittee within the company that has prepared the standard. Such subcommittees are populated primarily by in-the-field practitioners from throughout the company along with engineering specialists. This subcommittee composition is designed to achieve "user friendly" standards containing the best technical information available. In this regard, these subcommittees are analogous to the subcommittees of the Central Safety Committees.[3]

A second feature of these standards is that they are not mandatory. They represent the best general *guidelines* available within the company, but local managers—Central Safety Committees—are the responsible decision makers. This distinction

text continues on page 195

Utilities & Waste Management **Heating, Ventilation, Air Conditioning**	**Page 1 of 2** **Procedure No. U & WM-HVAC-1** **Issue Date xx/xx/xx** **Reviewed/Revised xx/xx/xx**
Approve this procedure	
____________________ Utilities Supervisor	____________________ Utilities & Waste Management Superintendent
JOB DESCRIPTION:	Air Filter Renewal
PURPOSE:	Renew air filters in supply fans when magnehelic, or visual inspection determines filters are dirty.
MINIMUM MANPOWER:	2, or (as required)
SPECIAL TOOLS OR EQUIPMENT:	Ground-Fault interruptor, ladder, extension light, Respirator (dust) mask*
SIGNIFICANT SAFETY PRECAUTIONS:	Wetfloor-Ground-Fault interruptor required.
REFERENCE PROCEDURES NEEDED:	Safety Procedure #118, Lock, Clear, Tag & Try Safety Procedure #128, Ladder Specification Procedure.

JOB STEPS:	SAFETY & HEALTH ITEMS:
1. Obtain permission to shut down supply fan from Building Supervisor or designated Building Service Supervisor.	1. Eye & toe protection during entire procedure
2. Shut down supply fan using stop-start station, open disconnect switch placing locks & tags on disconnect per Procedure No. 118.	2. Try operating start-station to confirm safe shut-down. * Both people assigned to job to lock out fan disconnect.
3. If filter chamber is damp or wet, ground fault interruptor must be used for electrical lights or electric powered equipment that may be required for job.	

Figure 6-12

Utilities & Waste Management
Heating, Ventilation, Air Conditioning

Page 2 of 2
Procedure No. U & WM-HVAC-1
Issue Date xx/xx/xx
Reviewed/Revised xx/xx/xx

JOB STEPS:

4. Remove upper filters first, using ladder if required. Person on ladder will pass filters to person on floor.
5. After new filters have been installed and chambers cleaned, remove locks and tags from disconnect, close disconnect and start fan from stop-start station. Observe and log readings of magnehelic, or write renewal date on card at filter section.
6. Take dirty, used filters to building platform and tag for landfill. Filters must be in boxed or polyethylene bags before calling dispatcher for removal.

SAFETY & HEALTH ITEMS:

4. If cartridge filters being serviced, hard hats must be worn.
   * Check drive belt condition.
   * Gloves required during steps 4 through 6.
   * Dust mask may be required steps 4 through 6.

* Available from Utilities Supervisor

6. Do not block platforms with large numbers of filters. Protect from weather.

Figure 6-12 (*continued*)

Utilities & Waste Management Powerhouse	**Page 1 of 5** **Procedure No. U&WM-PH-1** **Issue Date xx/xx/xx** **Reviewed/Revised: ________**
Approve this procedure:	
________________ Utilities Supervisor	________________ Utilities & Waste Management Supervisor
JOB DESCRIPTION:	Changing the Sulfuric Acid Drum to the Decarbonator
PURPOSE:	Sulfuric acid is used for decarbonation of boiler make-up water. Two drums of 66 Baumé sulfuric acid are kept in the refrigeration room, Bldg, ___. One is in service and one is on stand-by. As one drum becomes empty, the Shift Operator changes to the full drum. The following procedure is for transferring acid from a full drum to an empty drum.
MINIMUM MANPOWER:	2

SPECIAL TOOLS OR EQUIPMENT:

* 2 acid suits
* 2 Scott Air Packs
* 2 pr. rubber boots
* 2 long handle shovels
* 2 rubber aprons
* 2 stiff bristle push brooms
* 2 pr. rubber gloves
* 2 face masks
* 3 warning signs
* 2 pr. splash goggles
* long sleeve protection

SIGNIFICANT SAFETY PRECAUTIONS:

Protective clothing must be worn.

REFERENCE PROCEDURES NEEDED:

*Barricade Procedure No. 140.

DATE__________

Figure 6-13

Utilities & Waste Management	**Page 2 of 5**
Powerhouse	**Procedure No. U&M-PH-1**
	Issue Date xx/xx/xx
	Reviewed/Revised: ________

JOB STEPS:	SAFETY & HEALTH ITEMS:	INITIAL COMPLETE/TIME
1. Call "Solvent House" X1234 for delivery inside the refrigeration room of a drum of 66° Baumé sulfuric acid.	1. Mechanic's gloves must be worn throughout this procedure unless there is a good reason not to.	1. _____/_____
2. Check emergency materials required beforehand in case of acid spill in the refrigeration room: *400 lbs. of soda ash *2 pr. rubber boots *2 rubber aprons *2 pr. rubber gloves *2 face masks *2 splash goggles *2 long handle shovels *2 stiff bristle push brooms *Rope for barricading *Warning sign	2. Call Safety Office Ext. 2345 to contact Fire Chief. He will verify Scott Air Packs are available, before changing drum. If a spill occurs, bring Scott Air Packs to site spill.	2. ___/_____
3. After sulfuric acid drum has been delivered, barricade the following: * Door between No. 1 and No. 2 air compressors. * A safe working area from side of roll-up door.	3. Safety chains for barricading doors and areas. Use procedure No. 140. * Eye, toe and long sleeve protection required throughout this procedure. * Signs for doors and area. * Ear protection required when refrigeration machines are on normal powered operation.	3. _____/_____

Figure 6-13 (*continued*)

Utilities & Waste Management
Powerhouse

Page 3 of 5
Procedure No. U&WM-PH-1
Issue Date xx/xx/xx
Reviewed/Revised: ________

JOB STEPS:	SAFETY & HEALTH ITEMS:	INITIAL COMPLETE/TIME
4. Using 10-20 milliliters of distilled water in a graduate cylinder or other glass vessel, add one to two drops of the acid. After mixing, add a few drops of 10% barium chloride solution. A white precipitate will develop if the acid is sulfuric. Nitric acid or hydrochloric acid will give no precipitate. * If acid is not sulfuric, stop procedure and notify supervision.	4. Splash goggles, face mask, rubber gloves and rubber apron must be worn.	4. _____/_____
5. Set drum of acid in area that is designated as and marked acid area. Use Randolph pump with Tygon flexible plastic tubing to transfer acid to permanent barrel. These drums will not be removed or changed under normal conditions.	5. Splash goggles, face mask, rubber gloves & rubber apron must be worn.	5. _____/_____

Figure 6-13 (*continued*)

Utilities & Waste Management
Powerhouse

Page 4 of 5
Procedure No. U&WM-PH-1
Issue Date xx/xx/xx
Reviewed/Revised: ________

JOB STEPS:	SAFETY & HEALTH ITEMS:	INITIAL COMPLETE/TIME
6. Tag empty drum with properly made out Move Tag for _ Bldg. and notify transportation section.	6. * Be sure there is teflon gasket on the bung. * Flush Tygon flexible plastic tubing with water and discard tubing. * Lay drum on side so water will not collect on top of drum. * Lay bungs in the 3 and 9 o'clock position, in case they leak.	6. _____/_____
7. When all work has been completed, remove barricades and signs. Wash off all possible contaminated equipment that has been used. Note: Action to be taken in the event of an Acid spill:		7. _____/_____
* Leave immediate area	* Warn other personnel in area.	* _____/_____
* Notify supervision		* _____/_____
* Call Fire Chief-Ext._____ for Scott Air Packs.		* _____/_____
* Put on acid suit, gloves and boots.		* _____/_____
* Dam the spill with soda ash.		_____/_____

Figure 6-13 (*continued*)

Utilities & Waste Management
Powerhouse

Page 5 of 5
Procedure No. U&WM-PH-1
Issue Date xx/xx/xx
Reviewed/Revised: ________

JOB STEPS:	SAFETY & HEALTH ITEMS:	INITIAL COMPLETE/TIME
* Notify the first person you can rearch on the following list: 1. Joe Smith Ext. ___ 2. Jim Johnson Ext. ___ 3. Bill Jones Ext.___ 4. George Glass Ext.___ 5. Safety Office Ext. ___ * Broadcast soda ash on spill and shovel into plastic lined lever packs (20 gal. size). Take residue to the incinerator for burning.		_____/_____
* Restore area to original condition.		_____/_____

Figure 6-13 (*continued*)

HOTEL DIVISION - STANDARD WORK PRACTICES MANUAL

STANDARD WORK PRACTICE

AUTHOR: ____________ NO: III:7

REVIEWED: ____________ AREA: Kitchen/Stewards

AUTHORIZED: ____________ PAGE: 1 of 1

TITLE: Floor Mopping

SPECIAL SAFETY CONSIDERATIONS: Placement of Signs, Proper Equipment and Slippery Floors.

SAFETY HAZARDS: Falls & Slips

WORK STEPS	KEY POINTS
A. Required Equipment	° Buckets and equipment should be clean before process starts.
1. Cady with two (2) buckets - detergent with clean hot water - clean hot water with wringer. (clean and rinse)	° Detergent and clean rinse water must be changed every ½ hour.
2. Two (2) mops - clean 3. Wet floor signs.	° Must be clean, free of soils, grease and oils.
B. Placement of Signs	° Place signs in center of area to be marked.
1. Place signs at both ends of main area to be mopped.	° Signs must be in good condition.
2. Place signs at all cross traffic sections. 3. Remove signs when floor is dry.	SAMPLE: * Ends of main work sectio @ Cross traffic sections
C. Floor Mopping	
1. Pick-up large trash items in work area.	° Place in trash receptical.
2. With detergent and hot water, mop area (use left-to-right, right-to-left swing motion).	° Mop should be well soaked in detergent/water solution.
3. With second mop and clean rinse water: - place mop in wringer - mop area previously mopped with detergent solution.	° Mop should be placed in wringer in order to pick-up excess detergent and clean rinsed floor.

NOTE: A. Water must be changed every ½ hour.
B. Employee mopping floor must remain in work area until floor is dry.
C. Employee must warn others entering to use caution, floor is wet.
D. Signs must be removed when floor is dry.

Figure 6-14

STANDARD PRACTICE

AUTHOR: ____ DATE ISSUED: 7/25/85 NO.: ____

REVIEWED: ____ DATE LAST REVIEWED: ____ SECTION: Food Services

AREA: Cafeteria

PAGE 1 OF: 2

AUTHORIZED: ____

TITLE: Garbage Collection and Disposal

SPECIAL SAFETY CONSIDERATIONS: Wear white cotton work gloves or leather service operator gloves. HAZARDS: Use of mobile equipment, use of electric loading dock, proper lifting techniques.	FIRST AID:
MECHANICAL STEPS	**KEY POINTS**
1. Each a.m., Service Operator-General will go to each work station and empty trash and garbage.	1. This should be done the first time before production begins and regularly as per Service Operator Job Description routine.
2. Service Operator will use plastic mobile garbage cart and take with him a supply of new trash liners.	2. Caution must be used when operating mobile equipment. Follow these guidelines: • Always push cart forward. Do not pull cart behind you. • Cart must always be under control of operator. Never push cart and allow it to coast. • Walk slowly and watch where you are going. • Do not leave cart unattended. • Do not block aisleways with cart. • Be cautious of walking in areas where hot foods are being prepared. • If you walk behind someone, announce your presence so that he/she will not back into cart.

Figure 6-15

NO.: ________

PAGE 2 OF 2

MECHANICAL STEPS	KEY POINTS
3. Remove full trash liners from cans.	3. Pull up liner from edges which overhang can. • Do not compact trash with hands or feet. Sharp objects may be in bag and cuts may result. • Be careful not to spill garbage.
4. Tie plastic bag at top and place in plastic garbage truck. Repeat procedure at each station.	4. Do not overload truck.
5. When cart is full, get second cart and continue procedure.	5. Push first cart into garbage room.
6. When second cart is full, empty both into dumpsters outside building.	6. Push both carts onto loading dock and lower to ground level (see Standard Work Practice for Safe Operation of Loading Dock).
7. When at ground level, proceed to dumpster.	7. Watch out for traffic in parking lot.
8. Unload trash into dumpster.	8. • Keep cart out of traffic areas. • Be wary that cart does not begin to coast. • Open door of dumpster carefully. • Only lift one bag at a time.
9. When both carts are empty, return them to garbage room.	9. Place in room in organized fashion.

JWL/ksr

Figure 6-15 (*continued*)

PROCEDURE NO. 137
DATE
Revised ______________________
Page 1 of 2

STANDARD OPERATION PROCEDURE

Job Description: Use of Lapping Machine.

Purpose: To give smooth, flat finishes to metal surfaces.

Tools and Equipment: Rubber gloves, abrasive compounds of various grits, lapping vehicle, disc weights, felt, phenolic, small container, and measuring cup.

Significant Safety Precautions: Do not operate without protective cover. Wear rubber gloves for setup, handling material and cleanup.

Written by: Machine Shop

APPROVED BY: ______________________ DATE: __________

Job Steps	Safety Requirements
1. Place a container under collection port on right of machine.	1. Keep machine in "Off" position.
2. Get proper phenolic adapter.	
3. Place steel rings on surface of lapping plate against steel center disc and outer perimeter roller bearing.	3. Make certain to place ring on bearing in the direction of rotation -- counterclockwise.
4. Place phenolic adapter inside ring.	
5. Place work inside phenolic adapter space.	
6. Place disc weight on job, protect work with felt if necessary.	6. Be careful of possible pinch hazard.
7. Install abrasive dispenser on shaft.	
8. Mix lapping vehicle and abrasive compound to get proper grit. Use one measuring cup of abrasive compound to one quart of lapping vehicle.	9. Mix solution thoroughly.

(Over)

Figure 6-16

PROCEDURE NO. 137
Date Revised:
Page 2 of 2

Job Steps	Safety Requirements
9. Set timer to required lapping time.	9. Install cover.
10. Turn on main switch and push red timer switch on.	10. Do not allow plate to run dry. (Machine and dispenser capacity one-half hour maximum).
11. When lapping is completed, remove job and totally clean machine.	
12. Remove lapping plate and thoroughly clean. Take extreme caution to remove all grit from grooves and other machine parts.	
13. Remove container from collector port and empty in solvent waste tank.	
14. Return all parts to proper storage.	

Figure 6-16 (*continued*)

PROCEDURE NO. 138-A
DATE
Revised ____________
Page 1 of 3

STANDARD OPERATING PROCEDURE

JOB DESCRIPTION: Safe Operation of a Lathe

PURPOSE: Perform various machining operations.

TOOLS AND EQUIPMENT: Gloves, chip brush, chip hook, pliers.

SIGNIFICANT SAFETY PRECAUTIONS: Use available lifting equipment for heavy parts; i.e., chucks, steady rest, large work, watch for unguarded rotating parts. Never wear loose clothing. Wear gloves for setup, handling material and cleanup. Use Bargard covers to cover sharp tools.

Revised by: Machine Shop

APPROVED BY: ______________________ DATE: ______________

JOB DESCRIPTION	SAFETY REQUIREMENTS
1. Before starting work, see that machine and area are cleared to work safely.	1. Remove chips, oils and dirt from machine.
2. Mount work-holding device on spindle.	2. Use hoist for lifting heavy equipment and materials. Remove chuck key.
3. Chuck work securely.	3. Do not run lathe with empty 3 or 6 jaw or scrolled chuck unless lathe speed is 150 RPM or less. Remove chuck key.
4. Set jaws and when steady rest is used, tighten to lathe bed before releasing load and lock upper half of steady rest before starting machine.	4. Rope area for extended work, sharp chips, slippery floors, etc.
5. Rotate work by hand to see if work and chuck jaws clear ways and carriage and to minimize runout.	5. a. Counterweight (do not use lead weight), if work is mounted off center on face plate. b. Make sure lathe is not in high gear.

Figure 6–17

PROCEDURE NO. 138-A

PAGE 2 OF 3

JOB DESCRIPTION	SAFETY REQUIREMENTS
	5. c. Do not wear gloves while operating machine. Never wear loose clothing or jewelry which could become entangled in the machine or workpiece. d. Keep clear of all rotating equipment and work. e. Stop machine while measuring work, changing tools or when leaving area. f. Use recommended cutting fluids for specific materials. g. Never hold abrasive belt in one hand while polishing. h. Never use a rag to clean work or lathe during machining operations. i. Use polishing sticks, not fingers, for all holes or tight corners when polishing. j. Use chip hook (not pliers) to remove chips while machine is running. Exercise extreme care. k. Stop machine and remove chips from pan if there is a possibility that they might become entangled in the rotating chuck or job. Machine should also be stopped if entanglement does occur.
6. Set the speeds and feeds for material tool used.	
7. Start up and operate lathe.	7. Stand to one side when starting up.
8. When work is complete turn machine off: a. Remove all tools and center before cleaning. b. Remove all sharp burrs immediately.	

Figure 6–17 *(continued)*

PROCEDURE NO. 138-A PAGE 3 OF 3

JOB DESCRIPTION	SAFETY REQUIREMENTS
c. Clean machine and floor area of all chips, oils, and coolant.	
d. Return all attachments to normal storage locations.	
e. Make sure chuck jaws do not extend beyond outside edge of chuck.	

Figure 6–17 (*continued*)

PROCEDURE NO. 205
DATE
Revised ____________
Page 1 of 8

STANDARD OPERATING PROCEDURE

Job Description: Inspect TFE Tank Trailer, Building

Purpose: Biannual Inspection (2 years).

Tools and Equipment: 350 ft. lb. air operated torque wrench, 1,000 ft. lb. torque wrench, 1/2 ton chainfall, nylon slings, combination wrench set, 3/4" socket set, hex Allen wrench set, automative creepers, and ground fault interrupter.

Significant Safety Precautions: Hard hats are required throughout the inspection. When noted, an acid jacket, face shield, neoprene rubber gloves and/or a safety belt are required. Ground fault interrupter required on all electrical connections.

Written by: W. J. /B. W.

APPROVED BY: ______________________ DATE: ____________

Job Description	Safety Requirements
1. Operations will drain, purge, vent and attach a Contaminated and Hazardous Equipment and Facilities Release Tag.	1. Decontamination must be thorough or exception noted.
2. Pipelines connected to the trailer must be locked out, disconnected or blanked off per Lock, Tag, Clear and Try Procedure, No. 118.	
3. Barricade work area.	
4. Erect pipe or scissors scaffold on Creek side for access to manhole cover.	
5. Remove boot and protective cover from manhole. a. Two 7/16" combination wrenches required.	
6. Install 1/2-ton chain fall on monorail.	

Figure 6-18

PROCEDURE NO. 205
Revised ____________
Page 2 of 8

Job Description	Safety Requirements
7. Loosen and remove the manhole flange bolts.	7. Air line mask, neoprene rubber gloves, and acid jacket required for all mechanics in barricaded area thru Step 8.
a. Use 350 ft. lb. air operated torque wrench with a 1-3/4" socket wrench.	
b. Loosen bolts on far side of flange first.	
8. Remove and lower manhole flange with chainfall and nylon slings.	
a. Place flange on 4" x 4" x 2' wooden blocks.	
9. Disconnect air lines on the right side of the trailer to the air brake chamber.	9. Trailer must be chocked.
10. Loosen and remove bolts and lower air brake chamber with bracket.	10. Second man necessary to hold chamber while loosening bolts.
a. Located under trailer chassis.	
b. 11/16" combination wrenches required.	
11. Remove cover from orbit valve extension manhole on left side of trailer.	
12. Remove bolts holding valve cover in place under the trailer and remove valve cover.	12. Neoprene gloves, full acid suit with boots and hood required thru Step 17.
a. Use automotive creeper thru Step 17.	a. If any liquid is noticed thru Step 17, call Craft Supervisor before proceeding.
	b. Second man necessary to assist thru Step 17.
13. Remove insulation around orbit valve and handle.	
14. Remove orbit valve indicating rod.	

Figure 6-18 (*continued*)

PROCEDURE NO. 205
Revised ______________
Page 3 of 8

Job Description	Safety Requirements
15. Loosen and remove bolts from orbit valve extension handle clamp and remove extension handle.	
a. Use 7/32" Allen wrench.	
16. Loosen bolts from orbit valve flange.	
a. Loosen bolts on far side of flange first.	
b. Use 15/16" crowsfoot wrench.	
c. Remove all but two bolts from orbit valve.	
d. Shake orbit valve to loosen gasket and to allow trapped liquids (if any) to escape into process sewer.	
17. Remove remaining two bolts from orbit valve flange and lower valve.	
18. Remove 1/2 ton chainfall and install tackle block on trolley over manhole. Vessel is ready for inspection.	
19. Obtain three two-way radios from Building 236 supervisor.	
20. Review Safety Procedure No. 122 before entry.	20. a. Emergency rescue plan is to be developed by crew and supervisor.
a. Exceptions to Procedure are:	b. Review Decontamination Tag for protective clothing requirements.
1. Ankle harness required in addition to safety harness.	
2. Lifeline will not be attached until needed.	

Figure 6-18 (*continued*)

PROCEDURE NO. 205
Revised ______________
Page 4 of 8

Job Description	Safety Requirements
21. The inspector will lower himself into the trailer.	21. a. Inspector will not fully enter the trailer until backup man is in position on the scaffold. b. Turn 2-way radios on. c. Airline mask can be used if objectionable odors are detected in the trailer. Inspector and backup man to have masks suspended from neck, ready for use. d. 1/2" safety line to be installed thru tackle block and lowered to stand-by man on ground.
22. When backup man is in position on scaffold, inspector will fully enter trailer.	22. Hard hat must be worn inside trailer.
23. To inspect, inspector must crawl to the end of trailer and crawl backwards to inspect.	23. Maintain frequent radio contact.
24. When inspection is complete, exit thru manhole port and remove safety line from tackle block.	
25. Cut new gaskets for all flanged joints. a. Use 1/8" thick calcium fluoride filled Teflon supplied by customer.	
26. Position and install orbit valve on under side of trailer. a. Use automotive creeper thru Step #38.	26. Second man necessary to assist in installation.
27. Tighten orbit valve flange bolts. a. Use 15/16" crowsfoot wrench. b. Because of positioning, a torque wrench cannot be used.	

Figure 6-18 (*continued*)

PROCEDURE NO. 205
Revised ______________
Page 5 of 8

Job Description	Safety Requirements
28. Install orbit valve extension handle and clamp. a. Use 7/32" Allen wrench. 29. Remove tackle block and install 1/2-ton chainfall on monorail. 30. Position and install the manhole flange using chainfall and nylon slings. 31. Tighten manhole flange bolts. a. Use 350 ft. lb. air operated torque wrench. b. Final tightening is with 1,000 ft. lb. wrench set at 280 ft. lbs. 32. Release trailer to operations for leak test. 33. If a leak is detected, retighten flanges as necessary. a. Obtain a new or updated Decontamination Tag. b. The manhole cover cannot be tightened to a higher torque without permission from Project Engineering. 34. When leak test is satisfactory, prepare the trailer for off-site transportation. 35. Install chainfall on lifting eye over relief device. 36. Loosen and remove relief valve flange bolts. a. Loosen bolts on far side of flange first. b. Use 1 1/16" crowsfoot wrench.	

Figure 6-18 (*continued*)

PROCEDURE NO. 205
Revised ______________
Page 6 of 8

Job Description	Safety Requirements
37. Remove and lower relief valve using chainfall, nylon sling, and handline.	37. Have relief device tested by Cylinder Shop.
38. Position and install blind flange supplied by research.	
a. Tighten flange bolts on 119 ft. lbs. of torque.	
b. Use 1 1/16 combination wrenches required.	
39. Remove chainfall.	
40. Position and install air brake chamber and bracket.	40. Second man necessary to assist in installation.
a. Located under trailer chassis.	
b. 11/16" combination wrenches required.	
41. Connect air lines, on right side of trailer, to the air brake chamber.	
a. 11/16" and 5/8" tubing wrenches required.	
b. Move or disassemble scaffold for trailer removal.	
42. Notify customer trailer is ready for transporation off site for pressure testing.	
43. When trailer has returned and is released by operations to the crafts, repeat Steps #1 thru #4.	
44. Install chainfall over relief valve port.	
45. Loosen and remove blind flange bolts at relief valve port.	
a. Loosen bolts on far side of flange first.	
b. 1 1/16" combination wrench required.	

Figure 6-18 (*continued*)

PROCEDURE NO. 205
Revised ______________
Page 7 of 8

Job Description	Safety Requirements
46. Position and install relief valve using chainfall, nylon slings, and handline.	
47. Tighten relief valve flange bolts. a. Use 1 1/16" crowsfoot wrench. b. Because of positioning, a torque wrench cannot be used.	
48. Release trailer to operations for leak test.	
49. If a leak is detected, retighten flanges as necessary. a. Obtain a new or updated Decontamination Tag. b. Manhole cover cannot be tightened to a higher torque without permission from Project Engineering.	
50. Following successful leak test, disconnect airlines, on the right side of trailer, to the air brake chamber. a. 11/16" and 5/8" tubing wrenches required.	50. a. Second man necessary to hold chamber while loosening bolts. b. Trailer must be chocked.
51. Loosen and remove bolts and lower air brake chamber with bracket. a. Located under trailer chassis. b. 11/16" combination wrenches required.	
52. Insulate orbit valve. a. Use 1/2" thick closed cell urethane from Stores.	
53. Position and install valve cover. a. Can only be positioned one way.	53. Second man necessary to assist in installation.

Figure 6-18 (*continued*)

PROCEDURE NO. 205
Revised ______________
Page 8 of 8

Job Description	Safety Requirements
54. Position and install air brake chamber and bracket. a. Located under trailer chassis. b. 11/16" combination wrenches required.	54. Second man necessary to assist in installation.
55. Connect air lines, on right side of trailer, to the air brake chamber. a. 11/16" and 5/8" tubing wrenches required.	
56. Remove chainfall over relief device.	
57. Install manhole boot and protective cover. a. Two 7/16" combination wrenches required.	
58. Dismantle scaffold and remove barricades.	
59. Notify customer job is complete.	

Figure 6–18 (*continued*)

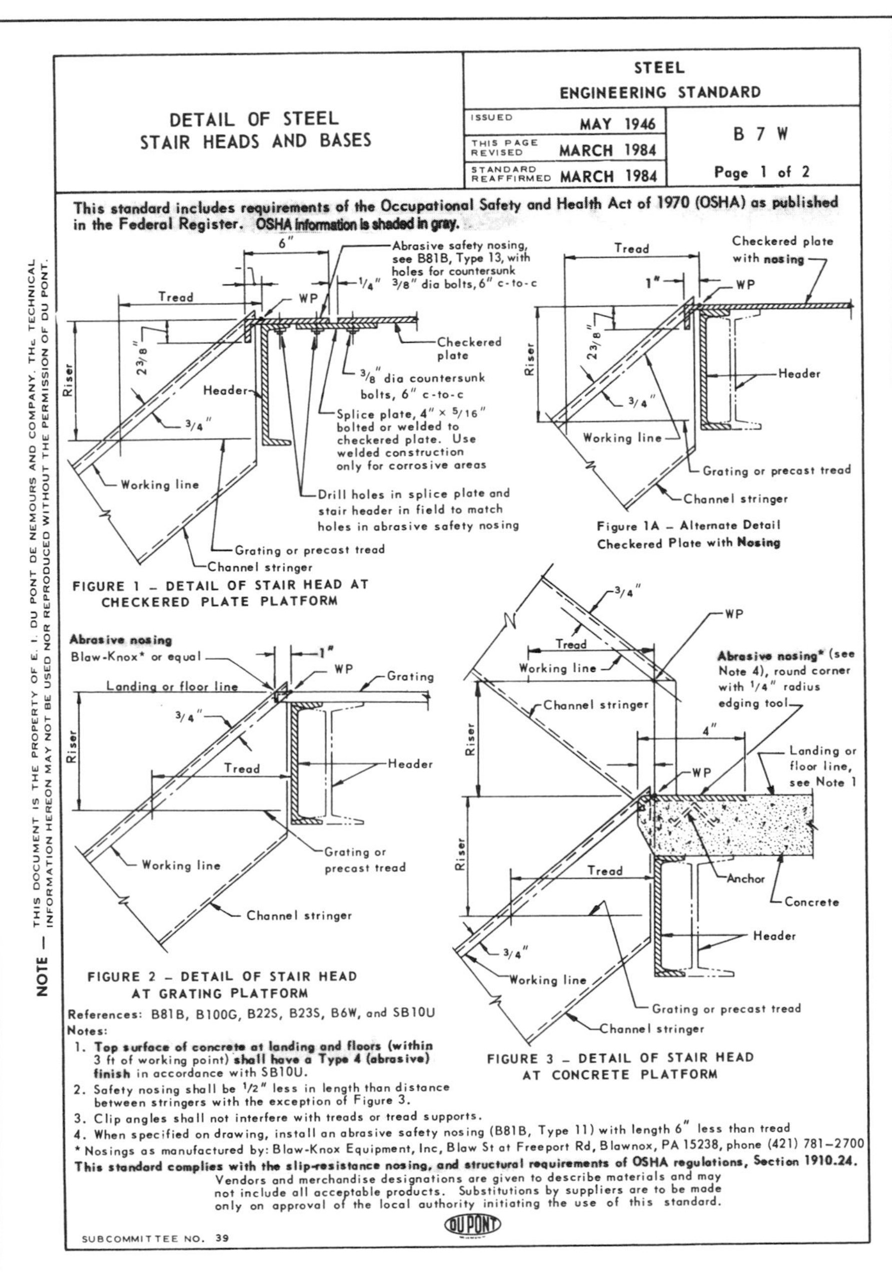

DETAIL OF STEEL STAIR HEADS AND BASES	STEEL ENGINEERING STANDARD	
	ISSUED MAY 1946	B 7 W
	THIS PAGE REVISED MARCH 1984	
	STANDARD REAFFIRMED MARCH 1984	Page 1 of 2

This standard includes requirements of the Occupational Safety and Health Act of 1970 (OSHA) as published in the Federal Register. OSHA information is shaded in gray.

FIGURE 1 – DETAIL OF STAIR HEAD AT CHECKERED PLATE PLATFORM

Figure 1A – Alternate Detail Checkered Plate with Nosing

FIGURE 2 – DETAIL OF STAIR HEAD AT GRATING PLATFORM

FIGURE 3 – DETAIL OF STAIR HEAD AT CONCRETE PLATFORM

References: B81B, B100G, B22S, B23S, B6W, and SB10U

Notes:

1. **Top surface of concrete at landing and floors (within 3 ft of working point) shall have a Type 4 (abrasive) finish** in accordance with SB10U.
2. Safety nosing shall be 1/2" less in length than distance between stringers with the exception of Figure 3.
3. Clip angles shall not interfere with treads or tread supports.
4. When specified on drawing, install an abrasive safety nosing (B81B, Type 11) with length 6" less than tread

* Nosings as manufactured by: Blaw-Knox Equipment, Inc, Blaw St at Freeport Rd, Blawnox, PA 15238, phone (421) 781–2700

This standard complies with the slip-resistance nosing, and structural requirements of OSHA regulations, Section 1910.24.

Vendors and merchandise designations are given to describe materials and may not include all acceptable products. Substitutions by suppliers are to be made only on approval of the local authority initiating the use of this standard.

SUBCOMMITTEE NO. 39

DU PONT

Figure 6-19

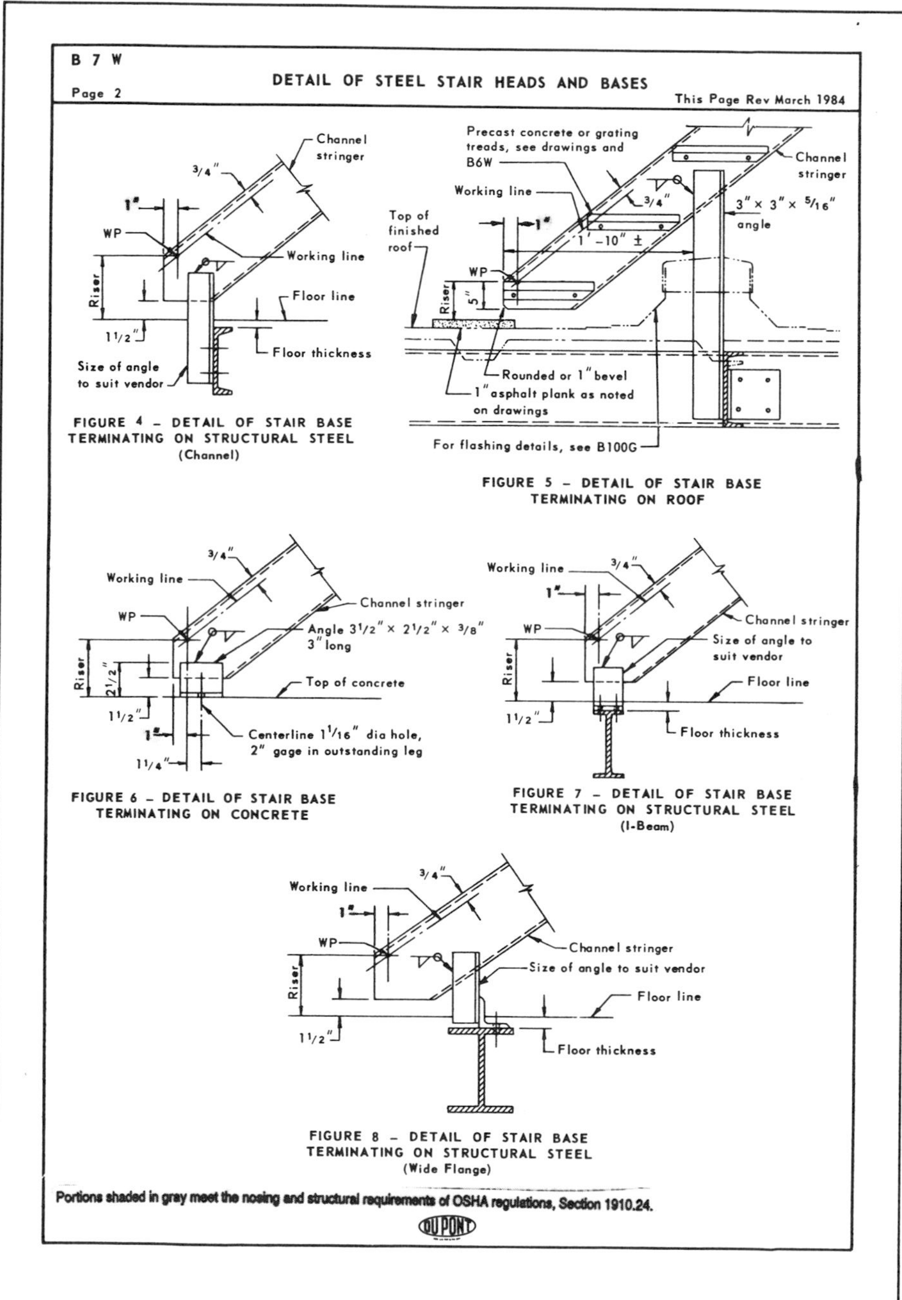

Figure 6-19 (*continued*)

STORAGE AND HANDLING OF LIQUEFIED PETROLEUM GASES	FIRE PROTECTION ENGINEERING STANDARD	
	ISSUED FEB 1951	F 8 J
	THIS PAGE REVISED AUG 1987	Page 1 of 4
	STANDARD REAFFIRMED AUG 1987	

This standard includes requirements of the Occupational Safety and Health Act of 1970 (OSHA) as published in the Federal Register. OSHA information is shaded in gray.

1. SCOPE

1.1 This standard provides information and guidance for liquefied petroleum gases stored aboveground as liquid under pressure at ambient temperature. Liquefied petroleum gas (LPG) is defined as any material which is composed predominantly of any of the following hydrocarbons, or mixtures of them: propane, propylene, butane, and butylene.

1.2 NFPA 58 and OSHA 1910.110 shall be reviewed for more specific detail.

1.3 State and local requirements shall be reviewed as they may be more restrictive.

2. CONTAINERS

2.1 Fabrication

2.1.1 Construction. LPG containers shall be designed, constructed, tested, and marked in accordance with Department of Transportation (DOT) or ASME Pressure Vessel Code requirements.

2.1.2 Capacity. Storage containers shall not exceed 90,000-gallon water capacity.

2.1.3 Supports. Tanks shall be provided with substantial structural supports of noncombustible material on firm masonry foundation. Exposed steel tank supports shall be protected with a 2-hour fireproofing system. Horizontal containers shall be supported on two saddles only and be designed to permit thermal expansion and contraction per B2R.

2.2 Location

2.2.1 Individual tanks shall be located with respect to the nearest important building, group of buildings, or line of adjoining property which may be built on, in accordance with Table 1.

2.2.2 Transfer of liquid from storage tank to portable containers shall be done at least 50 feet from nearest important building.

2.2.3 Transfer of liquid from motor-driven tank truck or tank car to storage should be done at an unloading spot which is 50 feet from the nearest important structure or adjacent property line.*

2.2.4 Tanks which are not separated by the distances specified in Table 1 shall be treated as a single tank for the purpose of determining separation distances to buildings, property lines, or other tanks. The capacity used in applying Table 1 shall be the sum of the capacities of all tanks in the group.

2.2.5 When dikes are used with flammable liquid tanks, LPG containers shall not be located within the diked area. The minimum separation between LPG containers and flammable liquid tanks shall be 20 ft, and the minimum separation between a container and the centerline of the dike shall be 10 ft. These provisions shall not apply when LPG containers of 125 gallons or less capacity are installed adjacent to Class III flammable liquid tanks of 275 gallons or less capacity.

2.2.6 Horizontal tanks should be placed parallel to each other and to important buildings or structures. Heads of tanks should not face toward other tanks or nearby buildings. Earthen or concrete barricades may be required to protect against rocketing tanks where this arrangement cannot be avoided.

3. VALVES, PIPING, AND ACCESSORIES

3.1 All valves, fittings, and accessories connected directly to the container shall have a rated working pressure of a least 250 psi and shall be of material and design suitable for LP gas service. Cast iron should not be used for container valves, fittings, or accessories. This does not prohibit the use of container valves made of malleable iron or nodular iron.

3.2 All connections to containers, except safety-relief, pressure gage, and liquid-gaging devices, shall have shutoff valves located as close to the container as practicable.

3.3 The filling connection at the storage tank shall be fitted with one of the following.

3.3.1 A combination back-pressure check valve and excess flow valve.

* See S22B and S27B for details of tank-truck and tank-car loading and unloading precautions recommended for flammable liquids.

Portions shaded in gray are from OSHA regulations, Section 1910.110.

SUBCOMMITTEE NO. 28

Figure 6-20

F 8 J

Page 2

STORAGE AND HANDLING OF LIQUEFIED PETROLEUM GASES

This Page Rev July 1989

3.3.2 One double or two single back-pressure check valves.

3.3.3 A positive shutoff valve in conjunction with either:

a. An internal back-pressure valve, or

b. An internal excess flow valve

3.4 For tank car or transport truck loading or unloading points and operations, a backflow check valve, excess flow valve, or a shutoff valve with means of remote closing, to protect against uncontrolled discharge of LP gas from storage tank piping shall be installed close to the point where the liquid piping and hose or swing joint pipe is connected.

3.5 All openings in the container shall be equipped with an approved excess flow check valve except the safety-relief connection, the liquid-level gaging device, the pressure gage connection, and the filling connection.

3.5.1 Excess flow check valves shall be designed with an opening to allow equalization of pressures not to exceed a No. 60 drill size (0.0400 in.).

3.6 The pressure gage connection need not be equipped with a shutoff or excess flow valve, if such openings are restricted to not larger than No. 54 drill size opening (0.0550 in.).

3.6.1 Gage glasses of the columnar type are prohibited on tank trucks, on motor fuel tanks, and on containers used in domestic, commercial, and industrial installations.

3.6.2 Liquid-level gaging devices which are so constructed that outward flow of container contents shall not exceed that passed by a No. 54 drill-size opening, need not be equipped with excess flow valves.

3.6.3 Gaging devices that require bleeding of the product to the atmosphere, such as the rotary tube, fixed tube, and slip tube, shall be so designed that the bleed-valve maximum opening is no larger than a No. 54 drill size, unless provided with excess flow valve.

3.6.4 Gaging devices of the flat, or equivalent type, which do not require flow for their operation and having connections extending to a point outside the container, do not have to be equipped with excess flow valves, provided the piping and fittings are designed adequately to withstand the container pressure and are protected properly against physical damage and breakage.

3.6.5 Excess flow, back-pressure check, and quick-closing internal valves described above shall be located inside of the container or, if outside, at a point where the line enters the container; in the latter case, installation shall be made in such a manner that any undue strain beyond the excess flow or back-pressure check valve will not cause breakage between the container and such valve.

3.7 Welded joints shall be used whenever possible; if brazed or soldered, material should have a melting point over 1000°F.

3.8 Flanges shall be fitted with high temperature type gaskets capable of withstanding exposure to fire temperature over 1500°F. Synthetic rubber, Teflon® TFE-fluorocarbon resin, and lead gaskets **are not** suitable for this service.

3.9 Valve outlets on containers of 108 lb (49 kg) water capacity or less shall be equipped with an effective seal such as a plug, cap, or an approved quick-closing coupling. This seal shall be in place whenever the container is not connected for use. Single trip nonrefillable, disposable, and new unused containers are excluded from this requirement.

3.10 A pressure-reducing regulator shall be provided at the tank prior to attachment of flexible hoses. This will prevent an excessive discharge of gas in case of hose failure.

4. RELIEF VALVES

4.1 Liquefied gas containers shall have one or more spring-loaded safety-relief valves of sufficient capacity to protect the container against overpressure under fire-exposure conditions. Total rate of discharge shall be computed according to Table 2.

4.1.1 These valves shall be arranged to afford free vent to the outer air with discharge not less than 5 feet horizontally away from any opening into the building which is below such discharge.

4.2 The discharge from the relief valve shall be vented upward from the container in such a manner to prevent impingement on the container (up to 2000 gal) or a minimum of 7 ft vertically above the top of the container (greater than 2000 gal). Loose-fitting rain caps and suitable drainage for liquid or condensate shall be provided.

4.3 Shutoff valves shall not be installed between the safety-relief valves and the container, except that a 3-way valve may be used where the arrangement of this valve is such as always to afford full required capacity flow through the relief valves.

4.4 Safety-relief values shall have direct communication with the vapor space of the container at all times.

4.5 A hydrostatic safety-relief valve shall be installed between each pair of shutoff valves on liquefied petroleum gas liquid piping so as to relieve into a safe atmosphere. The start-to-discharge pressure of such relief valves shall not exceed 500 psi.

DU PONT

Figure 6-20 (*continued*)

5. VAPORIZERS

5.1 Vaporizers may be of the following types:

a. Indirect-fired vaporizers utilizing steam, water, or other heated material

b. Atmospheric type using heat from the ground or surrounding air

5.2 The regulations of NFPA 58 for vaporizers shall be followed.

5.3 All vaporizers should have a stop valve between the storage container and the vaporizer.

6. FIRE PROTECTION

Appropriate facilities such as fire hydrants, hose, and nozzles shall be provided to cool aboveground tanks exposed to fire. Fire hydrant shall be so located that there are at least two hydrants within 150 ft of, and at significantly different directions from, each tank requiring protection, for unobstructed upwind approaches. A combination spray and straight-stream nozzle shall be provided for the hose line. Automatic water spray systems may be required for some installations. Consult the Safety and Occupational Health Division.

7. ELECTRICAL EQUIPMENT

7.1 All electrical equipment within fifteen feet of any liquefied petroleum gas container connection, shall be of the type approved for Class I, Group D, Division 2 locations. All electrical equipment within 5 feet in all directions from relief valve discharges and connections regularly made or disconnected, shall be of the type approved for Class I, Group D, Division 1.

7.2 No part of an aboveground LP-gas container shall be located in the area 6 ft (1.8 m) horizontally from a vertical plane beneath overhead electric power lines that are over 600 volts, nominal.

DUPONT

Figure 6–20 (*continued*)

F 8 J

Page 4

STORAGE AND HANDLING OF LIQUEFIED PETROLEUM GASES

This Page Issued Aug 1987

TABLE 1 – DISTANCE RESTRICTIONS[▲]

Water Capacity (gal.)	Minimum Distance to Building or Property Line (ft)	Minimum Distance Between Tanks (ft) (See 2.2.4)
Up to 125	0	0
126 to 500	10	3
501 to 2,000	25	3
2,001 to 30,000	50	5
30,001 to 70,000	75	One-fourth the sum of diameters of adjoining tanks
70,001 to 90,000	100	

TABLE 2 – RELIEF VALVE CAPACITIES FOR STORAGE TANKS

Surface Area (sq ft)†	Flow Rate CFM Air♦	Surface Area (sq ft)†	Flow Rate CFM Air♦	Surface Area (sq ft)†	Flow Rate CFM Air♦
20 or less	626	170	3,620	600	10,170
25	751	175	3,700	650	10,860
30	872	180	3,790	700	11,550
35	990	185	3,880	750	12,220
40	1,100	190	3,960	800	12,880
45	1,220	195	4,050	850	13,540
50	1,330	200	4,130	900	14,190
55	1,430	210	4,300	950	14,830
60	1,540	220	4,470	1,000	15,470
65	1,640	230	4,630	1,050	16,100
70	1,750	240	4,800	1,100	16,720
75	1,850	250	4,960	1,150	17,350
80	1,950	260	5,130	1,200	17,960
85	2,050	270	5,290	1,250	18,570
90	2,150	280	5,450	1,300	19,180
95	2,240	290	5,610	1,350	19,780
100	2,340	300	5,760	1,400	20,380
105	2,440	310	5,920	1,450	20,980
110	2,530	320	6,080	1,500	21,570
115	2,630	330	6,230	1,550	22,160
120	2,720	340	6,390	1,600	22,740
125	2,810	350	6,540	1,650	23,320
130	2,900	360	6,690	1,700	23,900
135	2,990	370	6,840	1,750	24,470
140	3,080	380	7,000	1,800	25,050
145	3,170	390	7,150	1,850	25,620
150	3,260	400	7,300	1,900	26,180
155	3,350	450	8,040	1,950	26,750
160	3,440	500	8,760	2,000	27,310
165	3,530	550	9,470		

† Surface area = total outside surface area of container in square feet.
When the surface area is not stamped on the nameplate or when the marking is not legible, the area can be calculated by using one of the following formulas:

(1) Cylindrical container with hemispherical heads:
Area = Overall length x outside diameter x 3.1416.

(2) Cylindrical container with other than hemispherical heads:
Area = (Overall length + 0.3 outside diameter) x outside diameter x 3.1416.
Note: This formula is not exact, but will give results within the limits of practical accuracy for the sole purpose of sizing relief valves.

(3) Spherical container:
Area = Outside diameter squared x 3.1416.

♦ Flow Rate – CFM Air = Required flow capacity in cubic feet per minute of air at standard conditions, 60°F and atmospheric pressure (14.7 psia).

The rate of discharge may be interpolated for intermediate values of surface area. For containers with total outside surface area greater than 2,000 square feet, the required flow rate can be calculated using the formula, Flow Rate – CFM Air = $53.632\ A^{0.82}$.

A = total outside surface area of the container in square feet.

Portions shaded in gray are from OSHA regulations, Section 1910.110.

[▲]Table 1 meets or exceeds these regulations.

Figure 6-20 (*continued*)

continued from page 165

is a fundamental one. It keeps responsibility for safety decision making congruent with responsibility for safety performance. No manager can absolve himself or herself from responsibility for performance by citing "I followed the engineering standard." To slavishly follow a standard is a mistake. Managers need to understand why they make the decisions they make, not only to assure themselves that the standard is being appropriately applied, but also to be able to explain to subordinates the rationale underlying the decision, gaining commitment of subordinates-leadership. By printing OSHA requirements in red, users are apprised of legal considerations that are distinct from otherwise desirable guidance. A manager may choose not to meet legal requirements, if in his or her judgment doing so would be a negative rather than a positive influence on employee behavior. Of course, if challenged, managers will be expected to defend their decisions. Decisions made in the context of a Central Safety Committee are very likely to stand the test of examination. One of the problems with legal codification of safety rules is that innovation is thereby stifled. It takes courage to decide to deviate from current legal requirements in order to improve, but such deviations have to be made if progress in improving employee safety behavior is to be accomplished on a continuing basis.

SUMMARY

Standards of performance regarding safety are established by management as the *requirements* that have become recognized as necessary to accomplish work without damage to employees, the public, or the environment. Because they are *requirements*, they must be strictly adhered to by all persons to whom they apply. These requirements are not optional. Performance standards must be communicated and understanding must be clearly established. They must be clearly written—written so as to convey an unambiguous meaning to all who are bound by their requirements.

The process by which standards of performance are created requires care, thoroughness, and the flexibility necessary to respond to changing circumstances in a controlled fashion. Creating standards that assist the safety effort rather than detract from this effort is hard, demanding work. Good results justify the effort. Safety pays.

NOTES

1. These examples, and others in this chapter, are not presented as "hot-off-the-press" examples. Word changes are continually being made to rules and procedures to reflect the most recent thinking on the subject. For example, the current wording of rule #13 in Figure 6-5 might remove the ten-minute exceptions as being unmanageable even though technically sound based on the actual noise level.
2. See Figure 5-1, pp. 94-97.
3. See Chapter 4.

Chapter 7

MANAGEMENT SAFETY AUDITS: PRINCIPLES AND TECHNIQUES

> "Oh, wad some Power the giftie gie us
> To see oursels as ithers see us!
> It wod frae monie a blunder free us,
> An' foolish notions."[1]

Burns immortalized the recognition that being able to see ourselves as others see us is a substantial asset. Being able to do so might improve our behavior. Management safety audits are designed to accomplish this objective. They also provide management personnel the opportunity to see and assess their own effectiveness in favorably influencing employee behavior. Management safety audits are the most important continuing management activity through which safety leadership is established and maintained. It is activity that is management initiated, not driven by crisis or by government-mandated regulations. It is therefore more creditable activity. But what are management safety audits? That is the subject of this chapter. Actual examples are recorded in Chapter 8.

Management safety auditing is the process in which management personnel observe employees performing tasks in the workplace, reach judgments regarding the safety behavior of the observed employees, enter into a discussion with the observed employees regarding these judgments, and then subsequently, anonymously, report the type of observed behavior in need of improvement. The benefits to be derived from this type of management activity are entirely dependent upon how management personnel behave while performing their auditing task. This chapter is devoted to describing the details that have been found to maximize the effectiveness of a formal auditing program.

AUDIT IN PAIRS

The efficiency and the success of management auditing are enhanced by auditing in pairs—two members of management audit together, as an ad hoc team for a particular audit. Whenever possible, at least one member of the team should be in the direct line of supervision of the employee(s) audited. The benefits of team auditing are:

1. The members of the team learn from each other because of their differing knowledge and experiences.
2. If the team is composed of boss/subordinate or high level/low level members of management, this interface brings additional opportunities for productive exchange of points of view. Communication of safety standards and needs can bridge organizational hurdles or impediments.
3. When actually observing, each team member is challenged to improve his or her powers of observation. Attention to details of actual employee behavior are enhanced—neither team member wants to appear to be a poor observer.
4. Standards by which employee safety behavior are judged are likely to be raised, as neither team member wishes to appear to be permissive or lax.
5. Team members can discuss their judgments and thinking among themselves prior to engaging in discussion with the audited employee(s). This procedure can save the embarrassment that can sometimes occur if a member audits alone.
6. During the discussion with the audited employee(s), the second member of the audit team, by his or her mere presence, makes a contribution toward keeping the discussion productive and "on-track."
7. It permits one auditor to be an observer during the discussion with the observed employee(s) and to step in, if needed, to keep the discussion constructive.
8. Team auditing permits the audit process to be a training experience when the team is composed of one experienced auditor and one inexperienced auditor.
9. Team auditing builds a sense of "oneness" in the organization by requiring some management personnel to visit and see operations that they may not have had any explicit reason for visiting. It provides management an opportunity to see and be seen by employees who may otherwise be strangers, in the accompaniment of a supervisor with whom employees are more familiar. It provides management an easy opportunity to "bridge the gap."

PREPARATION FOR THE AUDIT

Prior to actually observing employees, the audit team has some preparatory work to do.

1. It should review the summary of the previous period audit reports to find any major safety issues on which they may wish to focus.
2. It should decide the kind of work or the location in which work is being done that they want to audit.
3. It should briefly review the safety rules and procedures applicable to the work that they are likely to observe being done. This prepares them to be informed observers

but should also insure that the observers themselves are in compliance with the applicable rules and procedures.

4. If applicable, it should review and perhaps copy the standard operating procedure for the specific operation to be observed. (A copy of the procedure would provide a reference in the workplace, if needed.)

This preparatory process should normally take no more than ten to fifteen minutes.

OBSERVATION

After assuring themselves that they are prepared to meet applicable safety rules and procedures (safety helmets, safety glasses, safety shoes, ties tucked into shirt, no dangling bracelets, and so forth), the audit team should proceed to the location of the work that they have decided to observe. En route, the auditors should attempt to locate the first-line supervisor of the employee(s) to be audited. There are several reasons for contacting this first-line supervisor:

1. The auditing team is entering an operation for which the first-line supervisor is responsible. He or she should be shown the courtesy of recognition. In normal circumstances, extraordinary efforts to find the first-line supervisor are not warranted; the object is to avoid ignoring this important member of supervision.
2. There may be specific issues (not only safety issues) that are currently high profile ones. Auditors may be queried about these and should be prepared to discuss these to the appropriate extent.
3. In order to ensure a constructive discussion with the audited employee(s), it is necessary to have his or her (their) full attention. Thus, the work must stop. This is an event that directly affects the first-line supervisor's job performance. His or her nonobjection should be established prior to beginning an audit whenever reasonably possible. This is one of the reasons that one member of the audit team should be in the direct line of supervision responsible for the audited employee. The first-line supervisor, unless a member of the two-person audit team, should not, however, join the audit team.

Having a good constructive discussion sometimes requires the discussion to be held away from the actual workplace location, although a move should be avoided if possible. The best discussions can be held at the workplace, but if it cannot safely accommodate two additional people or is too noisy to have a conversation without yelling, then a move to a more reasonable environment is required. This more reasonable environment is preferably not the supervisor's office. Too often the supervisor's office is construed in a negative fashion not conducive to a constructive safety audit discussion.

If the audit team has no special type of work in mind, the team can simply walk into the plant, office, truck terminal, dock, road maintenance area, warehouse, or tank farm—any place work might be going on—and decide what to observe on an ad hoc basis. There is one caveat: if the observation process is started it must be completed. Do not start the process if it cannot be completed. If arrangements for providing relief have not been made when relief of the worker is needed, do not start making observations. Find another work activity. If "all is well," do not move on until mistakes are found. An important part of the audit system is the reinforcement of good behavior.

Auditors should use senses other than just their eyes; ears and noses can provide evidence of work underway. Nothing is quite so convincing of management's interest in safety as an auditor's climbing 7 or 8 levels of stairway grating to seek the source of the noise being made by a welder who is repairing a piece of equipment in 30° F weather and 30 mph winds. Go where the work is being done!

OBSERVATION OF THE EMPLOYEE AT WORK

The object of a safety audit is observation of the performance of work as it is being done, at least in part independent from outside influence, such as the presence of safety auditors. Thus, the work should initially be observed, if possible, without the worker's recognition that an audit is being conducted. This period of observation should continue for a few minutes. If still unrecognized by the employee, the auditing team should move to a position that will allow the employee to discover that he or she is being observed. This discovery of being observed can be of significant help to employees. It encourages employees to try to think back and re-examine their behavior for the period that they believe they might have been under observation. This re-examination is a constructive exercise; it is an inducement to "see ourselves as others have seen us."

Employees who are familiar with the auditing process quickly recognize an audit is underway. Those who are not familiar with the audit process wonder what is going on. However, the auditors should not allow work to stop while in the observation phase of the audit. The employee should be pleasantly urged to continue working, with perhaps an indication that the auditors would appreciate an opportunity to talk to the employee when he or she reaches a convenient stopping point.

During the observation period, the auditors should have made many safety-related observations and discussed whether or not these meet the auditors' standards, and, if not, what would represent improvements. The auditors' standards should, of course, include established rules, procedures, and requirements of SOPs to the extent these are known by the auditors, as well as those that come to mind as the auditors identify the hazards with which the employee must cope. The auditors should develop a mental inventory of all the actions of the employee that represent positive safety behavior deserving reinforcement by recognition. The audit team should also develop an inventory of actions for which improvement is appropriate. Written notes should not be made during the observation period. In fact, no evidence that note taking is taking place—clipboards or notebooks—should exist. The presence of such note-taking paraphernalia may intimidate or infuriate the employee being observed. Both are detrimental to the audit process. In addition, when writing, auditors cannot be observing. Tape recorders should also be avoided because of their possible adverse effect on the audit process. If auditors cannot remember what they see for thirty minutes or so, the observations must not be very important and not much will have been lost.

The ability to observe is enhanced by use of categories of employee actions. The categories, which should be memorized, are:

1. Personal protective equipment
2. Body position and motions
3. Tools
4. Equipment
5. Procedures
6. Orderliness

As the audited employee comes into view, each auditor should assess the status of the six categories.

1. Personal Protective Equipment

Is the employee's use of personal protective equipment consistent with the auditors's understanding of the applicable rules and perceived hazards of the workplace? That is, is the employee wearing a hard hat? Does a rule require the wearing of a hard hat? Does wearing a hard hat make sense? Is eye protection appropriate? Is face protection adequate? Hearing protection? Upper body protection? Arm protection? Hand and finger protection? Lower body protection? Leg or foot protection? Each of these should be mentally checked off against existing rules as understood by the auditors and against existing or realistically potential hazards recognized by the auditors. Some of these judgments may not be able to be made immediately because either the protective equipment or the work hazards cannot be seen adequately at this point. The auditors should recognize this fact and refine their judgments as they move closer to the employee and can see more. Assessment of some personal protective equipment, such as steel-toed shoes, may require waiting until the discussion phase of the audit, when close-up determination can be made.

2. Body Position and Motions

The next category is body position and motions. That is, are any body parts being put in jeopardy by their juxtaposition to hazards or is the employee's body position likely to bring about an injury? Consideration also needs to be given to awkward or repetitive body motions associated with the task. The objective is recognition of the possibility of both short-term traumatic injury and long-term damage to the body.

Some examples may help. Is an employee trying to hold a door steady with his left hand while trying to finish off a mortise? If the chisel slipped, is the left hand or wrist in jeopardy? Does the employee have his hands in his pockets while descending a stairway? Is the employee standing on the top step of a step ladder? Is the employee kneeling, putting his body weight on his knees against a concrete floor? Is the employee standing under a load while trying to guide it to the ground? Is the employee cutting toward his or her body? Is the employee pushing on a pipe wrench close to a wall so that if the wrench slipped his hand would hit the wall? Has the employee moved from one step ladder to another without descending to the ground? Is the employee standing or climbing on process equipment or piping? Is the employee facing switch gear while opening or closing it? Is the employee inappropriately inside a barricaded area? Is the employee repeatedly using the same finger-to-wrist motions? Does the task require excessive stretching? Does the task require twisting the torso while lifting? Is the employee lifting with his or her back or with leg muscles? How much reach is required? Ergonomic illnesses are increasingly[2] being recognized as important considerations in the workplace.

3. Tools

The questions to think about regarding tools are really three.

a. Are the tools in use the proper tools for the job or is the employee using some improvised or homemade tool?
b. Are the tools being used correctly?
c. Are the tools in use in good condition?

Some examples may help. Is a piece of pipe being used as a pry bar? Are conductive pliers being used to remove electrical fuses? Is a pipe wrench or pliers being used on a hexagonal fitting? Is a pipe extension, a "cheater," being used with a spanner or pipe wrench? Has a file been ground to fabricate a knife? Is a hand file being used without a handle? Is a sledge hammer being used with a splintered or loose handle? Are wood bits being used to drill into metal?

4. Equipment

The same questions can be asked about equipment as about tools. The distinction between tools and equipment is one of size and power source. Tools are generally "small" and hand operated. Equipment is larger and power activated. The distinction is made simply to assist auditors in identifying more clearly that item at which they are looking.

Again, some examples may help. Is a forklift truck being used as a makeshift man-lift? Has an automatic valve been blocked open? Has an interlock switch been blocked closed? Has a fire extinguisher been partially used, yet it remains in service? Are welding blinds in place? Is a hoist being side loaded by means of an inappropriate nonvertical lift? Is a step ladder being used in an unopened position? Is the equipment adequately locked out? Does the lock-out comply with written procedures? Has the equipment been properly decontaminated? Is there a record of decontamination? Have scaffolding erection procedures been followed? Are they documented?

5. Procedures

The questions for auditors in regard to procedures are similar to those for tools and equipment. Does a written procedure for the work exist? Is it adequate? Is it being followed? Is one needed? Is a work permit required? Does it exist? Is it being followed? Is it correctly executed? If not required, should a work permit be required? Is this really a tank entry? Are tank entry procedures being followed? Is this really a trenching operation? Should this work be barricaded?

6. Orderliness

Workplace hazards are compounded when the workplace is dirty, disorganized, cluttered or congested. These conditions in a workplace are not *normally* hazardous in and of themselves.

The unsafe aspect of disorderly workplaces is manifested when an employee begins to do work under these conditions. It is the employee's behavior, not the workplace, that is unsafe. Of course there are some exceptions to this fundamental concept. Oily rags that have been improperly disposed of (evidence of a previous unsafe act) do spontaneously combust.

Absence of expert knowledge regarding the work being observed should not intimidate or make an auditor feel unqualified to audit. The auditor's task as regards the employee is to get the employee to think about his or her behavior and what the employee can do to improve this behavior. It is not the auditor's task to be able to tell the employee what to do to improve. It has been my experience with workers around the world that lack of knowledge is not the major factor in determining safety performance. Rather, it is the lack of *using* the worker's knowledge in the performance of his or her work. In Third World or industrially emerging areas there is some lack of knowledge; that is, knowledge and training is needed. In the United States, Europe, and Japan, and in work forces that have been trained by companies from these areas, I have found very little lack of necessary knowledge to work safely. I have observed many unsafe acts[3] because knowledge was not being used.

The emphasis in management safety auditing should be creation of the opportunity to show appreciation for safe work practices being used and mutual recognition of what improvements are appropriate, not what is wrong or fault finding. Agreement between the auditors should normally be reached before discussing the audit with the employee. Gray areas should be minimized. Either a practice is acceptable, or improvement is needed, or the auditors simply do not know.

Management safety audits should be *mutual* learning experiences. Employees should learn what management thinks the employees have been doing well and recognize what changes they can make to improve their safety performance. Employees should also learn that management, as represented by the audit team, is interested in their safety and is willing to invest management time and effort toward improving the safety aspects of their work. The audit team should learn what employees are doing correctly as well as those areas needing improvement—that is, those areas in which management has not yet been successful in bringing about the behavior needed to establish an injury-free work environment. The audit team frequently learns something new about the actual work being performed and therefore becomes more knowledgeable not only in safety but also in what "goes on" in the workplace. The observation period of an audit is the opportunity to recognize employee behavior and act upon what has been seen.

DISCUSSION OF THE AUDIT

After the audit team has completed its observation period and privately discovered their standards regarding what they have seen, it is time for them to discuss their findings with the observed employee(s). If prior arrangements for relief have been made, these should be implemented and the employee be made available for discussion. As mentioned earlier, the discussion should occur at the workplace unless this is not feasible. In any event, the audit team should introduce themselves if they are not well known to the employee. Handshakes should be exchanged if in keeping with the local custom. One auditor should have been designated the chief spokesperson to avoid "double teaming" the employee and to allow the second auditor to monitor the progress of the discussion, contributing only when absolutely necessary. The designated auditor should explain that they have been observing the employee work as part of a safety audit and ask the employee if he or she has time to take a few minutes to discuss safety. The objective here is to obtain the employee's agreement to participate and to recognize that the employee may have priorities that temporarily are more significant than discussing safety.

I would not want to delay completion of a job that in turn would delay the start-up of a major facility. Indeed, some activities have a higher priority than a routine safety audit! Employees may want to know if disruption of their work has been approved by their first-line supervisor. These sources of employee anxiety need to be resolved to maximize the employee's full cooperation and participation.

After assuring that the conditions necessary for a good discussion have been established, the designated auditor should inform the employee of all the good things the auditing team observed. The auditor then goes through each of the six auditing categories identifying those that have met endorsement by the audit team. Some on-the-spot judgments must frequently be made because the full facts were not available through original observations. Negative observations should not be mentioned. No criticism should be expressed. If the employee volunteers some self-criticism on an item the audit team observed, the auditor should acknowledge that the team had made a similar observation. If the team had not made the observation, the auditor acknowledges this as well, and if one or both of the team members do not understand the item, they should get the employee to explain or otherwise not dwell on the item. The employee knows and recognizes that change is appropriate. Belaboring that point will only cause employees to withdraw from the process—a loss to all involved.

As a tactic, one or two good things may be withheld for use at a later time in the discussion when reinforcement of the employee's pride is needed. This portion of the discussion should proceed slowly. The employee should be given time to recover from the trauma of having been audited and an opportunity to think about his or her behavior. The auditors should proceed slowly and in a nonthreatening manner. This bears repeating! Many members of management are in a hurry, but this is one activity that must be timed to the needs of the employee.

After these positive reinforcements of desirable behavior have been completed, it is time to get the employee to self-examine his or her behavior for opportunities for improvement. This step can be accomplished in a number of ways, but always by asking questions, not by giving answers or instructions. Active thinking by the employee is the key, not passive acquiescence. For most supervisory personnel this is the most difficult portion of the audit process in which to become proficient. It requires patience, listening skills, and insight into the kinds of questions that can be asked to lead the employee to recognizing how his or her behavior can be improved while maintaining the person's self-esteem, confidence, and feeling that management thinks well of him or her even though there is room for improvement.

In addition, it is usually appropriate to tell the employee that this conversation will remain confidential. There will be no report to supervision regarding the employee's involvement in a management safety audit. The employee should be told that there will be a report on the kinds of activities that need some attention but no mention of names, or location and time such that names can be figured out. The team may want to reinforce the concept that they are auditing to help the employee see himself or herself as they have. The objective is to help the employee today, not tomorrow, through their supervisor.

The auditors can facilitate the self-examination portion of the discussion by asking questions similar to those listed below.

1. "John, I have commented on a number of items we noticed that you were doing well, in our opinion. We were particularly pleased to see that you were cutting away from your body all the time. You did not fall into the trap of cutting toward yourself. Those were the 'good' items. (pause) Were there any items upon which you think you could improve, now that you have had a chance to think about them a little?"
2. "John, we noticed one item that we think you might have done more safely when you were moving this box. Can you guess what we have in mind?"
3. "John, there was one item that we believe you did because of your skill in doing this job, but I don't think you would train a new man to do it that way. Can you figure out what it was?"
4. "John, you were checking the level of the battery water. Would you advise your daughter or son to do anything differently? What part of your body were you mostly using? How could that part of your body become injured?"
5. "John, is there a standard operating instruction for the job you are doing? Do you think you hit all the points it covers, or did you miss something? Are SOPs readily available to you? Could you get a copy to use out here in the field? Let's go look at the SOP and see if you can pick up what we believe was missed."

The entire effort is directed at getting the employee to self-examine his or her behavior. Auditors should avoid pointing out mistakes that have been made. They should lead the employees to make the discovery themselves. Occasionally, the effort to get the employee to think of what the auditors have in mind becomes embarrassing to both the auditor and the employee. The employee begins to feel he or she is stupid or is being made to feel so. At this point telling becomes acceptable. The employee is prepared to listen without becoming defensive. Occasionally the auditors will be in error; they should be prepared to listen and learn from the audited employee.

By means of a very determined and patient attempt to avoid *telling* employees what the auditors think, the auditing process allows employees to demonstrate their knowledge, if not their perfect performance. Employees appreciate this; none of us likes to be told something we already know. Being told implies we do not know. By not *telling*, the auditors avoid another problem. Their lack of knowledge does not become as obvious. They do not have to set themselves up as having superior knowledge. They can listen to the employee's opinion about how the job could be done more safely. This gives the auditors an opportunity to learn without fully disclosing their ignorance. Another objective that not telling accomplishes is the avoidance of confrontation. It avoids the temptation for the employee to defend his or her behavior. Defending behavior that, in fact, is in need of change is counterproductive; it impedes change. Yet another advantage of not *telling* employees is that auditors can avoid giving instructions. This removes one source of conflict between the auditing team and the responsible first-line supervisor. It is he or she who is primarily responsible for the employee's safety (beyond the employee himself) and the audit team should avoid interjecting itself into a supervisory role vis-à-vis the first-line supervisor.

Another tactical consideration is to avoid having employees make corrections during the discussion. Other employees will be watching. Making corrections that others can see can be embarrassing to the employee at the time, or perhaps later after supervision is out of sight. The employee should know that corrections can be made as he or she has the opportunity to do so. By showing consideration—by not expecting instant correction—auditors are also demonstrating trust, which in turn will beget trust. And the workplace climate will improve.

Sometimes it is useful for an auditor to re-enact, carefully, the action which the auditor is attempting to have the employee recognize. The employee should watch the auditor. This step frequently reveals to the employee an action of which he or she was completely oblivious. Employees sometimes cannot believe they did what the auditors observed; however, recognition and acceptance are improved by their seeing the acts re-enacted.

Inquiring why employees have behaved inappropriately can also be instructive. Again such an inquiry should be done with sensitivity. An employee may not be wearing safety glasses as required, but launching into an inquisition of why may be counterproductive. Leading questions should be asked. After an employee has recognized that he should be wearing safety glasses, a new item can be broached unless the employee volunteers an explanation. (If safety glasses are required, they are required; no explanation will be satisfactory. Without safety glasses the employee should not be allowed to work where safety glasses are required). After other items are discussed, and perhaps one of the "good" things mentioned that was earlier withheld for an occasion such as this, the employee can be asked if there are any mitigating circumstances or reasons why he is working without safety glasses. The audit team may learn that replacement glasses did not arrive as scheduled and that the employee's supervisor had told him that it was acceptable to work one day while wearing "street" glasses. The problem is not primarily the employee, but rather the supervisor, or perhaps, historically, just poor enforcement of the safety glasses requirement. It is remarkable what managers can learn by asking questions rather than by delivering lectures.

Audits take place in which the number of unsafe acts—undesirable safety behavior—are sufficiently large that to dwell on each of them is more than the employee can "take" and still maintain a constructive attitude. In these instances the major three or four items should be selected and the rest let go. This is not a condoning of unsafe acts. The purpose of an audit is to bring about a change in worker behavior. He or she is not likely to be able to react to more than three or four items.

All of these aspects of an audit take time—management time. Many managers who are new to the auditing process (some experienced ones as well!) find it very difficult to slow down enough to make effective audits. They view the process as inefficient. They are measuring what they are putting into the process and have little or no experience with what will be coming out of the process. Effectiveness should be the criterion. Getting people to change their behavior is not easy; it takes dedicated, persistent work. Backsliding in safety behavior is notorious. One concept that may help the impatient manager is that the audit team is not spending time only with the audited employee. Employees talk. And they will say nice things about the audit or ugly things about the audit. They will endorse the audit process and share what they need to do to improve or they will reject the audit process and become uncooperative. They will make the audit process a constructive force in the workplace or a destructive force. Their behavior will reflect management's behavior.

Take time. Care. Be sincere. Enjoy the audit and show that you enjoy it because you know you are trying to help people, to lead people, not to drive or manage them. Things and circumstances need to be managed; people need to be led.

EMPLOYEE SUGGESTIONS

The next step in the audit process is to give the audited employee a formal opportunity to make constructive suggestions for improving workplace safety. This portion of the audit also needs to be carefully handled.

Good listening skills are required. Some auditors may be tempted to record these suggestions and/or complaints and promise to "follow up" on them. This method is a mistake. Most workplace problems should be solved in the workplace. Thus, the employee should be asked what actions he/she has taken to bring about the suggested improvement. If the employee has not actively sought to bring about the suggested change, the auditors should try to redirect the employee into doing that which he or she can do. The auditing process should support the normal scheme for getting things done. Employees should be encouraged to "do business" through their direct supervisor and to show diligence in doing so. Only as a last resort should auditors take away work from a audit as a follow-up action.

When this part of the audit has been completed, the employee should be appropriately thanked for participation in and contribution to the audit process and to the safety of the organization. The auditors should then leave the workplace and the employee should return to work.

GROSS MISBEHAVIOR

In the event the audit team sees an event for which they believe disciplinary action should be taken, the audit should be terminated immediately. The employee should be approached, told of the observed behavior, and removed from the job if this can be safely accomplished. If this can not be safely accomplished, removal from the job should await circumstances when this can be done safely. Once the employee has been removed from the job, he or she and the responsible first-line supervisor should be gotten together in an appropriate place. The employee should then be asked to tell his or her supervisor why he or she is in this situation. Once the full story of what has happened has been communicated to the first-line supervisor, the audit team should depart and let the first-line supervisor do whatever needs to be done. This is not a disciplinary meeting and nothing should be said about discipline. It is simply a meeting in which the first-line supervisor responsible for an operation learns about a significant event first-hand, in a timely manner. Upper supervision will not know the employee or the work habits of employees or supervisory instructions to employees as well as the first-line supervisor. They should not be the disciplinarians of employees who do not report directly to them. This is the responsibility of immediate supervision.[4]

Upper management, of course, should follow up to determine what action was taken by first-line supervision and why. Based on this information, they can act, if needed, as they think best.

REPORT OF AUDIT RESULTS

After discussing their observations with the audited employee, listening to any employee suggestions, and thanking the employee for his contribution to the auditing process and to the safety effort in general (if warranted), the auditors should leave the workplace to review the audit. During this review, the audit team should record all the unsafe acts (actions that need improvement) that they observed during the audit. They may or may not have discussed these with the responsible employee. These should include any unsafe acts they observed, independent of who committed them.

This review process also provides the audit team an opportunity to think about what they saw and perhaps to recognize unsafeguarded hazards that they had not previously recognized. When in the workplace, the audit team should focus their attention on the employee they are observing and the team interaction with the employee. Occasionally they will develop new insights upon reflection during the recording phase of the audit.

In addition, during this part of the audit auditors can perhaps resolve differences in opinion that they had not resolved before or during the discussion with the audited employee. This is an opportune time to determine what standards of performance the auditors would like to see established. Actually establishing such standards is a separate activity. Deciding what the auditors "would like to see" should not be inhibited by the problems associated with implementation.

These unsafe acts should be described explicitly, not in general terms. If an employee was observed wearing his safety glasses down on his nose and thereby depriving himself of proper eye protection, the record should not be "employee not wearing safety glasses properly." The record should be explicitly descriptive—"employee was wearing safety glasses down on his nose, allowing eyes to be exposed while operating an engine lathe." If there is only one engine lathe operator, then this phrase should simply be deleted or be changed to read "craft employee was wearing safety glasses down on his nose, allowing eyes to be exposed while working." Including the words "engine lathe" identifies the employee.

The record of unsafe acts should be a record of unsafe acts, not who did them. There are auditors who believe the first-line supervisor should be apprised of the audit findings if he or she is not a member of the audit team. I believe this is a mistake. My experience has been, even with the best of supervisors, that supervision will advertently or inadvertently reveal to the audited employee an awareness of the audit results. This turns the auditors into policemen or umpires, not the coaches and leaders the audit system is designed to make them. Because many first-line supervisors correctly recognize that auditing of employee behavior is also auditing their effectiveness as a supervisor, they are often particularly anxious to know who has done what—to be able "to straighten him out." This act is sometimes done with considerable vengeance, because the supervisor has been embarrassed. Management safety audits provide only a sample of employee behavior. If a first-line supervisor wants to know what his or her employees are doing the supervisor has only to observe them for himself.

The purpose of this record of unsafe acts is to provide information for upper management to guide the safety effort. There is a tendency to want to record the favorable acts as well. This is a waste of time for both the audit team and anyone else who may feel obliged to read this material. The record should be the record of management failure to achieve the desired employee behavior. The record is created in order to remind management of the continuing effort that is necessary for achieving improvement and the direction in which this effort should go. The record is not designed to lull management into satisfaction that more actions were right than were wrong, for example. The employee actions that were observed to have been "good" are used to reinforce this good behavior when the audit observations are discussed with the audited employee, but afterward, there is no need to record these behaviors.

The audit records of each audit team should then be forwarded to a central collection point for analysis. This is usually the safety supervisor. However, a subcommittee of the Central Safety Committee might be utilized to make this summary analysis for the Central Safety Committee. The purpose of the summary is to extract, from the myriad observations made by many individual audit teams, the major observed deficiencies in employee safety behavior.

Statistical summaries of these audit results—in the form of number of deficiencies per unit time or persons audited—have also been found useful, particularly in large organizations in which observations tend to be numerous. If a record of the number of hours spent auditing is reported with each audit, the number of unsafe acts and/or safety rule violations per auditing hour can be calculated and used as a barometer of performance. In a one-hour audit, perhaps thirty minutes can actually be spent auditing. In another one-hour audit forty minutes may be spent auditing. If a record is kept of the number of people formally audited, the number of unsafe acts and/or safety rule violations per person audited can be calculated and used as a barometer of performance. Based on experience gained by actual use of such statistics, the CSC can decide whether or not such statistics are useful for their organizations. The question is, do these statistics relate to injury performance? Sometimes they do. Are they precursors or early-warning signals? Sometimes they are. The hazards of such statistics is that they are very likely to be biased, indicating improvement when no improvement has, in fact, taken place. These data are very subjective, particularly in the early years of a Management Safety Audit program.

These summary analyses are reported to the CSC as a guide to action and as an item to be communicated through line supervision down through the organization to employees in the workplace. This summary information augments the observations made by individual supervisors and provides them a broad base for discussions during "crew meetings" and/or during individual safety contacts with their employees (see Chapter 15). It also completes the management safety audit process.

FREQUENCY AND AUDIT ARRANGEMENTS

Individual management safety audits are a part of an overall management safety auditing program. Although the mechanics of successful programs can vary substantially, they do have some common elements: (1) audits are two-person audits, (2) they require written reports on observed deficiencies to be made and summarized for the Central Safety Committee, and (3) the frequency of and arrangements for auditing are predetermined, not left to ad hoc implementation. Items (1) and (2) have already been discussed.

The frequency and specific schedule of successful auditing programs vary. However, a program that has been particularly successful in organizations initiating a management safety audit program is organized as follows.

Every month, each manager, together with each of his or her subordinates, individually makes a one-hour audit of some work activities of employees for whom the subordinate is responsible. For example, a director who has three managers reporting to him can make three one-hour audits per month with subordinates—one with each manager. If a manager has three subordinate supervisors, he or she makes three one-hour audits—one with each supervisor—plus the audit with his or her director, for a total of four audits per month. The frequency of these management safety audits should be determined by the needs of the organization and the management structure of the organization. However, experience indicates that each member of supervision should participate in at least two hours of auditing per month as a maintenance level and up to four hours per month in circumstances in which a major increased effort is being made to improve performance. Thus, a manager with six direct subordinates might make an audit with each of these subordinates every other month, plus one audit bi-monthly with his direct superior—a total of seven one-hour audits every two months. Each manager should be held responsible for arranging for a substitute in those instances in which he or she cannot fulfill his scheduled audit assignment—because of vacation, a death in the family, and so forth.

As experience is gained in the auditing process, and its benefits have become widely accepted in the workplace, alternate arrangements have been successfully adopted. One such arrangement is simply to substitute a peer for the superior in the arrangement described above. This, of course, involves auditing personnel for whom one of the auditors has no direct or immediate responsibility. Such an arrangement does provide an "outside pair of eyes," which can be of value. This scheme has a scheduling advantage. All audits can be scheduled to occur at the same time and day of the week or month. Everyone recognizes that this is audit time and that meetings, for example, should not be scheduled during "audit time." Simultaneous scheduling of audits increases the awareness of employees that they may be audited. Some managers view this as a disadvantage. I have used this scheme and have found it satisfactory. The propose of audits is not to "catch" employees. A major purpose of the auditing process is to improve employees' awareness of their behavior. If specific prior notice of the possibility of being audited forewarns employees and as a result they are on "their best behavior" for an hour several times each month, I suspect this effectively contributes toward improving their behavior at other times.

In order not to lose the standards setting aspects of the boss/subordinate audit team arrangement, some organizations have found a combination of this scheme and the "peer pair" scheme to represent the best of both. Use boss/subordinate teams for part of the audits and "peer pair" teams for the rest.

One of the support functions the safety supervisor can provide an organization is to prepare the auditing schedule after the CSC has adopted a particular scheme. The audit schedule should show the audit team composition and the operation (employees) that each team shall audit. The schedule should be prepared on a monthly basis and copies provided to each scheduled auditor. If fixed times and days are part of the arrangement, these should also be specified.

THE SAFETY AUDIT SYSTEM

In the previous section, Management Safety Audits were described and their purpose elucidated. They constitute the cornerstone of a successful safety audit system. Two other sources of audits supplement this central auditing effort. These are: (1) first-line supervisor audits, and (2) safety supervisor audits.

First-line supervisory safety audits are formal safety audits, conducted in the same manner as described for management safety audits. These are conducted by a first-line supervisor alone or with a member of his or her "crew," within the "crew," or the organization for which the supervisor is responsible. The results of these audits are recorded, but only for future reference, by the first-line supervisor. The results are not reported up-the-line. These audits are designed to assure that first-line supervisors are making audits in addition to those they make as part of the management audit scheme and to increase the number of audits beyond those provided through management audits. The results of these first-line supervisory audits should be discussed—anonymously—in crew meetings. First-line supervisors should be prepared to discuss, in a general fashion, the results of these audits with *their* immediate supervisors.

The frequency at which these first-line supervisory audits should be conducted depends on a number of factors—injury frequency versus goal, number of employees per supervisor, and actual injury frequency experience. High injury frequencies, performance that is substantially poorer than the goal, and high numbers of employees per supervisor all indicate the need for more frequent rather than less frequent audits. A mid-point in the range of frequencies found reasonable is one one-hour audit per week.

Safety supervisor or safety coordinator audits are of two types: (1) regular safety audits—that is, personnel audits—and (2) compliance audits. Both of these types of audits can be done solo or with another person, a plant manager or operator. There is no need to be consistent in this regard, but the safety supervisor should have a reason for choosing someone to accompany him or her on an audit. The object of these safety supervisor audits is to provide management an assessment of (1) work practice safety, and (2) status of compliance with applicable statutory regulations. Reports on the results of both of these types of audits should be prepared for the Central Safety Committee. Anonymity should be retained regarding safe work practice audits. Compliance audits should be specific and should explicitly define what the safety supervisor considers is deficient and the statutory regulations upon which these judgments are based. The CSC has the responsibility for accepting or rejecting the judgments of the safety supervisor and for initiating corrective actions it deems appropriate. Responsibility for results remains with line management.

Full-time safety supervisors should be expected to make two to three one-hour work practice safety audits per week. In situations in which safety is a collateral duty, proportional reduction in this frequency is appropriate. Compliance audits should be made as required to achieve compliance.

Taken together, these three sources of safety auditing provide both management and the work force a powerful, systematic stimulus for excelling in safety—to their mutual benefit.

AIDS TO AUDITING

Some organizations have found it useful to keep the basic principles of management safety auditing readily available for management guidance. They have prepared laminated file cards outlining these basic principles. Figure 7-1 shows samples of the material that can be put on both sides of these cards. Figure 7-2 also summarizes some important features of the management safety audit process.

Aids to Effective Auditing

I. The Audit Cycle
   A. Decide—what activities to audit
   B. Stop—stand still long enough to really
      1. observe- truly see what is taking place, in detail
      2. discuss- with the observed employee(s)
      3. report- unsafe acts, no names (exception: gross misconduct)

II. The Observation Cycle
   A. Observe
      1. determine positive behaviors
      2. determine opportunities for improvement
   B. Discuss Observations
      1. go to where the action is, if possible
      2. provide for relief, if necessary
      3. introduce yourself, as appropriate
      4. positively reinforce the employee-take time, do not rush
      5. get employee to recognize areas of needed improvement. Ask leading questions; avoid "telling"; demonstrate, if necessary
   C. Provide employee his or her "turn"
      1. Provide opportunity for employee to express safety concerns
      2. Ask for ideas for improvement
      3. Thank employee(s) as appropriate
   D. Review and Report
      1. Review what was seen. Think about items that might not have been recognized
      2. Record items in need of improvement. Identify unsafe acts, rule violations, inadequate safety standards
      3. Do not record names
      4. Record items needing follow-up, if any
      5. Record recommendations of audit team

III. Observation Categories
   A. Personal Protective Equipment- head to toes
   B. Body Positions and Motions- Fail safe? Ergonomically sound?
   C. Tools- Proper? Properly used? Safe condition?
   D. Equipment- Proper? Properly used? Safe condition?
   E. Procedures- Followed? Existent? Needed?
   F. Orderliness- Would your mother-in-law approve?

Figure 7-1

Safety Audits

1. No evidence of note taking should be apparent.
2. Emphasis should be placed on people activity, not "things".
3. The audit does not generate a list of things to do.
4. Employees should be observed working prior to initiating discussion.
5. Employees should be "put-at-ease" early in the discussion. This takes time and should not be rushed.
6. Employees should be thanked or congratulated for their actions which reflect good safety practices, rule compliance, etc.
7. The audit team should ask questions, not deliver lectures. The object is to get employees to recognize personally the need to upgrade their safety performance. Discussions should be skillfully guided, but not be manipulative.
8. Discussion should be open, "honest", and direct, but not argumentative or confrontational. The discussion needs to be a mutual learning experience.
9. Employees should be encouraged to comment on any safety concerns they may have. These may be written down as evidence that follow-up will be made. The results of this follow-up needs to be subsequently communicated to the employee, by a member of the audit team. Employee follow-up should be encouraged.
10. It is almost always a mistake to inform the employee's direct supervisor of the specific results of a safety audit. The reason that communicating to the employee's supervision is usually a mistake is that it normally results in a contact with the employee which the employee is very likely to view as chastisement or criticism. This is destructive of the audit process. It does not support an atmosphere of **mutual learning and trust**. If the supervisor is aware that an audit has occurred and he/she wants to know what happened, he/she may ask the employee. This too, however, is usually a mistake for the same reasons.
11. Employees should be thanked for their constructive participation in the audit process.
12. Audits should not, unless the employee's conduct is particularly inappropriate, become the basis for disciplinary action. In cases of particularly inappropriate employee behavior, the employee should be informed that his/her behavior has been so inappropriate as to warrant supervisory action. The employee should then be escorted to his/her supervisor and asked to describe why he/she has been brought to the supervisor. This procedure avoids late reporting and opportunities for miscommunication. It also provides direct and timely participation by first-line supervision. Disciplinary action should be taken by direct supervision based on the evidence at hand, coupled with the employee's performance history.
13. The unsafe acts seen during an audit should be recorded at the audit wrap-up and forwarded to the Safety Office to be summarized with other audit reports for the audit period to assist in trend analysis, etc. These summary reports can be used throughout the organization as information to assist in safety discussions.

Figure 7-2

14. These safety audits become a powerful activity in support of the total safety effort. They require management presence in the work place, actively interacting with employees on a subject which is employee oriented (their safety). These audits are an effective means for improving morale in the work place.

Questioning Approach

* Questioning takes more time than "telling"
  but
  gets people to think.
* Questions lead people to
  - Recognize injury potential.
  - Do something to protect themselves.
  - Start questioning on their own.
  - Teach the questioner.
* Questions avoid
  - Arguments and confrontations.
  - Resentment.
  - Misunderstandings.
  - Displaying your ignorance in undesirable ways.

Figure 7-2 (*continued*)

THE SAFETY AUDIT: AN ADDITIONAL COMMENT

The propensity for supervision to criticize employee behavior (not always directly) appears to be a common phenomenon throughout much of the world. When conducting training courses in the management safety auditing technique, I show slides of the Observation Cycle which stress the importance of: (1) reinforcing good behavior by recognizing it, (2) getting employees to recognize areas needing improvement without telling them, (3) seeking employee safety concerns and suggestions, and (4) thanking employees for safety efforts. I then show some slides designed to encourage the development of powers of creative observation. These slides are followed by slides depicting various work activity. I ask "what do you see?" Almost without exception, the audience focuses on what is wrong! Finding fault continues until I stop the process after several slides and back up to review the Observation Cycle. Occasionally, after two or three slides, someone in the audience actually does mention something the employee is doing correctly. The slides show employees doing lots of things safely, just as most employees do most of what they do safely. However, supervisors have been conditioned to identify what is wrong, not what is right—management by exception. This propensity for criticizing employees for their mistakes is a major impediment in achieving excellence in safety. It makes safety an *imposed* behavior rather than an *induced* behavior. Yes, improvement in safety behavior can be effected by *telling*, but better results will be obtained by following the Observation Cycle. Tell the "good" news, and let the employee develop the "bad" news. Do not criticize.

Breaking the ingrained supervisory behavior of fault finding followed by criticism is not easy. Many supervisors simply find it difficult to say good things to subordinates, particularly when all they are doing is what they are supposed to do. Some significant percentage of supervisors do not see the mistakes subordinates make because they are too "busy" doing something else. Others simply do not want to watch employees work—they find the experience distasteful. Another set of supervisors does not watch employees work because they do not have the interpersonal skills necessary to avoid precipitating a distasteful confrontation—it is better that nothing is seen, for no corrective action will be needed.

SUMMARY

A primary objective of management safety audits is to improve the safety behavior of employees. *Telling* employees what they must do to behave more safely is usually counterproductive. *Telling* leads to defensive reactions and confrontations. *Telling* frequently tends to result in increased resistance to change, rather than inducing change.

A management safety audit process that reinforces good safety behavior by recognition of such behavior, coupled with a *questioning* approach that leads employees to recognize and talk about areas in which improvement is appropriate, is much more likely to achieve the desired change in employee behavior than is a telling process.

A second objective of management safety audits is continually to keep all levels of management aware of actual employee safety behavior that is in need of improvement. By conducting safety audits, as described in this chapter, management increases the opportunity to see, hear, and learn from employees regarding work procedures that are in need of change. The audit procedure is not one of finding fault, but rather one that leads to a *mutual* understanding and acceptance of improved ways of accomplishing tasks.

The behavior of management during safety audits has tremendous influence on the work force. Management should not underestimate this influence. The interpersonal skills of management representatives are critical to the results achieved. Management safety audits conducted as described in this chapter can assist in the development of interpersonal skills within the management group of an organization, while also accomplishing the task of creating an environment in which employees work free of injury.

NOTES

1. Robert Burns, "To a Louse—On seeing one on a lady's bonnet at church," *The Literature of England*, edited by G.B. Woods et al., Scott, Foresman, 1941, pp. 107-108.
2. OSHA definitions of damage resulting from long-term effects, as contrasted to traumatic or single incident effects, are classified as illnesses.
3. See Chapter 3, page 51.
4. See Chapter 12.

Chapter 8

MANAGEMENT SAFETY AUDITS: EXAMPLES

The process of conducting management safety audits and how to use the information developed during these audits was discussed in Chapter 7. This chapter presents examples of: (1) actual discussions during audits, (2) typical audit summary reports, and (3) some additional typical field observations of unsafe acts.

AUDIT DISCUSSIONS

Example 1

Auditor: "Hello, I'm Jim Thomen (if auditor is not known by employee) and this is Wayne Lucas." (Pause. Give employee a chance to introduce himself.) "Wayne is a supervisor in the fabrication department. We are making a safety audit." (Pause.) "We have been watching you work. Thank you. You were really working (if true). It is good to see you again (if employee knows auditor). Your name?" (if still unknown to auditor).

Worker: "Bill Jones."

Auditor: "Bill, we would like to talk with you for a few minutes about safety. Is this a convenient time for you?" (Pause.) "Will it be O.K. with your supervisor to take a few moments to discuss safety?" Or, if relief is needed, "We have talked to your foreman about getting you relieved so that we can discuss safety with you. When your relief shows up, we would appreciate your help. We just want you to know what we were up to. Go ahead and keep working while we wait."

When the observed worker is available, off the production line, as necessary, and the audit group has found a relatively quiet area in which a reasonable conversation can be held without the need to shout at each other, then:

Auditor: "As I was saying, we have been watching you work. Did you recognize that we were watching you?"

Worker: "Not really. I realized that you were looking at my job, but I didn't realize you were looking at me."

Auditor: "We were, and we wish you had realized it, because you may have given more thought to what you were doing. Anyway, I want you to know we saw you doing some *good* things regarding safety. For example, you are wearing hearing protection. Great!" (Pause.) "You have on long sleeves and they are buttoned down at the wrist. They are not rolled up half-way." (Pause.) "Why do you think we are pleased to see your sleeves buttoned?"

Worker: "Because, if they were not, they may become loose and be a hazard because a sleeve could catch on something and cause me to lose my balance, or something."

Auditor: "You got it." (Auditor might give a thumbs up signal. This communicates approval to the employee, but also to other employees who may be watching.) (Pause.) "We see that you have on steel-toed boots, as well. Good. Glad to see you using good judgment (or "following the rules" if steel-toed shoes are required). "We also noticed that you were using a fixed-end wrench. Good! What kind of wrench might you have been using which would have been less safe?"

Worker: "An adjustable-end wrench."

Auditor: "And why are adjustable-end wrenches less safe?"

Worker: "Because they slip."

Auditor: "And why else?"

Worker: "They round off the nut when they slip and make the wrench all the more likely to slip."

Auditor: "Right!" (Pause.) "Do you have any trouble getting (or keeping) the proper size of end wrenches for each job?"

Worker: "No trouble." Or "Not usually."

Auditor: "Bill, do you have a full set of fixed-end wrenches?"

Worker: "I have for American standards, but not for metric sizes. I have to get those from the tool room."

Auditor: "Does the tool room always have what you want?"

Worker: "Not always."

Auditor: "Is the problem just that the tool room does not stock enough or are mechanics keeping them in their toolboxes rather than returning them to the tool room?"

Worker: "Yes, I believe that is the basic problem."

Auditor: "Bill, I'll mention this in our report, but have you discussed this with your supervisor? (Pause.) "If not, I'm counting on you to do so. Give him a chance to correct the situation. If you have, have you brought this up at a safety meeting? What I'm getting at is that I would like you to try to make the 'system' work before we make an end-run around the system, by my getting involved too soon."

(Note: If worker has done all that is reasonable for a worker to do, then one of the auditors can volunteer to follow up in a way that does not produce negative feedback to the worker. This aspect needs to be very carefully considered. Unfortunately, not all first-line supervisors are sympathetic to the idea that an employee "go around" him or her by bringing up a problem to someone other than themselves.)

Auditor: "Bill, I'd like to move on and mention some other things for which we want to commend you. We noticed that when you picked up the hose you bent your knees rather than your back. Good! That habit is going to serve you well as you get older!" (Pause.)

Note: It is desirable to pause between mention of various topics to give the auditor time to choose words carefully but also to give the person observed time to reflect on his or her behavior/work practices, both "good" and "bad."

Auditor: "We also noticed that as you lifted the hose up above shoulder height to get it in place to be attached to the connection flange, you got help and had prepositioned a bolt so as to be able to secure the hose quickly. This really reduced the effort required to hold the hose in place as you made the connection." (Pause.) "I believe those were the items that we had identified for which we want to congratulate you." (Pause.)

Worker: "Well, I suppose now you are going to tell me the bad news."

Auditor: "No. We did see some things we believe you could have improved upon, but I believe you already know what most of them are if we give you the time to think about what you've been doing since we started watching you."

Worker: "Well, one thing. I don't suppose you like all these hoses lying around."

Auditor: "It is not really what we like or don't like. What we are asking you to do is think about how you can get this job done without getting hurt. Do you think the arrangement of these hoses can be improved?"

Worker: "Sure. If I had them out of the way, coiled up and then uncoiled them as I attached them, I would not have to step on them or over them as I got things ready."

Auditor: "Yes, we saw you step on the hoses several times and then you carefully stepped over the hoses several times. You avoided slipping or tripping. We agree, however, that your suggestion about better orderliness is a good one, and we support the time needed to make this work space more orderly. In fact, the job might even go faster, because you won't have your attention divided between trying to accomplish your work and having to watch so carefully where you are stepping. Good. You've gotten one of the items on our list."

Worker: "You mean there are more?"

Auditor: "Yes. We have an item relative to the risks associated with attaching the hose to the connection over here—above your shoulder height."

Worker: (Pause.) "I don't believe I see what you have in mind."

Auditor: "What is one of the risks associated with doing work above shoulder height?"

Worker: "Oh, you mean eye protection."

Auditor: "Yes, that's what we were concerned about. Bill, you mentioned draining the hose. Is there some aspect of that operation that could have been improved upon?" (Auditors are now looking at the work area, which has been covered with spilled liquid hydrocarbon material.)

Worker: "Yes, I should have drained the hose directly into the chemical sewer, rather than creating a job for someone else to clean up."

Auditor: "Yes, we agree, but also you would be providing yourself a cleaner workspace, right? Bill, we have two other thoughts. Back to your use of fixed-end wrenches for coupling these hoses. We were pleased to see you using that wrench rather than the adjustable-end type. However, we had a couple of thoughts about the operation in which you joined two lengths of hoses together by bolting the flanges together. Perhaps if I simulate what you were doing, you'll be able to see what we saw."

Worker: "Well, I know one thing. You think I should have worn gloves, right?"

Auditor: "Bill, it is not so much what we think, but what you think. Our purpose is not to tell you what you should do, but to get you to think about what you should do, and to give you an opportunity to see yourself and visualize what might go wrong and how you can help yourself. What about gloves?"

Worker: "No doubt about it. I should have worn gloves, but the storeroom was out of my size, and I lost mine last week."

Auditor: "Did you tell your foreman? He may have a pair or two in his desk, and he will undoubtedly want to follow up on this problem."

Worker: "No, I haven't, but I see your point."

Auditor: "Bill, we've covered the protective equipment item—but there was a work procedure or body position item that we have in mind. You were quite properly squatting while you were working on the flange connection, but your hand position was a problem. Do you know what we are thinking about?"

Worker: "I don't believe I do."

Auditor: "Take a look at what you see. I'll simulate."

Worker: "Oh, you mean if the wrench slipped, my knuckles might be scraped against the concrete. I was pushing down. But I don't see any way to avoid the problem—one hand has to be pulling up and the other must be pushing down."

Auditor: "There is no other way? In fact, on the last bolt, you changed your body position and avoided this problem. Do you remember what you did on that last bolt?" (Pause.)

Worker: "I believe I got the hose up in the air, off the concrete, and therefore had plenty of clearance between my hands and the concrete."

Auditor: "Good, that's right. Could you have done the same thing for all the bolts?"

Worker: "I believe so. (Pause) You guys really did watch me, didn't you?"

Auditor: "Yes, Bill, we did. We did because it is what people actually do or fail to do that gets them or a fellow employee injured. And sometimes it's tough to see yourself, so this safety auditing process is designed to help you see yourself. If you'll think back now, is there anything else that you can identify that we might have thought could be done more safely?"

Worker: "I don't believe I can think of anything else."

Auditor: "Bill, you got them all. You knew every one of the items we had on our minds—gloves, glasses, hand position, housekeeping and hose drainage. I hope we've been of some help, and again it was good to see you wearing long sleeves, and using the correct wrenches and good high topped steel-toed shoes." (Pause.) "Now, we have examined you and your work rather carefully. It is your turn now. Any thing about safety around this place that's on your mind? Any problems that are not getting solved? Any ideas for improvement?"

Worker: "Not that come to mind just now."

Auditor: "You're sure?"

Worker: "Well, you remember, I mentioned metric-sized wrenches. That's a problem—has been a problem—and my foreman, Jim, says he has asked about this several times but nothing seems to be happening."

Auditor: "Thanks, Bill. I'm not sure we'll be any more successful than Jim, but we'll look into it and see if this is something that can be improved upon—keeping in mind costs, etc. We appreciate your bringing it up. Anything else?"

Worker: "No, I don't believe so."

Auditors: "Thanks, Bill, we appreciate your efforts toward making this a good, injury-free workplace. We are still having some injuries which means we all need to keep working on our safety and keep safety at the top of our priority list. Thanks again, Bill. It's time to go back to work! Take care."

Upon completion of the field auditing portion of the safety audit, the two auditors should find an area away from the workplace, sit down, and review what they have seen and heard and what their thoughts are about these items. They should focus only on those items on which they would like to see improvements, and these items need not have been discussed with the employee who was audited. After reaching conclusions about what improvements would be appropriate, the auditors make their audit report by listing all the items in need of improvement. They then send the report to the safety coordinator (supervisor) for integration with all the other audit reports for summarizing and reporting to the Central Safety Committee (see Chapter 7).

Example 2

Auditor: "Hello, Bill. Wayne and I are on a safety audit; we've been watching you work. Thank you; we've been walking now for 4 or 5 minutes trying to find someone actively working. We caught you!" (Pause, smiling.) "Bill, are you on a rush or critical job—that is, will you be in any trouble with operations or your foreman if we take some of your time for safety?"

Worker: "No, I think it's O.K.—for safety. What have I been doing wrong?"

Auditor: "Bill, before we talk about anything you can do that would represent a safety upgrade, we'd like to point out some things we were pleased to see. You have your hard hat on, your ear protectors in, you are wearing safety glasses, and you are wearing safety shoes. You are also wearing gloves. You seem to have your protective equipment in full use." (Pause.)

Worker: "Why did you come see me? What's wrong?"

Auditor: "Bill, we are not here to find fault. We want to reinforce good behavior, good work practices, and if there are any changes which represent better practices we want to help you recognize them. It will be of more lasting value if you think of them rather than have us tell you. Beyond that, if all we did was tell you, it would suggest that we know of all the hazards of the job, and we don't. But, together, we may recognize some that were not apparent at first." (Pause.)

"Bill, while most of what we saw was very commendable, we did observe one thing we'd like to discuss. But before going on to that, we want to recognize that we believe you have adequately secured your work in the vise; you haven't misused the vise by supporting the piece only on one edge of the vise jaws. The vise is big enough to get a firm grip—you didn't pound on the handle or use a 'cheater' on the handle. Your work was at a convenient height. Did you have to disassemble this from the unit to get it at a convenient height?"

Worker: "Yes, but also I did not want to subject the unit to the hammering force I thought was going to be needed to drive this pin out."

Auditor: "Were there any other actions you took to make the job easier or safer?"

Worker: "Well, yes. Before lunch I put some penetrating oil on the pin, hoping this would loosen it some."

Auditor: "Good! Bill, do you know why we knew someone was working in here?"

Worker: "Because you could hear me pounding?"

Auditor: "Yes." (Pause.) "What about that pounding, any thoughts on the subject?"

Worker: "Well, I should not have been pounding steel against steel."

Auditor: "Why not?"

Worker: "Because the drift pin will become mushroomed and may have a piece broken off."

Auditor: "Looking at this pin and its mushroomed head, it appears that a piece has recently been broken off. Look how "fresh" that spot is."

Worker: "Believe you are right."

Auditor: "What would be a better way to accomplish this job?"

Worker: "Use of a wooden or bronze mallet would be safer."

Auditor: "Do you have a bronze mallet?"

Worker: "Yes."

Auditor: "Any problem with bronze?"

Worker: "No, not really, but it does require frequent 'dressing' of the mallet head."

Auditor: "What additional precautions might be in order?"

Worker: "I believe a face-shield would be a good idea, and also long sleeves."

Auditor: "Good! We thought so, too."

Auditor: "Bill, may I look at your hands?" (The auditor should extend his own hands, palms up.)

Worker: "Sure."

Auditor: "Bill, as I recall, you are married. I don't see a wedding ring."

Worker: "No, I don't wear my wedding ring, or any rings for that matter. I think they are very hazardous. I've seen what can happen when a ring gets caught on something."

Auditor: "You actually saw a finger injured from a ring?"

Worker: "Yes. I was out on the shipping dock looking at a forklift truck. One of the shipping operators was moving pallets around. He tried to remove one of those heavy oak pallets from the top of a pile that was about a foot above his head. He lost control of it, and as it fell to the floor a nail that was in the pallet caught this guy's ring and jerked his finger off. They did not find the finger until three days later when another operator found the finger inside a cotton glove in the pocket of his cloak."

Auditor: "That is a tragic story, particularly since the finger was not found in time to attempt surgical reattachment."

Auditor: "Do you know of any mechanics who wear rings?"

Worker: "Yes."

Auditor: "What do you think about that?"

Worker: "I believe they are making a big mistake. In most cases, it's their wedding ring and they or their wives don't want them to take it off."

Auditor: "What would you think about a rule around here that specified 'No rings are to be worn while inside the plant, except in offices and the cafeteria'?" (Pause.) "How much of a problem do you think we'd create if we established such a rule?"

Worker: "Most of the guys would react O.K. Even those that wear them know it's not a good thing to do. You might have a problem with one or two guys—probably depend on how you approach them. You might have better luck talking them into it, rather than just telling them they have to take it off."

Auditor: "Thanks, Bill, for the comments and your recognition of the hazards of mushroomed drift pins. The more I think about that pin, I don't believe you mushroomed that pin just now. Some other folks have been mistreating that pin also. How about talking up this hazard with the crew? Maybe we can save someone a tooth or even an eye—because safety glasses alone don't provide full protection." (Pause.) "Anything else on your mind, Bill, about safety?"

Worker: "I don't think so."

Auditor: "Well, we'll be on our way. Again, Bill, thanks for your safety efforts. The fewer injuries we have, the better off we'll all be, including the business itself. And that's good for us, too. We'll see you." (Shake hands.)

The auditors should now review what they have seen, comparing what they have seen vis-à-vis what they would have preferred to have seen. They should record these preferences and forward them to the site safety supervisor, or other supervisor, as outlined in Chapter 7.

Example 3

Auditor: "Hello, I'm Jim Thomen and this is Wayne Lucas. We are making a safety audit. We've been watching you work." (Pause.) "I need your help in this process; I am from Du Pont and I'm showing Wayne what I mean by a safety audit. Wayne works for ABC Company. Are you a contractor employee or are you an ABC employee?"

Worker: "I work for ABC."

Auditor: "Wayne is from operations. I hope you didn't mind us watching you. By the way, this will be painless, no feedback to your supervisor from us. Also, this is going to take a few minutes. Will you be in trouble with your boss if we delay your work a few minutes?"

Worker: "I don't think so, but I would appreciate your telling him, so he'll know I had a little interruption."

Auditor: "Sure, no problem. What's his name and where can we find him?"

Worker: "Randy Smith. His office is in the electrical shop."

Auditor: "Good, we'll let him know, but we won't discuss any details. That's just between us. Now, what's your name?"

Worker: "John Evans."

Auditor: "John, what we do on a safety audit is to look at what you are actually doing—check out your protective equipment, your body position relative to any possible hazards, the tools and equipment you are using, any procedures you are using or should be using, and the housekeeping situation."

Worker: "Well, I'm already in trouble. I'd be fired by now if I was working for Du Pont."

Auditor: "What do you mean? Have you worked for Du Pont somewhere?"

Worker: "Yes, I worked as a construction electrician on the Corpus Christi chlorine project."

Auditor: "What do you mean you would have been fired?"

Worker: "Well, to start with, I don't have my personal lock on the switch box for this circuit. Second, I'm not wearing safety glasses, and, third, I'm not wearing safety shoes."

Auditor: "Those would have all been required at Du Pont?"

Worker: "Oh, yes, and when we were working on the pier we had to wear life preservers. And those things were hot."

Auditor: "You mean, if you forgot one of those required personal protective items, you would have been fired?"

Worker: "No doubt about it."

Auditor: "Did you ever know or hear of anyone who got fired for not wearing the required safety gear?"

Worker: "No, I don't think they ever had to fire anyone for a safety gear violation. Everyone knew the rules and followed them. Du Pont was tough on safety."

Auditor: "Too tough?"

Worker: "No, it was for your own good."

Auditor: "John, would you work for Du Pont again if you had the opportunity—recognizing that they are tough on safety?"

Worker: "You bet."

Auditor: "You don't mind putting up with all that safety business?"

Worker: "Sure, I don't like it, but it makes good sense. I had the feeling that I would finish every day in good shape—no missing pieces."

Auditor: "If all those safety rules make sense, why don't you follow them here?"

Worker: "I don't know; they are such a bother and they don't *make* you here. I guess I just have to be made to follow them, even if they are for my own good."

Auditor: "Interesting discussion, John. Really a rather amazing discussion." (Pause.) "John, I don't want you to think that everything you were doing was wrong, and certainly shoes and glasses are under your individual and direct control—something you can fix yourself. Think about your Du Pont experience and see if you can use that experience to help yourself. The lock-out procedure is, of course, something you will have to work out with ABC. What do you think Randy's reaction would be if you asked him for permission to use your own lock on this circuit rather than rely on a tag that someone else puts on?"

Worker: "I don't know."

Auditor: "Why not give it a try; you may start something good! John, we did see some good things we'd like to comment on. Your housekeeping is excellent. You are cleaning up as you go. The debris you are creating you are putting into a waste box on your tool buggy. You are using a flashlight, so you can really see what you are doing. You have your circuit diagram immediately available and we saw you refer to it several times. You weren't trying to remember complicated circuitry. You were working from an appropriate ladder and were in good position on the ladder. You had your tools in your tool belt when they were not actually in use. You seem to have a great assortment of tools available. To the best of our knowledge you were using the right tool for the job all the time we were watching you. Are we right on this last item?"

Worker: "Yes, as a matter of fact, you may have noticed that I started to use an adjustable-end wrench at one point but replaced it with a small socket wrench."

Auditor: "Yes, we saw that. Do you think you changed because we were watching?"

Worker: "Probably—I don't know."

Auditor: "Well, if we helped, good! John, before we go, is there anything on your mind about safety?"

Worker: "Well, yes. It may seem silly, but I don't know why we don't have to wear a hard hat or perhaps just a bump hat inside the reactor area. I think it's because it is hot, the piping is crowded, and maybe it has something to do with radiation. I don't know. Hard hats are required out here, but in there where the hazard is greater they are not required. It doesn't make sense to me."

Auditor: "John, sounds like you have identified a tough one. Have you talked with your foreman?"

Worker: "Yes, but he does not know either."

Auditor: "John, we'll look into this. But I'm not at all sure we'll be able to resolve or get this issue resolved. It may be bigger than all of us. We will have a look—ask some questions—see if there are reasons we haven't thought of. We'll have to get back to you on this one. John, thank you. And Wayne, this was not planned. John was not a 'plant.' He is just a guy who has worked for Du Pont at a site where the safety effort was well directed. Again, John, thank you, and don't forget what you learned at Du Pont."

Following this audit, the auditors will want to discuss why safety rules at ABC Company don't get followed. Why are they treated as suggestions or recommendations rather than rules that must, as a condition of employment, be followed? (Note: safety glasses were required; safety shoes were not.) They will need to explore the head protection rule differences between inside and outside the reactor building. And then one of them must find John Evans and tell him what they have learned.

Example 4

Bringing about change is not easy. Old habits and ideas about work can be held onto tenaciously. I recall making a safety audit on Dick, a journeyman sheetmetal worker in Illinois one day. Two of his upper level supervisors were with me. The audit took place as follows:

Auditor: "Hello, Dick. May I have your attention for few minutes?"
Worker: "Sure, what's up?"
Auditor: "I'm Jim Thomen. Do you know these fellows?"
Worker: "Hi, Bob, Harry."
Auditor: "We have been making a safety audit. We've been watching you drill those holes. We noticed that you are wearing safety glasses, as well as safety shoes. Also, the sheet metal is well positioned and clamped so as not to move. And the lighting is good." (Pause.) "Dick, is there anything, however, that you could have done to improve the safety of the job?"
Worker: "Well, I could have center-punched the holes so as to help keep the drill from moving from the correct position."
Auditor: "Good, we noticed that as well."
Worker: "The reason I didn't was that the position of the holes was unimportant."

The audit team said nothing—just listened. When the craftsman finished his explanation, the audit team remained silent, thinking about what had been said. After a few seconds—it seemed like a minute or two—I continued.

Auditor: "Is there anything else that you might have in mind regarding the safety of the work you are doing?"
Worker: "Well, yes. The electric cord to this drill is a tripping hazard because it is always on the floor getting in my way."
Auditor: "I'm glad you recognized the cord as a hazard; it is one of the things we also noticed. Any thoughts about how this hazard might be eliminated?"
Worker: "An overhead retractable reel for the electrical outlet would solve the problem. In this way, only enough cord to do the job would be used, and it would be up on the table, not down on the floor. If it got in the way of the work, it could be retrieved by the reel, as needed."

Auditor: "Seems like a good solution. Have you discussed this with your supervisor?"
Worker: "No."
Auditor: "Is this something you would feel comfortable in discussing with your supervisor?"
Worker: "Oh, sure."
Auditor: "Will you do so?"
Worker: "Sure."
Auditor: "If your supervisor agrees that this is something that could be done, you may want to discuss this solution with the other fellows in the crew. What do you think?"
Worker: "Sounds great."
Auditor: "In the meantime, is there another way to keep the cord off the floor?" (While he was thinking, I looked over to the wall electrical outlet and then to the overhead area between the wall and the workbenches.)
Worker: "You mean, by tying the cord from above so as to make it pass overhead to the workbench?"
Auditor: "What do you think?"
Worker: "There is no way to support the cord once it gets over to the bench."
Auditor: "Any ideas for a solution to that problem?"
Worker: "Well, we could put removable stanchions at the corners of the bench and have a hook of some kind to hold the cord up."
Auditor: "Yes, I've seen the problem solved both ways. But what can be done now, today, to get the cord off the floor? If the problem is worth solving tomorrow or next week, or next month, it must be worth solving today, isn't it?"
Worker: "Well, I guess so."
Auditor: "What temporary solution could be put in place, until a permanent one is accomplished? "
Worker: "We could bring the cord to the workbench from the opposite side of the workbench and rope off the area where the cord is on the floor."
Auditor: "Dick, will you do that?"
Worker: "Yes."
Auditor: "Dick, this is a rather inexpensive solution. Could this be a permanent solution?"
Worker: "Yes, but it would be a pain in the butt and inefficient to have to give up that area as a passageway."
Auditor: "Yes, I see what you mean. As this is the case, I guess the cost of a retractable reel or moveable stanchion should be thought of as a cost to avoid irritiation or as an efficiency measure rather than as a cost of safety. I asked Dick for his reaction to this way of looking at things."
Worker: (Reluctantly.) "I guess, when you really think about it, that's the right way of looking at it."

Seldom will it be necessary to spend money for safety. Do what is necessary to accomplish the work safely and then spend money, if justified, to improve the efficiency of doing the work.

Worker: "Back to the hole-drilling. I should have prepunched those holes. Not only would the job have been done safer, but I probably could have done the job faster. I just didn't want to look for my punch. Also, the hammer I was using to bend those corners down wasn't the right hammer. I should have used a sheet metal hammer."

Auditor: "Why?"

Worker: "Well, these hammers (showing the hammer) are different and they affect the results obtained differently." (He demonstrated their use.)

Auditor: "I noticed the hammer you were using and wondered, but did not know for sure, whether it was the correct tool for the job. Thanks for the demonstration. I've learned something. Dick, we have one more item on our minds."

Worker: "You probably think I should be wearing gloves." (He waited for an answer.)

Auditor: "Well, as a matter of fact, the answer is yes, but I'd be interested in your thoughts."

Worker: "Let me tell you a story."

Auditor: "Okay, we'll listen."

Worker: "When I first entered this tin knocking trade, I was put with an old-timer—like me now—an experienced hand. After a few days, and a few cuts and knicks, I asked if I could get some gloves. The response was 'Boy, in this trade you don't *buy* gloves; you *grow* them!' He put his hands out to show me how tough his hands were. That was the end of the conversation. In this trade, you don't wear gloves."

Auditor: "Dick, it is time for the trade to change its view on how to protect hands. There is no need to have hands as hard and calloused as yours just because you are a sheetmetal worker. Dick, I know some very skilled craftsmen who do not have hands as rough as yours because they have been required by their supervisor to wear gloves. However, using gloves means getting gloves that fit each individual and that are flexible enough to get good hand 'feel.' Grabbing a pair of pipefitter's gloves is not adequate. But, Dick, I'm not telling you that you should wear gloves. There is no rule in this shop requiring you to wear gloves, so you are free to do what you want to do."

Poor work habits are passed from one generation to the next, unless management intervenes—intelligently. In this case, a lot of talk about gloves is going to be needed. A variety of gloves should to be made available and craftsmen should be encouraged to test them by use. Unfortunately, after all the talk and testing, it will probably require a serious hand injury before a requirement to wear gloves when handling sheetmetal can be successfully introduced in this workshop. Bringing about change is the essence of management. Successful managers are those who bring about change while securing the support of employees who are impacted by the change. This philosophy does not imply that support must always be established before the fact, but it helps.

Auditor: "Dick, thanks for your active and constructive participation in this audit process. Do you have any concerns or suggestions regarding safety in your work or on the site?"

Worker: "Well, yes, there is an item I'd like to bring up. I'm getting a little hard of hearing, and I know the shop is a noisy place in general, but some types of work are particularly noisy. Do you think there is a need for ear protection in this shop? I don't think I'd like to wear them, but what is your opinion? Should we wear earplugs in this shop?"

Auditor: "Have you discussed this with the other fellows or with your boss?"

Worker: "Not with the boss, but we've talked about it among ourselves."

Auditor: "I suggest you raise the question with your supervisor. See if the Safety Department can make something called a noise survey. This is a procedure in which actual noise levels are measured around the shop as well as the noise produced by specific operations in the shop. There are well-established, medically based rules to decide whether hearing protection is needed, depending upon the actual noise level. Measuring the noise level in the shop is the best way to start finding an answer to your question. Start by getting the facts. Dick, will you discuss this with your supervisor?"

Worker: "Yes."

Auditor: "Great. That's the way to go. This has been a really good audit. (Pause.) Now Dick, what are the items you are going to discuss with your boss?"

Worker: "The electrical cord and the noise survey."

Auditor: "Good. And thank you again for your efforts in working safely."

The audit team then went back to the office of one of the team members and reviewed the audit, recording those items that would represent improvements. This list is shown in Figure 8-4.

A copy of this report was then sent to the site safety supervisor. The safety supervisor receives a copy of all such audits, each month, and analyzes the findings. Based on the findings, he (or she) can recommend to the Central Safety Committee any actions he believes are appropriate. These recommendations flow from line supervisory observations and are therefore much more likely to gain approval and subsequent support than recommendations based solely on the safety supervisor's personal judgment. They are line management driven recommendations.

Several auditing techniques were demonstrated in this audit:

1. No instructions, just leading questions
2. No rule making on the spot
3. No arguments[1]
4. No criticism, but confirmation of acknowledged unsafe acts
5. No undercutting of the first-line supervisor[2]
6. Careful listening; patience; willingness to learn rather than instruct
7. Courtesy

AUDIT REPORTS

The audit reports for each of these audits is shown below. Differing formats are shown for each example.

Example 1

Figure 8-1

Manufacturing Management Safety Audit Report

10/1/90

By: J. R. Thomen
W. P. Lucas

Time: 10:00 A.M. to 11:15 A.M.
Number of persons audited: 1

Item:

1. Operator working in area cluttered with hoses, stepping on them. Unsafe act
2. Operator in the plant making overhead hose connection without eye protection. Rule violation
3. Operator drained liquid hydrocarbon onto concrete working area in plant. Unsafe act
4. Operator handling hose coupling without gloves. Unsafe act
5. Operator using spanner wrenches in a manner such that, if wrench slipped, hand would hit concrete floor—poor body position. Unsafe act

Summary: five unsafe acts, one of which was a rule violation.

Comments:

1. We believe it is time to establish a rule that "drainage of hydrocarbons from hoses and piping must be contained and disposed of in an environmentally sound manner."

Note: Availability of metric wrenches apparently needs improvement.

Example 2

Figure 8-2

Management Safety Audit Report

Area: ______________________

Date: ______________________

Auditors: ______________________

Items Observed:*	**Classification**
1. Mechanic hammering a steel drift with a steel hammer.	Unsafe Act
2. Mechanic using a drift with mushroomed head.	Unsafe Act
3. Mechanic hammering a drift without use of face shield.	Unsafe Act

Comments:

1. Mechanic supports a no ring rule. However, he suggests we start by "talking rings off" rather than immediately issuing an edict that rings may not be worn.

* All material in this report that is not in bold type should be handwritten.

Example 3

Figure 8-3

Management Safety Audit Report

Area: Electrical Craft
Date: 10/8/90
Auditors: J. R. Thomen
W. P. Lucas
Items needing improvement:*

1. Electrician not wearing safety glasses as required by rule.

2. Electrician not wearing safety shoes. Safety shoes are not required, but we believe they should be. The shoe policy has been a topic of discussion for long enough. A decision to require safety shoes in the plant and in all craft buildings should be made.

3. The question of head protection—hard hats are required outside the reactor area, but not inside it. This issue needs to be resolved and a clear explanation, in writing, of why our policy is what it is.

4. The question of use of personal locks for locking out equipment in addition to lockout tags was discussed. We recommend the creation of an ad hoc subcommittee of the Central Safety Committee to study this issue and make a recommendation. The Rules and Procedures subcommittee has discussed this, but can't seem to make up its mind. We would be pleased to serve on the ad hoc subcommittee. The government is beginning to make noises about requiring locks. We might as well be ahead of the game!

* All material not shown in bold type should be handwritten.

Figure 8-4

Management Safety Audit

Group: *Construction*
Date: 11/1/90
Observation:

1. Management does not know the noise levels of various areas and operations throughout the site. We believe management should know. A site noise survey should be m: starting in the sheetmetal shop.

2. No existing job procedure requires pre-punching of holes to be drilled in sheet metal. We believe there should be.

3. Electrical cord was draped onto floor, constituting a tripping hazard. This hazard needs resolution.

4. Mechanic was handling sharp-edged sheetmetal piece without wearing gloves. There is no rule or procedure requiring gloves to be worn, but we think this would be an improvement in work procedures.

5. Safety glasses did not have side-shields. Side-shields are not required, but we believe they would afford improved protection.

By: J. R. Thomen, A. B. Smith, J. F. Jones

The preceding four examples were taken from actual audits. They illustrate the technique and several ways of reporting results. The list that follows, Figure 8-5, is also taken from actual audits. They have been chosen as being typical of what will be seen during audits within well-managed companies.

This remark is not meant to be critical. It simply reflects the realities of the workplace even in organizations that are well managed, have better than average injury performance, and are sincerely trying to improve.

The standards expressed in the audits are those of my clients who accompanied me on the audits during which these observations were made. They are not necessarily a reflection of my standards. Standards should be established by line management, not staff personnel or consultants!

In many instances, these observers realized, for the first time, the appropriateness of the standards they espoused. Seeing *is* believing! The large number of notations that standards were inadequate is testimony that standards of performance—rules, procedures, standard operating procedures, design standards, and so forth—are significantly under-utilized by many companies as structural elements in their safety programs.

As with the Management Safety Audit reports shown in Figures 8–1 to 8–4, few unsafe conditions are listed in Figure 8–5. The emphasis in Management Safety Auditing is that of the behavior of people, not the condition of things. Therefore, the temptation to include unsafe conditions in audit reports should normally be resisted. Even so, unsafe conditions will creep into audit reports "without even trying." That is why these examples are essentially devoid of unsafe condition notations. Virtually every unsafe condition can be viewed as an unsafe act—failure to barricade an unsafe condition, locking-out, putting up warning signs, etc.—can be viewed as an unsafe act, as failure to correct it constitutes an unsafe act.

Figure 8-5
Typical Unsafe Conditions and
Unsafe Acts

Unsafe Conditions

1. A disk sander does not have a guard installed. The removal of the guard was an unsafe act, unless properly authorized. Failure to replace it was an unsafe act.

2. The bottom step of a new stairway has not yet been put in place. Stairway is not barricaded. Leaving the stairway in this condition was an unsafe act.

3. Laboratory apparatus is installed in such a manner that the fume hood sash cannot be lowered. This is evidence of a previous unsafe act.

4. Laboratory equipment is precariously stacked at edge of overhead shelf. The act of stacking was an unsafe act.

5. Pipe flanges are bolted together with bolts not long enough to engage all the nut threads. This is evidence of a previous unsafe act.

6. Diamond plate on floor of elevator is worn smooth—unsafe condition.

Unsafe Acts

1. Observed laborer hand digging directly under the scoop of a front-end loader. Unsafe body position.

2. Observed numerous contractor employees not wearing safety glasses as required by rule. Only reluctantly did they comply.

3. Observed a mechanic without eye protection while grinding. Rule violation.

4. Observed loose tools stored on top of gear box on lathe. Unsafe storage of tools—unsafe act. Inadequate housekeeping procedures.

5. Observed first-line supervisor not wearing safety shoes as required by rule. Rule violation.

6. Observed many mechanical craft personnel and their supervision wearing rings in violation of written rule prohibiting the wearing of rings. This is evidence of extremely poor safety discipline and failure to enforce established rules.

7. Repeatedly observed management personnel ascending and descending stairs without holding onto hand rail. Unsafe acts. Inadequate safety rules.

8. Observed several supervisors driving cars on site without wearing seat belts. Rule violation.

9. Observed several injuries that had not been reported to supervisors or medical. Unsafe acts. (No rule existed for reporting injuries that were thought not in need of treatment.) Inadequate safety rules.

10. Observed contractor employee checking railroad rails not wearing safety glasses as required by rule. Employee was allowed to continue to work even after need for glasses had been estabished. Inadequate rule enforcement; supervisor did not know how to enforce.

11. Observed office personnel using filing cabinets that were not bolted or weighted to prevent tipping. Unsafe act because of use. Equipment inadequately restrained. Inadequate standards.

12. Observed supervisor riding a bicycle with only one hand free to use on handle bars; other hand and arm were supporting a large collection of papers. Unsafe act. Inadequate standards.

13. Observed a manhole cover being propped open by a valve handle to permit hoses to enter manhole. Work site was not barricaded. Unsafe practices. Inadequate standards.

14. Observed a nitrogen hose being used as a water hose. Rule violation.

15. Observed process operator remove a process probe from a process line which was thought to have been completely depressurized and vented. In fact, flare gas pressure was present. Inadequate shutdown procedures. Existing procedures not strictly followed by direction of supervisor. Inadequate supervisory safety discipline.

16. Observed contractor personnel removing bolts from a flange by pounding on wrench handle with a sledge hammer. Unsafe act.

17. Observed a group of contractor employees performing electrical work. Employees were standing and walking on electrical cables, some were not wearing safety glasses as required, and some had no goggles on their hard hats as required, some were wearing rings. Tool boxes were located at the edge of an elevated permanent platform that had no toe-boards. Unsafe acts; rule violations. Inadequate standards.

18. Observed a forklift truck being operated with elevated forks without a pallet on them. Rule violation.

19. Observed stores operator opening a box with knife that was not equipped with hand guards. Gloves were not being worn and knife was not sheathed after use. Unsafe acts. Inadequate standards.

20. Observed scissors with pointed ends in desk drawer, unsheathed. Unsafe act. Inadequate standards.

21. Observed contract welder welding from a ladder approximately 3 meters off the ground. Area was not barricaded. Unsafe act.

22. Observed welding being done without a designated fire watch. Unsafe act. Inadequate standards.

23. Observed two contractor electricians working on an outlet box. They had not personally established that circuits were de-energized. Unsafe act. Inadequate standards.

24. Observed welding being done in close proximity to other employees who were involved in the job. Eye protection from welding flash burns was not being worn. Unsafe acts. Inadequate standards.

25. Observed a contract electrician preparing to make a cable splice. He was sitting on top of a control cabinet, sawing a piece of cable while holding it barehanded against his thigh for support. He was not wearing eye protection as required. Multiple unsafe acts and rule violation.

26. Observed the unfinished installation of new grating steps. Steps were not barricaded; one step was missing! Unsafe condition created by the unsafe acts of installers.

27. Observed employee cleaning parts in an acid bath. Safety glasses were being worn, but because of hazard potential face shield should have been worn. Unsafe act. Employee did not understand composition or hazards of bath. Material Safety Data Sheets not available. Unsafe act. Inadequate standard operating procedure.

28. Observed employee cut tygon tubing with open razor blade. Unsafe act. Inadequate standards.

29. Observed two craftsmen on a mezzanine area approximately 15 feet above the concrete floor below. One was standing at the edge of mezzanine with one foot on an electrical distribution conduit (wire-way) and the other on a heating duct beyond the edge of the mezzanine. He steadied himself by hanging on to an overhead pipe with one hand while he attempted to "sweat" in a copper tube joint with a torch in the other hand. He was not wearing a lifeline.

The second craftsman was standing with his left foot on an A-frame step ladder at about the fourth step and was leaning over the top of an electrical cabinet with his right knee on top of the cabinet. He was trying to provide solder for the first craftsman. Rings were being worn. No gloves were worn. Multiple unsafe acts. Inadequate standards.

30. Observed silicon wafers being cleaned by two operators. Glove length was inadequate to provide wrist protection; safety glasses were worn down on nose, providing inadequate eye protection. Unsafe acts. Inadequate standards.

31. Observed "professional" employee descending stairway with both hands fully occupied in carrying materials. Unsafe act. Inadequate standards.

32. Observed laboratorian using chemical fume hood with sashes continuously left open. Unsafe act. Inadequate standards.

33. Observed employee entering manhole. While facing the manhole, employee twisted one leg enough to engage foot on first rung of vertical ladder within manhole. His next step was accomplished by completing this twisting motion until other foot could be placed on rung of ladder. No hand supports were available. Unsafe act, induced by equipment inadequacy.

34. Observed the unloading of a truck at an unloading dock. Truck was not chocked. "Sneaker" shoes were being worn by some storesmen. Unsafe acts. Inadequate standards. Supervision did not think they could enforce safety shoe rule because of presence of outside drivers.

35. Observed a laboratory scale extrusion operation. Technician was handling polymer in the quench tank without gloves. Safety glasses were worn well down on nose. Technician burned back of hand as we watched because he allowed it to touch extruder discharge port. Fume exhaust ducts were poorly positioned above feed hoppers and no dust mask was being worn. Unsafe acts. Inadequate standard operating procedures.

36. Observed welder working in an open area in which several other persons were also working. No "blinds" were in place to shield others from hazards of welding. Unsafe act. Inadequate standards.

37. Observed a high-speed winder in operation from which the cover of a gear box had been removed. Unsafe act. Inadequate standard operating procedures or rules.

38. Observed laboratory technician working at several fume hoods in different laboratory modules. She wore no safety glasses and carried glass beakers in bare hands while using the building corridor to move between hoods. The internal laboratory route was excessively congested. Rule violation. Unsafe acts. Inadequate standards.

39. Observed truck drivers routinely exiting their cabs while facing outwards. Unsafe act. Inadequate standards.

40. Observed storesmen jump from truck bed to ground. Unsafe act. Inadequate standards.

41. Observed burn on research professional's hand. Employee acknowledged she had burned it with nitric acid because she was not wearing gloves. Injury had not been reported. Unsafe act. Rule violation.

42. Observed electricians working approximately 10 feet above floor level climbing and standing on process piping while not wearing safety belts. Unsafe acts. Inadequate standards.

43. Observed water treatment operator. Ensuing discussion revealed he had "never seen a written job procedure" and had experienced an incident in which he "got a good snootful" of chlorine gas as a result of not switching chlorine cylinders in proper sequence. Unsafe acts. Inadequate standard operating procedures and/or training.

44. Observed a number of office personnel with both feet upon their desks. Unsafe acts. Inadequate standards.

45. Observed laboratory technician place entire head inside fume hood while reactions were taking place. Tubing was not clamped securely to associated glassware.

She was not knowledgeable concerning a serious injury that had occurred the previous day in an adjacent laboratory. Unsafe acts. Inadequate safety communication.

46. Observed extruder operator. He wore no arm protection, although evidence of small burns on his arms was present. Unsafe act. Inadequate standard operating procedures.

47. Observed a laboratorian using a hood in which the manometer showed no liquid whatsoever. By use of tissue, laboratorian demonstrated the inadequacy of the airflow in this hood, commenting, "It's been this way for over two years." Unsafe act; use of defective equipment. Inadequate safety management.

48. Observed "member of road gang" jump from road to bed of truck while the truck was moving with a tank wagon in tow. Unsafe act. Inadequate standards.

49. Observed craftsman using portable grinder in tank farm area with guard removed and plugged into a two-prong receptacle at the end of a long series of extension cords in a 220 v electrical service. The ground wire had been "lost"; the last extension cord was a 110 v two-wire cord. The fire watch occasionally let water splash into the receptacle. Unsafe acts. Inadequate safety management.

50. Observed jackhammer operator using jackhammer without eye protection, hearing protection, or gloves.

QUESTIONS FOR USE IN AUDITING

Experienced auditors develop a repertoire of questions for use during auditing. They have found these questions valuable in stimulating productive thinking and discussion during an audit. Some of these are directed to supervision (as when supervisor/subordinate audit teams are utilized, or when the audit team discusses safety with the responsible supervisor prior to proceeding with the audit); most are directly usable with employees during the auditing process.

Figure 8-6

Questions for Use in Auditing

1. Can you think of anything you did that could have been done more safely?
2. What hazards exist in the work you were doing? How could you have improved your protection from these hazards? How about the protection of others?
3. If you were training a new employee or your son or daughter, would you have done anything differently?
4. What safety rules are you most tempted to violate?
5. Are there any safety rules or procedures that you think are inappropriate? Unnecessary? Make things worse rather than better?
6. We have several items that we think could have been improved upon. Can you think what they are?
7. Which safety rules do you think are most frequently violated? Why?
8. Which safety rules do you have the most trouble following (enforcing)? Why?
9. May I see your hands? (Look for callouses, small untreated injuries, oil, grease or product contamination, rings, etc.) Anything different between my hands (show

hands) and yours? Are these differences necessary? How could these differences be minimized?

10. What was the last injury in your work group?

11. What was the last lost-time injury on the site?

12. What was the most hazardous thing you have done since getting out of bed today? (Desirable answer is: "Drive to work.") What did you do to protect yourself from the hazards of being on the public roads? (Desirable answer: "Wore my seat belts.")

13. Are you a sometimes wearer of seat belts or an always wearer of seat belts?

14. Do you always require passengers to wear seat belts? What about rear-seat passengers? What about when you or your spouse is dressed in "party" clothes?

15. Where do most fatal injuries occur? (Answer: roads). What can you do to protect yourself? (Answer: several defensive driving items, including seat belts.)

16. Why don't you wear seat belts?

17. Do you feel you have the authority to enforce our safety rules? What obstacles do you see to enforcement of safety rules? (Addressed to supervision.)

18. Are there safety rules around here that are not adequately followed?

19. Does supervision pay enough attention to compliance with safety rules, standard operating procedures, lockout procedures, etc.? Do you think supervision is too lax? Too tough? Any examples you care to mention?

20. How is your safety at home different from here at work? Is that good? Why do you think this difference exists? Do you wear your safety shoes and safety glasses when you cut your grass?

21. What do you think about the way injuries are investigated around here?

22. Are employees reluctant to go to medical with a minor injury? If so, why?

23. Do some employees keep Band-aids available for self-treatment? Why?

24. What is your personal safety audit schedule? (Addressed to first-line supervisor.)

25. Any particular safety items you would like for us to look for or emphasize? (Addressed to first-line supervisor.)

26. What safety items have you been stressing lately? (Addressed to first-line supervisor.)

27. What do you think about the quality of recent safety meetings? What was the subject of the last meeting? How are these meetings conducted?

28. How many lost-time injuries have we had so far this month? This year? Is this record better or poorer than our historical one?

29. What do you think is the most serious safety problem we have? That you have?

30. What part of your job do you worry most about? What part of your body is most affected by your work?

31. What was the last injury you had? How could it have been prevented? What steps were taken to prevent reoccurrence? Do you think these were adequate to actually prevent reoccurrence?

SUMMARY

Safety auditing is an acquired management skill. It is acquired through thoughtful practice. Acquisition of the skill is enhanced by conducting the audit in supervisory pairs so as to provide monitoring of the process while it is taking place. Members of the audit team can increase their auditing effectiveness by discussing how an audit turned out—what went well and what led to development of unproductive or defensive responses. Stick with the basic rules:

1. Observe.
2. Recognize good behavior.
3. Ask open-ended questions that lead the employee to recognize opportunities for improvement.
4. Listen to employee concerns. Guide the employee toward self-initiated corrective steps.
5. Thank the employee for his or her efforts to work injury free.

NOTES

1. Dick's initial explanation of why prepunching was unnecessary presented an opportunity for argument. The auditors knew the explanation was faulty; so did Dick. By not challenging the explanation, the auditors did not put Dick on the defensive. But Dick could not stand to let the auditors go away thinking that he, Dick, really was such a poor craftsman that he really believed his own initial explanation. He had to come forth with the correct explanation. Given time and no criticism, Dick could be fully honest.

2. Referring the audited employee to his supervisor not only avoids undercutting the supervisor, but also puts pressure on the supervisor to do something. He cannot really afford to slough off an idea that has found some support from his upper management.

CHAPTER 9

INJURY/INCIDENT INVESTIGATIONS: PRINCIPLES AND TECHNIQUES

PURPOSES OF INJURY/INCIDENT INVESTIGATIONS

Figure 4–2, page 63, depicts the Organization for Safety. The Central Safety, Health, and Environment Committee and its subcommittees are the keystone of this organization. The two supporting activities are Management Safety Audits (Chapters 7 and 8) and Injury/Incident Investigations.[1] Management safety audits are designed to reduce the frequency of occurrence of employee (contractor) unsafe acts. Incident investigations are designed to discover and correct the weaknesses in the organization which permitted the incident to occur. Incident investigations unfortunately constitute a major need in most organizations because of the large number of incidents occurring within the organization. *Investigations of incidents should lead to the recognition of the need to strengthen the other, preventive, portions of the Continuous Safety Management Process* (Figure 4–1, page 62).

This objective has not been the goal of most injury/incident investigations. An examination of thousands of client injury investigations reveals, based on the stated conclusions and actions taken, that the major reasons for undertaking these investigations fall into one of the first six of the categories listed below. Rarely is reason 7 the basis of an incident investigation.

1. To satisfy an organizational need to "investigate injuries" and get the paperwork done.
2. To find out what went wrong, and fix it.
3. To find out who made a mistake so as to assign responsibility.
4. To find out who made a mistake, so as to identify the responsible person and to determine what action regarding this person should be taken—discipline and/or training.

5. To find out what went wrong in the specific instance, but also what else may have been "wrong" that needs fixing.
6. To find out *who* was wrong in the particular instance and also *who* else may have been wrong and in need of "fixing."
7. To analyze the incident as an undesirable event that the safety management process failed to prevent.

Flawed Purposes

The purpose of an injury investigation should not be to fill out injury forms to fulfill insurance or governmental requirements (item 1 above). A good investigation results in the ability to fill out these forms, but that should not be the motivation for injury investigation.

Lower level supervision who frequently see no upper level management participation in the investigative process, and who see no real changes as a result of injury investigations or little to no follow-up on investigations, quite logically conclude that the purpose of an investigation is, indeed, to fill out these forms. This interpretation is a tragedy. Because nothing will be learned from the injury, employee behavior generally, is not likely to be altered and therefore employees will continue to be injured in a similar fashion.

When filling out forms is the motivating factor in injury investigation, the information gathered is frequently fragmentary, superficial, and in error. The supervisor may simply interview the employee and record the person's understanding or version of what happened. In some organizations, the injured is simply asked to fill out the forms himself or herself; then the supervisor confirms correctness of the report by signing the form, with no real investigation being conducted.

All of these categories, with the exception of reason 7, while having some positive aspects, are essentially negative in outlook. The widespread concept that the primary reason for injury/incident investigations is to determine the *cause* of the injury raises a basic question: Why conduct injury/incident investigations? This is not a trivial question. Is the purpose of an investigation to determine cause or to determine what can be done to prevent reoccurrence? If the reason for an investigation is not clearly understood and accepted by potential contributors to the investigation, their contributions will fall short of their full potential. Investigations will therefore fall short in providing the organization the full benefits of the effort expended.

Many safety professionals and others who have devoted time and energy toward injury reduction may respond to this basic question by suggesting that the question is improperly framed—that the issue is not either/or, but both. That is, unless determination of cause is established, removal or abridgement of causal factors cannot take place. Determination of cause is thought to be essential to the taking of informed preventive actions.

Determining Cause: Fixing Blame

My own experience has been that identification of cause, per se, is of little value in injury/incident investigation and may sometimes have a counterproductive effect.

Because injuries arise out of the unsafe act of someone, most frequently the injured himself or herself, establishing cause normally fixes blame (see Chapter 3). It is virtually impossible to separate determining cause from assigning blame, even if it is unspoken. The association is too close to achieve separation, even if desired. This is not a process in which employees normally feel free to contribute all they know about a situation because of concern for themselves or fellow employees. Fixing blame is expected to be followed by appropriate chastisement or discipline. Why else is *who* determined? A procedure that is recognized as a blame fixing one produces a chilling effect on getting the facts of an incident.

Unfortunately, many organizations when seeking causes investigate incidents with an adverserial mentality. This atmosphere may also arise if they are being excessively conditioned by advice from legal counsel. When incident investigation takes place in this fashion, management becomes like a private detective, hunting for the person responsible for the injury and halting the search when the "culprit" has been established. It is as if identifying cause will somehow lead inexorably to cause elimination. After the "demon" is identified, it miraculously, by some unseen hand, is excized. Figure 9-1 is a sample of a management report that also reflects this phenomenon. The guilty party is usually the injured party. This approach is a mistake. Many investigators who look for causes during an investigation deny that they are seeking culprits or establishing guilt. This is wishful thinking! In an atmosphere in which cause(s) is determined, it is unlikely that those who have made the mistakes will not feel as though they have been found guilty. It is unavoidable.

Actual experience indicates that this approach to injury investigation promotes a "see no evil, hear no evil, speak no evil" behavior. It promotes contentiousness and litigation, and prejudices employees, unions, hearing officers, administrative law judges, and juries to see the injured as "the little guy" fighting a battle against the "big guys"—big guys whose losses are insured. The actual direct payor (insurer) is not normally present in litigation procedures (except where large sums of money are involved on an individual case basis); even if present, the payor realizes that losses represent "pass throughs" that it can ultimately recover—from the insured (employer) through premium increases.

Determining cause sounds logical. It is, however, a trap—a trap that can be avoided.

Punish Behavior, Not the Injury

The approach described above is a rather unproductive view of injuries/incidences and their causes. Most injuries/incidents occur because people are trying to do something, trying to accomplish something. Most of the time the "something" is a task associated with their job assignment; that is, they are "good" employees trying to get their jobs done. Injury investigations that conclude by informing the injured "to take more care" normally are not only ineffective and a waste of effort but also, in fact, counterproductive. This admonition is, of course, the next logical step in an investigation based on cause identification. The guilty party has been identified and supervision has quite correctly admonished the employee "to be more careful." Such investigations are generally counterproductive because they let the supervisor or

Monthly Accident Report
Summary Of Occupational Injury Cases

04/01/90 to 04/30/90

Date	Employee/ Supervisor	Body Part/ Injury Type/ Severity/ Rec Basis	Description of Accident	Primary Cause	Secondary Cause
04/16/90		Wrist Contusion First Aid N/A	PULLING ON PIPE WRENCH; NIPPLE HE WAS TURNING BROKE; WRENCH SLIPPED; HAND FLEW FREE AND STRUCK NEARBY U-BOLT	APPLYING TOO MUCH TORQUE ON NIPPLE, CAUSING NIPPLE TO BREAK	
04/18/90		Nose Laceration OSHA Other Sutures	FIRE ON P-5 PUMP; WENT TO HELP PUT IT OUT; GOT SPRAYED BY STREAM OF WATER FROM TURRET; TURNED HEAD; STRUCK HEAD ON NEARBY VALVE STEM	NO PIPE PLUG IN IVN SAMPLE POINT; DRAIN VALVE LEFT CRACKED OPEN; IVN FLASHED	HASTE AND CONFUSION IN FIGHTING FIRE
**04/11/90		Toe Contusion Restricted Duty Restrictions	TWO EMPLOYEE'S WERE TRYING TO UP-RIGHT FALLEN BARREL; ONE LET GO TO AVOID PINCH POINT; BARREL FELL ON OTHER EMPLOYEE'S FOOT	FAILURE TO INSURE WORKER'S WORK METHODS WERE COORDINATED	FAILURE TO WEAR SAFETY SHOES
02/21/90		Teeth Fracture OSHA Other Fractures	PULLING ON A WRENCH IN TIGHT QUAR-TERS; WRENCH SLIPPED OFF THE NUT AND STRUCK EMPLOYEE IN THE MOUTH	DIFFICULTY SECURING WRENCH ON NUT IN TIGHT QUARTERS	POOR BODY POSITION
**04/19/90		Knee Sprain/Strain Lost Time Inj Lost Time	WALKING ON REACTOR CATWALK; STEPPED OVER HORIZONTAL SCAFFOLD MEMBER; CAUGHT ONE FOOT ON SCAFFOLD MEMBER; FELL AND TWISTED LEG	SCAFFOLD MEMBER OBSTRUCTING WALKWAY	FAILURE TO STEP OVER SCAFFOLD MEMBER WITH DUE CARE
04/23/90		Leg Contusion First Aid N/A	HOOKING UP STEAM HOSES; TRYING TO ELIMINATE POSSIBILITY OF A FIRE; VISION IMPAIRED BY SMOKE; SLID ON OIL AND TRIPPED OVER SCAFFOLD PIECE	OIL SPILL CAUSED BY HOLE IN CONTROL VALVE	SLIPPERY WALKING SURFACE
04/04/90		Hand Laceration First Aid N/A	WALKING ON UNIT; LOST FOOTING ON STEP; FELL; HAND STRUCK PROTRUDING SHEET METAL INSULATION COVERING; CUT HAND	FAILURE TO STEP WITH DUE CARE	FAILURE TO INSURE INSULATION COVERING IS SECURE

** Indicates Restricted Duty or Lost Time Injuries

Figure 9-1

injury investigator think he or she has done something useful. In fact, nothing useful has been accomplished. The injured already knows he or she should have "taken more care." Telling the employee provides no new information to the employee as guidance for the future.

Even explicit disciplinary action is also normally of little value to the employee who injures himself or herself or another employee. He knows the mistake he has made and recognizes the adverse consequences of his actions. Most employees do not need disciplinary measures to understand this message. Disciplining the injured may be of some benefit to others as an example of what can be expected if one becomes injured or causes someone else to be injured. The message transmitted to employees by such action is "Don't get injured." This goal sounds good; however, it focuses on punishing the injury, not correcting the behavior that resulted in the injury.

If indeed discipline appears appropriate, the more useful approach is to discipline all employees who exhibit behavior that is a sufficiently serious breach of safe behavior, independent of whether or not an actual injury has occurred. It is *behavior* that discipline is designed to change, not the healing rate of the injury. The people who most need to learn are those who have engaged in an unsafe act (behavior) but who have thus far been fortunate in avoiding injury. Many of these people will have demonstrated to their satisfaction that the involved act is not unsafe, for they have not become injured! Management must react to unsafe behavior, injury related or not, if progress on safety is to be achieved.

Flawed Injury Report Forms

Figure 9-2 shows a better than average investigation report form of the type widely used by many organizatiions. It suffers from a number of significant deficiencies, however:

1. It combines reporting of the injury with the results of the injury investigation. As a result, distribution of findings is severely restricted because of the employee's right to privacy.
2. Item 12 suggests that normal injury treatment is other than that performed on site by site-employed personnel. Recording only who provided the treatment makes available no information regarding the actual treatment or the work restrictions the injured should recognize. The important information to be obtained from medical personnel is: (a) time, date, place, and provider of treatment; (b) symptoms and diagnosis; (c) treatment, including use or nonuse of prescription medication and dosage; and (d) work restrictions, if any.

   Many forms of this type provide for a medical determination of "fitness-for-work." This is inappropriate. Medical personnel should restrict their views to the condition of the patient and actions necessary to effect speedy and full recovery. Whether or not there is work available that meets the required conditions is not a medical matter and should not be decided by medical personnel. This is a supervisory matter to be decided by supervisory personnel, at an appropriate level (see Chapter 13).

ACCIDENT INVESTIGATION REPORT

INSTRUCTIONS: Must be filled out by employee's Manager, Supervisor, or Foreman. Mark N.A. (not applicable) items that do not apply to case. Write "none," "unknown," or "don't know" for applicable items for which there is no answer. Never leave a blank.

1. Employee's Name (Last Name First)

2. Employee's Home Address (With Zip Code)

3. Social Security Number	4. Date of Accident	5. Time of Accident

6. Age	7. Sex ☐M ☐F	8. Marital Status	9. Time Worked at Present Occupation	10. Job Title

11. Component No.	Manager, Supervisor, or Foreman

12. Treatment at
☐Industrial Clinic ☐Other — Specify (Doctor and/or Hospital) ______
(If treated by outside doctor or hospital, Employee's Notification of Injury/Illness form must be completed)

ACCIDENT DESCRIPTION

13. Location of Accident

14. Witness(es) (Attach Statements if Available) ______

15. How did the accident happen (if applicable, indicate right hand, left foot, etc.)? Employee alleges that ______

16. Description by Manager, Supervisor, or Foreman to include extent of injury (second degree burn, fracture, etc.) and type of treatment (sutures, diathermy, etc.):

17. TYPE OF CASE
(Check Below)
01☐First Aid
02☐Injury No Lost Time
03☐Injury Lost Time*
04☐Restricted Work
05☐Occupational Illness
06☐Fatality

18. ACCIDENT TYPE
(First Event in the Accident Sequence)
010☐Struck Against
020☐Struck By
030☐Fall from Elevation
050☐Fall on Same Level (Trip)
060☐Caught In, Under, or Between
080☐Abraded or Rubbed
100☐Bodily Reaction
120☐Overexertion (Muscle Pulls, etc.)
130☐Contact with Electrical Current
150☐Contact with Temperature Extremes
180☐Contact with Radiations, Caustics, Toxic, and Noxious Substances
☐Other (Explain): ______

19. PART OF BODY
(Check Most Serious One)
100☐Head, Face
120☐Ear(s) (Right, Left, Both)
130☐Eye(s) (Right, Left, Both)
200☐Neck
310☐Arm (Right, Left, Both)
320☐Wrist (Right, Left, Both)
330☐Hand (Right, Left, Both)
340☐Finger(s)
400☐Trunk
420☐Back
450☐Shoulder(s) (Right, Left, Both)
510☐Leg(s) (Right, Left, Both)
520☐Ankle(s) (Right, Left, Both)
530☐Feet (Right, Left, Both)
540☐Toe(s)
800☐Body System
☐Other (Explain): ______

20. NATURE OF INJURY OR ILLNESS
(Check Most Serious One)
100☐Amputation
120☐Burn (Heat)
130☐Burn (Chemical)
160☐Contusion, Crushing, Bruise (Intact Skin Surfaces)
170☐Cut, Laceration, Puncture (Open Wound)
180☐Dermatitis
200☐Electric Shock
210☐Fracture
220☐Freezing, Frostbite
250☐Hernia
270☐Poisoning, Chemical
290☐Radiation (Ionizing, Nonionizing)
300☐Scratches, Abrasions (Superficial Wounds)
310☐Sprains, Strains
☐Other (Explain): ______

*On lost time accidents only complete Lost Time Accident Follow-up Report

Figure 9-2

ANALYSIS OF ACCIDENT CAUSES

21. What did the injured (or other person) do or fail to do that contributed directly to the accident? Be specific. (Example: "Used ladder too short for job;" "Stood on the top rung of ladder.") Don't say "Careless," "Poor judgment," etc.

22. Answer only if Item 21 applies. Check those below judged responsible for what was done or failed to be done, thereby contributing to the accident. More than one item may apply. Write in the information for the direct causes not listed.

- 01 ☐ Unaware of (job) hazards
- 02 ☐ Inattentive to hazards
- 03 ☐ Unaware of safe method
- 04 ☐ Low level of job skill
- 05 ☐ Tried to gain or save time
- 06 ☐ Tried to avoid extra effort
- 07 ☐ Acted to avoid discomfort
- 08 ☐ Influence of emotions
- 09 ☐ Influence of fatigue
- 10 ☐ Influence of illness
- 11 ☐ Influence of intoxicants
- 12 ☐ Defective vision / hearing
- 13 ☐ Indirect cause(s) other than those listed. Explain.
- 14 ☐ Unable to judge nature of indirect causes. Explain.

Explanation:

23. Check the primary type of unsafe action and / or condition in each column and circle any secondary.

UNSAFE CONDITIONS

- 000 ☐ Hazardous defects of tools, equipment, etc.
- 210 ☐ Inadequate aisle space, exits, etc.
- 220 ☐ Inadequate clearance for moving objects, etc.
- 240 ☐ Inadequate ventilation (not due to defective equipment)
- 260 ☐ Improper illumination
- 299 ☐ Fire and explosion hazards
- 300 ☐ Hazardous methods or procedures
- 410 ☐ Improperly piled
- 420 ☐ Improperly placed (includes housekeeping)
- 430 ☐ Inadequately secured against undesired motion (not unstable piling)
- 510 ☐ Unguarded
- 520 ☐ Inadequately guarded
- 540 ☐ Ungrounded
- 550 ☐ Uninsulated
- 590 ☐ Unlabeled or inadequately labeled materials
- 999 ☐ Other (Explain):

UNSAFE ACTS

- 052 ☐ Cleaning, oiling, adjusting, etc., of moving equipment
- 057 ☐ Working on electrically charged equipment
- 100 ☐ Failure to wear personal protective equipment
- 150 ☐ Failure to wear safe personal attire
- 200 ☐ Failure to secure or warn
- 250 ☐ Horseplay, distracting, teasing, etc.
- 300 ☐ Improper use of equipment
- 350 ☐ Improper use of hands or body parts
- 400 ☐ Inattention to footings or surroundings
- 450 ☐ Making safety device inoperative
- 500 ☐ Operating or working at unsafe speed
- 550 ☐ Taking unsafe position or posture
- 750 ☐ Using unsafe equipment
- 999 ☐ Other (Explain):

ACTIONS TO PREVENT ACCIDENT RECURRENCE

24. Mark with a (✓) those actions taken to prevent recurrence. Circle other corrective actions decided upon or planned but not yet carried out. NARRATIVE COMMENTS REQUIRED ON PRIMARY ACTION.

- 01 ☐ Reinstruction of person(s) involved
- 02 ☐ Conversation record with person(s) involved
- 03 ☐ Discipline of person(s) involved
- 04 ☐ Reinstruction of others doing job
- 05 ☐ Temporary reassignment of person
- 06 ☐ Permanent reassignment of person
- 07 ☐ Action to improve inspection
- 08 ☐ Action to improve clean-up
- 09 ☐ Order job safety analysis done
- 10 ☐ Equipment repair or replacement
- 11 ☐ Action to improve design
- 12 ☐ Action to improve construction
- 13 ☐ Installation of guard or safety device
- 14 ☐ Correction of unnecessary congestion
- 15 ☐ Improvement of personal protective equipment
- 16 ☐ Order regular pre-job instructions
- 17 ☐ Order use of safer materials
- 18 ☐ Check with manufacturer
- 19 ☐ Inform all departmental supervision
- 20 ☐ Other than above

Describe details of primary corrective action:

25. Additional Comments:

Manager, Supervisor, or Foreman's Signature: ______ Date of Report ______

ORIGINAL SHOULD BE RETURNED TO SAFETY OFFICE. WITHIN 24 HOURS. PLEASE MAINTAIN A COPY FOR YOUR RECORDS

FOR SAFETY OFFICE USE ONLY

OSHA Recordable ☐ No.: ______ Non-Recordable ☐ Compensation Forms Required ☐

Additional Comments:

Reviewed by: ______ Date: ______

Figure 9-2 (*continued*)

3. Item 14 uses the pejorative term "witnesses." It suggests that the "witness" knows what happened and may become involved in a legal proceeding. These perceptions have a chilling effect in securing employee perception of what they think happened and what they saw, heard, smelled, felt, or tasted. Employees frequently do not want to become "witnesses"—because it suggests that they may have to "testify" against a fellow worker who may have done an unsafe act. On the other hand, an employee may want to be a witness in order to testify against the company. In either situation, the unbiased seeking of the truth is hampered.

   The investigative process should be undertaken so as to include all personnel who may have something of significance to contribute and should foster an open exchange of opinions, recognizing that it is highly unlikely that one person is going to have a perfectly clear and unambiguous understanding of all the facts of the situation. A cooperative evaluation of all the facts that can be brought forth for consideration should be the desired goal. Establishing written records of "witnesses" is counterproductive to this objective.
4. Item 15 uses the word "alleges." This also is a pejorative word. It suggests that an employee may be misrepresenting the facts. This is provocative and counterproductive. Alternative wording might be; "employee said . . . " or simply an employee description of what happened. As will be stated later, this, too, is usually a mistake. A brief description of the incident by supervision—only two or three sentences—can be useful for early communication purposes. No attempt to record facts that may suggest causes or fault should be included in the description of the incident.
5. The information called for by items 17, 18, 19, 20, 22, 23, 24, and 25 should not be sought in this check-the-item fashion. This method requires only a minimum of thought with little or no analysis. Many safety professionals endorse the use of such check-the-item responses because these are "better than nothing." This is a poor excuse. What is required is a thorough investigation based on reason 7.

The requirement that the injury be reported to the Safety Office is appropriate. Someone needs to classify the injury both for internal records and for governmental records (OSHA forms 101 and 200 log). Reports to state agencies are also required. The Safety Office is an appropriate organization to recommend injury classification, subject to approval by line management. Some organizations make injury classification a function of the medical group. This is usually a mistake; it too closely couples injury treatment with injury classification. An adverse result may be a tendency to undertreat, thus reducing the injury classification severity. Medical personnel should not normally be subjected to this temptation or the intimidating discussions with line managers that may arise regarding why an injury was classified as it was. Although the challenge of injury classification may be quite legitimate an activity, medical personnel should not normally be put in a position that invites challenges regarding "overtreatment" of injured employees.

Injury classifications made by safety personnel should be subject to review and revision by upper line management, as are the decisions of other functional groups within the organization. However, proper injury classification requires a detailed understanding of the applicable rules/regulations. Line management cannot be expected to be an expert in injury classification; line management should expect to receive cogent explanations from safety personnel regarding the considerations which lead to specific classifications. Line management should retain the authority to make final classification if differences of opinion arise. However, such differences in opinion should be rare. Unanimity of opinion normally results when all the facts are made available for the decision-making process. In circumstances in which line management feels compelled to overrule the safety officer, the reasoning involved should be clearly established and recorded to maintain credibility with the work force as well as with some future OSHA compliance review.

The better practice is to require direct supervision to classify injuries. They, of course, should seek advice and guidance, but not decision-making, from their safety supervisor. If the safety supervisor is dissatisfied with the classification decision of the direct supervisor, higher level management review of the classification should be sought. This process keeps responsibility within the line management organization organization where it belongs.

However, the requirement to report the results of an injury investigation to the Safety Office within 24 hours is inappropriate. It is unlikely that a reasonably good injury investigation is going to take place within 24 hours. Such a time requirement communicates that the paperwork is more important than the substance of the report; it encourages cursory investigations having little real value.

In addition, the "For Safety Office Use Only" section advertises that there may be interesting additional notations on record. These also mitigate against wide publication of the report.

In Figure 9-3 is shown yet another version of commonly used forms. This form provides for the signature of the employee. Why? So that he cannot change his story later? That is, management does not trust him? What a message to give an employee! If the employee chooses not to sign, what will happen? Nothing. Signing this form is neither a condition of employment nor a requirement to file a worker's compensation claim. Employee signing is a bad idea.

SELF-RENEWAL INCIDENT INVESTIGATIONS

Avoidance of Negatives in Determining Cause

The negatives associated with incident investigations based on determining cause and the use of reporting forms that focus on determining cause can be avoided. By focusing incident investigations on determining the facts of a situation and an analysis of the failings of the Safety Management Process (see Chapter 4). The emphasis of the investigation shifts from individuals to defects in the safety system and its functioning. It shifts from finding fault with individuals to how the safety process can be improved

text continues on page 254

ACCIDENT INVESTIGATION FORM

INSTRUCTIONS

Use this form to help you investigate each near-miss or work related accident. The purpose of the form is to help you determine the cause(s) and the corrective action(s) needed to prevent recurrence of similiar accidents. As part of this investigation, you must conduct a site visit and inspection, and interview witnesses and the involved employee. Do not draw any conclusions until you have thoroughly reviewed all details associated with the accident. This investigation and report should be completed within 24 hours of the accident while the facts are still fresh in everyone's mind.

Completing this form serves as documentation that an employee has notified the Company of an occupational injury. A visit to a medical or other treating facility should be made if warranted or requested by the employee, but is not required to document the occurrence of the injury.

EMPLOYEE'S NAME:__________ P.R.#__________ S.S.#__________ SEX: M F

EMPLOYEE'S AGE__________ YEARS SERVICE__________ OCCUPATION__________

UNIT OR M&E GROUP ASSIGNED__________ DATE ASSIGNED TO UNIT OR M&E GROUP__________

INJURY/ILLNESS

When did you first learn of the injury and/or illness?__________

What body parts appear to be injured/ill?__________

What physical evidence of an injury/illness did you observe?__________

____

Who treated the injury?__________

Do you know if this employee had previous trouble with the injured/ill body part? Yes____ No____

If yes, describe:__________

What restrictions if any were issued?__________

Is employee approved to return to work? Yes ____ No ____

ACCIDENT/OCCURENCE

State facts of accident and your understanding of how the accident occurred. (1) Indicate exactly what employee was doing when the incident occurred, (2) What substance or object caused the injury, illness or near-miss, (3) What were work site conditions and work equipment conditions like?__________

____

____

____

____

____

____

____

____

Witnesses: __________

At what unit or facility did this accident occur?__________

Identify the exact location on the unit or facility __________

Give day of the week, date and time of day when accident occurred__________

____

Was this an overtime shift? Yes____ No____. If no, when did this employee last work an overtime shift?__________ How many days prior to this accident did this employee have his last two days off?__________

Has this employee had a similar accident like this in the past? Yes____ No____

Figure 9-3

CAUSES (UNSAFE ACTS):

What (If any) was/were the unsafe act(s) or practice(s) of this accident?____________________

Were any tools or pieces of equipment used improperly? Yes____ No____ Explain how__________

Who is principally responsible for performing the unsafe act(s) or practice(s)? __________

As best as you can determine, why did that person perform the unsafe act(s) or practice(s)?

CAUSES (UNSAFE CONDITIONS):

What unsafe conditions contributed to the accident?____________________

What tools or equipment aids were involved?____________________

What was their condition?____________________

When were they last inspected?____________________

Should the injured employee have identified and corrected the hazard? Yes____ No____ Explain your answer.____________________

Who do you think should have been responsible for identifying and correcting the safety hazard?

CORRECTIVE ACTION

What action has been or will be taken to correct the hazard? ____________________

Who is responsible for completion?____________________

On what day was it completed?____________________

If not corrected, when do you anticipate completion?____________________

What action are you taking to insure an accident occurrence like this will not recur?__________

What is your anticipated completion date?____________________

MISCELLANEOUS

You must review this report with the involved employee. When was/will this be done?__________

When will you/did you review the incident with the rest of your crew?____________________

Date of report____________________ ____________________

Supervisor

cc: Division Manager
Unit Operating/Maintenance Superintendents
Safety Department
Medical Department

____

Superintendent

Figure 9–3 (*continued*)

Medical Analysis & Reporting System
Initial Visit

Name | Case Date | Case Type ☐ V ☐ W

Social Security Number | Dependent Code | Activity Date (*Same as Case Date*) | Activity Location

This record started as a result of ☐ 1 Personal Visit ☐ 2 Emergency Call ☐ 3 Phone Call ☐ 4 Other

☐ Non-Employee | **Type of Visit** ☐ 1 Illness ☐ 2 Injury ☐ 3 Other Only Requires Treatment

☐ Return to work evaluation

Date: First Missed Work / Returned to Work

Hospital Days

Blood Pressure

Initial /

Resting (Required if Initial B.P. Greater than 149/89) /

☐ Check (✓) if Patient Taking B.P. Medicine

Temperature . °F | Pulse

Disposition
☐ 1 Full Duty
☐ 2 Limited Duty
☐ 3 Sent Home
☐ 4 Referral
☐ 5 Hospital
☐ 6 Other

Disability
☐ 1 None
☐ 2 Temporary Total
☐ 3 Temporary Partial
☐ 4 Permanent Total
☐ 5 Permanent Partial
☐ 6 Fatal
☐ 7 Undetermined

Diagnostic Procedure
☐ 1 X-Ray
☐ 2 Urinalysis
☐ 3 Blood Drawn
☐ 4 ECG
☐ 5 Audiogram
☐ 6 Vision
☐ 7 Pulmonary Function
☐ 8 Other

Follow-Up Requested | Date

Reason

Illness/Injury require •Disposition •Principal Type •Disability •Treatment

Illness/Injury Description
☐ 1 Occupational ☐ 2 Non-occupational
☐ 1 Major* ☐ 2 Minor*
☐ Recordable for OSHA

*Required for Injury only. See reverse for definition.

Principal Type of Illness/Injury
▼ Must match Type of Visit—only one response. System will generate a diagnosis code based on Illness or Injury—**Not both.**

Illness
☐ 01 Dysmenorrhea
☐ 02 URI
☐ 03 Common Cold
☐ 04 Sore Throat
☐ 05 Headache
☐ 06 Nausea/Vomiting
☐ 07 Diarrhea
☐ 33 Other Illness**

Injury (*One or more sites must be shown*) ►
☐ 20 Abrasion
☐ 21 Amputation
☐ 22 Burn - Chemical
☐ 23 Burn - Thermal
☐ 24 Concussion
☐ 25 Contusion
☐ 26 Crushed
☐ 27 Dislocation
☐ 28 Foreign Body
☐ 29 Fracture
☐ 30 Laceration
☐ 31 Puncture
☐ 32 Sprain/Strain
☐ 33 Other Injury**

Location
☐ 01 Head
☐ 02 Face
☐ 03 Ear
☐ 04 Eye
☐ 05 Nose
☐ 06 Mouth
☐ 07 Teeth
☐ 08 Neck
☐ 09 Shoulder
☐ 10 Arm
☐ 11 Elbow
☐ 12 Forearm
☐ 13 Wrist
☐ 14 Hand
☐ 15 Finger
☐ 16 Chest
☐ 17 Back
☐ 18 Abdomen
☐ 19 Hip
☐ 20 Pelvis
☐ 21 Genitalia
☐ 22 Thigh
☐ 23 Knee
☐ 24 Leg
☐ 25 Ankle
☐ 26 Foot
☐ 27 Toe
☐ 28 Other**

Enter DX for Other. System will **not generate diagnosis code for Other Illness/Injury.

Treatment (Multiple)
☐ 01 Blood Pressure Check
☐ 02 Consultation
☐ 03 Dressing of Wound
☐ 04 Ear Plugs
☐ 05 Ear Wax Removal
☐ 06 Foreign Body Removal
☐ 07 Immobilization
☐ 08 Incision/Drainage
☐ 09 Irrigation
☐ 10 Medication - External
☐ 11 Medication - Injectable
☐ 12 Medication - Oral
☐ 13 Observation
☐ 14 Physical Therapy
☐ 15 Pregnancy Check
☐ 16 Safety Glasses
☐ 17 Support, e.g., elastic bandage
☐ 18 Suture
☐ 19 Suture Removal
☐ 20 Other

Immunization
☐ 25 Allergy
☐ 26 Tetanus Toxoid
☐ 27 Tetanus/Diphtheria

Type
☐ 1 - Basic 1
☐ 2 - Basic 2
☐ 3 - Basic 3
☐ 4 - Basic 4
☐ 5 - Booster

Amount

Lot Number

Manufacturer

☐ Allergic Reaction

ICD DX Code	Date	Diagnosis
.		
.		
.		
.		
.		
.		

Physician/RN Signature X | Provider Code / | Opr. Code | Date Key Entered

Figure 9-3 (*continued*)

Time | In ☐ AM ☐ PM | Out ☐ AM ☐ PM

Name

Job Title | Extension

Age | Sex | Social Sec. No.

To be Completed by Patient (Not computer recorded) | Complaint or Allegation

Patient Signature | Date

X

Physician (If Referred)

Address

City | State | Zip

What Employee was doing

What Happened

Object or substance which allegedly injured employee
(Full chemical or trade name(s), if applicable)

Supervisor's Name | Ext.

Address *(Non-Employees Must Complete)*

City | State | Zip

Location of Alleged Accident, Exposure or Event
(Always complete if occurrence not on premises)

Description *(Company Name, Etc.)*

Address

City | State | Zip

Medical Department Use Only | Date

Comments

Physician/RN Signature

X

Major injuries include

- Those requiring the employee to leave the plant before the end of the scheduled work shift.
- Those requiring a change of job, regardless of length of time involved.
- Lacerations requiring any sutures, butterfly closure, or similar technique.
- Eye injuries requiring an eye patch, and those where loss of sight is distinct possibility.
- Burns more severe than first degree.
- Injuries requiring a sling, cane or crutches, or otherwise interfering substantially with locomotion or use of limbs.
- Hernia cases.
- Injuries producing loss of consciousness or shock.
- Fractures and amputations.
- Others of comparable severity.

All injuries not considered "Major" by this definition should be coded as "Minor."

53-600 Back (05-86)

Figure 9–3 (*continued*)

continued from page 249

for the benefit of all employees. It shifts from telling employees "to be more careful" to designing management actions to actually achieve this result. It shifts from fault-finding to a quest for management self-renewal.

We always know two things about every injury. One is that someone did something unsafe. We do not need an investigation to determine this. This is true for every injury. The only thing an investigation can do about this item is to determine who. The second item we know about every injury is that the safety management process—that is, management—has failed. An investigation can and should determine the failings (there are usually multiple failings) of the process and what can be done to correct these failings by improving the process.

Examination of the Safety Management Process

When reason 7, page 242, becomes the basic reason for investing time and effort in investigating incidents, the negatives associated with the search for causes vanish. To be sure, a good set of relevant facts will reveal undesirable employee behavior and probably other significant factors that contributed to this undesirable behavior. The focus, however, shifts from the individual to the broader question of what needs to be done to or through the "system" in order to achieve the desired employee behavior in general. Even injured employees will more willingly and openly contribute to an inquiry based on this reason.

An organization must be prepared to challenge its own safety and operating philosophies, standards, and operating style to ensure that it has not, in fact, created a workplace culture that invites or conditions employees to "cut corners" or take chances, thus undermining the best of management intentions.

Objectives of Incident Investigations

Reason 7 focuses on the safety management process. As a consequence, it directs attention to the following objectives:

1. To **examine** the circumstances or operation in which the incident occurred in order to determine safety strengths and weaknesses.
2. To **determine** what changes or strategies appear necessary to reinforce strengths and correct weaknesses.
3. To **take steps** designed to prevent reoccurrence of similar injuries by bolstering the safety management process.
4. To **demonstrate** management's commitment to the welfare of employees, the public and the environment.

Objective 1 drives the investigation toward developing a set of clearly stated facts regarding the circumstances under which the injury occurred—the "good" things that were present as well as the items needing improvement.

Objective 2 drives the investigation toward an action plan or response that is focused on the organization, not the injured. Objective 2 drives the investigation toward institutional considerations, not individual failures. These goals reinforce the concept that, although the specific injury was undoubtedly caused by an unsafe act on the part of someone, the reason for the unsafe act transcends (normally) the specific individual responsible for the particular injury under investigation.

Objective 3 drives the investigation toward identifying specific actions that the investigation team thinks will be effective in precluding the occurrence of a similar injury to anyone in the organization, any time in the future. This goal requires widespread dissemination of the full results of the investigation.

Objective 4 drives the investigation toward really doing something—not just performing lip service. In order to increase this sense of "doing something," injury investigations should include not only recommendations for actions to be taken to prevent reoccurrence, but also identification of the person responsible for carrying out each action as well as a proposed date of completion. By identifying an expected completion date, follow-up against a published criterion can be made. In addition, actions that have completion dates are much more likely to be identifiable as realistic.

In order to further enhance the prospects of achieving a productive investigation, the investigation team should be held responsible for the results of their efforts. An excellent way of doing this is to include the names of the team members on the investigation report, which is widely circulated.

There are risks associated with widely publishing incident reports. Management negligence may be revealed and the report may subsequently find its way into the public media or other adverserial hands. Management negligence makes good "copy." However, when an investigation adequately achieves objective 4—management commitment to safety—investigative reports lose much, if not all, their appeal to adverserial interests. The write-ups demonstrate dedication to seeking the truth and dealing in facts, not suppositions. They demonstrate that management knows what it is talking about. This sort of situation is not nearly as interesting to the media as is a situation in which management can be put on the defensive by claims of "cover-up."

Some managers will be concerned that acknowledging that corrective steps are needed will be an admission of guilt upon which adverserial legal action can be based. Existing law recognizes that society would not be well served if employers were encouraged to avoid corrective measures out of fear of legal actions regarding evidence that could then be used against them.[2]

Report Forms and Instructions

The forms shown in Figures 9-4 and 9-5, together with the instructions contained in Figure 9-6, provide the basic structure around which productive incident investigations based on Reason 7 can be conducted.

When thoroughly carried out and widely communicated, incident investigations are an effective channel through which the "safety message" can be communicated. By investigations of incidents, an organization can develop a fuller understanding of the fundamentals of safety. Incident investigations led by line management provide management with opportunities to:

text continues on page 261

OCCUPATIONAL INJURY/ILLNESS REPORT

CASE NO. ______
EASI REPORT ______

FULL NAME OF INJURED (Last, First, Middle Initial)		IMMEDIATE SUPERVISOR	DEPT./BUILDING
DATE OF INJURY/ILLNESS	TIME ____ A.M. ____ P.M.	NATURE OF ILLNESS OR INJURY	
DATE OF TREATMENT	TIME OF TREATMENT ____ A.M. ____ P.M.	TREATMENT	
WORK RESTRICTIONS (IF ANY)			RX MEDICATION ONLY DOSE ______
SIGNATURE—MEDICAL SECTION	R.N. M.D.	☐ RETURN TO MEDICAL ON	PREVENTION ______ PAIN ______ TREATMENT ______

JOB TITLE	SECTION/DIVISION	DATE OF BIRTH	SEX Male ☐ Female ☐	MARITAL STATUS Single ☐ Married ☐
ADJ. SERVICE DATE	SOC. SEC. NUMBER	HOW MANY MONTHS WAS INJURED FAMILIAR WITH WORK HE/SHE WAS DOING?		
INJURED'S HOME ADDRESS, ZIP CODE				

BRIEF DESCRIPTION OF INCIDENT—(INCLUDE LOCATION, PROTECTIVE EQUIPMENT USED.)
(IF ADDITIONAL SPACE NEEDED, USE SEPARATE SHEET)

THIS IS A FOUR-PART "NO CARBON REQUIRED" FORM TO BE USED FOR REPORTING ALL INJURIES AND FOR REPORTING INVESTIGATIONS OF FIRST AID CASES. INVESTIGATIONS OF OSHA RECORDABLE INJURIES ARE REPORTED SEPARATELY.

ACTION TAKEN TO PREVENT RECURRENCE

INVESTIGATION DATE	INVESTIGATED BY	REPORT BY	TITLE

INSTRUCTIONS FOR COMPLETING OCCUPATIONAL INJURY/ILLNESS REPORT

I MEDICAL SECTION—
A. COMPLETE FORM TO BOLD LINE
B. DISTRIBUTION: 1. DETACH AND RETAIN BLUE COPY
2. DETACH AND ROUTE PINK COPY TO SAFETY SECTION.
3. GIVE REMAINING 2 COPIES TO INJURED EMPLOYEE FOR DELIVERY TO HIS/HER SUPERVISOR.

II INJURED EMPLOYEE'S IMMEDIATE SUPERVISOR
A. COMPLETE 2 COPIES RECEIVED FROM INJURED EMPLOYEE BY FILLING IN ALL INFORMATION BELOW BOLD LINE.
B. DISTRIBUTION: WHITE—SAFETY SECTION GREEN—LINE MANAGEMENT INFORMATION AND FILE

Figure 9-4

Incident Report

REPORT NO. 82-1
DEPARTMENT: PHOTO PRODUCTS REPORT DATE: 7/12/82
DIVISION: R&D INCIDENT DATE: 6/11/82
LOCATION: /126

NATURE OF INCIDENT

The outer race of a bearing fractured while an attempt was being made to remove it from a small armature shaft. A piece of the bearing broke the right lens of an employee's safety glasses. The employee suffered a laceration of the right eye.

DESCRIPTION OF INCIDENT

Technicians had diagnosed the problem of a motor that became inoperable in the middle of a run as a bearing failure. The Electrical Shop was contacted, and while the electrician was on his way the bearing was removed and inadvertently replaced with an undersized bearing. A technician was attempting to remove the second bearing with a wheel puller clamped in a vise. When a second technician approached the bench to assist in the operation, the outer race of the bearing failed. A piece of the broken bearing, struck the right lens of the employee safety glasses at high speed, fracturing the lens.

FACTS BROUGHT OUT

- The technicians had experience removing bearings from shafts, but it was the first time they had attempted to remove a bearing from a small armature shaft.
- The wheel puller arms were exerting force on the outer race of the bearing, instead of on the inner race. (see figure)
- The outer race is of hardened steel and brittle, and the force exerted caused it to fail.
- An attachment to be used with the wheel puller is available so that force is exerted on the inner race rather than the outer one.
- The small I.D. of the inner race (inside portion of bearing) of the wrong size bearing and the resulting interference fit was a major factor causing the outer race to shatter.
- Employees were not aware of the potential failure of the hardened steel.
- An arbor press with shield would have been more appropriate for the job.
- There was no written procedure for the task.

Figure 9–5

- Failure of bearings when being removed by the above method are rare, but have occured in industry.
- The employees safety glasses met the standards for industrial eye wear, were about one year old and in good condition. It is felt that the glasses prevented a more serious and, perhaps, permanent eye injury.

CORRECTIVE ACTION	RESPONSIBILITY	TIMING
• Develop a written procedure for removing bearings from shafts. The procedure should include requirements for using the proper tool, the correct method and shielding.	J. Smith	July 30, 1982
• Develop written procedures for other definable mechanical-type work.	J. Smith	July 30, 1982
• Work closely with specialized mechanical shops in all cases.	All personnel	Effective immediately
• Publicize incident	P. Alden	With this report.

INVESTIGATED BY

J. Smith - Chairman, P. Alden, C. Bronte, C. Columbus, C. Dickens, A. Einstein, H. James, E. Sullivan, H.M. Thackery, H.D. Thoreau

DISTRIBUTION

Photo Products Department - all personnel
Safety Offices of all Photo Products off-site locations
CR&DD - Serv. Div., all exempt personnel
CR&DD - Res. & Feedstocks, Supervisory personnel
Other Depts. on Site - Lab. Directors, Lab. Administrators, Research Supervisors in ETL, C&P, Petrochemicals and Polymer Products

Figure 9-5 (*continued*)

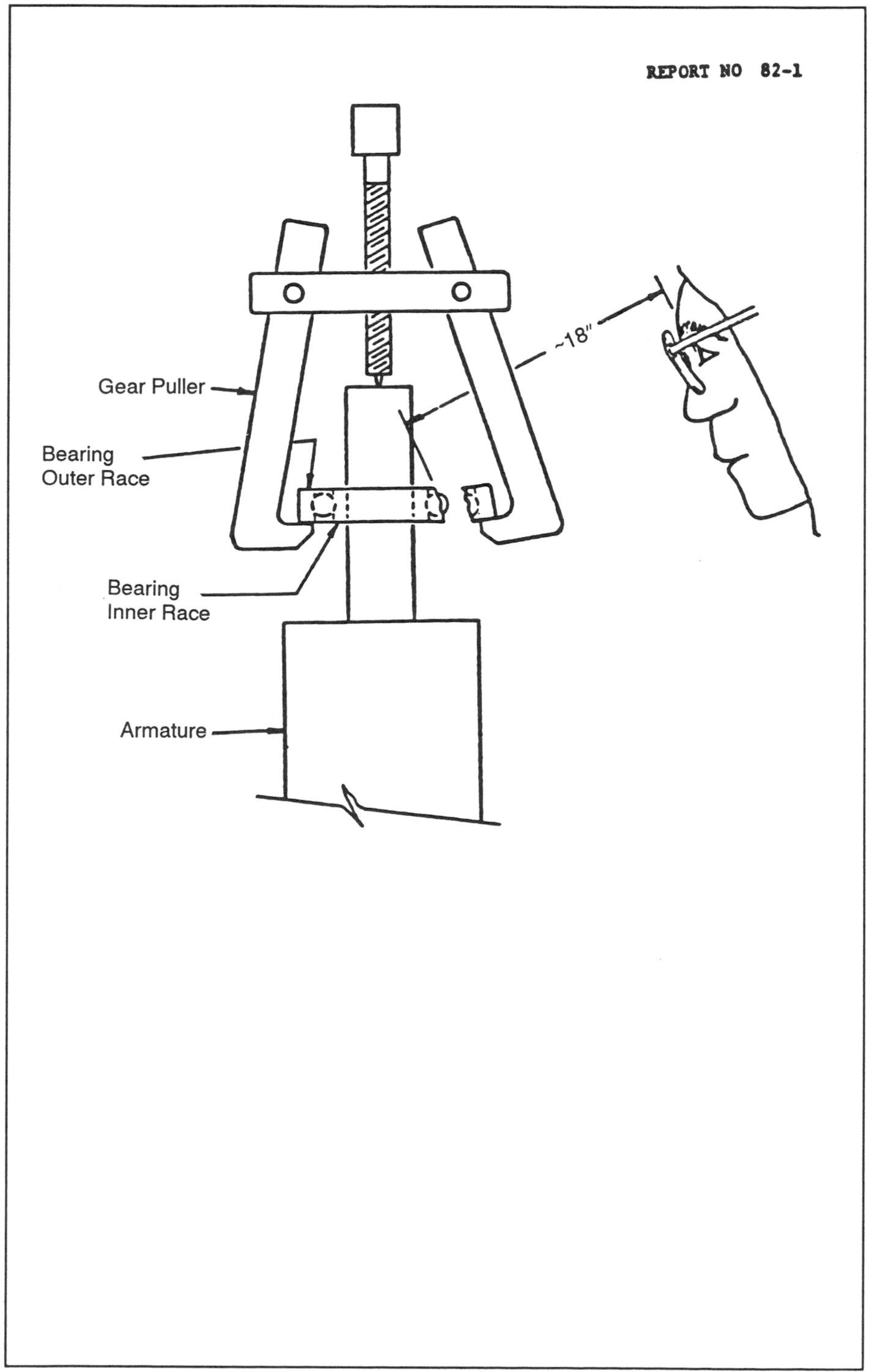

Figure 9-5 (*continued*)

SAFETY PROCEDURE

PROCEDURE NO. 108
ISSUED ______
REVISED August 12,

INCIDENT REPORTING

INTRODUCTION

Unexpected occurrences, whether or not they result in injury to personnel, but which had potential for serious injury are called Incidents. It is important that these incidents be investigated promptly. Useful lessons can be learned from these investigations, and publicizing them throughout the location may prevent a similar incident happening somewhere else. If incidents are not thoroughly investigated and reported, an important safety tool is lost, leaving a door open for someone else to do the same thing, perhaps resulting in a serious injury.

OBJECTIVES

The objective of investigating and reporting incidents is to prevent recurrence by:

- Identifying and correcting hazardous conditions and/or practices through a detailed analysis of the incident.
- Promptly communicating the findings to others who may benefit from the specific information and understanding developed through the investigation.
- Broad application of the findings to update rules and standard practices by all groups.

DEFINITION

An "incident" is an unexpected occurrence which interferes with the orderly progress of work and which caused, or might have caused, one or more of the following:

- a serious injury or adverse effect on the health of one or more employees
- actual or potential significant loss of physical facilities even though potential for injury was small
- an environmental problem
- a situation which could have an unfavorable impact on the public

INVESTIGATION

As soon as possible after the incident has occurred, it is the responsibility of the area or group supervisor most directly affected by the incident to convene an investigating committee to study the circumstances surrounding the event, and to prepare a report of their findings, including recommendations to prevent recurrence.

The investigating committee shall include the area or group supervisor, a member of the Safety, Industrial Hygiene and Fire Protection Section, and other personnel who can contribute to the investigation. In addition, the committee should include one member from an area or group not involved with the incident. Comments from the employees directly involved in the incident are usually very important and the employees' inputs should be included in the investigating committee's findings.

The investigating committee should compile all the relevant facts at the scene of the incident. If possible, the scene should not be changed until at least a preliminary investigation can take place. In addition to the reported facts, the committee should consider making a photographic record of the scene for future reference.

INCIDENT REPORTS

After the committee has completed the investigation (normally not to exceed 7 calendar days), the area or group supervisor or their designee will issue an Incident Report as soon as possible using the attached format, including the following:

1. **Nature of Incident:** A brief (one or two sentences) statement of what happened.
2. **Description of Incident:** A detailed, essay-like and technically sound analysis of the circumstances leading up to the incident and a full description of what happened. Use photographs and diagrams when they will contribute to an explanation of the incident.
3. **Facts Brought Out:** A listing of key facts, brought out by the investigation, which are the basis for the corrective action recommended.
4. **Corrective Action:** A list of all recommendations the committee makes, together with the designation of a specific individual who will be responsible for carrying out each recommendation. The timing for the corrective action must also be shown.

   In situations in which disciplinary action is thought appropriate, this activity should be dealt with by the appropriate member of supervision, independent of and separate from the incident investigation.
5. **Investigated By:** The committee chairman and all committee members are listed.

PUBLICITY

Prior to final publication, a draft of the report should be sent to all committee members for their review and comments. The committee chairman is responsible for having the final draft approved by a level of management required to gain implementation of all recommendations,then typed and sent to the Safety Office for final review. The final copy will then be sent to the Printing Section.

Each department should publicize the incident by sending copies of the report to all personnel they believe will profit by the information. Minimum distribution for an Incident Report is shown on the attached sample. If additional distribution is deemed necessary by the department responsible for the report, it should be noted on the report and the Printing Section advised.

Figure 9-6

continued from page 255

1. Assess its own inadequacies regarding safety.
2. Assess the status of employee safety morale.
3. Demonstrate to subordinates management's dedication to employee safety and health.
4. Develop a better understanding of why injuries occur.
5. Learn more about existing rules and procedures.
6. Develop improved rules, procedures, and educational efforts designed to preclude repeat injuries or incidents.
7. Prepare appropriate communication materials that can be widely and openly used throughout the workplace.

Neither form (Figures 9-4 or 9-5) provides for recording an employee description of what happened or a supervisory description of what happened. Forms that provide for two versions of what happened should be avoided. (See Figures 9-2 and 9-3.) They promote divisiveness, a "me" and "them" environment. Incident investigations should promote a mutually shared understanding of the events that resulted in the incident. Report forms should guide investigation participants toward this goal. They should not promote behavior motivated by personal protectiveness. Immediate supervision and medical personnel should fill out the injury report forms, which they should consider primarily as instruments for use in injury prevention and only secondarily for use as legal instruments. These purposes are not antithetical; the issue is one of emphasis. A better legal document and better employee responses will result with the use of a form designed to foster thorough, open investigations. This approach to investigations develops an atmosphere in which all members of the investigative team can reach a common understanding of the facts surrounding the incident and the appropriateness of the required corrective action.

The form shown in Figure 9-4 has two purposes: (1) recording all occupationally incurred injuries/illnesses, and (2) reporting the results of the investigations of first-aid cases that are thought to have no significant potential for more serious consequences—that is, not worth communicating to other employees. In this regard, care must be taken that communications to employees be pertinent and of such a frequency that employees will show interest rather than simply ignore the message.

The form in Figure 9-4 provides for recording the necessary personal data regarding the injured, the medical description of the injury, the medical treatment provided the injured and any restrictions that should be observed in order to facilitate recovery, and identification of the nature of the treatment. (This latter information is essential for proper classification of the injury.) Medical initiates this form after treating the injured. As indicated on the form, two copies go to the injured person who gives them, in turn, to his or her supervisor. The supervisor completes the remainder of the form (1) if the injury is a first-aid case with no significant potential for a more serious event, by recording the results of an informal investigation and the resulting recommendations; or (2) in the event of a more serious injury or an incident with potential for a more serious injury, by indicating in the investigation report section of the form that a formal incident investigation will be held and reported upon as an Incident Investigation. This procedure requires that the supervisor make a decision as to which course of action is to be taken. The supervisor should seek guidance, as needed, from the safety supervisor or higher line supervision. After completing the form in either of these two ways, the supervisor forwards one copy (white) of the report to the safety supervisor. The second copy (green) is sent to his or her supervisor for information and review.

Medical keeps one copy (blue) for its records and use in bringing the injured employee's personal medical record up-to-date following the injury. Medical sends one (pink) copy to the safety supervisor. This informs the safety supervisor of the injury and provides the information upon which an injury classification can be based. Upon the safety supervisor's receipt of a copy (white) of the supervisor's notated report, the "loop" is now complete, unless a formal incident investigation is to be held. If such an investigation is to be held, the safety supervisor is thereby alerted to this fact. Informing both the safety supervisor and higher line supervision of the decision regarding the degree of investigation allows this decision to be reviewed in a timely fashion and additional action to be taken if differences of opinion exist regarding the correctness of the previous investigative action.

The safety supervisor should recommend the classification of the injury, subject to review and final decision by line management. The safety supervisor should be expected to provide line management with explanations of the classification criteria as needed for line management to knowledgeably approve the classification. Actual classification authority should not be delegated to the safety supervisor. Classification is a line management responsibility and the line should not be allowed to divest itself of this responsibility. Having the line make the classification removes the opportunity for the line to "blame" the safety supervisor for the resulting classification; it also keeps the safety supervisor in a staff role—as should be the case. Keeping the classification decision in the line organization also results in a better informed line organization.

Medical, safety, and the line organization need to stay abreast of the injured's recovery progress, both from a personnel basis and for assurance that subsequent events (for example, changes in treatment or work assignments) are recognized in relation to the appropriate classification of the injury.

Some professional safety personnel will object to the forms shown in Figures 9-4 and 9-5 on the grounds that they do not contain the data necessary to maintain an adequate injury data base as do the forms in Figures 9-2 and 9-3. The forms in Figures 9-4 and 9-5 are designed to help line management demonstrate leadership while discharging their management responsibilities. They are not designed to minimize the clerical work required by the Safety Office, nor should they be. The Safety Office will need to do its own clerical work. By doing so, perhaps the safety professional can help line supervision understand that injury investigation is more than filling out forms.

The format shown in Figure 9-5 is used to report the results of an incident investigation in which the simple report on the form in Figure 9-4 does not suffice. This form contains no personal information regarding the injured, in injury cases, and only a brief description of the injury—no invasion of privacy. The remainder of the report is devoted to disclosure of the facts developed at the investigation and the actions to be taken for improvement. In actual practice, Figure 9-5 is not a form to be filled out but rather a *format* for reporting the results of an investigation. Each report will have its own spacing as required by the report. This is a report that can be widely publicized througout the work force.

When an Injury Occurs

Care for the Injured Upon learning of an injury, the direct supervisor of the injured should see the injured employee to quickly determine, firsthand, the extent of the injury and the potentially worst reasonable injury that might have occurred. The supervisor will also want to assure himself or herself that the injured is receiving appropriate medical attention and that appropriate communication with family members has taken or will take place. The supervisor should be expected to demonstrate leadership in these two activities. He should suggest or even insist on additional or alternate medical treatment if this appears needed. If medical treatment is being provided by a third-party medical source such as the emergency room of a local hospital, he should normally be there. The supervisor is the employer's agent and should be expected to act responsibly vis-à-vis this third party. If this is not likely to occur, management with sufficient authority and skill should accompany the direct supervisor as needed to be effective. The task is to obtain the best possible treatment available in a timely fashion. Effort expended at this point can save a lot of "second guessing" later on.

Notification of Family and/or Government Agencies Family notification needs to be accomplished by a well thought out plan. The injured may not be able to do so because of either physical and/or emotional impediments. The direct supervisor is the key person; he or she can be of enormous help in facilitating this communication. Transportation problems may need to be resolved. After dealing with all the immediate personal concerns of the injured, it may be appropriate to ask, what happened? If the incident involves a fatal injury or an environmental incident, perhaps a chemical spill, notification of appropriate governmental agencies and other provisions of an Environmental Emergency Response Plan should be executed. Standard Operating Procedures should specify the communication plan for such events—what, when, by whom, and to whom.

Preliminary Fact Gathering Preliminary questioning of the injured assists in determining who should be a part of the investigation team and in obtaining a brief understanding from the injured as soon after the injury happened as is reasonably possible. Only the broad outlines of the event should be determined at this point. These will establish the expected framework in which a thorough investigation, if warranted, can be conducted. Other questions might be, "With whom were you working? What was happening when you got injured?" The injured should be encouraged to talk. The correctness of the statements should not be challenged. This can be sorted out later. Nor should intimidating questions be asked. This is not the time for an interrogation, just a quick, spontaneous response. There should be no criticism that causes the employee to become defensive.

In circumstances that warrant it, conditions in the workplace need to be given attention.

Immediately following the injury, while the injured is being treated, someone should be designated to study the scene of the injury with two objectives in mind:

1. To be able to describe in great detail at the subsequent injury investigation meeting the facts of the workplace:
   - positions of switches, set-points, valves, "blanks," recorders, and so forth
   - position of parts of various pieces of equipment
   - location of any blood
   - location of adjacent personnel
   - presence of warning signs/devices and machine guards
   - tools in use
   - odors and evidence of spills
   - housekeeping, orderliness

To assist in this step and to improve recollection, detailed notes must be taken, sketches drawn, photographs taken, and records written of conversations with persons who were close to the incident. These notes of conversations should not be recorded at the time of the conversation, but should be recorded as soon as possible, privately. The objective here is to avoid the appearance of legalism, or establishing eyewitness accounts. "Eyewitness" accounts frequently are in error—not in accord with the actual facts—and can therefore impede the understanding of what happened. The objective is to "capture" thoughts of employees as quickly as possible, yet to recognize that these thoughts may not adequately represent the full and correct facts of the case. In fact, these "thoughts" should be handled for what they are—initial impressions, subject to modification as the investigation reveals a better understanding of events.

2. To prevent the workplace from being disturbed, cleaned up, or altered if this is reasonably possible to accomplish. Maintaining the workplace "as is" provides the investigating committee the opportunity of seeing the workplace as it actually was at the time of the injury. However, if this would be a costly decision, this step may not be justified. Rescue operations may preclude maintaining the status quo. The seriousness of the injury, the complexity of the circumstances, the financial consequences, and the uncertainty of equipment condition are all factors that should be considered before action is taken regarding the workplace.

The Investigative Team All injuries should be investigated to a degree appropriate to their seriousness or potential seriousness. An investigation of a superficial paper cut on the finger of a secretarial employee arising from ordinary handling of a sheet of paper may be no more than spending a moment reviewing precisely what the employee was doing and reaching a mutual agreement that the use of a sliding motion with the hands needs to be avoided in order to avoid such a cut. An investigating team consisting of the injured and the first-line supervisor is all that is needed. The report of this investigation can be made directly on the form in Figure 9-4. No publicity is warranted.

In circumstances in which the injury or potential for injury or damage to health or to the environment is substantial, greater attention and analysis are appropriate.

After obtaining the employee's initial report of what happened, when circumstances make this possible, the supervisor and others can begin to think about who the chairman of the investigation team and the members of the team should be. Depending on the seriousness or potential seriousness of the event, the chairman of the investigation team can range from the first-line supervisor to a direct report of the site manager or functional head (for example, marketing, finance, or research) of an operating safety unit or organization.

It is usually not wise for the top person in the organization to serve as chairman of the investigation committee. His or her role is best reserved for monitoring the conduct of the investigative meeting and/or providing critical review of its thoroughness and the adequacy of its recommendations. The seriousness of the event should serve as a guide to the appropriate degree of direct involvement of the top person. In a large organization in which lower levels of supervision are fully capable of handling the investigation, the manager may want merely to make a few opening remarks in which he or she reminds the committee members that the purpose of the meeting is to develop recommendations that the committee believes will prevent reoccurrence of similar events. The manager can also confirm his or her conviction that all injuries/incidents can be prevented and that the task of the committee is to discover what can be done to make this a reality. The manager can also make clear that management shortcomings, including his or her own, are not "off limits." After such remarks the manager may choose to leave the meeting, or, on the other hand, remain present to assist as may be needed. The manager should, however, normally not run the meeting.

If the organization is a small one, the manager may be the only member of management who can adequately chair the investigating committee. In fact, if the unit is a very small one and the incident is of sufficient seriousness, it may be necessary for someone off-site to serve as chairperson. The critical consideration in determining the chairperson is whether or not the prospective chairperson has the leadership skills and influence within the organization to lead the committee to a useful outcome. The chairperson should be the lowest level supervisor who can meet these criteria.

Membership on the committee should be determined by two criteria: (1) whether it is likely that the person has something unique to contribute—some unique information or viewpoint, and (2) whether it is likely that the recommendations that are developed will significantly affect this person or the organization he or she represents. These criteria suggest that the chairman needs to make some preliminary estimates of what will take place during the investigation and, therefore, who should be present. The committee should, however, not be so large as to make impossible a good cohesive working group; perhaps eight persons is a practical maximum, even for complex situations. Several meetings may be necessary to reach an understanding of modes of equipment operation, operating instructions, training records, and materials. It is usually better to work a small committee harder than to enlarge the committee.

All OSHA recordable injuries (because of their seriousness, not because of their recordability) and most illnesses should be investigated by a team of no less than four persons: (1) the injured, when available; (2) a peer of the injured—a fellow worker, who is familiar with the work involved, perhaps from a different work crew; (3) the injured's direct supervisor; and (4) this supervisor's supervisor. Each of these committee members has a unique contribution to make to the investigation.

Possible candidates for addition are: (1) safety supervisor, (2) additional higher level supervision, (3) site physician or other medical personnel, (4) additional representation from the injured's peer group, and (5) anyone who may be expected to become responsible for an anticipated recommended action item—for example, purchasing personnel, if shortages of materials or supplies appears to be a factor contributing to the event.

The *injured* can contribute personal understanding of what happened, prior experience, training, state of mind, perceived and actual job pressures for production, quality, costs, customer contacts, and so forth.

A *peer* of the injured can report how he or she normally does the task involved, specific training, job pressures, close calls not involving an injury, equipment malfunctioning, and inadequate or out-of-date performance standards. In the event that the injured has difficulty in being objective, the presence of a peer can be helpful in "keeping the story straight." The presence of a peer also dilutes the proportion of the team who are management representatives. This team makeup puts a constructive restraint on supervisory behavior that may otherwise turn the investigation into an inquisition. When well chosen, the peer representative also will be seen by those not at the investigation as a reliable reporter of the committee's deliberations.

The injured's supervisor should be present primarily because it is he or she who is directly responsible for the well being of the injured employee. The supervisor needs to come face to face with any of his or her own shortcomings as contributing factors to the injury. As such, the supervisor may be the most useful person in developing corrective action steps.

The *second-level supervisor* should be present for at least the following reasons: (1) he or she can become more fully aware of the performance of the injured's supervisor, (2) he or he should be able to contribute to the corrective steps from a broader point-of-view than other participants, (3) he or she can more creditably represent upper management's commitment to employee safety, (4) he or she has access to more resources than other members of the team in the event that resources appear as limiting factors in developing recommendations on action items, and (5) like the injured's peer, the second-level supervisor can normally be more objective concerning the events leading to the injury because he or she is normally less intimately involved than are both the injured and the injured's direct supervisor.

There are several reasons for the desirability of upper management's direct, active participation in the investigation of serious injuries or incidents with potential for serious adverse consequences:

1. Lower management and hourly employees can see management's concern for and commitment to the well-being of employees, the public, and the environment.
2. The incident investigation is likely to be more thorough because the higher level manager is able to ask more probing questions on the basis of his or her experience.

3. The higher level manager, by example, trains lower level managers in incident investigation techniques.
4. Recommendations to prevent recurrence carry more weight and are more likely to be implemented.

To be actively involved means to review the scene of the injury, and to actively participate during the investigation. Simply signing the report form is not being actively involved!

The proposed committee members should be informed of their selection as members and be asked to come to the investigation meeting as well prepared as possible to contribute to establishing a full understanding of the events leading to the incident. In complex operating situations, operating personnel should review any existing standard operating procedures, machine speed records, and sequence charts, operating logs, and other records that may be of value in improving their understanding of what happened as well. Maintenance and engineering personnel can contribute by examining equipment involved for evidence of malfunctioning switches, valves, hydraulic lines, and other evidence that equipment failure may have been an important factor.

STEPS IN CONDUCTING THE INCIDENT (INJURY) INVESTIGATION MEETING

1. All the participants on the investigation team should be welcomed, and be assured that each has something to contribute to the meeting and that the investigation will prove useful. Participants should be made to feel as much "at ease" as possible. All members should be introduced or they should introduce themselves—giving a brief statement of their job assignment. Upper supervision should arrive at the meeting early, to have time to exchange a few "pleasantries" with as many of the participants as possible, before the chairman calls the meeting to order.

2. The chairman should then remind the group that the reason for getting the group together is that an employee has been injured or a noninjury incident has occurred, and that the purpose of the meeting is to develop an understanding of what happened in order to be able to take actions to prevent a reoccurrence of this specific incident, as well as other ones that may be similar to the one that has just occurred. The chairman should express management's support for this effort and its dedication to operating the activity free of employee injury or other types of incidents.

If higher level management is present, its representative should take the opportunity to express concern for employee welfare and personal support for measures that may need to be taken to assure nonreoccurrence. Management should restate support of the concept that "all injuries can be prevented," emphasizing that the very reason for the investigation is to develop plans for preventing future potential injury. Thus, the meeting will not end until recommendations for adequate action have been established. In fact, the group may need to be reconvened if this objective cannot be accomplished at the first meeting.

3. A medical report on the status of the injured should be made. This can be made by the injured, if available. In addition, the medical prognosis should be brought forth.

Participation by the facilities medical advisor is desirable. First-line supervision may be the only source of this information if neither the injured nor the physician/nurse is present; however, the condition of the injured must be established. In order to develop real action plans, the group needs to understand that it is investigating a real situation—that the investigation is not an just academic exercise or a bureaucratic requirement.

4. The injured, or—if he is not available—someone who is knowledgeable about the injury, should tell the group what happened—**without interruption**. Questions can be asked later, but the "stream of consciousness" of the injured must not be interrupted. After the injured has presented his understanding of what happened, the chairman—who should have been taking brief notes, not a verbatim transcript—should then restate "what happened" in summary form, that is, the chairman's understanding of the injured's description. He should seek and obtain the injured's concurrence, adjusting the description as necessary. Upon hearing this restatement of the description, the injured may want to change or clarify the description. He should be encouraged to make sure that all correctly understand the facts. He should not be challenged or induced to behave defensively. That the "story" does not seem to "hold water" can be addressed later, not at this time. Now is the time to get the clearest possible description from the injured, without questions or inferences denoting fault. The injured should be allowed "to tell his story."

If anyone on the investigation team feels some point needs clarification or elaboration, he should ask his questions after the reporting employee has told his story. Questions should be restricted, however, to the facts surrounding the injury or incident. They should not explore its causes. The following types of questions do not help in determining facts and often actually hinder the search for facts regarding events related to the injury: "Were you trained in this part of the operation?" "Didn't you know you had to wear goggles?" "Why didn't you get another ladder?" "You mean you didn't know the safety rule which prohibits the use of that type of match on this plant?"

5. After a clear understanding of the injured's report has been established, inputs from others who may know something about what happened should be requested. Again, this information should be given without interruption. Again, the chairman should restate each person's contribution to establish that the chairman, at least, has a full, complete, and accurate understanding of what the "reporter" has reported. Having received reports from all who have some information to report, the chairman should then move on to step 6.

6. At this step, any conflicting or apparently conflicting views should be discussed and resolved. Eyewitnesses are notorious at reporting fact, assumptions, and conclusions all wrapped up as "facts." The chairman needs to recognize this phenomenon and to remind the group that as this is a common human tendency it would be most unusual for all "witnesses" to have "seen" the same thing. The chairman might also illustrate the point by the story of three blind men who describe an elephant while touching the elephant on different parts of its body. Getting a common understanding of a complex phenomenon is a demanding effort, requiring patience and skill in getting full and cooperative effort from all. The desired net result must be a description with which all participants agree. If disagreement persists, the chairman may need to pursue additional facts in order to resolve differences in points of view. There may be cases in which these differences cannot be

resolved resulting in more than one version of "relevant facts," and thus the need for action plans to cover all of the plausible versions of "relevant facts."

In order that the chairman can guide the committee in developing all the relevant facts, the investigation should include inquiry into at least the following categories of events or circumstances:

a. General environment, both physical and operational
b. People, and their positions and activities
c. Organizational factors
d. Procedures
e. Equipment and its status

A significant factor to examine is evidence of recent change. In many incidents some change in status of one of the above categories constitutes a major fact contributing to the onset of the incident and subsequent injury or damage to health or the environment. Changes in personnel, equipment, or procedures should be thoroughly examined, particularly the transfer of controls, instructions, or information about changes that must be known.

7. After the final version (or versions) of relevant facts has been established and stated by the chairman, or preferably recorded on a blackboard or easel pads, each participant should be specifically asked, one at a time, if he concurs with this understanding of what happened. Is the person "comfortable" with "relevant facts"? Does he have any questions to raise for clarification? Does he believe that all possible information of help to the inquiry has been brought forth? Is there anything about which he wants to know more? Does he need to inspect the workplace again?

The chairman should express the view that if there are any members of the group who do not fully understand what happened, there will almost certainly be other employees who will not understand what happened after reading the investigative report. As a result, some employee, somewhere, sometime, is not going to have been helped by this investigation and he or she will be similarly injured. This possibility needs to be avoided.

Finally, the chairman should meticulously ask each person if he believes all the facts have been developed. The chairman should be assured of recognizable positive response from each participant. It is now time in the investigative process to develop specific recommendations for preventing reoccurrence, that is, an action plan.

You should note that "causes" of the injury or incident have not been identified. This omission is by design. A well-developed set of facts will make the cause(s) obvious. The cause(s) will undoubtedly be the result of unsafe acts (commission or omission) of someone. **"Accidents don't just happen; they are caused"**—by someone. A well-investigated incident will have developed an adequate set of facts, making specific identification of cause(s) only a finger pointing exercise. This practice should be avoided for it has a chilling effect on the development of a full set of pertinent facts. This conclusion regarding "causes" will surprise many people, including numerous safety professionals I have known. "If you don't know the cause, how do you know what to do to fix things?" The above discussion does not suggest that the cause(s) should not be discovered and recognized, but only that it not be explicitly identified as such. What good does it do to point out the indiscretions or mistakes of particular employees, when the "facts" have made these clear? The inquiry should move directly from fact development to recommendations for prevention.

Another significant aspect of not identifying causes is the beneficial effect it has on future readers of the report. By not providing cause identification, readers are enticed into doing their own thinking, their own analysis of what the causes were and the degree to which they believe the proposed corrective actions are adequate.

Furthermore, avoiding explicit identification of causes removes an item from the investigation that would frequently develop contentiousness within the investigative team. Participants may become defensive and try to prioritize causes in order to place their indiscretions low on the list.

Before developing recommendations, the chairman should find an excuse to have the meeting "take a break." The participants can leave the room—go to the restroom or get some coffee—and reconvene in ten minutes or so. This break allows members, on an informal basis and perhaps a private basis, to express concerns that may still exist and to develop confidence to express them when the meeting reconvenes. It also gives the chairman an opportunity to thank, privately, any individual who has contributed unusually well to the understanding of the group, or whose contribution may have taken considerable courage or insight.

8. After reconvening the meeting, the chairman should make another "round" to seek any new ideas regarding the facts of the situation that may have arisen during the break. These should be explored and incorporated into the previous set of facts.

Because the injury investigation report is prepared to assist in the education of those not participating in the investigation, it is important to record all the facts brought out during the investigation which an interested person who was not on the investigation team might logically want to know. Doing so accomplishes several goals:

a. It provides enough information to the reader to learn and be able to have an informed point of view regarding the adequacy of the "facts" developed and recommended corrective action.
b. It demonstrates the degree to which the injury was investigated.
c. It helps train all readers in injury investigation procedures.
d. It establishes that management will vigorously pursue the investigation of injuries until a clear understanding of "what happened" has been developed or, in the absence of understanding, until possible alternative hypotheses of "what happened" have been developed. This position will encourage early and complete revelation of facts regarding future investigations in which readers may become involved.
e. It provides evidence that management seeks the truth, regardless of where this search leads.

Many of such "facts" may not be important regarding the particular injury under investigation; however, readers may want to know certain information so that they can independently reach their own conclusions. It is therefore useful to include such facts.

The facts should be itemized in simple sentences, not scenarios or paragraphs. Each fact needs to be dealt with singly. Each statement that represents a circumstance thought to need improvement can then be balanced by a corresponding corrective action in the "Recommendations" portion of the report.

9. The chairman can now begin the process of developing the recommendations for actions designed to prevent reoccurrence of the incident—not just for the injured, but for all employees. All suggestions from the committee should be recorded without judgmental or practicality comments from anyone, and also why a suggester thinks a recommendation will be effective in prevention. There should be no editorial comment, no negativism, at this point. The full range of possible actions should be listed, including who (person or employment category) is to take action or carry out each recommendation. Some recommendations may not make sense after the implementers are identified. These can be dropped, or substitute actions can be added. An example is, "Tell the injured to work more safely." Who should tell him? If he is in the meeting, the facts have already been established that the employee should have acted in a safer manner. Perhaps the injured is in the hospital because of an unsafe act he had committed. How often will telling such an injured person "to be more careful" make sense? Almost never. Yet many injury investigation reports state under the "action taken" space that the employee was "informed to be more careful."

Although usually desirable, it is not necessary that all the persons being assigned responsibility for taking action be at the investigative meeting. If they are not present, the chairman should see that these people learn of and accept responsibility for taking the recommended actions.

During the development of the recommendations portion of the investigation, each itemized fact must be examined and a determination made whether or not some improvement is needed. If it feels competent to decide what corrective action will achieve the desired improvement, the investigation team itself should record the corrective action as a recommendation.

Because management is responsible for the prevention of injuries and, more broadly, for all incidents, recommendations will largely be actions that management should undertake. Recognizing this aspect of injury investigation clarifies why it is so important to have representatives of all subunits of the organization which may have corrective actions to accomplish be present at the investigation meeting.

If the investigative team does not feel competent to specify the needed improvement, its recommendation should take the form of "consider such and such," or "issue a design request," or "develop a training program." Again, responsibility and timing must be specified. If it requests additional investigative work, the team must specify the specific short-term action it recommends as a stop-gap action so that the company can continue to safely operate, while awaiting a more permanent or economic solution.

Each recommendation is thus associated with an identifiable "fact" that needs to be changed. If recommendations cannot be identified as arising from specific facts, the "facts" portion of the report is probably deficient. And, that some "fact" is thought to need improvement by a reader and there is no recommended action for improvement suggests an inadequate set of recommendations.

It is not unusual, particularly in large organizations in which the bottom line may be remote, to seek solutions to safety problems by expenditure of money—modifications to facilities or additional or different equipment. These are enticing solutions. They frequently avoid the need to recognize current failings in individual people or the safety management process (the sources of all injuries). As hardware solutions take time to implement, no changes to people or management systems need be made during the wait for the new equipment! However, if employees and management cannot operate existing equipment safely, they are unlikely to be able to operate new equipment safely. The expenditure of money is seen by some managers as a way to demonstrate their commitment to safety. And, because of an organization's stated commitment to safety, approval of expenditures for safety is relatively easy to obtain. In fact, in some organizations safety is the "open, sesame" for obtaining funds that cannot otherwise be justified. In some, by recommending expenditure of funds, the investigating team purposely passes its responsibility to another party—that is, higher management—which may be reluctant to turn down a request for funds based on safety.

Recommendations that involve the expenditure of funds, in contrast to a managers' time and effort, should be viewed with considerable skepticism. The acid test is simply to look at the interim solution, if there is one, and question why it cannot be the permanent one. A review of the interim solution normally reveals that its shortcoming is not safety but rather inconvenience, inefficiency, and so forth. This being the case, funds are needed not for safety, but for convenience or efficiency. Let them be justified on this basis—not for safety! If there is no interim solution, the operation has presumably been shut down until facilities that can be operated safely have been made available. This approach usually generates acceptable interim solutions.

Recommendations from good incident investigations should focus on improvements to the safety management process, only rarely on facility changes.

10. The next step is to review the recommended action steps to see if there is a reason for accomplishing them in some particular sequence, rather than in parallel. If there is a logical sequence, this should be recognized and then acceptable, but realistic, completion dates should be assigned to the accomplishment of the steps.

It may not be possible to establish specific dates at this stage of the investigation. The investigative meeting might be adjourned and reconvened in a day or two, if this postponement will permit satisfactory dates to be established. If not, it is normally a better practice to get the report written and published, listing a date as "to be determined" rather than delaying issuance of the report. When the missing completion date(s) have been determined, a revised report should be issued.

Occasions arise when recommendations should be made in the form "consider taking the following action . . . " This permits the report to be expeditiously issued while preserving the fact that some additional thinking, and perhaps approvals, is going to be required. If the situation is handled in this fashion, ideas are not lost, follow-up is indicated, and, indeed, the readers of the initial report may be able to contribute to the "consideration." Again, the name of the person who is to be responsible for the "consideration" is recorded and published in the initial report.

11. The last item of business for the investigative team is to determine the distribution of the report. In general, the report should be sent to all employees who reasonably may be expected to profit from reading the report. More specifically, this may mean all employees (on the site), or *all maintenance and operations personnel.* Consideration should also be given to providing off-site personnel in a large organization an opportunity to learn from the incident. This is frequently best accomplished by sending a copy to other site managers and their location safety supervisors.

It is also sometimes appropriate to send copies or abstracts of the report to trade journals and professional societies, if unusual or new phenomena have been involved.

A significant aspect of wide dissemination of incident investigations is that readers are provided an opportunity to reach an independent judgment about the adequacy of both the investigation and the developed recommendations. Some readers may have, or believe they have, pertinent information regarding the incident which was apparently not recognized by the investigating team. By discussing such information with a member of the investigative team, the reader can assure that this information is appropriately recognized.

Secretary

The chairman of the committee has a lot of work to do during the meeting. While he or she may want to take a few notes to help recall critical facts, it is desirable that the chairman not also be responsible for producing the report. The chairman should normally appoint one of the committee members to serve as secretary assigned the task of producing and publishing the final report, subject to the chairman's approval.

Witnesses' Testimony

The procedure outlined above is an open, cooperative effort to discover the truth. Some people—in particular, some safety professionals—will find fault with this procedure because it does not provide a formal opportunity to interview individuals on a confidential basis. The belief is that by providing confidentiality some information will be obtained that otherwise would not become available. In an adverserial environment, this may be correct. However, an incident investigation should not be a criminal investigation in which, perhaps, much is to be gained by withholding information.

Formally obtaining confidential information is counterproductive to achieving good incident investigations. Doing so fosters a sense of lack of trust in the organization that is antithetical to the cooperative, nonthreatening environment necessary for establishing trust, mutual respect, and support for the investigative process itself. A few safety professionals may even feel personally threatened, because one of the "arrows in their quivers" is the establishing of good relationships with employees on a confidential basis.

Of course, there may be occasions in which an informant desires anonymity. He or she should be encouraged to be more forthright, with an explanation that the greater good will be served by being so. In spite of such encouragement, openness may not prevail. The supervisor who has received such confidential information has been put in an awkward position. The truth of the information cannot be tested by open discussions. Even when true, if the information is not disclosed its veracity cannot be defended. The one thing a supervisor may be able to do is to use the information to assist in his or her own search for understanding and thereby to develop the information independent of the informer. Knowing an answer frequently can assist in finding the path to the answer. My own experience suggests that this confidentiality route should be avoided, if possible.

REPORTING THE RESULTS OF THE INVESTIGATION

Figure 9-5 provides an outline for reporting the results of an investigation that are to be made available to the work force. Each of the sections of this outline is discussed below.

Nature of Incident. This section is a brief statement of what happened. It provides the reader with enough information to decide whether the report is of sufficient interest for him or her to proceed further or not.

Description of Incident. This section describes the incident but avoids, as much as possible, enumeration of facts; it must avoid statements relative to conclusions. The extent of the injury or other negative results of the incident usually are included.

Facts Brought Out by the Investigation. This section of the report lists the facts, as developed by the investigation. They should be simple, clear, short one-sentence statements, each containing only one specific fact. The section should include relevant "Good" facts, as well as "Bad" facts. The test for inclusion is, "Would a reader reasonably need to know this fact in order to understand the investigation and its recommendations?"

Corrective Action. This section lists all recommendations, along with who is responsible for implementing the recommendation and an expected completion date. The chairman of the investigative committee should be kept informed about implementation of each recommendation. The chairman in turn should keep his or her line management informed so that members of the Central Safety Committee are able to report, if called upon to do so, the status of recommendations at their meetings. As is indicated in Figure 4-3, page 69, this is a responsibility not of the Safety Office, but of line management.

Investigated by . . . This section lists the names (no position titles) of the investigative committee in alphabetical order. Providing readers with the identification of the members of the investigative committee accomplishes at least three desirable results:

1. It provides readers of the report an opportunity to discuss the report with someone who participated firsthand in the investigation.
2. It provides incentive for the investigative team to do a thorough and competent job.

3. It provides readers information relative to the importance attached to the investigation by upper management (presence or absence) and the level of management support for the developed recommendations.

The alphabetical order of the list also supports the anonymity of an injured person.

Publicity. In this section the investigative committee specifies what distribution will be given the report. As is indicated in Figure 9-6, reports should be centrally issued to assure similarity in format and style. This is an appropriate task for the Safety Office. One additional benefit of issuing investigative reports through the Safety Office is that this affords the safety professional one last chance to offer informed staff advice to line management prior to issuance of the report. However, formal approval of the report by the Safety Office should not be required. Again, this is a line management responsibility, not a staff responsibility.

USE OF THE REPORT

1. Each person receiving an incident report should read it, understand it, and assess any changes needed in his or her own situations in view of the reported circumstances and recommendations.

2. A second use of these incident reports is conducting "crew" safety meetings (see Chapter 15). Enhancement of employee understanding and commitment to safe working practices is an essential objective of crew safety meetings. Discussions of incident reports during these meetings contributes to achieving this objective. In addition, when incident reports are thorough, including development of meaningful action steps, they provide an important vehicle for demonstrating management's commitment to the safety and health of employees and the environment.

3. A third use of incident reports is follow-up by supervision on recommended action steps. It can bring out these reports from "tickler files" on a timely basis. It is also useful to review the status of incomplete action steps of reports at the monthly Central Safety Committee meetings as indicated in the sample agenda for this meeting (Figure 4-3). It may not be feasible to review the status of all reports. The chairman of the CSC should indicate which reports are to be reviewed. Those not individually reported on may simply be noted as "all items completed" or "6 of 7 items completed." The report provides an easy means for tracking follow-up.

One use that some have found for these reports is to measure performance. The fewer their number, the better the performance. This approach is almost always a mistake. To do so discourages the recognition of and reporting of incidents in which no injuries have occurred and deprives the organization of important learning opportunities. In fact, strong safety organizations expect to have incidents occur, be recognized, and be investigated. As performance improves, events that in the past may not have been considered as incidents become considered as such. The definition of incident is not static. It is the severity of events classed as incidents that may be a measure of performance, not their number.

THE "INDEPENDENT" INVESTIGATION

Many organizations have established the practice of "independently" investigating serious injuries and incidents not involving personal injuries. The premise is that through an unbiased investigator more will be learned about "what happened" than would through an investigation conducted by representatives of management responsible for the operation involved.

Strengths of an Independent Investigation

There are some identifiable inherent strengths associated with the use of an "independent" investigator. I have identified below those that I recognize:

1. The independent investigator may be a more experienced investigator than any available management representative. He or she may bring a more inquiring attitude, may make a more tenacious effort to ferret out important details, may have a more knowledgeable understanding of how events occur, and therefore may be better able to sift through available facts to piece together the most likely sequence of events that ultimately resulted in the incident.

2. The "independent" investigator may be more "open-minded" and therefore better able to recognize inadequacies, both organizational and individually. He or she may be more "objective" in evaluating the "facts" developed by his or her investigation.

3. Beyond these possible superiorities of investigative skill and knowledge, the "independent" investigator may simply be less likely to "cover up." A greater measure of honesty is presumed to be available from an "independent" investigator.

4. By prescribing the use of an "independent" investigator, upper management may be able to better project an image of "seeking the whole truth," unadulterated or diminished in culpability, as might not be expected of an investigation undertaken by representatives of management responsible for the operation.

5. Lastly, as suggested under "Flawed Incident Investigations," many management investigations are undertaken to satisfy an institutional requirement to conduct an investigation. Little of value is expected; little is obtained. This is, for some, a convincing reason for using an "independent" investigator.

Weaknesses of an Independent Investigation

There are, however, many disadvantages associated with the use of "independent" investigators.

1. The use of "independent" investigators communicates to participants and others that direct line management cannot be relied upon to conduct an "open" inquiry—that there is a significant risk of a "cover-up" of important facts. It also communicates a lack of trust in direct supervision at all levels. If upper level management demonstrates lack of trust in their subordinate supervisors, why should subordinates of these supervisors have trust in their superiors? An adverse consequence of the use of "independent" investigators is diminishment of the trust needed to develop and

maintain an effective, efficient organization. If lack of trust or the perception of lack of trust exists, safety performance will deteriorate rather than improve.

Management that cannot be trusted or is treated as though it cannot be trusted, should be removed, not circumvented by the use of an independent investigator. Such management will not be able to provide the leadership necessary to achieve improved safety performance—or improvement in anything else, for that matter. Trust, as Drucker[3] has indicated, is a prerequisite to leadership.

The use of "independent" investigators destroys organizational morale. In turn, this environment often results in the development of defensive attitudes—attitudes that lead to noncooperation with the "independent" investigator. This frequent situation is seen as justification for the need of a skilled "outsider" who is capable of digging out the facts in an uncooperative environment. That is, the use of an "independent" investigator creates an atmosphere justifying the practice.

2. The use of an "independent" investigator denies management the opportunity of directly experiencing and recognizing the shortcomings of the organization which an investigation may reveal. Thus, management is undesirably shielded from the discomfort or sense of failure that is essential to the development of the commitment to improvement needed to actually bring about change. Third parties, "independent" investigators, simply do not normally achieve management stimulation or the advantages management gains by "seeing for itself."

3. Even in those situations in which an organization does not consciously develop a defensive attitude and behavior, an "independent" investigator is often viewed as an outsider, and as such may be denied important information. For example, local employees might rally together and not be as critical of the "local" organization as is necessary to obtain a full understanding of all pertinent facts. Local employees have to live with each other after the "independent" investigator has gone, and their participation in the investigation may reflect this reality.

4. It is not only local employees who may develop defensive attitudes in the presence of an "independent" investigator. Line management frequently responds defensively to recommendations developed by an outside, "independent" investigator. Their attitude can also complicate achieving the degree of commitment to the recommendations needed for implementation.

5. "Independent" investigators do not have the responsibility for implementing their recommendations. Recommendations of "independent" investigators may be viewed as "unrealistic," or may reflect a degree of zeal that is viewed by management as unacceptable, or is accepted reluctantly and unenthusiastically. If the "independent" investigator is a "safety expert," the risk that recommendations will be viewed in this manner is particularly high. Safety experts frequently feel obliged to recommend perfection rather than a degree of improvement that will be actively endorsed by management and positively acted upon. This problem is inherent in a system that uses a safety expert as an investigator, "independent" or not. To expect a safety expert to recommend less than perfection is to expect the expert to abandon his or her knowledge—to abandon professionalism. Recommendations by safety experts, though valid, can be successfully discredited by an unsympathetic management. They

can be categorized as unrealistic, representing a lack of appreciation for the peculiarities of "our" business. Recommendations die for lack of enthusiastic sponsors.

6. Another weakness of the "independent" investigator arrangement is that line management is denied the opportunity of using an incident investigation as a vehicle for demonstrating its commitment to the safety and health of its employees, the public, and the environment. It denies line management an opportunity to demonstrate leadership.

7. Another significant weakness of the "independent" investigator approach is that pieces of information gleaned from the investigation are frequently both confidential and in conflict with each other. Resolution of conflicting evidence received in confidence becomes difficult to accomplish. Such investigations are prone to take on the characteristics of an inquisition in an attempt to identify the responsible or guilty parties. This negative aspect of some incident investigation practices was discussed under "Flawed Purposes," page 242.

8. Another consequence of confidentially secured information is that it cannot be included in the investigation report if the report is to be widely circulated. Alternatively, such information is included in the report, and the report is made confidential; thus its usefulness throughout the organization is presumably greatly restricted. This practice further compounds the issue of trust that the use of "independent" investigation raises.

9. Lastly, information obtained confidentially may be difficult to verify. It frequently cannot be easily tested by disclosure and subsequent challenge.

These are significant weaknesses inherent in the practice of "independent" investigations in contrast to investigations conducted by responsible management personnel. The use of an "independent" investigator not only sends the message of distrust, but also denies line management all the benefits that flow from a thorough, management-led investigation (see Self-renewal Incident Investigations, page 249).

An Example of an Independent Investigation

I know of an instance in which an "independent" investigator, an upper level supervisor from another plant, was named chairman of the investigation committee. The incident to be investigated was a major fire that resulted in loss of facilities but no fatalities. In fact, there were no injuries and no loss of capacity (facilities were redundant), only substantial loss of property.

The members of the committee were both on-site and off-site personnel. None reported directly to the local plant manager regarding normal assignments. The committee met, called witnesses one at a time, made their analyses, developed recommendations, and issued a report to the senior management to whom the plant manager reported. Copies of the report were also issued to all committee members on a confidential basis—all independent of the manager and his direct subordinates, the plant top management group. As a result of this arrangement, the manager and his immediate staff were in the position of having a report issued on an incident at his plant, copies of which were provided to some of his lower level supervisors, but which he did not receive until some six months later—after the recommendations had been approved by his superiors. Neither he or his staff was asked for input to the investigation or the resulting recommendations. This was truly an "independent" investigation.

Leadership cannot be developed or demonstrated in this type of environment. The local manager's credibility as a leader had been undermined by the public demonstration of lack of trust in him by his superiors. This "independent" investigation was not unique regarding this manager. It was simply the normal thing to do when this organization investigated a serious safety event. Instead of providing the manager an opportunity to demonstrate leadership, this organization has institutionalized a system that assures development of nonleaders.

Avoiding Cover-Up

The one weakness of self-investigation is, indeed, the possibility of actual or perceived "cover-up." This weakness can be easily overcome by management including on the investigation committee a person or persons of such independence and character to assure that the investigation is "open" and is perceived as "open." This is not an excuse; it is an act of leadership. By following this practice, line management maintains responsibility for investigating events for which it is responsible while maintaining "openness" in the process.

Investigation by Governmental Authorities

In situations in which legally authorized governmental authorities elect to conduct their own investigation of an incident, management should provide a liaison of adequate stature and authority to effectively assist such outside investigators. This liaison should also be available to answer employee questions regarding their involvement in investigations by governmental agencies.

Despite the involvement of governmental authorities, management should conduct its own independent investigation. The fact that a governmental agency is conducting an "independent" investigation should not deter line management from gaining the benefits to be derived from its own self-investigation using the principles and techniques presented here. However, if relevant information is available from governmental sources, management should seek it.

SUMMARY

Injury and incident investigation provides management at all levels an effective means for demonstrating its interest in and dedication to protection of the safety and health of employees, the public, and the environment. Line management led investigations require active, visible line management participation in the process of discovering deficiencies in the safety management process and in developing management action steps to remedy these deficiencies. They provide management an opportunity to heal itself. In short, they provide management an opportunity to demonstrate real leadership on a continuing basis.

Investigations of untoward events is an integral part of *The Continuous Safety Management Process* (Figure 4-1, page 62). They represent opportunities to discover the means for achieving continuously improving safety performance. Injury and incident investigations should be welcomed and enthusiastically pursued; they should not be shunned or participated in begrudgingly.

The results of injury and incident investigations should be:

1. *Discovery* of all relevant facts regarding the event in an atmosphere of open cooperation.
2. *Development* of management action steps that are expected to actually prevent reoccurrence of the event.
3. *Assignment* of responsibility for accomplishing each of the action steps, together with an expected completion date for accomplishment.
4. *Dissemination* of these facts, corrective action steps, responsibilities, and accomplishment schedule openly and widely throughout the organization.

These results are not easily achieved. However, success is more likely to be achieved if the principles and techniques outlined in this chapter are accepted and practiced.

Beyond achieving improved safety performance, management-led injury and incident investigations have demonstrated their positive influence on the profitability of the enterprises in which they have been rigorously pursued.

NOTES

1. Undesirable occurrences—injuries as well as events that did not result in injury to personnel but that had potential for serious injury or illness, or damage to the environment—are called Incidents. Injuries constitute a subgroup of Incidents.
2. See Rules of Evidence for United States Courts and Magistrates, Article IV—Relevancy and Its Limits, Rule 407 (Pub. L. 93-595.1, Jan. 2, 1975, 88 Stat. 1932).
3. Peter J. Drucker, "Leadership: More Doing Than Dash," *The Wall Street Journal*, 1/6/88, Chapter 2, Figure 2-1.

CHAPTER 10

INCIDENT INVESTIGATIONS: EXAMPLES

Chapter 9 discussed the principles and techniques for investigating and reporting incidents which have been found effective for demonstration of management leadership in achieving excellence in safety. But what about the product that is produced by the use of these principles and techniques? Achieving excellence in safety is not an academic exercise in understanding; it requires *doing*. The incident reports that are shown in the following pages have been selected to illustrate the product to be produced by applying these principles and techniques. They cover incidents both with and without injuries.

CASE 1

This case is reported via a letter from a mastic asphalt operative to his employer.[1]

> Respective Sir,
>
> When I got to the top of the building I found that the storm had pushed a pile of asphalt blocks over the edge.
>
> I rigged up a beam with a pulley at the top of the building and hoisted up two more barrels of blocks—I carried out the job—When I had finished there were a lot of blocks left over—I hoisted the barrel back up again and secured the rope at the bottom. I then went up and filled the barrel with the surplus blocks—then I went to the bottom and cast off the rope—Unfortunately the barrel of blocks was heavier than I was and before I knew what was happening the barrel started down—jerking me off the ground—I decided to hang on—
>
> Half way up I met the barrel coming down and received a severe blow on the shoulder, then continued to the top—banging me head on the beam and getting me fingers jammed in the pulley—When the barrel hit the ground it burst

its bottom allowing all the blocks to spill out—I was now heavier than the barrel and so started down again at great speed—half way down I met the barrel coming up—and received severe injuries to my shins—when I hit the ground I landed on the blocks getting several painful cuts from the sharp edges—At this point I must have lost my presence of mind—because I let go of the rope—the barrel came down giving me another heavy blow which landed me in hospital—I respectfully request you send me an Accident Report Form—

Not all reports of injuries are so thoroughly itemized as the above one. It is clear that this employee has been well trained to understand that filling out the Accident Report form is really the important item of business to accomplished as noted in reason 1, Chapter 9 (page 241).

CASE 2

Refer to Figure 9-5, pages 257-259.

Analysis of Incident Report in Case 2

1. The report has been prepared and issued as specified in Figure 9-6. The paper used is preprinted with red hash marks around its perimeter. The actual typing of the report for publication was done in the safety office where a report number was assigned—report 1, for the specified year, for Photo Products Department, for this site.

2. The *Nature of Incident* is described in three brief sentences—what was being done, what happened, and what injury occurred (not its classification). These sentences provide the reader with enough information to determine whether or not additional reading is warranted. They provide the data necessary for indexing or cataloging the event and for transmitting to others who may have an interest in it. They focus on the event, not on the bureaucracy of injury classification—and thus keep the "message" to employees nonjudgmental. That is, the event has been investigated because of management's interest in employee safety, not because management is required to investigate all injuries of a specified degree of injury.

3. The *Description of Incident* provides a short but detailed narrative of the circumstances under which the event occurred and an amplification of what happened. A diagram is attached to assist in achieving understanding.

4. The *Facts Brought Out* section is a series of "single thought" sentences that are statements of facts (as determined by the investigation) of interest to a reader who wants to gain an understanding of what happened and how it happened and to form an independent viewpoint regarding possible corrective actions to be taken. An important aspect of reporting of incident investigations is to keep in mind who the readers of the report are likely to be. The purpose of the report should be to communicate to these readers, not simply to substantiate that an investigation was made.

In reading this report, I have some questions that were not answered by the report, for which I believe the investigative team had answers. They simply did not report them. Was the attachment designed to exert force on the inner race available in the laboratory? Did the technicians know of the existence of such an attachment? Answers to these questions would assist in understanding whether the event occurred because of lack of knowledge or lack of use of knowledge. The distinction clarifies the corrective actions needed to prevent reoccurrence.

A second area in which the "facts" section could have been improved is the statement that the safety glasses were in good condition. The only judgment the investigation team can render is in regard to what remained of the glasses; the prior condition of the lens that was fractured is indeterminable. The remaining statements seem appropriate. The statements were carefully crafted to be factual, not judgmental.

5. The *Corrective Action* section focuses on "system" failures, not employee failures. Employee failures are already known, and presumably the employees involved in this event and those who learn from this event will have the knowledge necessary to prevent reoccurrence. What is needed now is an improvement in the safety management system which enhances the likelihood that employees with the requisite knowledge use this knowledge and that future employees both obtain and use the knowledge required to accomplish the task without injury. Written job procedures and standards, are essential to achieving these results (see Chapters 5 and 6).

An improvement to this section of this report would be the requirement to develop a list of "other definable mechanical-type work" as a separate identifiable corrective action. Such a list would establish a quantitative definition of the task. This will help to develop all the needed procedures, so that the procedure development effort continues after enthusiasm has waned.

6. The *Investigated By* section of this report identifies the members of the investigative team. In this case the team is larger than might appear necessary. However, each of these people had something significant to contribute. The presence of the involved individuals and their supervision as well as a safety representative needs no explanation. However, the presence of two additional levels of research supervision, as well as supervisors of both electrical and mechanical crafts and their supervisor, may need explanations regarding their possible contributions.

First, the report was not issued until a month after the event. This timing suggests either a late starting investigation, an investigation in which considerable controversy was involved, or both. This was the first incident to be reported in this laboratory organization of approximately 100 people six months into the year. It was therefore the first injury opportunity for research management to demonstrate its concern about safety, and to lend its support to the actions to be taken and to the importance of timely response to such events.

This event relates to mechanical work on electrical equipment being done by laboratory personnel whose background and experience is largely, but not exclusively, chemical in nature. Electrical and mechanical supervision were present to provide their knowledge regarding the work to be accomplished. Their supervisor's contribution, together with upper level reseach supervision, was to assure that the recommended action was not that such work be done by craft personnel rather than by laboratory personnel. The event had opened the broader question of what was the reasonable way to accomplish this type of work. A tentative conclusion had been reached by upper supervision that training technicians for this type work was more efficient than calling for craft assistance with its attendant disruption of other work. They wanted to be present to better judge whether this conclusion was a correct one.

By direct participation in the investigation, first-line craft supervision were kept in an informed position regarding any questions that members of their crews may have raised about accomplishing this type work. The recommendation "to work closely with specialized mechanical shops" was undoubtedly included in recognition that the craft organization should not be ignored.

The investigation was chaired by the first-line research supervisor, who took on the responsibility for most of the recommended corrective actions. This line of action is as it should be, for direct supervision is responsible for the safety of all its employees. This chemist is going to have to learn some mechanical procedures! But if he is wise, he will obtain the assistance of his technicians and craft supervision in the task of preparing the required written procedures.

7. In the *Distribution* portion of the report is shown the distribution for the report. This distribution should include all groups who have requested such reports, generically, as well as any group the investigation team may think could benefit from seeing the report. Publicizing the distribution list permits recipients to judge whether all who they think can benefit have been afforded the opportunity of doing do.

CASE 3

TO: Those Listed [list not shown] January 28, 1989
FROM: J. B. Cordosa

Minor Incident Investigation: January 18, 1989

On January 16, 1989, there was a five-gallon spill of waste amines in the tank farm area of the Amines Process development pilot plant. The spill was cleaned up quickly, and we had no odor complaints from outside the plant.

Facts

A pipefitter had removed a bleed valve handle on the waste amines tankwagon in order to cut the stem. This particular bleed valve was located close to the valve used for charging waste amines to the tank wagon. Because of its location, it is very easy for the operator to accidentally bump it open during a waste amines transfer. This had happened on the previous day, causing a small drip, which resulted in the decision to cut the stem. We suspect that when the valve handle was reinstalled, the bleed line was left slightly open. Another possibility is that the bleed valve was bumped open by the operator as she went to open the valves.

An operator began preparing to transfer amines waste. She opened the internal valves and checked the pressure on the tankwagon. Everything looked normal, so she walked over to the amines shed area and began to open valves and pressurized the waste amines receiver for transfer. She then walked back to the tankwagon to open the external valves. She noticed a stream coming from the bleed valve, and immediately returned to the amines shed to cut off the waste amines flow. She then called for a second operator to help in the clean-up.

The lead operator came out and immediately shut off the bleed valve, stopping the flow of waste amines. Both operators then put on respirators. The lead operator went inside, put on an acid suit, and returned with scrubber solution (1% sulfuric acid) in order to neutralize the waste. The other operator began to use buckets of water to dilute the stream and also began to construct a dike with bags of sand. During the spill clean-up, the first operator splashed herself with dilute waste amines. Because she did not have on acid gear, she went in and changed clothes, but did not feel the need to shower. She had on regular leather work shoes, not acid-resistant shoes, and it was noted that these shoes should be checked for contamination and tossed if necessary, as leather shoes can absorb amines.

The third operator during this time shut down the process.

Contributing Factors

1. The lighting in the area was bad, making it difficult for the operator and the mechanic to work with the external valves.
2. The location of the bleed valve makes it easy to bump it open.
3. The lack of appropriate gear could have resulted in an injury, but did not in this case.

Recommendations to Avoid a Similar Spill

1. Improve the lighting in the tankwagon area (John Jones).
   Temporary changes already made, permanent changes to be made by January 31.
2. Cap off the bleed valve after pressure testing new tankwagons (John Jones). Done.
3. Modify the new tankwagon procedure—add a note to cap off the bleed valve (Dave Smith). January 31.
4. Review the procedure for mechanic handover to the operators (Bill Porter/John Jones/Dave Smith, with operators and mechanics). January 31.

Recommendations on Safety Gear

1. Review the current spill procedure. We decided that perhaps it is too restrictive (requiring full acid gear and SCBA for any spill, no matter how small). Modify if necessary (Bill Porter/John Jones/Dave Smith). February 15.
2. Retrain operators and emergency response team on spill procedures (Dave Smith). March 15.
3. Consider locating emergency gear closer to the amines shed and the tankwagon (John Jones). January 31.
4. Reinforce with the operators the need to change clothes and shower after being splashed (John Jones). January 31.

5. Determine if operators should report to the dispensary if splashed (Bill Porter/John Jones). Reinforce with operators (John Jones). January 31.

6. Consider if our policy should be that acid shoes are required at all times. Check to see if the new acid shoes are comfortable and whether or not they come in various styles. Inform everyone of the decision (Dave Smith). March 1.

Conclusion

The overall response to the spill was very good, with the exception of taking the time to put on the right safety gear. Operator response showed a good understanding of the process and the need to work together as a team in order to contain the spill.

(Signed) Janet Cordosa

J. B. Cordosa

Analysis of Incident Report in Case 3

The incident investigation reported in Case 3 contains many of the essential elements of an excellent incident report:

1. Description of what happened
2. Facts relevant to the incident
3. Recommendations, responsibility, and timing
4. Distribution list for report

However, the effectiveness of the investigation and the usefulness of the report of the investigation can be substantially improved:

1. The introductory paragraph of Case 3 is appropriate. Labeling this paragraph is a preferable practice—it tells the reader what the paragraph is designed to do. "Nature of the Incident" is an appropriate label. This paragraph should always be brief, as is the one in Case 3. The absence of odor complaints from off-plant sources is properly noted. The absence of personnel injuries is not noted but should be.

The size of the spill is mentioned; this item is inappropriate for this section of the report. To do so introduces a detailed, secondary fact too early in the report. The "Nature of the Incident" section should be analagous to an indexing entry—a key to the subject, but not the subject. See **Case 3, Rewritten**, p. 287.

2. The second paragraph of the report should be a "Description of the Incident," which, while brief, provides an overview of the incident preparing the reader for the kinds of issues he or she should anticipate in the "Facts" section of the report. It is an abstract of what is to follow. See **Case 3, Rewritten**, p. 287.

Case 3 as originally written does not provide this description independently of the **Facts** section of the report. The description is blended into the **Facts** section.

3. There is a *Facts* section in which a narrative report of the facts of the case are recorded. This third section of the report should be a series of, preferably, one-sentence, stand-alone factual statements that are, or may reasonably seem to be, of

relevance in providing the reader with the information necessary for a good understanding of the incident. The objective is to provide the reader with enough information (1) to understand the reasoning behind the recommendation contained in the report and (2) to develop an independent judgment regarding the adequacy of the proposed recommendations. See **Case 3, Rewritten,** p. 288.

4. The fourth part of the report of investigation is the "Recommendations" section. This section contains the actions believed appropriate (necessary and sufficient) to prevent reoccurrence of the incident or similar incidents, together with who is responsible for carrying out the recommendation and the time by which the recommended action is expected to be completed. If approval or concurrence by higher management or organizations not represented at the investigation is required, the recommendation should read "seek approval of . . . " or "Consider . . . " The point here is that a recommendation should be worded such that it can, in fact, be accomplished by the person designated as "responsible."

5. Part five of the incident report should contain the names of all members of the investigation committee, in alphabetical order, without titles or job assignments. Case 3 does not provide this information. See **Case 3, Rewritten,** p. 292.

6. Part six of the incident report should indicate who should receive copies of the investigation report. Case 3 indicated this inadequately on the front page. Copies should go to all personnel and/or representatives of organizations who may profit from knowing about the incident and the corrective steps being taken to prevent reoccurrence. See **Case 3, Rewritten,** p. 292.

CASE 3, REWRITTEN

Incident Report

Report No. ____*xx*____
Incident Date: 1/16/89
Report Date: 1/28/89
Location: 456 Tank Farm

Nature of Incident

A waste amines spill occurred while transferring waste amines to a tankwagon. An employee's clothes were splashed, but no injuries were incurred. No off-site odor complaints were received.

Description of Incident

At approximately 5:15 P.M. on 1/16/89, during an attempt to transfer waste amines from the waste amines receiving tank adjacent to the outside shed of Building 456 to a tankwagon in the tank farm area, a stream of waste amines was observed coming from a bleed valve at the tankwagon. The operation was shut down, the bleed valve closed, and the spilled material cleaned up and properly disposed. The spillage is estimated to have been about five (5) gallons. No waste materials entered the sewer system.

Facts Brought Out

1. It was dark outside; the lighting in the area of the tankwagon was poor and has been determined to be inadequate.
2. Because of the close clearances between the external valve and the bleed valve in the liquid line at the tankwagon, shown on the attached sketch (Figure 1) [see Figure 10-1], the valve stem on the bleed valve had been removed and cut shorter by a steam fitter on 1/15/89. This corrective action had been taken because the bleed valve had been bumped open earlier during operation of the external valve in the liquid line, resulting in a "small amine drip."
3. In preparation for transferring waste amines from the waste amines condensate receiver to the tankwagon, both tankwagon internal valves (liquid and vapor) were opened and the pressure on the tankwagon was observed as ___XX___ psi, and judged to be "normal."
4. Valves, to assure delivery from the condensate receiver to the tankwagon and to no other destinations, were opened or closed as necessary. Pressurization of the condensate receiver was effected, which in turn pressurized the entire liquid line to the external valve at the tankwagon.
5. Returning to the tankwagon to open the external tankwagon valves, the operator observed a stream of amines waste coming from the liquid line bleed valve.
6. The operator immediately returned to the amines shed and closed valve ___T4___ to cut off the waste amines flow. A second operator was summoned to assist in the clean-up.
7. The second operator proceeded immediately to the tankwagon and closed the bleed valve, stopping the amines flow.
8. Both operators put on respirators. The second operator put on an acid suit and acid-resistant boots and returned to the tankwagon with scrubber solution (1% sulfuric acid) with which to neutralize the spilled waste amines.
9. A third operator shut down the amines process at ___?___ P.M.
10. The first operator, who had not put on an acid suit, began using buckets of water to dilute the spilled waste and also began to construct a dike from sand bags available for this purpose.
11. Some dilute waste amines were splashed on the first operator's clothing. She changed clothes, but not the leather shoes she wore. No skin contact was thought to have occurred. Operator did not report to Medical or shower.
12. The diluted waste amines were successfully contained by diking and use of sand, and were scooped up and put into a drum for disposal. None entered the sewer. The sewer opening had been covered with rubber sheeting to

prevent entry of waste amines had this material not been adequately contained.

13. Subsequent evaluation by the first operator confirmed that no skin contact with waste amines had occurred.
14. Operating Instruction No. 102 specifies that full acid suit and acid resistant safety shoes shall be worn when waste amines spills are being handled.
15. There was not a clear "turnover" from operations to maintenance and then from maintenance back to operations. Procedures for accomplishing this exist but were not in use.
16. Some concern was expressed that the requirement for full acid suit and acid resistant safety shoes is excessive and unnecessarily delays taking remedial action in cases of spills of this type.
17. Emergency safety gear is stored *inside the pilot plant building*, which is 125 feet from the tankwagon and approximately 75 feet from the amines shed. Operator commented that remoteness of this gear was a contributing factor in not using full acid suit and acid-resistant safety shoes.
18. The emergency response team from the plant arrived at xx, but were not needed.
19. Written Procedure No. 102, dated 10/19/88, "Batch" Transfer of Amines to Temporary Tankwagon Checklist," exists but was not being used. It has not been normal practice to actually use this procedure checklist when making waste amines transfers. Procedure did not have piping diagram attached to it.
20. Procedure No. 102 makes no mention of the existence of bleed valves.
21. Three tankwagons are in use. One has no bleed valve in the liquid line (see note on attached schematic). [See Figure 10-1]
22. Some bleed valve discharge lines have been capped; others have not.
23. A procedure exists for pressure testing "new tankwagons."
24. Acid suits and acid boots are "group" apparel. Individual operators do not have their personal gear.

Recommendations

	Responsibility	*Timing*
1. Improve lighting in the tankwagon area.		
Temporary	J. Jones	Done
Permanent	J. Jones	1/31/89
2. Modify the "New Tankwagon" procedure to include capping off bleed valve after pressure testing new tankwagons.	J. Jones	Done
3. Cap off all bleed valve discharge lines.	J. Jones	Done

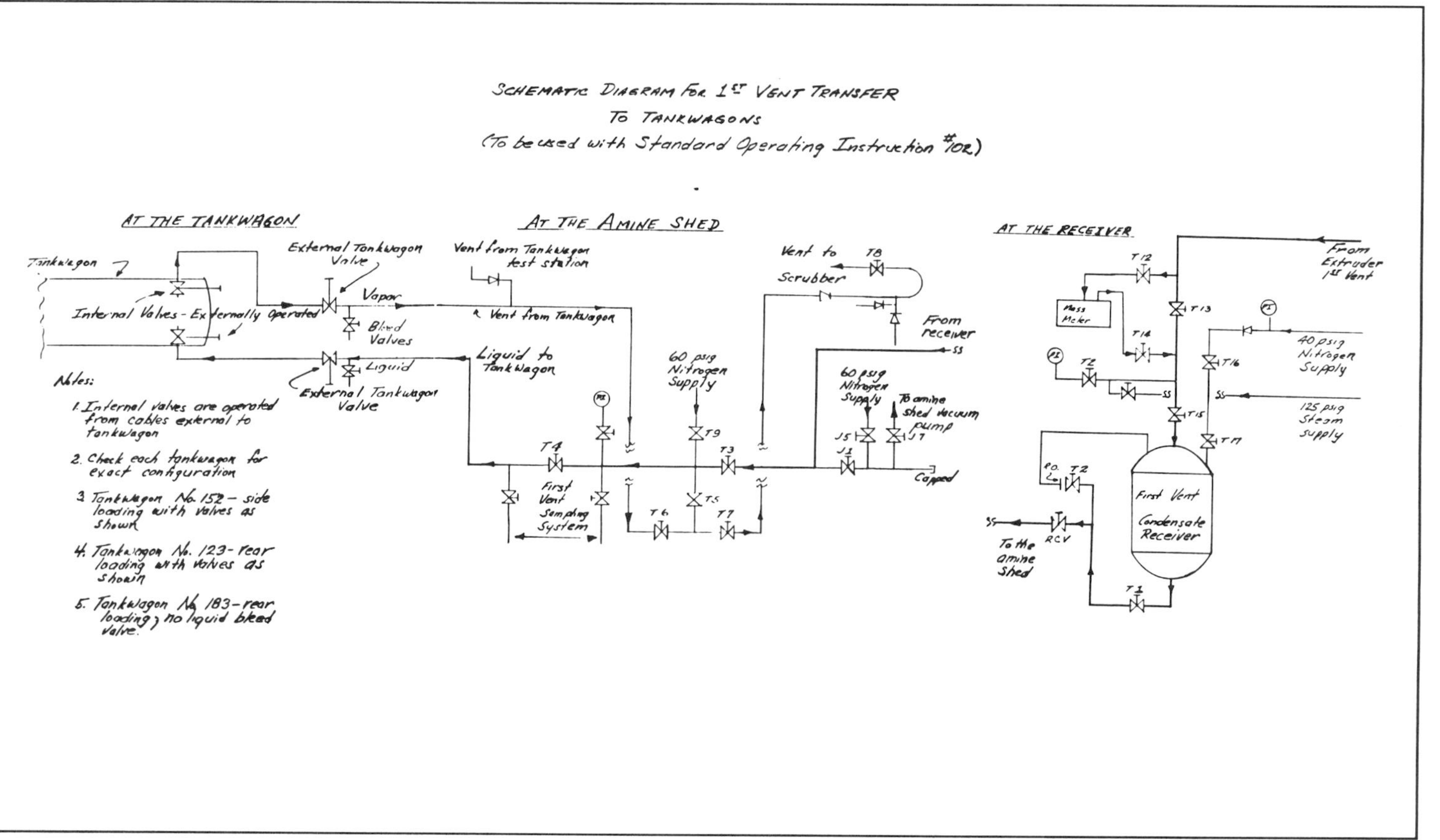
SCHEMATIC DIAGRAM FOR 1ST VENT TRANSFER
TO TANKWAGONS
(To be used with Standard Operating Instruction #102)
AT THE TANKWAGON
Tankwagon
Internal Valves - Externally Operated
External Tankwagon Valve
Vapor
Bleed Valves
Liquid
External Tankwagon Valve
Notes:
1. Internal valves are operated from cables external to tankwagon
2. Check each tankwagon for exact configuration
3. Tankwagon No. 152 - side loading with valves as shown
4. Tankwagon No. 123 - rear loading with valves as shown
5. Tankwagon No. 183 - rear loading, no liquid bleed valve.
AT THE AMINE SHED
Vent from Tankwagon test station
Vent from Tankwagon
Liquid to Tankwagon
60 psig Nitrogen Supply
T4
T9
T3
T5
T6
T7
First Vent Sampling System
Vent to Scrubber
T8
From receiver
SS
60 psig Nitrogen Supply
To amine shed vacuum pump
J5
J7
J1
Capped
AT THE RECEIVER
From Extruder 1st Vent
T12
T13
Mass Meter
T14
T2
SS
T15
T16
40 psig Nitrogen Supply
SS
125 psig Steam supply
T17
P.O.
T2
First Vent Condensate Receiver
RCV
To the amine Shed
T1

Figure 10-1

4. Review Procedure No. 85 "Mechanical/Operator Handover Procedure" with all operators and mechanics in the amines area. Establish the use of Procedure No. 85 as a normal job requirement.	W. Porter	1/31/89
5. Reinstruct all amines pilot plant operators on the need to wear personal protection gear when handling amines.	W. Porter	2/2/89
6. Review Spill Procedure No. 90 with particular attention to personal protective gear requirements, clothes changing, and showering requirements, and reporting to supervision and Medical.	D. Smith	3/15/89
7. Retrain all operators in amines pilot plant on requirements of revised spill procedures.	W. Porter	
8. Consider relocating and personalizing emergency gear to facilitate availability.	W. Porter	2/15/89
9. Consider the need for making acid-resistant shoes (boots) a standard requirement for all amides pilot plant operators.	D. Smith	3/1/89
10. Alter Procedure No. 102 to include:		
a. piping diagram.	D. Smith	3/27/89
b. reference to bleed valves and explicit requirement that all downstream valves be in closed position prior to pressurizing the liquid line to tankwagon.	D. Smith	3/27/89
11. Establish as a job requirement that Procedure No. 102 be routinely used when transfers of waste amines are made to a tankwagon.	W. Porter	4/1/89
12. Review all amines pilot plant operations to determine where existing operating procedures are not currently in routine use and where additional operating procedures need to be prepared. Establish that the use of operating procedures is a job requirement.		
a. Start using existing procedures.	J. Jones	4/1/89
b. Identify pilot plant operations for which operating procedures do not exist.	J. Jones	3/1/89
c. Prepare needed operating procedures and put into use.	J. Jones	5/1/89

Investigation Committee

J. Cordosa, S. Hasse, J. Jones, F. Knight, W. Porter, D. Smith, L. Taylor.

Distribution

All research managers; division director
All pilot plant supervisors, section heads
All members of investigation committee
Safety office, Newark
Safety office, Austin

CASE 4

The following report of an accident was received by mail.

1. Accident report. On returning from a workplace in Bristol County (30 miles from the depot) in a rented truck, two laborers of the installation department fell down a road embankment approximately 12–15 feet. They reported that the truck had skidded off the road on a curve. The driver received various cuts and bruises, none of them serious. The other worker had extensive bruises and cuts over most of his body, but particularly on his right leg which was very damaged because of the overturn of the truck.

2. Accident cause. In a first evaluation, the causes that may have produced this accident are:

a. Bad weather conditions (rain)
b. Bad road pavement
c. Human mistake on braking
d. Besides, they were not wearing their seat belts.

3. Immediate measures to be adopted:

a. Obligatory use of seat belts in all vehicles.
b. Issue safety rules for road travel:
   i. Use of seat belts
   ii. Maintain speed appropriate for the actual road conditions, not just posted speed limit
   iii. Driver must be in physical condition to drive safely
   iv. Establish maximum load for each vehicle
   v. Verify that rented equipment is fully equipped.

c. Verify that all workers know the safety rules, specially in the installation department.

d. Periodic verification that workers are following these rules by the safety supervisor.

This was a report from a depot manager of a highway maintenance organization. There is a depot in most of the counties in which the company does road work. The depot crews vary from a norm of 5 to 15 employees but are augmented by temporary hires to approximately 10 to 30 employees as needed. Depot managers report to regional managers who are responsible for approximately five depots.

Judged by the standards required to achieve excellence, this is a rather poor report. Judged by the standards found in everyday real life, this is an unusually good report to come from a gang-boss in a road maintenance organization. What has the regional manager learned about this "accident"? What information is obviously missing? What information is alluded to but not provided?

CASE 4, REWRITTEN

Incident Investigation

No. 89-xx
Injury date: 12/30/89
Report date: 1/20/90

Nature of Incident

On 12/30/89, two employees were thrown from a van in which they were riding when the van skidded off the highway. Both employees received multiple bruises throughout their bodies. Both employees lost time from work as a result of these injuries. Full recovery of both employees is expected.

Description of Incident

Two employees were returning from a work site in Bristol county (one driver, one passenger) during wet weather. On a curve in the road, the driver lost control of the vehicle, which tumbled down an embankment resulting in a total loss of the vehicle. Both employees were ejected from the vehicle.

Facts Brought Out

1. The driver was a long-term employee.
2. The driver was an experienced driver.
3. It had been raining. Both moisture and mud were on the highway.
4. Both employees denied that either had had a "drink" or a beer before starting the trip back to the depot.
5. There were significant skid marks remaining on the highway. Both tires showed skid marks. Based on these facts it is judged that the vehicle's brakes were functioning properly. No post-accident investigation of brakes was conducted. Post-accident investigation of tires revealed adequate tire tread.
6. This was a single vehicle accident.
7. The vehicle was not equipped with seat belts. It had been rented from XXX Company.

8. No post-accident evaluation of the vehicle was made to determine if the cab of the vehicle was still intact, i.e., no determination was made which may have indicated that injuries to employees would have been reduced if seat belts had been worn.
9. Neither employee has returned to work as of 1/18/90.
10. Driver blood tests for alcohol were taken by state police and subsequently reported negative.
11. The load being carried in the van was not in excess of its capacity, based on visual inspections.
12. The speed of the van was reported to have been within the posted speed limit.
13. Condition of injured employees relative to being able to do some alternative useful work has not been determined.
14. Driver's driving license was valid.
15. How employees were gotten to medical treatment facilities and subsequently returned to their homes was not determined.

Recommendations

	Responsibility	*Completion Date*
1. *Establish* a policy that all vehicles used by employees while on company business must be equipped with seat belts (lap belts and shoulder harnesses) for all persons riding in the front seat of the vehicle. This means *all*—company owned, privately owned, rented, customer owned, etc. Trucks having gross weights of more than xxx tons would be exempt from this rule.	Regional Central Safety Committee	2/1/90
2. *Consider* removing the truck exemption recommendation in #1.	Regional Central Safety Committee	3/1/90
3. *Consider* extending the requirements of recommendation #1 to all employees in over-the-road vehicles (tractors, road graders, etc.)	Regional Central Safety Committee	4/1/90
4. *Review* with every employee the need to adjust speed to road conditions, including conditions that can reasonably be expected under adverse weather conditons. Braking ability should be verified by cautious application of brakes as conditions change.	Each supervisor with each employee	2/1/90

5. *Review* with every employee the responsibility of the driver to keep his or her vehicle under control at all times. This is a driver responsibility that cannot be abandoned.	Each supervisor with each employee	2/1/90
6. *Determine* condition of injured employees and availability of alternative useful work that can be done by employees. Return employees to work when appropriate.	Depot manager	1/23/90
7. *Review* with each employee their need to know location of medical treatment facility nearest to their work sites.	Depot manager	1/23/90
8. *Contact* vehicle rental agency to advise them of need of seat belts in front seat of all vehicles rented to the company.	Company Purchasing Organization	1/28/90
9. *Consider* extending the requirement to use seat belts to *all* passengers in vehicles (includes back seats).	Regional Central Safety Committee	4/1/90

Investigation Committee:

Mark Baker, Tony Ikeda, George Johnson, Tommy Thompson, and Bill Sullivan

Distribution

All Bristol depot employees
All Region 2 depot managers
Region 2 manager, Dick Mackenzie
Corporate safety office, Phillip Strauss
Corporate Purchasing office, Linda Castle

Comments on Case 4, Rewritten

1. Uncertainty about the driver's experience has been removed.
2. The question of "alcohol" has been raised and dealt with as thoroughly as possible.
3. The speculation regarding vehicle loadweight as a causal factor has been corrected. Placement of load was not addressed.
4. Condition of vehicle (tires and brakes) has been established as satisfactory.
5. The fact that vehicle was not equipped with seat belts has been established.
6. The existence of a dangerous road conditon has been factually established.
7. The reason that the employees were not back at work, doing something useful, was not addressed.
8. Each of the facts that are in need of change is addressed in the recommendation portion of the report.

9. Areas of concern that the investigating committee did not feel competent or authorized to act upon independently were put forth as "Consider" recommendations. These have been referred to the Regional Central Safety Committee. The depot manager is a member of this committee.
10. There is no recommendation for which there is not a corresponding related "fact."
11. The speculation of possible causes included in the original report has been resolved.
12. No cause of the accident has been specified; every reasonable reader will come to the conclusion, however, that the driver either was driving too fast for the road condition and/or was not paying enough attention to adequately control the vehicle. By not specifying this as a cause, the investigation team avoided an argument from the driver or the inappropriate introduction of a fact such as he was trying to dodge a stray dog. First, it did not put the driver on the defensive; second, it avoided the "trap" of telling the driver "to be more careful" and concluding the investigation without having developed recommendations for improving the safety management system.
13. It allows the reader to decide the question of drinking as a factor, without introducing speculative statements that would inhibit distribution of the report.
14. Wide distribution of the report has been provided for, in particular to other depots in the region and to both regional and corporate safety offices. Thus, it is available to other groups as considered useful by these staff support groups. The corporate purchasing office has been included because it is this group that negotiates the contract with vehicle-leasing organizations.

CASE 5

Case 5 involves an employee fatality outside the United States. Because the case was a fatality, local management was not allowed, by corporate policy, to investigate. A corporate safety specialist was dispatched to make an independent investigation (see Chapter 9, p. 276). Also, because of the fatality, government representatives appeared on the scene to make their independent investigation. The government's investigative report is unavailable for review; it is being used in court action against the company. The investigative report of the corporate safety specialist is approximately eighty pages in length and it has been made available to a select few people on a confidential basis. This report represents a thorough collection of testimony (two weeks) from various employees, including managers up through the plant manager. The employee was found dead; no testimony is available from him. Based on all the testimony available, some of which is inconsistent, the report developed a plausible sequence of events that resulted in the death of the employee. Because of both its volume and the confidentiality of witness's testimony, the report is not generally available. The report was issued four weeks after the fatality.

Although local management did not have the results of an investigation available to it, it did begin to take some corrective steps; however, it did experience some difficulties in doing so because of the restraints on making changes imposed upon it by the two formal investigations taking place, and the prohibition placed on management discussion of the events with employees. Neither of these independent investigations appeared to be concerned for the economic consequences of a delayed start-up and its related loss of income to both the firm and its employees.

Because of the absence of an accident report as in Cases 1-4, the "story" as developed by the safety specialist is summarized below.

> On the morning of April 13, 1990, a holiday, Mike Krumm came into work on an overtime basis to descale a viscose ripening tank. He "clocked in" at 7:30 A.M. using a clock card that had his employee number on it but the name of another employee. He apparently got his tools about 8:30 A.M. and was seen entering the "chemical building" at approximately 9:00 A.M. He was also reported to have been seen at approximately 9:30 A.M. outside the "chemical building" laboratory. Although Mike was "missed" at lunch time, his absence did not prompt concern. Bill Lamont had spoken with Mike early in the morning and had reminded him that he should not go into a viscose ripening tank "too soon."*
>
> All "regular" viscose ripening room (VRR) employees had turned down overtime, apparently as a concerted effort to express their job dissatisfaction. Mike was an experienced operator who had previous experience in cleaning ripening tanks—presumably under supervision, which was the normal practice. Employees generally were aware of the hazards of viscose, including the possibility of excess exposure to carbon disulfide or oxygen deficiency in enclosed spaces.
>
> The tank to be cleaned had been taken out of service so that work could take place on the vacuum system, in order to improve its effectiveness. The system appeared to have some leakage, because vacuum pumps were running more often than normal. The vacuum system was complex; several valves had been replaced without noticeable improvement in system integrity.
>
> Although thorough standard operating instructions were available for the operator of the ripening tank, no instructions existed regarding the descaling operation. No written tank entry procedures existed at this location. Normal practice was that two men accomplish the descaling after the tank had been sufficiently vented. Venting was accomplished by opening the access manhole at the lower side of the tank as well as the manhole at the top of the tank. "Overnight" venting was apparently the normal practice.
>
> Several contractor organizations were on the site doing work unrelated to the descaling work that Mike was brought in to accomplish. The contractors' permit-to-work system had "broken down." It could not be determined with certainty when and to whom such permits were issued on the day of the fatality.

* In the manufacture of rayon, viscose is "ripened" by retention in vertical tanks in a chilled ripening room. Vacuum de-aeration is also accomplished during ripening. Viscose is a caustic solution of cellulose that has been treated with carbon disulfide, CS_2. The ACGIH TLV for CS_2 is 10 ppm. The odor threshold for CS_2 for most individuals is much lower.

Mike was found at 3:45 P.M. when he was sought by another employee. He lay at the bottom of the ripening tank, partially covered by a large section of viscose "skin."

After Mike was extricated from the tank, resuscitation was attempted and continued until arrival of a doctor from the City Hospital at 4:00 P.M. The doctor pronounced Mike dead shortly after his arrival. The doctor estimated death due to oxygen deficiency had occurred at approximately 10:30 A.M. Some "skin" material was found external to the tank. Mike was not wearing a fresh air mask as was normal custom.

Plant management notified Mike's wife by personally going to Mike's home. The production manager flew in from headquarters on the evening of April 13, and visited with the family, expressing his condolences. Assurances were given employees that when the investigation of the safety specialist was completed, management would take the steps necessary to prevent reoccurrence of such an event.

Analysis of Case 5

While management and employees came to know what happened in general, neither investigative report has been made public. As a consequence, employees do not know the facts upon which management has based its understanding of the fatality or the actions it intends to take to prevent reoccurrence. Of course, employees will therefore judge "what happened" for themselves, basing their opinions on less than all the available information. They will also watch changes instituted by management and reach judgments regarding the adequacy or appropriateness of these changes. Employees have not been put in position to support management, on a timely basis, in discussions of the fatality with neighbors and the public in general—particularly representatives of the media.

On the contrary, they have had testimony extracted from them but no official "feedback" of what others may know about the situation. Under these circumstances, it is reasonable to expect that some employees will take negative positions vis-à-vis management.

All of these negatives can normally be avoided if management conducts itself appropriately. **Case 5, Rewritten** demonstrates a more appropriate management response to this fatality. Some government investigators may not like this approach because it is different from the investigative approach to which they are accustomed. They may even object to discussion of the situation in a group by "witnesses." So be it; management is still responsible for results and should proceed as described in Chapter 9.

CASE 5, REWRITTEN

If the investigation of the fatality outlined above had been investigated by a group of people as described in Chapter 9, the results could have been presented as follows, and be available for *any* interested party to read and study. Such a practice does run some risk that a company adversary will attempt to use the report to embarrass the company and/or its management. However, secrecy is worse. As pointed out in Chapter 9, what is unknown is more titillating and likely to be speculated about than are honest facts and evidence that real preventive efforts will be undertaken. By having a group investigation, the participants can inform their subordinates and/or fellow employees of all the facts available to the investigative team, and hence management. They are also prepared to talk about corrective actions that have been recommended. In other words, knowledge and understanding are shared with employees as soon as they are available. Dissemination of this information should not be held up pending issuance of the report. This means that a good understanding of the facts must be achieved by the entire investigation team.

INCIDENT INVESTIGATION

Report No. 90-5
Injury Date: 4/13/90
Report Date: 4/20/90
Location: XXX

Nature of Incident

On April 13, 1990, an employee was found dead inside a viscose ripening tank. Medical examination supports a presumption of oxygen deficiency as the immediate cause of death.

Description of Incident

An experienced viscose ripening room operator had been assigned the task of descaling a ripening tank, which in normal operation is a CS_2-rich, oxygen-deficient "confined space" in which viscose is both "ripened" and de-aerated. The descaling operation is normally done on a regular schedule. In this instance, descaling was to be accomplished in conjunction with some maintenance work to improve the vacuum system integrity. Work was being done on an overtime basis.

Facts Brought Out

1. April 13, 1990, was a plant holiday.
2. The deceased had been requested by his supervisor to come in to the plant to do the needed work because all the operators assigned to the VRR had turned down the opportunity to work overtime. They had refused to come in even when urged to do so. It was not normal to request employees assigned to the chemical building to work in the VRR.

3. The deceased was an experienced employee who had descaled tanks in the past, apparently always under the direction of a supervisor; however, he was currently assigned as a member of the chemical building crew.

4. The tank had been taken out of service prior to the "day" shift of April 13, in order to isolate certain valves in the vacuum system for diagnostic purposes. Difficulty in maintaining vacuum was being experienced, suggesting a loss in system integrity.

5. The deceased's supervisor was not on the site on April 13.

6. The deceased picked up some descaling tools from the toolroom at approximately 8:30 A.M. The tool room was open because of maintenance work being done.

7. The deceased was next reported to have been seen outside the chemical building laboratory at approximately 9:30 A.M., at which time he was reminded not to go into a VRR tank alone.

8. The deceased was "missed" at lunch time by some of the employees who had seen him, but his absence did not prompt concern that something may have happened.

9. Another employee, who wanted to talk to the deceased, went into the VRR at 3:45 p.m to look for him. This employee observed pieces of "skins" on the floor outside the tank and then saw the deceased inside the tank, partially covered by a large piece of "skin." He immediately reached into the tank, pulled the deceased out, turned in the fire alarm to summon help, and began administering mouth-to-mouth resusitation.

10. The City Hospital was called at 3:50 P.M.; a doctor arrived at the plant and was escorted directly to the VRR arriving at 4:00 P.M. The doctor pronounced death immediately upon his arrival.

11. Civil authorities were called and, with their concurrence, the deceased was transported by the hospital ambulance to the city mortuary.

12. The deceased's supervisor and the plant manager were called about 4:15 P.M. and informed of events.

13. The immediate supervisor and plant manager went to the deceased's home and informed the deceased's wife of his death and what they knew of the events leading to his death.

14. The production manager was called and flew into town, arriving at the deceased's home at 8:30 P.M.

15. The plant manager had come to the plant at 8:10 A.M. to see what was going on and to check "clock-cards." Because the card the deceased had used had his clock number on it but not his name, the manager did not know the deceased was at the plant.

16. There is no written requirement that two men must be used to perform descaling work. Descaling has been done both singly and in pairs.

17. No confined space entry permit system is in use on this site; specifically, none was used in this instance.

18. The man-hole entryway at the top of the viscose ripening tank was closed, not open as "everyone" knows it should have been.

19. The general practice has been to open both access openings, top and bottom (side), for twenty-four hours before entering the tank, and then only after the CS_2 odor is "low enough." Meters for measuring CS_2 and oxygen concentrations are available but are not often used. There is no evidence that a "gas" test was made in this case.

20. The VRR tank was not completely isolated as is the usual practice before entry is made. Water, caustic, air, steam, and vacuum lines were still connected to the tank.

21. There is a well-developed set of operating instructions covering operation of equipment on the plant; in particular, the de-areation procedure is meticulously specified. (Failure to de-areate properly results in breakage of filaments in the subsequent spinning operation.) There is no system for assuring that these procedures are up-to-date.

22. The deceased was not wearing a fresh air mask when found, although one was hanging on the side of the tank.

23. The vacuum system work was being done by outside pipefitters. The permit-to-work system documentation for contractors was not adequate to determine, with certainty, when and to whom such permits had been issued on April 13.

24. The deceased left a wife and two children.

Recommendations

Item	*Responsibility*	*Expected Completion Date*
1. Prepare confined space entry procedures appropriate to site.	B. Tobias	6/1/1990
2. Have the new confined space entry procedures reviewed by corporate safety professionals. (Note: No on-site safety professional.)	B. Tobias	6/15
3. Issue Confined Space Entry Permit procedures. Discuss with every employee.	R. Piccard B. Tobias	6/29
4. Establish training requirements and licensing procedure for use of air sampling meters.	B. Tobias	6/1
5. Prepare a list of all "confined spaces" on the site.	D. Wojcik B. Tobias	5/4
6. Communicate to every current employee and to every contractor employee entering site that no "confined space" shall be entered until the above recommendations (1–5) have been completed unless individually permitted by the plant manager.	R. Piccard	4/27

7. Review existing permit-to-work procedures for contractors. Revise as appropriate. Ensure adequate records on issue and compliance.	D. Wojcik	5/1
8. Prepare detailed Standard Job Procedure for descaling ripening tanks.	S. Kaiser	4/27
9. Prepare a list of other plant tasks for which additional Standard Job Procedures shall be prepared.	Each first line supervisor; B. Tobias; D. Wojcik	5/4
10. Establish a time table for preparation of detailed standard procedures for jobs identified in recommendation 9 above.	B. Tobias D. Wojcik	5/11
11. Incorporate the above rules and procedures into a site safety manual. Develop a site safety manual. (Note: No site safety manual exists.)	R. Piccard	6/15
12. Begin a systematic program that ensures review of existing operating procedures on a specified frequency.	B. Tobias	5/18
13. Review "clock card" procedures; report any changes needed.	L. Mueller	4/27
14. Review this report with every site employee.	Supervision	4/27

Investigation Committee

Bruce Giuliani
Stephen Kaiser
Brian Lohmeyer
Bill Lamont
James Messick
Linda Mueller
Howard Osborne
Robert Piccard
Bobby Tobias
David Wojcik

Distribution

1. Every site supervisor (to be discussed with every site employee)
2. All plant managers
3. All investigation committee members
4. All corporate "officers"

End of Report

Note: The *titles* of committee members listed below should not be shown on the report. They are listed *here* to illustrate the composition of this committee:

Corporate safety professional	Giuliani
First-line supervisor, VRR	Kaiser
Operation Supervisor, chemical building and VRR	Lohmeyer
Operator, chemical building	Lamont

First-line supervisor, maintenance	Messick
Office manager	Mueller
First-line supervisor of deceased	Osborne
Plant manager	Piccard
Manufacturing superintendent	Tobias
Maintenance and engineering superintendent	Wojcik

Comments on Case 5, Rewritten

1. The report, containing the known (to a representative group of site employees) facts and management-initiated and -endorsed recommendations—a preventive action plan with responsibilities and a time table for accomplishing—was published one week from the fatality. It was concise and short enough that most employees would read the report.

2. The investigation was promptly completed, within two to three workdays following the funeral. All members of the investigation committee have the same set of facts—facts over which there is no disagreement among the committee.

3. Many employees got some creditable verbal facts from members of the investigation committee during the week following the event; written facts and the action plan were available one week from the event.

4. If any person has additional information he or she believes relevant, this information can be brought to the attention of any member of the investigation committee. A wide choice of a communication channel is available.

5. Management "took charge" of a "bad" situation and demonstrated its resolve to prevent reoccurrence.

6. Management made public "who" and "when" things were expected to happen. Employees were provided the information upon which to judge management's performance vis-à-vis this resolve. These actions build trust and confidence as management meets the time table.

7. No blame was placed on the deceased for doing such a "stupid" thing; no employee has been exhorted to refrain from making the same "dumb mistake."

8. Management has implicitly taken responsibility for the fatality; it is management that has recognized its failures, and management that has the corrective actions to accomplish.

9. An "outsider," the corporate safety officer, was a full participant in the investigation. Everyone, from the operators to the plant manager, understands that the top officers of the company will have the opportunity to make inquiries directly to the corporate safety professional. This will help ensure there are no "secrets"; but, more important, it is an opportunity for local management to "recover" and to guide the corporation to higher safety standards. (This site is typical of other sites within the corporation as regards "safety.")

SUMMARY

These five case histories demonstrate how injury and incident investigation and reporting can be used to effectively improve the safety management process, including open and thorough communication with all employees. They illustrate the technique of discovering relevant facts without fault-finding. Defensive employee behavior is thereby diminished.

They demonstrate that the final objective of such investigations is to develop a management action plan designed to improve the safety management process, rather than to determine what went wrong in the particular event. The particular event was used as a means of improving the way management carries out its safety responsibility, broadly.

These case histories illustrate how all employees can learn from the mistakes of other employees, including supervision. They also illustrate a way in which every employee can contribute to the safety management process to the extent of his or her ability.

They provide models that can be used in improving the usefulness of injury and incident investigations.

NOTES

1. This case has been adapted for the Mastic Asphalt Industry from an original Gerrard Hoffnung speech to the Oxford Union in 1954. I am indebted to Mr. Albert R. Stones, Managing Director, Towson Asphalt, Bolton, England, for this "letter."

CHAPTER 11

GOAL SETTING

Along with determining and establishing the mission of the organization, taking responsibility for results, endorsing strong associates and subordinates, and earning trust, a leader must set goals for the organization—criteria by which to measure performance and targets to shoot for—which, if achieved, represent real achievements, and thus success (see Figure 2-1, page 37.) Successful leaders are careful in setting goals. Goals need to be challenging but attainable. The organization needs to *believe* that goals can be reached and that they are worth reaching. The effective leader establishes goals and communicates the plan by which he or she sees these goals being reached. The effective leader establishes credibility of these goals and enlists the energy and support of the organization in searching to attain them.

MEASURING PERFORMANCE: ON-THE-JOB

In safety, goals are normally stated in terms of the number of injuries per exposure hour—that is, frequency rates. This provides an opportunity to make direct comparisons between different organizations and the same organization over time, even though organization population may significantly differ. Because of OSHA reporting requirements, in the United States the standard reporting rate is the number of injuries per 200,000 exposure hours. This is roughly the number of injuries in a year per 100 employees (100 X 40 hours/week X 50 weeks per year). The rest of the world, to the best of my knowledge, uses injuries per million exposure hours.

Because a fatality quite properly is considered more serious than a simple first aid case, an injury classification system based on seriousness has been developed. Figure 11-1 provides definitions of terms used in the U.S. classification system. These definitions are essentially those developed by the U.S. National Safety Council prior to enactment of OSHA legislation.

OSHA Injury Classifications

1. "Lost workdays—days away from work. The number of workdays (consecutive or not) on which the employee would have worked but could not because of occupational injury or illness."

2. "Lost workdays—restricted work activity. The number of workdays (consecutive or not) on which, because of (occupational) injury or illness: (1) The employee was assigned to another job on a temporary basis; or (2) The employee worked at a permanent job less than full time; or (3) The employee worked at a permanently assigned job but could not perform all duties normally connected with it."

3. "Medical treatment. Includes treatment of injuries administered by physicians, registered professional personnel, or lay persons (i.e., non-medical personnel). Medical treatment does not include first-aid treatment . . . even though provided by a physician or registered professional personnel." In explaining this definition more fully the Guideline expands the definition to include not only actual treatment provided, but also "should have been provided."

4. "First aid treatment. Any one-time treatment, and any follow-up visit for the purpose of observation of minor scratches, cuts, burns, splinters, and so forth, which do not ordinarily require medical care. Such one-time treatment, and follow-up visit for the purpose of observation is considered first aid even though provided by a physician or registered professional personnel."

5. "Occupational illnesses. Any abnormal condition or disorder, other than one resulting from an occupational injury, caused by exposure to environmental factors associated with employment."

Source: U. S. Department of Labor, Recordkeeping Guidelines for Occupational Injuries and Illnesses, September 1986.

Figure 11-1

This classification system appears to be becoming commonly accepted around the world. Thus, frequency rates for various degrees of seriousness will be more easily compared on a global basis.

These classification terms are normally abbreviated as:

LWC—lost workday case, *with* days away from work.

RWC—lost workday case, *without* days away from work.

MTC—medical treat case.

FAC—first aid case.

TRC—total recordable cases. This is the sum of LWC + RWC + MTC for both injuries and illnesses, including fatalities.

All U. S. occupationally related injuries and illness must be *recorded* on the OSHA 200 log and reported annually to the Bureau of Labor Statistics.

There are measures of safety performance other than employee work-related injuries and illnesses. Damage or potential damage of the environment has increasingly become an important criterion of performance. Injury and damage to the health of the public, or the potential to do so, are also a measure of an organization's safety performance. Damage to facilities is yet another safety performance measure. Injuries to employees occurring off-the-job sufficiently serious to preclude their coming to work are becoming more fully recognized as an important measure of safety performance. The frequency of occurrence of first-aid cases is also a possible candidate for measurement of performance.

The frequency with which untoward events—incidents—take place which may or may not have resulted in injuries or damage to health, environment, or facilities, is also a possible measure of performance (see Chapter 9, page 280).

Another measure of performance that is sometimes used is "days away from work," either cumulative or averaged on a per injury/illness basis. OSHA requires reporting the "days away from work" statistics. This is presumably a measure of the seriousness of lost workday (LWC) injuries. Unfortunately, these data are the result of both the seriousness of the injury and the manner in which the injury is managed (see "Total Disability Performance," p. 311 ff).

No single measurement has been accepted, generally, as the preferred criterion for measuring performance. Fatalities must certainly be the most important, followed by injuries sufficiently serious to prevent reporting for work—any work. Using seriousness of injury as the criterion creates a hierarchy of criteria, each of which can be a measure of performance. This presents an array of yardsticks that can be confusing and that can sap the energy goal setting should generate. One solution that many organizations have found successful is the use of a two-tiered criterion for on-the-job performance. The first and most important of these criteria is the LWC (including fatalities) frequency rate. The second, and subsidiary criterion is the TRC frequency rate. Adoption of this two-tiered scheme places focus on the most serious injuries without implying the concept that if an injury or illness is not really serious it is not important. Two criteria for on-the-job performance are not too much for most employees to comprehend and react to positively.

Some organizations—for example, large international petroleum companies whose operations require extensive over-the-road driving of petroleum tank trucks in "difficult" environments—may find it desirable to have the first tier of a two-tier system measure only the fatality rate. The second tier might be either the LWC or the TRC rate.

Selection of the most useful performance measures reveals the leader's sensitivity to what criteria stimulate employees.

MEASURES OF PERFORMANCE TO BE AVOIDED

The first-aid case (FAC) frequency rate has been mentioned as a possible measure of performance. While changes in the frequency of first-aid cases certainly reflect changes in performance, the use of FAC frequency rates as a goal is virtually always counterproductive. In the best of reporting circumstances, the validity of reported FAC rates is suspect. Becoming injured, even slightly, is evidence that someone has done something unsafely. In the absence of a well-established workplace culture that demands that "all injuries, regardless of how slight, must be reported," injuries that the employee believes can be successfully self-treated will frequently simply not be reported. Such injuries are considered by many, including a significant percentage of supervision, as simply not warranting the time of the employee or the medical personnel—certainly not worth going through the "hassle" of an injury investigation.

Even in organizations believing that all injuries including first aid cases should be reported, it is unwise to use first aid cases as a performance measure. To do so establishes a temptation for not reporting to which some employees will simply fall victim. This denies supervision the opportunity of learning what there is to be learned as well as foregoes the opportunity to have the injury more appropriately treated. In any event, quantitative measurement of first aid cases is a statistic in which most work forces will place no credence. It is therefore useless as a criterion for performance measurement or goal setting.

Another tempting variable for measuring safety performance is to calculate an incident rate. This method ostensibly would measure the frequency of untoward events, or near misses, which might serve as an early warning or leading indicator useful in directing the safety effort. This, too, is a "confessional" for which the confessor will be admonished. It also requires that a static definition of what constitutes an incident be developed. I have seen definitions based on value of property damage, volume of uncontrolled hazardous materials that are released, and degree of injury that might have reasonably resulted if circumstances had been only slightly different. If such definitions are used in conjunction with incident rate as a measure of performance, seldom do the judgment calls err on the side of calling an untoward event an incident. There seems to be a predisposition to assure that the criteria for incident status are *not* met. "Legalism" prevails. A better practice is to encourage reporting of all such incidents with the goal of investigating those that seem worthy of investigating. These would be classed as incidents and, indeed, investigated.

This method suggests adoption of a flexible definition for what is considered, at the time, serious enough to be investigated and hence to be classed as an incident. I recommend this as sound policy. It encourages full reporting and serious consideration of the question; it avoids "playing games" with pre-established but ambiguous definitions; it allows management to raise standards as performance improves. What may not have been considered an incident worthy of investigation yesterday can be considered so today without bureaucratic discussion regarding definition changes. An event becomes an incident because a leader says it is!

MEASURING PERFORMANCE: OFF-THE-JOB

Injuries

A major source of personal pain and suffering as well as financial loss to the employer are injuries that occur off-the-job. Because of their interest in employees as well as stockholders, many managers have come to recognize the virtue of devoting attention to off-the-job injuries. Some have incorporated off-the-job lost workday cases (time away from work) frequency rate as part of the safety goals for the organization for which they are responsible. I know of none who have incorporated less severe off-the-job injury rates as part of a goal setting effort. Developing a workplace culture that recognizes and supports management's interest in the off-the-job activities of employees, and holding supervision responsible for performance results is a complex and challenging task. Suffice it to say that excellence on-the-job is not likely to be achieved if off-the-job injury performance is ignored. Passing through the workplace gate does or can improve the safety behavior of employees, but the less change that is needed, the better. In 1953, Du Pont began using off-the-job injury performance as a performance criterion for supervision. After a "rocky" start, this concept is now a well established and accepted one; employees understand that the basic thrust is to encourage them to "take their safety home and with them on vacation." In 1990 off-the-job injury frequency rate for Du Pont employees was 0.48. A goal of 0.40 has been established for 1991.

As mentioned earlier, "days away from work" is a possible measure of performance useful for goal setting. It is probably the measurement most directly related to costs and hence an important element of the safety program. However, it does not appear to be a statistic that generates enthusiasm or support in the organizations in which it is used. Because of this liability, it is unlikely to be useful as a challenging goal. However, such a reaction by employees is not unchangeable. In circumstances in which employees are genuinely concerned about costs and maintenance of productivity, "days away from work" can and has become a motivating criterion.

Illnesses

Off-the-job illness performance is another major area of employee health and safety which affords managers who aspire to leadership an opportunity to lead. (See a more detailed discussion under Total Disability Performance, p. 311 ff.)

MEASURING PERFORMANCE—SUMMARY

From the numerous performance measures possible for goal setting, four emerge as being reasonable: (1) number of fatalities, (2) LWC rate, (3) TRC rate, and (4) off-the-job LWC rate. For convenience of communication, frequency rates may be converted into whole numbers for a particular work force. Use of actual frequency rate is a rather esoteric criterion for most employees. In addition, rate statistics do not enlist concern and interest as readily as whole numbers of individually identifiable injuries.

These rates, and corresponding whole numbers of injuries, are normally stated on a per year basis, and in practice the whole numbers are allocated on a monthly basis to permit monthly assessment of status. Thus, for a work force of 1000 employees, a goal for LWC = 2.4 is equivalent to twenty-four LWC injuries and illnesses in the annual goal period, or two per month. Thus, employees can be kept abreast of how the organization is doing on a monthly basis.

ESTABLISHING SAFETY GOALS

Establishing safety goals is not a task that management should take lightly. Establishing safety goals that generate energy within the organization to achieve superior results requires a sensitive appreciation for employee understanding of safety performance criteria and measurement. Astute leaders should avail themselves of the built-in "intelligence" system that the Central Safety Committee and its subcommittee system provides (see Chapter 4). The Program and Activities subcommittee can be an excellent vehicle through which to develop the required sensitivity to employee understanding. Some organizations have found that creation of an ad hoc Goals subcommittee of the CSC has contributed successfully toward setting overall goals for the organization. In large organizations, divisional goals are also established for each division of the full organization. These divisional goals, of course, must "fit" the total goals for the entire organization as ultimately established at the top. Leaders should seek help but not abdicate their responsibility to lead; an important part of this philosophy is their setting goals.

Organizations that have enthusiastically and knowledgeably adopted the management of safety ideas as outlined in this book have consistently reduced their injury/illness statistics by 50 percent during the first two years of adoption.[1] These organizations have included chemical research laboratories, railroads, barging operations, bakeries, slaughter houses, oil refineries, and chemical plants in the United States and around the world and across significant cultural barriers. The system works—when it starts at the top!

There are other safety related events that do not involve injuries or illnesses in which responsible management will have an interest and for which goals are appropriate. Goals should be established only for those events that can be measured by yardsticks that remain essentially constant. The *number* of specific events meeting a fixed definition—such as emissions to the atmosphere or spills—may be useful for goal setting; these should not be overlooked as important measures of safety performance. Total volume of classes of emissions is also appropriate. On the other hand, "incidents" would not meet the criterion of being measured by a constant yardstick. As performance improves, organizations will find it possible and useful to consider as serious events that in the past were not thought of as such. In the absence of serious injuries over long periods of time, organizations tend to develop smugness or become lax. One way of avoiding these undesirable behaviors is to recognize, investigate, develop constructive action for, and report to employees events that, while not as serious as some in the past, nevertheless represent opportunities for learning, improving, and keeping employee attention to safety at a high level. Organizations are normally either progressing or regressing; a status quo is unlikely to continue. Most organizations do not have this problem because most organizations have plenty of injuries/illnesses to recognize, investigate, develop corrective actions for, and report to employees.

Communicating Goals, Plans, and Performance

Once annual goals have been set, they should be widely publicized throughout the work force. Publication of these goals simultaneous with the announcement of activities developed by the Program and Activities subcommittee and any other safety initiatives stemming from CSC decisions will emphasize the new frequency rates set for the coming year together with some plans for "making it happen." Employees will understand this as a coordinated plan that has resulted from careful consideration by the CSC after it received input from the entire organization by way of its subcommittees. A smoothly functioning organization for safety results in the development of goals and programs from within the entire organization, with stimulus and approval coming from the "top."

"Report cards" should be periodically issued. Monthly reporting is both timely and convenient from a record-keeping point of view. Monthly performance data, along with year-to-date compared to goal year-to-date performance data, should be widely publicized. Congratulations and appreciation or spurs to improved performance can accompany such communications as appropriate. The Program and Activities subcommittee can arrange for these communications, which need not be complex. Short messages on easels at lunchrooms or site entrances can frequently suffice.

In summary, goal setting is an act of leadership. Goals should be established thoughtfully and thoroughly. Report cards should be provided to the work force.

TOTAL DISABILITY PERFORMANCE

The foregoing discussion has focused on work-related injuries and illnesses and off-the-job injuries. A fourth area of employee health and safety is off-the-job illnesses. When viewed from a financial perspective, employee illnesses constitute a major business cost and therefore a major cost to society. Medical cost containment is a well-recognized rallying cry. Most cost containment efforts are being directed at control of costs *after* the illness has been recognized. Many organizations are beginning to recognize that efforts to *prevent* illness also "pay off" in reduced employee absenteeism and its associated medical and productivity costs. "Quality-of-life" issues become important. Corporate leaders are demonstrating that sustained but gentle efforts to get employees to adopt life-styles more conducive to good health can be successful. Routine, good medical examinations, health or fitness centers, stop-smoking programs, walking and/or running facilities, low fat diets, and alcohol and drug abuse rehabilitation programs are all being introduced by employers who recognize that employees are indeed "our most important asset." Both Johnson and Johnson and Du Pont are marketing their successful experience with such programs to outside clients on a for-profit basis.

The existence of workers' compensation programs (social programs, in Europe) for work-related disabilities and disability insurance programs for nonwork-related disabilities has been and continues to be an important aspect of income protection for employees. These two categories, and medically related absenteeism in situations in which there is no disability insurance, add up to the *total disability performance*—all absences for medical reasons.

Total disability performance can be a useful guide by which management measures its total safety and health performance. In some organizations, total disability performance is also being successfully used with the entire work force. Its usefulness is directly proportional to the degree to which the people involved have been brought to understand its importance and the factors that determine its magnitude. Leaders develop followers!

Disability Insurance Programs

To achieve good employee relations and cost control, these programs require adequate supervisory attention and a clear understanding of the programs by all the major participants, who include:

1. Employees
2. Supervision
3. Site medical (or off-site employer medical provider)
4. Private physicians
5. Insurance carriers—if applicable
6. Unions—if applicable

Three fundamental principles underlie a well-administered disability plan. If these are not properly understood, they can appear to the participants to be in conflict with one another.

Principle 1. Employees who, because of illness or injury, are unable to work should remain away from work for the purpose of "recovery," with the objective of returning to work as soon as his or her condition permits, consistent with the best medical judgment available. The health of the employee is of first consideration.

Principle 2. Income continuity during periods of disability should be authorized by supervision only after assuring that absence from work is appropriate to the recovery objective. In this regard, a clear understanding of why the employee's presence at the workplace would be detrimental to the health of either the employee involved or other employees in the workplace must be established. In the absence of a sufficient understanding of the reasons for absence from the workplace, supervision should not authorize income continuity.

Principle 3. Employees must cooperate with supervision and employer medical personnel in order to be eligible for income continuity during periods of disability. Principle 3 puts a significant responsibility on the employee to permit such examinations and inquiries by employer medical personnel which in their judgment may be necessary to determine the employee's condition. The employee is expected to follow advice and directions given by employer medical personnel in order to remain eligible for income protection coverage.

These principles are not easy to establish in practice. They are sound principles, nevertheless. The difficulty in establishing them in practice relates to the desire by one or more of the major participants to maximize what is or is perceived to be its own unique interests. An examination of the role of each of these participants and their motivation for preserving or expanding their roles reveals how much, in practice, most organizations fail to manage their disability programs. For most organizations, adoption of these principles requires a major overhaul of existing understanding and administration of their income protection programs.

Even when these principles are recognized and accepted by all the participants, Principle 3 puts a significant responsibility on supervision to establish employee understanding of all three principles, preferably well before the incidence of a disability period. It also places responsibility on supervision to sufficiently understand the medical situation and to be innovative regarding possible useful work that is consistent with the employee's return to perform an activity that is not detrimental to the recovery process.

Employer medical personnel are a significant source of guidance for supervision in disability cases and should be freely consulted in cases on which professional medical advice is needed. Employer medical personnel are also important in regard to a necessary understanding on the part of employee private physicians. A complicating factor in obtaining understanding of the principles of disability administration is that private physicians frequently (1) do not have a realistic understanding of work available for employees, and (2) have both a physician/patient relationship and a business/client relationship with their customer/patients (see Chapter 13).

In regard to the health of the employee, the six possible participants in disability plans have the health of the employee as a common interest. However, commonality of interest may not exist regarding such related concerns as: nature of available work, inconvenience rather than health of the patient/employee, malpractice considerations, costs to the company, equitable treatment of employees, need of insurance carriers to protect their claims base, and need of unions to "represent" employee constituents.

It is in these latter categories that most differences of opinion and attitudes arise—and negative and unproductive attitudes and behavior develop among and between the six participants—employees, supervision, employer medical personnel, private physicians, insurance carriers, and unions (when applicable).

Early identification of possible areas of conflict can assist in avoiding conflict, particularly if all parties understand Principles 1, 2, and 3. The prime responsibility for employee understanding of these principles rests with supervision and is best achieved well before disability occurs. Establishing appropriate employee behavior regarding personal health and motivation in situations in which these are deficient is an important supervisory function. The prime responsibility for an understanding of these principles by private physicians rests with employer medical personnel. The prime responsibility for gaining union understanding of these principles normally rests with both direct supervision and site (corporate) Personnel, Human Resources, or Industrial Relations personnel. Supervision and site medical (employer medical personnel) are mutually responsible, cooperatively, with keeping each other informed and knowledgeable regarding the degree to which they have carried out their respective responsibilities. Management personnel are also responsible for keeping union representation informed—within the bounds of privacy desired by the employee involved and union contractual considerations. Insurance carriers are normally best dealt with by Human Resources personnel. Proper management of the disability program is required to achieve both first-class medical treatment and minimum time loss from the workplace, while providing income protection for employees.

These basic principles are no less appropriate regarding supervision of attendance problems of employees who may not yet be eligible for income continuity during periods of absence from work due to disability. In fact, the achievement of a thorough understanding of these principles by new employees during their early (probationary) employment is essential to long-term success of the overall program.

Workers' Compensation Programs

The management of employee absences arising from work-related injuries/illness differs from the above only in that some employees may seek to abuse the provisions of worker compensation laws. This difference does not change the management task; it simply makes it more difficult. Absences from work for medical reasons must be managed consistently, independent of whether the medical problem is or is not work-related. Employees cannot be expected to understand and accept two different standards for determining their need to be at work. The source of their medical problem—work or nonwork—should not be the determining factor. It is the employee's condition that should be the determining factor regarding return to work.

If employees' income payments are substantially different depending upon the origin of their medical problems, administration of return-to-work procedures and achievement of desired employee behavior are substantially complicated because pay, not the employee's medical condition, becomes the central issue. An employee may find it difficult to "get to work" when workers' compensation is being paid but the employee is not fully disabled—that is, he or she could do some productive work. In fact, many employees, if not fully disabled but drawing workers' compensation payments, find productive work to do—but not with the employer whose workers' compensation rates are being adversely affected!

In the absence of a disability insurance program (nonoccupational) at least equal in value to the workers' compensation program, nonoccupationally incurred injuries and illness will often be claimed as occupationally incurred. Where these motivating sources exist, the opportunity for contentiousness and adversarial behavior are fostered. Well administered medical disability programs which provide full normal income protection to full-time employees for a specified period of time who are unable to do *any* productive work can provide a much-appreciated employee benefit at very reasonable employer cost.

Such programs, when well understood by all the participants, and when well administered, can result in total disability (all reasons) rates of 2% or less of actual hours worked. Compared to the results actually achieved by apparently less generous programs, more "liberal" programs can, in fact, be less costly to both the employee and the employer because of their resulting improvement in productivity.

Reporting and Analyzing Total Disability Performance

As with other measures of safety and health performance, each member of the Central Safety Committee should report the disability performance statistics for the operation he or she is responsible at every meeting of the CSC. This should be part of the standing agenda for the CSC. The medical representative can report the total performance data. These reports should be in terms of disability hours divided by total hours (in percent). It is important that line managers base their individual reports on the reports that their subordinates have made to them. Although having the numbers available is important, at least as important is verbally reporting the numbers up-the-line in the presence of peers.

Another feature of reporting up-the-line that is useful is requiring a report of the number of employees failing to pass some arbitrary performance screen—for example, the number of employees who have missed more than eight days of work or who have missed work more than four times the previous twelve months. Each of the employees who are "picked up" by the screen can then be identified as a "problem case" or not. A verbal report on what is being done to resolve a "problem case" should then be expected from each reporting manager. By adopting this procedure, the chairman and other members of CSC learn what each manager is doing in his or her respective organization toward resolving problem cases.

A long-service employee who suffers a temporarily disabling heart attack yet has had an excellent attendance record would be a nonproblem, even though he misses more than eight days of work. On the other hand, a long-service employee who has begun to miss days and finally "breaks through" the screen, signals to supervision that something has apparently gone awry with his or her health. This would be a problem case that warrants supervisory attention and an action plan designed to correct the deteriorating performance.

The screen should be set at a level at which local management (CSC) is willing to discuss individual cases. Also, the existence of the screen should not be widely communicated because it is likely to become a de facto employee "right." Such screens, in fact, do become widely known and should therefore be changed slightly from time to time—for example, instead of a criterion of 8 and 4, one of 9 and 5. Such screens are tools that assist supervision to focus its attention on employees whose health appears in need of improvement.

Just as management has found means for focusing attention on employees whose health needs improvement, some part of its attention should be focused on those employees whose performance has by some criterion been outstanding. This recognition can take many forms. Members of the CSC can join employees who have achieved five years or more of perfect attendance for "coffee and doughnuts" and photographs of the five-year, ten-year, etc., record holders. Innovative organizations have found a wide variety of ways to recognize unusually good individual performance. Peer group disability performance recognition has also been found useful.

SUMMARY

The goal setting process requires:

1. Selection of meaningful safety, health, and environmental measures of performance
2. Selection of a limited number of measures of performance that can be explained to and understood by the work force
3. Recognition that other measures of performance may be of value to management
4. Actual goal setting to involve all employees whose actions will determine performance
5. Understanding and administration of income protection programs as significant factors in determining performance
6. Reporting and evaluation of performance on a timely (monthly) basis as an integral part of goal achievement

NOTES

1. *The Wall Street Journal* advertisement, Safety Management Services, E. I. du Pont Co., 1986.

CHAPTER 12

DISCIPLINE IN SAFETY

The word *discipline* has a number of meanings that differ importantly. One definition of discipline is (1) "punishment; chastisement"; or another is (2) "control gained by enforcing obedience or order, as in a school or army; hence, orderly conduct, as troops noted for their *discipline*." Others are (3) "rule or system of rules affecting conduct or action," and (4) "training which corrects, molds, strengthens, or perfects." All of these definitions have applicability to achieving excellence in safety.

The basic message in this book has been that "you will catch more flies with honey than you will with vinegar." Education, demonstrated interest in and direct personal support of the safety effort by line managers at all levels, gentle persuasion, constructive, no-blame injury investigations, a well-developed set of safety rules and operating procedures, and other means of demonstrating leadership are the principal tools for establishing and maintaining a work force that will perform safely. Definitions (3) and (4) apply here.

However, a few employees always seem to be either unable or unwilling to work safely—that is, to work in a manner consistent with established rules and procedures or recognized safe practices in the absence of established rules and procedures. Definitions (1) and (2) become operative in these situations.

In definitions (3) and (4) we are presumably doing something *for* an employee. We are training, explaining, or coaching in order that the employee see and understand how certain behavior is not in the best interest of his or her safety and/or health. In definitions (1) and (2) we are presumably doing something *to* an employee—for failing to behave as we want him or her to behave. This reversal presents supervision with a major obstacle to determining how it should be acting at any particular point in time.

Under these circumstances, supervision frequently waffles, is indecisive, and procrastinates. It becomes unpredictable, threatening, authoritative, and confrontational, and—when slight improvement is noted—it reverts to coaching. In short, it is simultaneously sweet and sour. Although this characteristic may make some Chinese dishes appealing to the palate, as supervisory behavior it confuses subordinate employees, particularly employees whose behavior is in question. The better concept is to look upon all four definitions as a continuum, with no reversal between definitions (3) and (4) and (1) and (2). How can this goal be accomplished? The procedures are really quite straightforward.

From a sense of "fair play" and good employee relations as well as from strictly legal considerations, clearly established personnel procedures must exist. Such procedures should provide for the documentation of supervisory actions as supervision moves, as needed, from definitions (3) and (4) to definitions (1) and (2), based on factual evaluation of employee behavior.

Supervision needs to keep each employee fully informed regarding his or her thinking about the employee. To accomplish this the supervisor must reveal his or her thoughts and therefore open the door to questions about the validity of the supervisor's thinking process and facts. This is as it should be. We no longer live in an environment in which supervisory motives, factual knowledge, and actions are above review. Thus, supervision should put all its cards on the table for examination by any person who has a legitimate reason to do so. As a result, any defects in the supervisor's position will be discovered early in the process and not become an impediment to the disciplinary process. Such an impediment may only be an embarrassment to the supervisor and his or her management. However, it may be fatal to the process. And failure of the process will discourage all supervision from undertaking the process at all.

In fact, I have seen supervisors in order to avoid acknowledging that they are afraid to undertake the disciplinary process, simply not "see" behavior that needs modification. Others may recognize the behavior but merely suggest that the employee change the behavior. Either of these supervisory reactions to unacceptable employee behavior—behavior persisting to the point that a "punitive" as contrasted to a "training" reaction is called for—is devastating to a safety program, and to employee morale in general. These difficulties emphasize the need for a sound discipline procedure and the need for supervision to understand a sound, constructive disciplinary procedure and to use it with confidence. The five-step procedure described below is one that supervision can use effectively.

DISCIPLINARY PROCEDURE

Step 1: Informal Employee Contact

Employee behavior that, while unacceptable, is in need of only modest change can usually be dealt with through normal supervisory training and coaching activities. The procedure begins with supervisory recognition of the unsafe (unacceptable) behavior, followed by an informal discussion of the behavior. However, if the undesired behavior persists, the employee and supervisor should have a full discussion of the behavior, the reasons for its unacceptability, and need for a change. The employee's agreement should be sought regarding these basic facts and thinking. Agreement is not necessary on all points. However, there can be no ambiguity regarding the employee's behavior and the need for this behavior to change. The purpose of this discussion is to have the employee see his or her behavior as the supervisor has seen it. The purpose is not to coerce or threaten the employee. In trying to achieve this objective, the supervisor should explain that his or her responsibilities include training employees, coaching employees, trying to have employees see themselves objectively, and ultimately not allowing an employee whose behavior endangers his or her own safety or health or the safety and health of others to continue to work.

Formal written documentation is not desirable at Step 1. However, the wise supervisor makes some informal personal notes regarding the date, place, and content of this Step 1 discussion with the employee. This informal note is not part of the employee's personnel file, but is only a "memory assist" for the supervisor in the event that the verbal contact proves to be ineffective. Such a note is the personal material of the supervisor.

If the required changes in behavior occur, everyone wins. The employee works safely; there is no "record" to be concerned about, and the supervisor has successfully "coached" the employee.

If, however, the required changes in behavior do not occur, the procedure of Step 2 will be necessary.

An example of a Step 1 unsafe act that results in verbal contact might be failure by a mechanic to wear approved eye protection while using a grinder. In this example, it is presumed that there exists a safety rule specifying that employees must wear safety glasses when using grinders. The rule may also specify the use of safety glasses with side shields, or the use of a full face shield in addition to safety glasses with side shields. The safety rule must be a written rule and must clearly specify the detailed meaning of "eye protection." The employee cannot be expected to understand what management considers approved eye protection if management has not expressed its standards in writing. Effective communication of these written standards is also required if the goals of "fair treatment" and success in third-party review are to be achieved.

Step 2: Formal Employee Contact

A repeat failure of an employee to wear required eye protection while grinding may properly move the disciplinary effort to improve the employee's behavior to Step 2 of the progressive disciplinary procedure. In fact, *any* direct violation of a well-established and enforced safety rule might well move the disciplinary action to Step 2. The decision to move to Step 2 should include consideration of the time interval between the occasions of unsafe behavior and the seriousness of the behavior. In addition, the decision to move by supervisor A to Step 2 for employee A1 should be consistent with other actions by supervisor A in regard to his or her other employees. In this regard, it is unwise to overlook unsafe acts by an employee because of unusually meritorious performance in some other aspect of performance. To do so reveals a supervisor's use of safety as punitively based, not as being based on genuine concern for the offending employee's (and others') safety and health.

The goal is to treat employees equitably, showing the same concern for the safety of each employee independent of other considerations. This goal is more likely to be achieved if the supervisor really understands that disciplinary action is taken in order to do something *for* the employee, not *to* the employee. Supervisory action should be predicated on acceptance by all parties that the desired behavior change is in the best interest of the employee involved as well as of others in the workplace. Application of discipline should be motivated because of real concern for the employee's well-being, not because the supervisor is irritated that the employee is not following instructions.

If the decision is to move to Step 2, the employee should be sent to the supervisor's office or some other off-the-job location, in which a private discussion can be undertaken in a relatively calm environment. The employee should be told why he or she is being "sent to the office," together with an indication that the supervisor will join him or her in a few minutes. This time lapse will give both the employee and the supervisor an opportunity to think things over before discussing the matter.

Because disciplinary action is likely, the employee should be offered union representation if the work force is unionized. If the work force is not unionized and the employee desires the presence of another employee, this request should be granted. Contractual agreements may be such that union representation may be required, or at least should be invited to be present. Depending upon the employee relations environment in the facility, management may *want* union representation to be present and should therefore arrange this. After all of the above have been considered and acted upon, the supervisor can then proceed to the "office" to conduct the Step 2 discussion.

Normally, Step 2 is sufficiently early in the multistep disciplinary procedure that the best results are obtained by a direct, private discussion between the employee and his or her supervisor. However, if the group must be enlarged as outlined above, arrangements should be made such that management personnel are not outnumbered by the employee and other nonmanagement personnel.

Step 2 discussion should begin with supervisory expression of concern for the employee's well-being (in this case, eyes) and then proceed to establish the factual reasons that the employee is in the office. These should include the instance of specific unacceptable behavior and mention that a similar unsafe behavior had been discussed with the employee in the recent past. The facts regarding both instances should be established. Agreement on the facts should be attempted before the discussion is continued. If no agreement is obtained, an attempt should be made to establish sufficient supporting evidence such as time, place, and details of discussion, as may be needed in the future to establish credibility with an unbiased third-party review.

If clearly stated and convincing supporting evidence is lacking, the supervisor should establish such facts as can be adequately supported and proceed accordingly. This may require return to a Step 1 position. If the facts are sufficiently supportable, the procedures of Step 2 can be continued.

The employee should be asked if there are mitigating factors that he or she wishes to bring forth. Similarly, if union or other employees are present, they should be asked if they are aware of mitigating factors that should be considered. These should then be recorded and considered during the discussion. The record needs to reflect that factors thought by some employees to be mitigating ones, have been considered by the supervisor in reaching a decision regarding appropriate disciplinary action.

At Step 2, normal disciplinary action is to record the discussion of Step 2 in the employee's personnel record. It will serve as the base point for any future disciplinary action that may become appropriate. The purpose, again, is to convince the employee that his or her behavior must change if he or she expects to remain an employee.

This record should become a permanent part of the employee's record. It is a recorded statement of fact and management reaction. With the passage of time, these events become less relevant. However, experience indicates that it is preferable to let some future supervisor under some future set of circumstances make the judgment regarding relevance. Some union/management agreements and even some managment decisions in the absence of a union set forth a statute of limitations on material in an employee's record. Where such provisions exist, it is better practice to restrict availability of the record beyond a specified time period than to actually remove material from the file.

After it is established that the employee has been put in Step 2 of the disciplinary procedure, the remaining steps of the disciplinary procedure should be reviewed with the employee, with an indication to the employee that what happens next is up to him or her—that supervision will react to his or her behavior and that this reaction can be counted upon. The end-point for Step 2 is usually just this—an explanation of the remaining portion of the disciplinary procedure and a clear picture of how far the employee has traveled down the disciplinary route.

Several other points might well be made: (1) A second offense is beginning to look like deliberate intent not to follow safety standards, rather than mere oversight. Thus, the evidence is beginning to demonstrate possible insubordination. If so, this would constitute a more serious breach of acceptable conduct. The purpose in mentioning this possible interpretation of the employee's conduct is to get the concept "out in the open" at this time, rather than to wait until a future date when action is being based on an actual charge of insubordination. The object is to secure a change in employee behavior, not to surprise the employee. Best results are obtained if the employee is accorded a full understanding of management's thinking and that upon repeated failure to follow prescribed safety standards the employee should *expect*[1] to be moved to Step 3, Warning of Probation. This expression does not *promise* a move to Step 3. The decision to go to Step 3 should be based on the facts at the time of a future indiscretion. The point here is not to *promise* because circumstances surrounding some future failure may be such that it is inappropriate to proceed to Step 3—for example, the performance of a very minor, temporary oversight. However, the employee's behavior should take into consideration the *expectation* that Step 3 will be taken at the next failure to perform his or her work safely.

Step 3: Warning of Probation

Should future behavior result in movement to Step 3, the same preliminary procedure should be used as in Step 2: (1) the employee is sent to the "office," (2) the appropriate persons are gathered together for a discussion with the employee, and (3) the facts are established—including the instance of unsafe conduct and the discussion of Step 2 as recorded in Step 2 proceedings. At Step 3, the supervisor may wish to discuss what action he or she should take with higher direct management and/or someone in the personnel organization prior to proceding beyond the facts of the offense. If so, the meeting should be recessed, to be reconvened after the desired consultations have been accomplished. The employee should not be allowed to return to regular work or work similar to that in which the unsafe behavior occurred. Until Step 3 is concluded, the conditions under which the employee is to be permitted to return to normal work assignments have not been determined.

After obtaining the needed guidance, the supervisor should reconvene the meeting and take the action that has been agreed upon. This may be to formally place the employee on Warning of Probation, along with a full explanation of the kinds of action the supervisor may take if the situation does not improve. The next escalation of the disciplinary procedure is Step 4, Probation, or Warning of Termination.

The object of the discussions at Step 3 is (1) to again inform the employee of the need for a behavioral change, and (2) to give the employee a clear understanding of the kinds of action management may take if Step 4 becomes necessary. Should Step 4 become necessary, the employee should not creditably be able to express surprise at what happens at Step 4. Step 3 is normally still a "talking" or discussion step in which supervision attempts to secure an agreement with the employee about the needed change in behavior without resorting to overt punitive action, although punitive action is discussed in relationship to possible escalation of the disciplinary procedure to Step 4.

If agreement regarding the needed change in behavior cannot be established, the employee should not be allowed to return to work. Agreement to work safely as defined by management is required prior to allowing the employee to return to work. Failing to secure this agreement, the employee's employment pass should be retrieved and the employee "sent home" in anticipation of discharge—a direct move to Step 5, Termination, skipping Step 4.

If agreement is reached but the employee's behavior does not become totally acceptable, progression to Step 4 is in order. This is the last step prior to termination of employment. The standard of *totally acceptable* needs emphasis. The standard by which the employee is judged will establish the minimum level of behavior acceptable to management. In thinking about this minimum acceptable behavior, it is useful to think about the health of the organization, if all employees were performing at this minimal performance level. If the results would be unacceptable to management, it suggests that the minimum acceptable standards have been set too low. They should be raised, and the employee should be informed of the supervisor's revised view of the situation and the new, more demanding, standards which are being established. This discussion can take place during any of the steps in the disciplinary procedure except the last step, termination. The standards to be used at Step 5 must have been established at Step 4 or earlier.

Step 4: Probation or Warning of Termination

The preliminary action taken by the supervisor at Step 4 is the same as that with the earlier steps:

1. Send the employee to office.
2. Arrange for other appropriate persons to participate in the discussion.
3. Establish all the relevant facts—review the case from its inception, clearly and meticulously reciting documented evidence of management's efforts to salvage the employee (by seeking a change in behavior, not by lowering of standards), including all the actions management has undertaken in its efforts to "turn the employee around." Restate the absolute need for the employee to work safely, follow established rules, and so forth. Explain that ultimately removal from the workplace may be the only way to prevent the employee from injuring himself or herself, another employee, or the public. Express regret that these previous efforts have failed.
4. Adjourn the meeting as in Step 3, if needed.
5. Seek advice/counsel.
6. Reconvene the meeting in a timely fashion and inform the employee and union, if present, of the supervisor's decision—presumably to place the employee in Step 4 of the disciplinary procedure.

There should be no "bargaining" at this point. The union and, presumably, the employee both have the option of filing a grievance over the supervisor's action. This is as it should be. The threat of such a grievance filing should not, however, influence supervisory action in using the disciplinary procedures for changing employee behavior. The grievance procedure should operate; threats of its use, however, should not intimidate supervisory action. If the supervisor has acted properly, he or she should not attempt to "second guess" the outcome of a grievance.

The terms of Probation or Warning of Termination should be thoroughly explained to the employee and union representatives as appropriate to existing union/management relationships. In both union and nonunion situations, a representative of the Personnel or Human Resources Department should be present as an observer, not as an active participant. This is a line management meeting.

During the Probation step, the supervisor should formally review performance status with the employee on at least a monthly basis. The discussion of the review should be documented and read by the employee and then made a part of the employee's official employment file.

The duration of the Probational or Warning of Termination period should not be specified. It should be rescinded only when the supervisor is satisfied that it no longer serves a useful purpose because the employee has sufficiently demonstrated fully acceptable performance.

At Step 4, the time has come for more than just talk. Specific corrective actions that immediately impact the employee should be taken. Consideration should be given to establishing new "rules" in some areas of the employment relationship, for example:

(1) appropriateness of overtime work, if the employee needs more than ordinary supervision which may not be available on an overtime basis, or, if management is not willing to risk the employee's working with another supervisor and/or crew; (2) requirement that the employee prepare a short write-up of why he or she can work safely and his or her intention of doing so; (3) reassignment to a task that is less hazardous or provides more supervision, with or without a change in pay; (4) removal of "bidding" rights to other assignments while in a probational status. It may be necessary for upper supervision to impose item (4). Unfortunately, some supervisors solve their problem by encouraging the problem employee to seek an assignment in some other supervisor's organization.

The last item to be communicated is an explanation that failure to achieve acceptable behavior will result in termination of employment.

Step 2 is an attempt to effect a change in employee behavior through talking. Step 3 involves talking, but talking that involves a warning, not a threat or "promise," that he or she should *expect* more stringent action to be taken if behavior does not change sufficiently. Step 4 also involves talking, but also fulfilling the expectations established at Step 3. Step 4 involves demonstration that management can and will do more than just talk. At Step 4, management demonstrates it will take specific punitive actions to discomfort the employee and to establish management credibility for action. By taking punitive measures at Step 4, management prepares the employee, and others as well, for the ultimate punitive action, Termination, at Step 5.

Some organizations include time off without pay as a corrective action. This appears to me to be excessively punitive. It is apt to be viewed as a *quid pro quo* for the unacceptable behavior and would appear to undermine the progressive discipline procedure with the suggestion that the employee is being punished twice—once by escalating the degree of jeopardy of job loss and, secondly, by denying pay. At best, denial of pay adversely affects the employer/employee relationship in a way that has a lasting detrimental effect long after the desired change in behavior has been achieved.

Some employers have found useful a practice of giving employees time off *with* pay to *think* about the employer/employee relationship in order to come to a non-emotional decision regarding the employee's ability or willingness to accept the employer's expectations. This procedure is reported to have a high probability of problem resolution. The employee either returns to work exhibiting the required change of behavior or quits. The issue is resolved, and, if the employee has quit, discharge has not been necessary. If the employee returns to work with the stated intention of working safely but fails to do so, management can proceed directly to Step 5, Termination.

One source of advice and counsel during the determination to proceed to Step 4, Probation or Warning of Termination, is, for example, the plant manager, site manager, research manager, or marketing manager, who represents the highest level management representative to which the employee can appeal for consideration. The personnel policies of the organization should be such that identification of this management representative has been clearly established through previous communication to employees, past practices, or union bargaining. The best results will be obtained when this person both is competent to handle employee discharge responsibilities and is "on site." In small organizations within larger organizations, this may not be possible. In any event, the person who will be the final voice for management should thoroughly understand the case and give his or her nonobjection to the proceedings prior to going to Step 4.

The nonobjection from the site manager (top management level to be involved) should be sought by the first-line supervisor in accompaniment with his or her supervisor and appropriate representation of the personnel organization. Obtaining this nonobjection accomplishes several desirable results:

1. It assures that the top person is kept abreast of developing discharge cases in which he or she may become involved. This provides the opportunity to alter the course of events to a pattern which is judged to be more appropriate.
2. It prevents the supervisor from arriving at the brink of discharging an employee, Step 4, without being sure he or she has the suppport of his or her superiors. Failing to provide a formal means to secure this support, lower levels of supervision either will not act when they should out of fear they will not be "backed" or will act and merely hope they will be "backed." To hope is not enough. Under a situation in which hope is relied upon, there will be a sufficient number of cases in which the site manager will not support a discharge that supervision will retreat to the "do nothing" position rather than risk making a mistake.
3. It secures nonobjection from the site manager and keeps the responsibility for disciplinary action with direct supervision—without directly committing the site manager to a specific course of action. This position allows flexibility by both the site manager and direct supervision to adjust their thinking (position) as events develop. It does secure the site manager's agreement that the case has been handled well enough up to this point to support a discharge case, should the next step (discharge) become necessary—provided that this step is also adequately handled.

In short, securing the site manager's nonobjection prevents a fatally defective case from proceeding to the discharge stage. Few, if any, personnel cases are handled with perfection. Securing nonobjection establishes what degree of imperfection the site manager is willing to accept. In this, the site manager should avail himself or herself of the advice/counsel of the head of the personnel department or from whomever else he or she may want to seek counsel, including off-site superiors. Normally, the best results will be obtained when this person, the site manager, can lead his or her organization without any visible or routine reliance on others outside the immediate organization.

The immediate organization needs to recognize that its actions may place the larger organization at risk. By the seeking of counsel from sources within the larger organization, the needs of both the larger organization as well as the immediate organization are more likely to be met.

Employees who do not respond appropriately to being placed in Step 4, Probation or Warning of Termination, and those whose conduct has been grossly unacceptable should be terminated from employment. They should be removed from the risks of employment. This act should not be one based on management irritation or pique. Discharge should be the result of careful, objective consideration of the facts of each individual case. A well-established procedure designed to assure that such consideration is achieved is essential to successful termination of employees who are no longer desired. The end point of such a procedure is described in the next section—Step 5, Termination.

In Step 4 as in Step 3, the supervisor should review performance on a monthly basis and put documentation of this discussion in the employee's file after the employee has read the writings.

Step 5: Termination

It is important that all employees—supervised and supervisors—understand this fundamental tenet. Management does not initiate the termination process. Employees do. Whether or not the process is initiated is the responsibility of individual employees, not supervisors. Thus, supervision must be dependable in regard to their reaction to unacceptable behavior. If unacceptable behavior is tolerated and then acted upon, it is supervision that has initiated the process. When this occurs, the process is seldom successful. A successful termination process is one that has been put in place and understood by employees before it is triggered into action by the behavior of an employee—it is employee initiated.

The termination process is set in motion when supervision becomes aware of a verifiable unacceptable behavior of an employee—preferably, the result of direct observation by first-line supervision. If the observer is not the direct first-line supervisor, the employee should be escorted to his or her direct first-line supervisor. The employee should be asked to explain to this supervisor why he or she has been summoned. Upon hearing a satisfactory explanation, the observing supervisor should depart. The direct first-line supervisor is now able to deal with the situation based on clearly established facts, not heresay. The employee has established the facts to the satisfaction of the observer in the presence of the employee's supervisor.

Failing to get the employee to relate the facts, the observer (member of management) may do so himself or herself, seeking concurrence by the employee. Failing to get employee concurrence does not invalidate the observer's testimony. The employee's reaction or "version" should be sought. The "facts" should be made as clear and uncontrovertible as circumstances permit. Care must be taken to assure that the employee has been given appropriate time and opportunity to be heard. This is a fact-establishing meeting; the employee is not to be disciplined in any way during this meeting. No chastisement or expression of disappointment, or comments involving judgment should occur. This discussion should be only a dispassionate recitation of facts.

Depending upon the seriousness of the inappropriate behavior and the disciplinary status of the employee, and past practice regarding other employees, the direct first-line supervisor must now determine what to do. If the supervisor does not know what to do, he or she should seek advice. The employee should not be returned to work until the case has been handled. The purpose of discipline is to change employee behavior so as to make the employee "acceptable" in the workplace. If an employee is returned to work, the employee is presumably "acceptable."

Allowing an employee to return to work is an act confirming a supervisor's opinion that the employee is "ready" to work. Administering discipline after the employee has returned to work suggests that the employee was prematurely returned to work or that the discipline fundamentally is not designed to make the employee "ready" to work, but rather is punishment for punishments sake—not an action designed to change behavior, but rather, a *quid pro quo*. This is not corrective discipline, but merely the "price" of an unacceptable act. A schedule of penalties for specific inappropriate conduct achieves the same undesirable results. This scenario should be avoided if excellence in safety is to be achieved.

If the inappropriate act in itself or in conjunction with the employee already being in a disciplinary status leads to a decision to proceed toward termination, the employee should be "sent home" immediately, if the case is a strong one and the site manager is not immediately available. If the manager is immediately available, the employee should remain in an office—not be allowed to return to the work area—while the case is briefly reviewed with the site manager. This is not a termination-determining review, but merely a preliminary review that gives the site manager the courtesy of expressing any concerns or offering advice on how to proceed. Of course, if the manager believes, based on the data available, that termination is not an option, then he or she should explore available options and the employee handled in accordance with the selected option. Sending an employee home is a significant action and deserves reasonable attention prior to taking the action. A possible termination case should not *demand* immediate attention of top management; top management has many important activities, but employee welfare should be high on the list. Site managers who are physically available should be given the opportunity to decide their level of participation in a decision to "send an employee home." In the absence of top management, there may be others with whom a direct first-line supervisor should consult, prior to sending the employee home. This should be a consultation; it should not be "getting permission."

In the absence of higher supervision, or behavior sufficiently unacceptable, the first-line supervisor can and should be allowed to act independently. The employee should not be retained on site for a long period of time (an hour?) while supervision seeks advice, nor should the employee be allowed to work. Sending an employee "home" is not a decision to terminate, it is a decision to consider termination (or time off) and the employee should not be allowed to work while this decision is under consideration. As is discussed earlier, the act of allowing an employee to work establishes that the employee is ready or approved for work. Allowing an employee to work is not consistent with consideration of termination.

If the employee is subsequently returned to work—that is, not terminated—the question of pay for time not worked arises. If a union contract exists, contract terms normally govern this question. In the absence of contractual requirements or personnel policies in nonunion situations, the following guidelines have proved effective and are viewed as "fair" by employees and supervision alike. If the decision to "send home" was based on a clear need to consider termination, then the employee is not paid. If the decision to "send home" was faulty—that is, if there was no reasonable basis to consider termination—then the employee is paid. This arrangement will restrain overeager supervisors, without rewarding employees who are not terminated but whose cases legitimately deserved consideration.

Once the employee is off site, the top management group of the unit or site in which the employee is employed is gathered to "hear" the case. The group is called, when meeting for this purpose, the Termination Review Board. At a manufacturing site, this group would be the site manager and all his or her immediate subordinates. In other organizations, the group would be the Laboratory Director or Marketing Manager, for example, and his or her immediate subordinates. The top person present should be the senior manager from whom a review can be obtained within the company. That is, this group "speaks for the company." They should be empowered by the company to do so. No further review should be available within the company; further review should be available only through third-part participation—arbitration or courts of various jurisdiction, of which there are many—state unemployment compensation commissions, state and federal labor boards, Federal Office of Contract Compliance, EEOC Commissions, and civil courts.

The object of this concept is to get all parties involved in the termination procedure to understand that termination is not a bargaining process that can be pursued to higher and higher levels within the corporation. This termination procedure provides direct first-line supervisors a clear, functional disciplinary procedure through which to favorably influence the behavior of employees for whom they are responsible.

The timing of the meeting at which the "case" is heard is important. Preparation of the case will take some time. The employee is off-site and presumably will not be paid for time not at work. If the employee is not terminated, this loss of pay is the consequence of the termination procedure and should not be thought of or considered a "penalty." Thus, the case must be heard expeditiously. At most, two days usually represents a reasonable balance between providing sufficient time to prepare the case and minimizing the loss of pay should the employee be returned to work.

The case is prepared by the employee's first-line supervisor with the help of his or her supervision and someone from personnel. The pertinent facts of the case and the employee—age, length of service, "protected class" status, work history, record of supervision, previous and existing disciplinary status—are all important factors. A good case presentation includes all the facts that the participants in the meeting may bring up. These might include action taken in similar cases by this supervisor, action taken on similar cases by other supervisors, mitigating circumstances, involvement of others—a whole host of questions designed to bring out all facts relevant to achieving a fair and unbiased management response.

The meeting should be opened by the senior manager with some introductory remarks that outline the purpose of the meeting. These should include:

1. Establish that all the pertinent facts are available to the supervisor involved, even though embarrassing to supervision.
2. Assure that the employee has been treated fairly.
3. Commit upper management to the chosen course of action. This step gives confidence to the first-line supervision that he or she has his or her management's support.
4. Establish, for third-party review in the event this becomes necessary, that the termination process was an orderly, well thought out, fair, consistent process.
5. Make clear that, if new or different facts are discovered after the meeting, supervision should not be afraid to postpone final action until these new facts have been evaluated.
6. Recognize that the case will not have been handled with perfection. Hindsight almost always provides an opportunity for recognition that certain supervisory action could have been better. It is most important that all the facts be revealed. If supervision has made "fatal flaws," these need to be recognized. There is little likelihood of such flaws at this point, because the case will have been previously reviewed, briefly, with the senior manager prior to proceeding to Step 4.

The presentation of the case should be done verbally by the first-line supervisor, using overhead projections and/or easels to keep the facts clearly in front of the "audience." Chronological presentation of the data assists in accomplishing this.

In addition to the presence of the senior manager and his or her immediate subordinates at this meeting of the Termination Review Board, others who can be of assistance, as well as those who can gain some experience are: "personnel" people, other members of management including other first-line supervisors, and supervision from other areas of the plant. The object is to have a good cross-section of the organization present to provide their knowledge and reaction to the facts and proposed termination action and to evaluate the proposal to terminate. Their role is not to decide whether to terminate or not. This is not a play on words. The first-line supervisor is the person who is determining whether or not he or she is going to terminate the employee. The supervisor has reached a decision based on personal knowledge and understanding of how the "system" works. He or she has had preliminary support from the site manager if the employee has been previously placed on Warning of Termination (Probation) and if the present case was briefly reviewed by the site manager prior to "sending the employee home." The supervisor has also had the support of the personnel department in preparing the case and surely has had the support of his or her direct line management or at least their nonobjection. The purpose of the review of the case with the Termination Review Board is to seek its nonobjection to the proposed action by the first-line supervisor. This concept keeps the decision making at the first-line supervisory level, albeit with a lot of help or guidance.

After the case has been presented, all the questions asked and answered, and the information from others at the meeting brought forth, the site manager should then ask the first-line supervisor if, in view of what he or she has heard during the meeting, it is still his or her plan to terminate the employee. The manager should then publicly poll each of his direct subordinates for their thoughts and ultimately their decision to object or not object to the final plan of the first-line supervisor. When this has been accomplished, the manager then asks other members of the group for their thoughts. In addition, the manager might specifically ask first-line supervisors who may be present questions such as:

1. Can you support a decision to terminate? If not, why not?
2. Can you support a decision not to terminate? If not, why not?
3. Are there any other facts, situations, or "history" of which we should be aware?
4. What do you think the reaction of your people will be if the employee is terminated?
5. What do you think the reaction of your people will be if the employee is not terminated?
6. What do you think the reaction of the "protected class" of employees will be?

The attempt here is to get all possible reactions "on the table" so that no surprises arise when the final decision becomes generally known.

The manager should now ask his or her direct subordinates if they care to adjust their positions and if so, why.

The manager should then ask the first-line supervisor who has presented the case whether he or she desires to change his/her mind regarding termination. This is not an invitation to change positions, but rather an opportunity to do so based on any information not previously available to the supervisor. Cases that have been thoughtfully brought forward seldom have to change course at this point, but it is better to do so now than to proceed with a case recognized to be fatally defective. To do so is normally poor employee relations, even if the case is not challenged. It communicates the wrong standards to supervision, and it invites third party review.

Finally, the manager must cast a vote, which is, of course, the vote that counts. This is not a vote to terminate or not, but a vote to object or nonobject to the course of action being pursued by the presenting supervisor.

Managers who lead will not simply follow the majority position of their subordinates. They have the ultimate responsibility. The task of the leader is to make the crucial judgment. This procedure clearly places the mantle of leadership on the manager. Virtually no case will be free of all blemishes after this review process. The ultimate decision will rest on achieving both fair treatment of employees and reasonable standards for guiding supervision in handling disciplinary cases. This judgment should not be left to the personnel group. Only the top manager can integrate all of the considerations that affect such decisions, for example: (1) the need to support supervision in their effort to get work performed safely; (2) the need to afford fair treatment for employees; (3) the desire to avoid adverse public notoriety; (4) the desire to avoid legal entanglements that may produce unfavorable decisions and thereby adversely affect future management flexibility in leading the organization; (5) the possible desire to avoid union/management conflict (where union representation is present); and (6) the impact of the decision on the larger (corporate) organization.

Having cast a vote, the manager should then thank the first-line supervisor for having gone through what is clearly an ordeal. The manager should then thank the other participants for their help in the effort to determine the proper course of action, and make any explanations regarding his or her final decision which may be helpful to others in understanding the final outcome and the important issues involved. It is critical that each participant understand the issues and be able to explain these to others who may make inquiries concerning the Termination Review Board meeting. Ideally, all participants would also be able to conscientiously support the action taken.

The supervisor then goes forth with either the "blessings" of the manager or guidance for alternative action, if nonobjection is not obtained.

This is a long arduous task. Treating employees appropriately is an important function of supervision. Keeping first-line supervision in a leadership position is critical to establishing and maintaining a strong, productive, high morale organization. Members of supervision who cannot manage a fair and considered disciplinary program should not remain as supervisors.

No termination case is likely to have been handled perfectly. Supervision will have taken some action or failed to take certain actions which, in retrospect, were errors. Some may have been recognized as errors at the time. Cases need not be perfect, supervision should understand this. They should not be stymied into inaction because of fear that their mistakes will be revealed, to their detriment. A wise manager will recognize this and will let others know he or she recognizes this. These mistakes should be recognized as mistakes from which all can learn rather than used to embarrass the supervisor.

The primary purposes of the Termination Review Board are:

1. To assure fair and considered treatment of the employee.
2. To recognize any fatal flaws in the case which may result in an adverse ruling by third-party review in the event this occurs.
3. To provide an opportunity for upper management to demonstrate its interest in employees and supervision, while clearly communicating to the organization required standards of performance.

As a general rule, it is undesirable to "lose" cases upon review by third parties. Employees and supervision will not normally recognize that the case was overturned because of inadequate procedural aspects of the case in contrast to the standard of behavior involved. Review agencies seldom rule on the standards of conduct required by the employer. The question to be answered is "Has the employee been fairly treated? Has the employer reached an unbiased, considered judgment?"

Meetings of the Termination Review Board are frequently long, by their very nature. This length is not all bad. It allows time for participants at the meeting to become more rational and less emotional regarding the facts of the case. It is evidence that management has attempted to get all the relevant facts and has earnestly tried to objectively evaluate them. Long meetings provide an opportunity to "take a break" during the meeting. This provides participants an opportunity to ask questions of each other privately, and to encourage lower level supervision to participate more actively.

Before adjourning the meeting, the manager should remind the group that no one should discuss the case with others at the present time. The termination process is not over. The union, if any, needs to be recognized. The details of such recognition/bargaining are so varied that no attempt is made here to describe union/management discussions. This in no way diminishes the importance of such discussions. In fact, it is recognition that these discussions are important, appropriate, and complex; hence, any attempt to discuss this issue here would, of necessity, be superficial. However, under the heading Union Relationships I have outlined some important concepts that will be helpful.

The employee should now be contacted by the supervisor and asked to come to the site to discuss his or her employment status. No discussion should take place on the telephone. If the employee is interested, he or she should come in for this discussion. If not, the employee can simply be terminated "for cause" and any monies owed the employee mailed to the employee by registered mail accompanied by a letter confirming the employee's termination of employment.

This outcome is not the preferred one. It leaves unresolved such issues as returning the employee's company pass and disposition of the employees personal belongings that may remain on the site, and a possibly desirable exit medical examination.

The preferred and normal sequence of events is that the employee comes to the site and gains entrance as a visitor. If a gate-house exists, gate-house personnel must be alerted not to permit use of the employee's pass as a means of securing entrance (if the employee still has the employment pass).

The employee is then met by the first-line supervisor along with a representative of the personnel department or, if no personnel department personnel are available, another supervisor—one in whom the employee should have some confidence. If the employee requests that another employee also be present, this request should be honored. However, no nonemployee should be permitted to participate in this meeting. This group should then meet in a quiet, comfortable, private location—an office or conference room—to discuss with the employee his or her employment status. The case should be factually and thoroughly reviewed with the employee, describing the episodes that have occurred as well as management's response to these events and the disciplinary steps that may have been taken previously. The employee knows all these facts already. It should be summarized again for him or her so as to enable the employee to see the case as objectively as possible. This review should not be rushed; it should be a thorough one.

The meeting of the Termination Review Board should then be discussed. The composition of this board, together with some of the questions that were raised and their answers, should be explained to the employee. The employee should be allowed to take notes, but should not be given any papers or allowed to copy "verbatim" any material. The notes that he or she takes should be the employee's understanding of what is being said.

The employee should then be asked if he or she disagrees with any of the *facts* of the case or believes that there are important mitigating circumstances that have not been brought out or considered. If there are none, the first-line supervisor should inform the employee that he or she is terminating the employee's employment as of a specified time (normally shortly after this meeting). The employee should be asked to surrender the company pass as well as any other company-owned objects. This step usually requires going to a locker room, where the employee can retrieve personal belongings. The group should then return to the meeting place (office) at which time a check for wages owed should be presented to the employee. This check should be specially prepared based on an estimated time of termination and exit from the site. It should reflect any monies owed to the company by the employee in accordance with local legal requirements.

At this point the supervisor may express any regrets he or she may have regarding the fact that "things" didn't work out any better, or indicate that the employee should go forth and not make the same mistakes again. However, no indication should be given to the employee that re-employment is a possibility at some time in the future. Any statement concerning re-employability will almost certainly be expressed or heard in a more favorable context than it should be. It will also sorely complicate some future supervisor's or employment officer's task!

After the check has been presented, the employee's pass has been retrieved, and the employee is prepared to leave, the direct first-line supervisor should volunteer the following. "I have terminated you today. I believe the process by which I have reached the decision to do so has been fair and based on sound data. The site manager has said that he [or she] will speak with you or allow you to speak to any other member of management if you care to do so. He may be contacted by telephone at _____." If the invitation is accepted, the manager or other selected person should be available at his or her convenience, not on the same day, but within one or two days subsequent to the termination, if possible.

The direct first-line supervisor should then depart the meeting. The remaining supervisor should then ask the terminated employee if there is anything he or she would like to say. The supervisor might ask, "What could have been done differently so that things could have 'worked out' better?" The object here is twofold: (1) to get all the thoughts of the employee on top of the table—as it is not desirable that management be "surprised" some time in the future; and (2) to assist the terminated employee to understand his or her actions and why they need to be changed if the person expects to work for another employer. In the event that some new development arises in this meeting that the second supervisor believes needs to be considered before the terminated employee departs the site, this supervisor should ask the employee to remain in the office while he or she gets the direct first-line supervisor to return and hear the new development. Then the first-line supervisor should react in the same manner as though the development had arisen during his or her meeting with the employee.

The employee should also be informed regarding the company's response to inquiries from other firms at which he or she may seek employment. This should normally be only confirmation of dates of employment, without "editorial" comments.

If, on the other hand, the employee disagrees with the factual basis of the termination as initially explained, the direct first-line supervisor will need to record the details of these differences and then determine their validity and consequences. If the direct first-line supervisor is confident that the employee is mistaken, he or she should be straightforward and say so, including a *brief* statement of why. If the direct first-line supervisor is not certain regarding these allegations, but recognizes that even if the employee is correct he or she would still reach the same conclusion, the supervisor should make a straightforward statement to this effect—that is, the factual differences under discussion are not material to the outcome.

On the other hand, if the supervisor is uncertain regarding the facts, and if as a consequence he or she wants to postpone a decision until a more thorough understanding of the facts can be accomplished, then he or she should simply say so. The supervisor should acknowledge that the employee has raised an issue that warrants further consideration before a final decision is reached, thank the employee for bringing up this apparent new information and state that this information will be reviewed. The supervisor then escorts the employee off the site with a comment that "I will stay in touch," or "I will call you in a day or two."

The supervisor now has work to do: to inform the Review Board of this new development and see that the issue is quickly resolved.

The direct first-line supervisor, with help from any sources he or she can muster, must now evaluate the new information and make a decision as to what course of action he (or she) wishes to take. Having made a decision, the supervisor should request a reconvening of the Termination Review Board, bring them up to date regarding the new information, and inform the Board of his current plan for dealing with the employee. He seeks nonobjection from the Board as before. If the plan is to terminate and nonobjection is obtained, he proceeds as outlined before. If termination is not planned and he receives nonobjection to some alternative plan, he proceeds with the alternative plan. It should be executed in a manner similar to that outlined for the termination situation. If the direct-line supervisor does not obtain nonobjection to his plan of action, he should seek the Board's direction and then faithfully and skillfully execute the Board's decision.

In my own experience (far more than 100 nonsafety cases—I have not had a safety case proceed to discharge), I have never felt the need to override the position of the first-line supervisor *at the end of the meeting.* I have had a very few cases in which new facts were brought to the supervisor which altered his or her judgment regarding his own employee. There obviously have been some very close calls. Supervision does not always do the job as well as desired. On the other hand, supervisors also find themselves trying to raise standards, hoping for support from their upper management. These, because of the burden of "past practice," are the more difficult and sensitive cases. The procedures outlined here can provide the structure and ultimate forum to assure high standards of fair treatment of employees while strongly supporting lower supervision in getting the job done safely. I have never had a decision reached in this fashion overturned by third party review, although many have been tested.

Organizations differ in their assessments of what is to be communicated concerning the reasons for an employee termination. Employees will want to know "why" and in some sense they should understand "why"—the "why" is a part of their workplace. On the other hand, a very high priority should be placed on the "right-to-privacy" of the terminated employee. Philosophically, these are conflicting considerations. In practice, in most cases, they need not be. The "grapevine" is usually healthy and vigorous, without needing to be nourished by management. It should be used, and one way to do so is outlined below.

As a result of the "grapevine," employees will normally ask supervision "why" or "if" an employee has been terminated. Supervision should be knowledgeable about the fact of termination and should straightforwardly answer this question. However, the question of "why" is considerably more complex. The supervisor may ask the employee his or her own current understanding of "why," and then respond by saying that this "understanding" is "essentially correct" or "not." Additional details should not be discussed. If asked why "not?" the supervisor's response should be, "We believe it serves no useful purpose to go into further detail. You have the big picture; that's enough" or "you don't have a complete set of facts, but I believe the terminated employee has a right to some privacy."

If the "grapevine" is wrong, which it seldom is regarding termination cases, supervision will simply have to wait until a more nearly correct supposition arises from within the "grapevine." It gives the grapevine an opportunity to work its magic. The object is to achieve employee understanding without invasion of an ex-employee's right to privacy by management.

This termination procedure has many desirable features:

1. It keeps the direct first-line supervisor directly responsible for handling the disciplinary aspects of his or her role as supervisor.
2. It requires the direct first-line supervisor to be continuously fully informed on what is happening.
3. It clearly establishes the direct first-line supervisor as being "in charge." It keeps the supervisor in a leadership role, not a "messenger" role.
4. It provides the direct first-line supervisor the opportunity to reassess his or her decision, should new facts develop either during the Termination Review Board meeting or during the actual termination discussion with the employee.
5. It provides a mechanism for keeping upper management fully informed regarding the specific case in point, but also provides a forum in which to learn of related practices within the organization.
6. It provides upper management a forum through which organizational values—fair treatment, high standards, and so forth, can be reinforced in a "real" setting, not an academic or contrived circumstance.
7. It provides employees assurance that every termination case will be "heard" by upper management.
8. It keeps the process moving. It does not permit negotiation or interjection of grievance procedures to sidetrack the process. Management acts, and it acts responsibly; if others chose to do so they will need to react—not just

stall the management decision-making process and thereby wear down management resolve to act.

9. It provides each of the site manager's direct subordinates first-hand knowledge of events, thus enabling them to communicate appropriately and knowledgeably down the line to their organizations both the specifics of a case to be communicated and the specifics regarding reinforcement of organizational values, standards, and goals that may have emerged from the Termination Review Board meeting.

The above procedures may appear to be excessively demanding of management time and energy. They do require time, energy, and thought. Beyond these, they require discipline—a disciplined behavior on the part of management. If management expects to have a well-disciplined work force (definitions 3 and 4), it must be well disciplined itself. These procedures provide the framework for exercising and demonstrating to the work force and interested third parties appropriate supervisory discipline. Because they are effective, they are efficient. They will result in substantially improved employee performance, in safety as well as in other important performance criteria, for those employees who can and want to improve. They will result in termination of employment for those few individuals who will not or cannot behave acceptably.

The termination of those few employees who are terminated through these procedures frequently marks a positive turning point in their lives. They recognize that they have been treated fairly, and that because of their behavior and their behavior alone they have lost something they wanted. Many resolve never to allow this to happen again and go on to become productive members of society, frequently in much more responsible positions than they were likely otherwise to have attained. More than once, I have had the fathers of employees who have been terminated tell me years later that "being terminated was the best thing that could have happened" to their sons. "You did something which his mother and I could never do." This is the result of demonstrating genuine interest in employees in a thoroughly dispassionate manner. These guidelines will assist supervision to remain dispassionate under circumstances in which many become emotional and indulge in less than clear thinking and effective behavior.

UNION RELATIONSHIPS

I have purposely avoided discussing in detail the role of a union if union representation exists. I do not mean to diminish in any way the importance of a union in disciplinary procedures. The role of unions and the union/management/employee interfaces are so varied in U.S. organizations that no adequate treatment of the subject could be achieved in the context of this book. However, some simple concepts can be of help.

1. A union has a right to become involved; honor it.
2. A union has a right to express its views; facilitate its doing so.
3. There will normally be contractual provisions related to disciplinary procedures, including discharge; honor them.
4. In the absence of contractual provisions and/or "past practices" that management considers binding, management determines the requirements

for continued employment. Do so. Do not bargain away additional management "rights" during discussion of a discharge case.

5. Understand the existing disciplinary process and the appropriate union role; develop a fair, considerate game plan by which to gain control of this process (if management does not have control of the process) and execute the game plan well. Be sure the union understands the disciplinary process and that management will execute it well. Miscalculations by the union frequently arise because management has been less than forthright. Management must not allow itself to be outmaneuvered in the conduct of the process. However, management must be open-minded to new *relevant* facts. Consider them!
6. Prepare and execute the process such that it will withstand third-party review; if management is wrong, decide on an alternate course of action that will not be successfully challenged while minimizing the adverse consequences of an earlier wrong decision. Fatally flawed cases, when pursued, only magnify the problem. Third-party review will normally focus on the process by which discipline has been administered, not on the absolute standards of conduct involved.
7. Unions have a right to be present at meetings with employees in which discipline reasonably can be expected to arise as a topic of discussion. Recognize this right forthrightly; invite union participation when the right exists. Do not do so grudgingly, or attempt to exclude.
8. Maintain control of the process. Anticipate union reaction; know what management action is to be taken to deal with each anticipated or possible union reaction. Do not let extraneous matters divert the disciplinary process. Remember that disciplinary action is initiated by employee behavior; management is simply reacting to employee behavior as it has previously said it would. There should be no surprises. The time for union objection to the process was at the time the process was established, not when it is being put to use.

   If the union desires a change in the process, it can certainly bargain on the issue, but not as part of a disciplinary proceeding. Do not allow "bargaining" to become part of an individual disciplinary process. Keep these proceedings simple and straightforward. Do not allow confusion to arise between the disciplinary process and generalized "bargaining." To do so will result in compromise of the process, uncertainty regarding outcome, inadvertent bargaining away of principles, confusion, deterioration of morale, and tarnished leadership. The process becomes a degenerative one. Avoid this outcome.

CASE HISTORY

The normal outcome of systematic and consistent application of a well-established progressive disciplinary procedure to employees who demonstrate an inability or unwillingness to work safely is either that (1) behavior becomes acceptable—investment in the employee is salvaged, or that (2) behavior does not change sufficiently—the investment in the employee is lost.

There is a third outcome. Although rare, occasions do arise in which employees exhibit uncontrollable unsafe behavior that can be corrected by moving the employee to another assignment. I recall an operator, Bill, whose job assignment required him to operate a cellophane coating tower. This was complex, high-speed equipment within which rolls of uncoated cellophane weighing approximately 800 pounds, 30 inches in diameter and 50 inches wide, were unrolled, and the film was pulled through a coating bath, transported six floors through a drying oven, and returned to a windup on the ground floor. The process variables were many and interrelated in complex ways. Bill was a hyperactive individual, prone to taking actions reactively, with little thought to or understanding of what impact these actions might have one or two steps beyond the immediate result that triggered his reactive response. In short, he was an "accident waiting to happen" around complicated, high-speed equipment that required close and continuous personal involvement of the operator.

Bill was an experienced operator; although he had not been seriously injured recently, he had experienced some small nicks and cuts. He had also experienced several "close calls" and had been observed engaged in unsafe acts upon many occasions. Supervision had discussed these and his hyperactivity, with him. Supervision had also discussed his hyperactivity with Medical, which was already aware of this hyperactivity because of his frequent trips to Medical for "attention" of some sort or another.

Following the steps outlined above, including a one-week stint with one of the better operators in the crew, discussions with Bill reached the point that, after two crying episodes, he asked to be reduced to an assignment as "helper," which required much less responsibility and personal involvement with the equipment. As a consequence of a reduction in his hyperactivity (presumably because of less anxiety as a result of less responsibility and the reduction of the hazards of the job assignment), Bill's safety performance was subsequently judged to be acceptable. Had Bill not been acceptable on the "helper" assignment, supervision had already thought through the next step and had communicated this next step, informally, to union representatives. The next step?—mail clerk. The mail clerk's assignment was an assignment well below Bill's mental abilities, but was the only appropriate assignment to which Bill could be assigned without negating the "rights" of other employees. Fortunately, Bill performed acceptably and several months after reassignment reported to his supervision that he was "getting more out of life with less money." He thanked his supervision for taking the action; he "knew he wasn't a tower operator, but could not remove himself from the job."

As might be expected in the case of Bill, as an operator his production volume and quality were the poorest in the crew. This is the usual situation. Jobs being performed unsafely do not get done well. Bill might well have been handled as a production or quality problem. Volume and quality were not ignored in discussing his safety performance. However, in this instance, the key point used by supervision was safety. Safety should not be used as a shield behind which to do things that need to be done but that are really motivated by other considerations. However, where safety is a dominant issue, the use of safety as the driving force for action sends a constructive message to all employees.

Some may ask: "Would the same action have been taken if Bill had been an outstanding operator, using only production and quality as a performance criteria?" Who knows? It all depends on what management wants. What does management really believe? Does it believe it can run a productive, high-quality facility unsafely? Does it believe it can get employees to behave appropriately in regard to volume, quality, and costs, which are areas in which management's interest may be higher than employees' interest, but be unable to have them behave appropriately in an area that is clearly in *their* personal best interest—their safety and their health?

SUMMARY

An essential aspect of leadership is establishing disciplined followers. Safety leadership results in a work force that not only adheres to established work procedures but also continuously seeks to improve these procedures. Management activities that have been demonstrated to be successful for the development a well-disciplined work force are discussed and illustrated in this book. Only one has been identified as a disciplinary activity.

A progressive disciplinary procedure and its practical application have been the management activities discussed in this chapter. The administrative procedure is designed to secure the employee behavior necessary to avoid workplace injuries, or damage to health or the environment. It should be used when employee behavior has been inadequately responsive to other motivating efforts.

The procedure is composed of five steps:

Step 1—Informal Employee Contact
Step 2—Formal Employee Contact
Step 3—Warning of Probation
Step 4—Probation, or Warning of Termination
Step 5—Termination

Each step is initiated by unacceptable employee safety behavior and represents supervisory efforts to favorably influence the employee's future behavior. Steps can be skipped if the employee's behavior represents a particularly serious breach of safety discipline.

The procedure requires the first-line supervisor to be in charge at each step, while providing timely upper management review and response to the plans of the first-line supervisor. When carefully administered as illustrated, the procedure assures equitable treatment of employees while providing the employee the opportunity to demonstrate the required level of performance. The procedure has clearly defined end points. The employee's behavior becomes fully acceptable or the employee is reassigned to a job on which it is believed performance will be fully acceptable. In the absence of the availability of such an assignment, the employee is terminated "for cause"—unacceptable safety performance.

This disciplinary procedure has been used in well over 100 cases that resulted in employee termination. None of these cases was based on safety; all safety based cases secured the desired change in employee behavior without termination. Many of the termination cases were challenged through third party review, none successfully.

NOTES

1. The choice of the word *expect* is by design. The intent is to convey the idea that the employee should expect a particular supervisory action yet to avoid a management commitment to a specified action based on some future set of circumstances. This avoids the trap that many supervisors set for themselves by making statements such as "one more instance, or mistake, and you are gone." The problem with such statements is that the next "instance" will occur, but will do so under mitigating circumstances in which termination becomes ill advised. Thus, supervision is put in the position of having made a statement, a promise which it does not deliver. This situation undermines supervisory credibility and in many cases confidence because the mitigating circumstances may have been defined by higher level management! Use of the term *expect* accomplishes what needs to be accomplished without the attendant risk.

Chapter 13

THE ROLE OF EMPLOYER MEDICAL PERSONNEL IN ACHIEVING EXCELLENCE IN SAFETY

Safety leadership comprises all those activities undertaken by members of an organization which are designed to favorably influence: (1) the avoidance of injury to people, and damage to facilities and the environment, (2) the minimization of the seriousness of such events that do occur, and (3) the rapid recovery of personnel and their subsequent return to work.

Medical personnel have a significant contribution to make in achieving excellence in safety. Their responsibility begins with the employment process and ends, for employees, upon termination of employment. For nonemployees, such as medically terminated former employees and pensioners, this responsibility may continue until death.

THE EMPLOYMENT PROCESS

An important part of the employment process is the determination of suitability of candidates for employment, including medical suitability. Employees should not be assigned to work in situations in which they cannot, or are not expected to, perform satisfactorily except perhaps, on trial bases. If fully understood and carefully monitored, such trial assignments can be successfully managed. However, trial periods should generally be avoided because the management of unsatisfactory outcomes is often quite difficult.

Hiring the "handicapped," when the degree of handicap is well understood and the requirements of the job permit, can frequently lead to notable successes. Job modification can facilitate such successes. In addition, "handicapped" employees frequently bring with them greater determination, energy, dedication, and loyalty to the aims of the organization than do some nonhandicapped candidates. The key to success is to establish a clear understanding of expectations before-the-fact and to begin the work activity with a reasonable expectation of success on the part of all the parties involved. Hiring the handicapped for assignments in which they can be successful is not only morally sound and legally required, but also "good business."

Candidates whose medical conditions dictate that employment, at the tasks available, is ill-advised should not be hired. However, these decisions need to be carefully and conscientiously reached.

The structuring of the employment process can make a significant contribution to achieving careful and conscientious evaluation of employment candidates. Unfortunately, many employment processes are sequential, accommodating the desire to minimize evaluation costs. If the evaluation is conducted in a sequential fashion, the testing or evaluating is continued until the candidate fails. In this way, no costs are incurred beyond the point of failure on one item, and more expensive items—such as medical testing—are avoided. A more desirable procedure will determine the relative strengths and weaknesses of each candidate who is likely to be successful, thus enabling the choice to be made from among a larger pool of candidates.

The first type of evaluation, sequential testing, has at least three defects:

1. It does not permit the "whole" person to be adequately considered, allowing judgment to be exercised in evaluating weaknesses in one area against strengths in other areas.
2. It reveals which test was the determining test for failed applicants and thereby focuses on a single criterion of employment.
3. Medical personnel frequently lose objectivity as to the actual work potential of the candidate because they may in essence be making the hiring decision. Their evaluation is the only obstacle yet to be cleared prior to the job offer.

The better practice involves establishing a battery of tests, each part of which is randomly applied to all candidates. Selection is then based on all the evidence available. To avoid testing all applicants with a full battery of tests, a practice of using one test or criterion as a preliminary screen is an advisable compromise. All applicants who are successful on the screen would then be fully tested. Of course, the screen as well as other criteria, must be validated as having an adequate relationship to expected future job performance. The term "validated" is used in a very technical sense; studies designed to "validate" must be done by skilled persons.

The confidentiality of medical records becomes important in this process. The task of medical personnel is to determine suitability for employment; that is, they need to "know" the candidate medically as well as to understand the tasks to be performed and the degree of proficiency in task performance expected by management. The medical person needs to communicate to management his or her assessment regarding the candidate's relative ability to do the tasks involved but not the detailed medical reasons (maintenance of confidentially) for any inadequacies. This procedure demands the use of reasoned judgment both by medical personnel and by members of management involved in the hiring decision; general medical evaluations should not be simply "pass/fail" but should provide management sufficient insight regarding the candidate's health to allow this information to become a part of the greater picture. An exception to this general rule are tests specifically designed to be pass/fail, for example, drug screening tests.

In order to keep employment costs down, some medical personnel have found it useful to have a post-hiring medical examination which is more thorough than a pre-employment examination. The purpose of the post-hiring examination is to establish more broadly employees' health characteristics at time of hire. This practice provides a baseline set of data, which may not be cost-justified for candidates, in contrast to employees. By establishing such a baseline medical record, both employer and employee may be better able to make informed judgments regarding work-relatedness of future health problems.

The acquisition of new employees is significant in determining the caliber of the work force, yet it is frequently undertaken under the pressure of current human resource needs, with consideration of only current costs/profits. However, the long-term health of the business is largely determined by the capabilities of the work force. Medical personnel, as well as others involved in the hiring process, should fully recognize their obligation to the future of the business when making current hiring decisions. The consideration should be: Is this an employee we want for the long haul? Mistakes made in initial employment are very costly in the longer run. The article in Figure 13-1, taken from *The Wall Street Journal*, 8/8/83, expands this consideration to the entire employment process.

MONITORING OF EMPLOYEE HEALTH

Although not directly a safety issue in the narrow sense of the word "safety," clearly the health of employees is one aspect of their "safety," hence the term "occupational health and safety." Monitoring employee health is another area in which medical personnel have a contribution to make, not only to the safety of employees, but to the efficiency with which the organization functions. Periodic medical examinations provide this on-going monitoring of employee health. Changes in functional competence in areas such as respiratory capacity, hearing and seeing acuity, and laboratory testing, as well as other indicators may signal occupationally incurred deterioration in health. In any event, the earlier a deterioration in health is detected and preventive action taken, the better both the employee and employer are likely to be.

TREATMENT OF INJURIES

The most dramatic contributions medical personnel can make to the safety management effort are the treatment of injuries and the management of the treatment process. A good employee medical record materially assists in maximizing this contribution.

Most employer medical personnel and physical facilities are not intended to replace employees' personal physicians or specialists in narrow fields of medicine. However, employer medical personnel should be expected to make a positive contribution to the proper management of injury cases—obtaining timely and appropriate medical attention and minimizing loss of productivity. All injuries or suspected injuries, regardless

Choosing a Crew That'll Stay the Course

Manager's Journal

by C.R. Reagan

Picking the right employees is always an uncertain process, particularly when you have to make a judgment about how someone will perform over his lifetime. But in 30 years of personnel work at DuPont, I learned some hiring principles that help you improve your batting average. Prior to my retirement last September, I spent a quarter of a century at the company's cellophane plant at Topeka, Kan., where the turnover rate has averaged less than 3.2% per year. I'm convinced that the following 10 principles in hiring were an important factor in this exceedingly low rate.

1. Don't rush. Recognize the magnitude of the investment involved in hiring people. For those who remain for 30-plus years until retirement—a large percentage in our case—the company will be investing about $1 million each in wages and benefits. Considerable study and discussion takes place before purchasing a machine or making a capital investment of that magnitude. The wrong person on a job can have far more harmful effects than a faulty machine. Machines can be repaired or replaced more easily than people, and a machine doesn't upset other machines in the way a disgruntled worker can affect other employees.

2. Decisions shouldn't be made by personnel alone. It is best for those who will supervise the employees to have a direct role in interviewing and evaluating candidates. This avoids the later charge, "He wasn't any good to start with. Personnel sent him to me." Supervisors will take a more active interest in making sure their employees succeed if they have a part in choosing them. Multiple opinions about candidates are also advisable: We found it useful for at least three people to talk with each candidate who advances to the interview stage. Individual evaluations and opinions would be discussed and reconciled at a meeting where summary evaluations would be made.

3. Properly validated aptitude tests can be useful. For some jobs, it isn't possible to predict a candidate's aptitude from his application form, from interviews or even from reference checks with previous employers. The more complex the job, the more importance aptitude tests assume. Appropriate aptitude tests are essential in choosing employees for electronic or instrument maintenance and computer operation, but they are of little benefit in filling routine manual jobs.

4. Don't hire someone out of pity because he needs a job. An employment decision has long-term consequences for your employer and for all those who will be working with the person hired. Altruism is an admirable quality, but it is wrongly placed here.

5. No one should be selected simply because his father, brother or other relative has worked out well. In our experience, the performance of a good employee has little predictive value about his relatives.

6. Current employees are an excellent source of recommendations. Allowance must me made for possible partiality when relatives or friends are involved, but we have found that most employees are quite cautious and consider very seriously whom they recommend. Also, they have firsthand knowledge of what it takes to be successful in the kind of work involved.

7. Study the school record carefully. Of all the reference checks normally made, the school record has proven most valuable. It is the best barometer for predicting attendance, work habits and personality characteristics. It is difficult to disguise one's true nature for the number of years spent in school.

8. Maintain a hiring priority list. Keep a good backlog of top candidates. Include as many notes and records as possible, and set up a "priority to hire" list similar to the "draft" list used by professional sports teams. Some of your candidates will find other jobs and won't be available when you call them, but decisions to hire often must be made quickly, and having candidates preselected avoids the necessity of making hurried judgments.

9. Select employees; don't reject applicants. Our policy has been not to *reject* anyone. Instead, we have *selected* those who best meet our needs. This is a distinction that makes a difference in the company's public relations image and the various laws bearing on employment.

10. Cover job requirements thoroughly. During pre-employment interviews, be sure to explain completely the specific requirements of the job. Before accepting the job, the candidate should fully understand what is required regarding shift work, overtime, etc., and how wage and promotion policies operate. This can avoid problems and dissatisfaction later.

Mr. Reagan, now retired and living in Topeka, Kan., was an employee relations supervisor for DuPont.

Figure 13-1

of how slight, must be reported to medical and to supervision as soon as practical. Adoption of this fundamental policy regarding injury or suspected injury reporting results in several benefits.

1. It assures proper treatment of even small injuries, and thereby reduces the incidence of complications, which can result in greater pain, suffering, and loss of productivity.
2. It provides employer medical personnel an opportunity to diagnose the injury, treat the injury, and/or refer the injured to a specialist of the employer's choice as deemed appropriate.

Occupationally incurred injuries are clearly an employer responsibility. The employer has a "right" to protect its interest if the need arises. In many political jurisdictions, the injured employee also has a "right" to chose his or her medical personnel. This right, or course, must be acknowledged and complied with if the issue arises. However, by provision of first-rate medical attention, with obvious real interest in seeing that such care is provided in a timely manner, in most cases the question concerning choice of medical personnel need not arise. In any event, by having the injured employee see employer medical personnel first, employer medical personnel maximizes its ability to manage the treatment and return-to-work process. The employee's private physician can be expected to remain more objective in dealing with the patient/client if he or she has input from the employer medical personnel prior to seeing the employee patient. An injury should not be an excuse to avoid work. Absence from work should be a medical necessity rather than a convenience for the employee. In fact, the presence of medical personnel at the workplace often can provide a measure of convenience as well as safety for the recuperating employee who otherwise may be at home, perhaps alone. Being at the workplace, when not inhibiting to the recovery process, often is therapeutically beneficial. Doing normally assigned work may not be possible or advisable, but doing productive work—work that would otherwise be done by someone else, or not done at all though useful—might be. "Make work," even though not detrimental to the recovery process, is a ruse detrimental to the morale of the injured as well as others who recognize it for what it is. It is counterproductive to achieving excellence in safety.

RETURN TO WORK

Another significant area for employee medical personnel to contribute to the safety program is authorizing the return to the workplace for employees who have been absent for medical reasons. The employee's injury or illness need not have been occupationally related. Determination of the appropriateness of returning to the workplace following a period (even one day) of absence for medical reasons is best done by competent medical personnel. Because the employer has concern for the employee and legal reasons to determine fitness for presence in the workplace, employees should have to obtain authorization for their return from employer medical personnel prior to being allowed to do so. Although each individual undoubtedly has a point of view regarding his or her fitness to return to the workplace, the management process is best served by requiring the opinion of trained employer medical personnel. Such personnel will undoubtedly consider the professional opinions of any "private" medical personnel who may be involved in the case.

It is undesirable that employees return to work prematurely. By doing so, they may endanger their own health or the health of other employees. Beyond preventing inappropriate return to the workplace, the practice of requiring employer medical personnel authorization to return to the workplace makes it possible for employer medical personnel to maintain a much more thorough and therefore useful medical history of each employee. Thorough medical histories are of great help in early recognition of occupationally induced illnesses (or the lack of their symptoms) and in the formation of a factual basis for situations that may arise in the future. Such a practice also provides an opportunity for "guided" or "modified" work assignments to be developed which will prove productive and therapeutic to the recovery process if full recovery has not been accomplished prior to return to work (regular or normal assignment).

Cooperation between employer medical personnel and direct supervision can frequently lead to "modified" work that an injured employee can accomplish without in any way interfering with the recovery process. As mentioned above, such work is often therapeutic and makes a contribution to the recovery process.

Determination of the medical condition of an employee is a medical responsibility and should be fully communicated to the employee. Within the rules of ethical medical practice, the employee should be told the detailed medical diagnosis, treatment options, prognosis, and restrictions regarding work. Medical personnel have a major role in determining fitness-for-work. However, medical personnel should not be allowed to unilaterally determine "fitness-for-work"; they should be expected to determine what restrictions, if any, must be observed during a recovery period. Determination of "fitness-for-work" implies a knowledge of available work that is frequently not available to medical personnel on a timely basis. Medical personnel should stay within the bounds of describing medically related restrictions. The determination of the availability of productive work within the restraints imposed by medical restrictions and the desirability, from other points of view, of using employees in such work are management responsibilities. These responsibilities should not be abdicated to medical personnel, nor should medical personnel be allowed to usurp management of them. In the presence of open cooperation between medical personnel, the injured, and management personnel, the decision regarding return-to-work can be an intelligent one. This decision will recognize the legitimate interests of all the parties involved, while maintaining the welfare of the employee as the foremost objective.

The logistics of coming back and forth to work sometimes becomes a stumbling block to return to the workplace. All involved parties should be innovative in finding ways to reasonably accomplish the objective. It is sometimes useful, particularly in situations in which full wage protection is offered the injured employees, to consider what arrangements would appear reasonable if the personnel policy did not provide wage protection. Sometimes, because the cost of injuries is borne, from an accounting standpoint, by an overhead account, direct supervision is not supportive of the "modified" work concept. This same exercise of considering what could appear reasonable in the absence of income continuity, can also get supervision to view the need for "modified" work more objectively. Charging the costs associated with injuries directly to the operational cost center will make a positive contribution to the safety program. Such a practice also more correctly assigns costs to the operation responsible for their inccurrence.

Permanent disability cases need to be handled in a manner consistent with personnel policies covering such cases. State worker's compensation laws may be of significance and should be known and recognized.

Rate of pay while the employee is temporarily doing "modified" work may be a consideration. Where contractual arrangements permit, maintenance of normal earnings during performance of "modified" work is a significant positive contribution to the safety program. Reduction in rate of pay is seen as an additional penalty (injury is the first penalty) and should normally be avoided where employee/employer relationships permit protection of rate of pay for a temporary period.

The article in Figure 13-2 taken from *The Wall Street Journal* is instructive to this issue. Consultation with supervision regarding the diagnosis and prognosis of employee health conditions is another important area in which employer medical personnel can be of assistance. With full confidence established between supervisory personnel, medical personnel, and employees, the process can be managed so as to avoid premature return to the workplace on the one hand and malingering by employees on the other hand. Employees should be at work, doing something useful, unless to do so is harmful to the recovery process. The purpose of being absent from work should be timely and effective recovery; being injured should not, per se, be an acceptable reason for not being at the workplace.

TERMINATION OF EMPLOYMENT

Upon cessation of employment, the exiting process should include an exit medical examination. Such an examination (1) provides the employer and employee a factual record regarding employee health in those areas examined, and (2) provides employees an opportunity to discuss any concerns they may have regarding their health. This opportunity for discussion also provides the employer a reliable record of such concerns or their absence. It can be of help in future claims, and in preempting future claims. The exit examination also demonstrates management's interest in the employee even though he or she is leaving. This philosophy is frequently desirable as an item of good employee relations, as well as a prudent business practice should questions arise in the future. Employers should be held responsible for occupationally incurred injuries or damage to health; they should protect themselves from being saddled with costs simply because they are the only source available with resources to pay.

Reprinted from THE WALL STREET JOURNAL.

TUESDAY, MARCH 17, 1987

A Doctor's View of Disability Claims

By Philip R. Alper

The patient's eyes brim with tears.

"Couldn't you give me a month off work?" she asks pleadingly.

This is the world of disability evaluation and certification, one of medicine's lesser-known byways where art, science and ethics blend in sometimes mysterious ways.

Only a handful of physicians earn their livings determining disabilities. And in a sad incident last month, a doctor died that way: Peter-Cyrus Rizzo III, a New York surgeon, died Feb. 6 after being shot the day earlier by a retired firefighter whose request for an additional disability pension allowance had just been rejected by a panel of doctors. For the rest of us, the task of figuring out degrees and lengths of incapacity constitutes one of many relatively distasteful bureaucratic chores.

Sometimes that task is very straightforward. The loss of an eye or limb, for example, may be directly related to the requirements of a job and periods of disability may be determined objectively. More often, however, the issues are blurred. The emotional status of the patient, how the patient feels about the job and particularly about relations with supervisory personnel, and the cultural biases of both patient and physician all combine to produce a result that is likely to be more impressionistic than definitive.

There is a wide variation in thinking about how sick one is and how important time off is in order to get well. The patients' responsibilities outside of work also vary. It's hard to say to what degree these factors should influence disability status. Most physicians probably consider them important.

"Why do you feel you can't work?" I ask my patient. Her condition is an unusual affliction of the scalp, causing hair loss, itching and pain.

"I'm ashamed to be seen and I can't stop scratching," she answers. The woman, who is known to me as hard-working and responsible, clearly isn't herself.

When confronted with debatable disability requests, doctors face a great temptation to please the patient. Doing so also keeps the patient coming back to the office and maintains a steady stream of fees. This temptation, however, is not different from those faced in other areas of medicine where professional ethics remain the principal barrier against providing unnecessary or improper treatment.

There are certainly places where sick-slips are for sale. Pseudo-injuries and pseudo-illnesses leading to phony insurance claims provide grist for the mills of investigative reporters. No doubt there are also lesser degrees of dishonesty. But everyday reality is much more humdrum.

Given the patient's opportunity to play the system for personal gain, I've been surprised at the comparative infrequency of fanciful requests for time off. Perhaps this stems from my own middle-class background with its resulting vibes that stifle them in advance. Or since physicians are known to attract patients who resemble them, it may reflect the similar work ethic of my patients. As many patients push me to return them to work sooner than I think advisable as want to drag their heels.

One of my patients, a disability-claims examiner, is much less sanguine. She fumes at disability rip-offs, at what she sees as a trend for alternative health practitioners, such as chiropractors, to stand behind them, with their opinions receiving equal credence with those of physicians at hearings.

That may be, but there *are* tough calls. Emotional upset, headaches, backaches and other subjective symptoms are hard to quantify. Besides, someone who truly feels disabled may as a result actually be disabled. A well-timed period of time off with stress reduction and an effort at better understanding may prevent a much worse disability later. It may also uncover factors at the workplace that can be improved. I try to give the patient the benefit of the doubt within reason. Not doing so is more than unkind; it risks harm to the patient and lawsuits that neither the physician nor employer would welcome.

After a major illness, fears about employability and ability to handle stress are commonplace. They have to be addressed in order to ensure a good outcome. I've been frustrated by lack of a formal job description furnished by the employer. Too often I've been told by the employer that an initial trial period of part-time or light duty can't be accommodated. "My insurance doesn't allow it" shuts me up but doesn't help the patient's transition from illness to health.

One final aspect of the disability scene bears mention: It is loaded with absurdities that result from mixing science with politics. Hereditary disabilities of patients in the military are considered service-connected if discovered while on active duty. Heart attacks of California police and firemen are statutorily deemed related to job stress and compensible even if they occur at the gambling tables in Las Vegas.

In the absence of an exact science and lacking the descent of a professor of disability ethics from Mt. Olympus, I've developed a rule: Coddle people a little but aim to keep them active and productive.

As for our patient, persistence and persuasiveness got her two weeks off, and a later one-week extension.

Dr. Alper is a clinical associate professor of medicine at the University of California at San Francisco, and an internist in Burlingame, Calif.

Figure 13–2

SUMMARY

Employer medical personnel have an important role in establishing management safety leadership. This role begins with the employment process and ends with the death of former employees. The key to maximizing the effectiveness of this role is to establish clearly that medical personnel make their contribution by providing management and employees timely medical advice and guidance and maintenance of good employee medical rcords, not by making operational decisions.

Management decisions regarding employee presence in the workplace are, indeed, management decisions, not decisions to be made by medical personnel. Supervision should not be allowed to abdicate such decisions to medical personnel, nor should medical personnel be allowed to usurp supervisory responsibility for employees and employee contribution to the success of the enterprise. For their part, supervision must keep themselves fully informed regarding employee health and ability to work. In doing so, supervision must understand and fully evaluate advice and guidance available from employer medical personnel.

Medical personnel should provide *staff* assistance to the operational or executive part of the organization—line management. This distinction is crucial to establishing leadership in safety management.

CHAPTER 14

FINANCIAL ACCOUNTING PROCEDURES AND SAFETY LEADERSHIP

Accounting procedures affect the safety management process in two important ways: (1) by facilitating or providing impediments to acts of management leadership, and (2) by distancing or linking monetary expenditures to the benefits derived from these expenditures.

INFLUENCE ON ACTS OF LEADERSHIP

The degree of freedom to act, which an enterprise's accounting procedures provide managers, directly influences the perception of subordinates regarding the leadership qualities of a manager. Accounting procedures that delegate little or no decision-making authority regarding expenditure of funds in comparison with the expectation of subordinates rob the supervisor of a significant means of demonstrating leadership. This limitation is most significant when it is an impediment imposed upon a local site manager. Employees rightfully look to the top management they can see and know for action, particularly when their personal safety is involved. A response that "I'll have to check headquarters" undermines the local manager's leadership position. When accounting procedures require "checking with headquarters," any other less "damaging" response will eventually be recognized as disingenuous and will undermine employee trust and thus also undermine the manager's ability to lead. The manager's leadership position is eroded either way.

Some managers attempt to cure this problem by authorizing funds in violation of accounting procedures, but then quickly obtaining the needed headquarter's authorization. They may even do so with tacit approval of headquarters personnel. For some employees this behavior can present a macho, person-of-action image, that enhances the perception of managerial leadership. However, such management action also communicates that procedures viewed as excessively restrictive can be ignored, at least temporarily, in the name of expediency. For safety, this is a devastating leadership example to set. The temptation to deviate from established safety procedures in the interest of expediency is always present. Shortcuts always seem to be appropriate, "under the circumstances." Achieving excellence in safety requires achieving excellence in safety discipline. This is not likely to occur in an environment in which a manager undermines this concept by his or her own behavior. Employees cannot be expected to understand and believe that safety procedures must be held inviolate, but deviation from accounting procedures is acceptable.

In a broader sense, managers who do not adhere to established accounting procedures do themselves and the organization, generally, a much greater harm than the damage done to the safety effort. A manager who does not follow the rules on accounting matters signals that he or she may not follow other rules. Such a manager may not be worthy of subordinate trust in following certain personnel rules or procedures, particularly those that may not be widely known—for example, salary, promotion, and transfer policies, which are most personal for each subordinate. By not following the rules, even accounting rules, such managers shoot themselves in the foot and do not develop the trust needed to be leaders. Accounting procedures should adequately recognize this need for managerial freedom of action while also providing for financial accountability.

Accounting procedures (practices) classify expenditures of funds into two broad classes: (1) Capital Expenditures and (2) Expense Expenditures. Expenses are costs that are borne by the enterprise on a current basis for which current management can be held accountable in the short run. Capital expenditures are costs that can be "capitalized" and amortized or depreciated over a period of years and taken as expenses each year.

Monthly cost sheets should reveal expenses expended each month and authorizing managers should be expected to explain their actions upon request. I see no reason for any formal limitations to be put on local top managers regarding authorization of individual Expense expenditures. There are normally, or should be, other restraining influences within most organizations that effectively control management decisions regarding Total Expenses. Expenditures of large sums of money normally take time; such expenditures become apparent in monthly cost information and can be challenged. Alternatively, because expenditures of large sums of money take time, there is ample time to seek authorization from higher levels of management who may need to understand the appropriateness of the expenditure under existing circumstances. A third alternative is simply to seek nonobjection from upper management; this solution communicates the intent to spend a significant amount of money, but does not open the door to negotiation of a revised current expense budget. Upper management simply indicates that if the expenditure can be made within existing cost budgets or forecasts, it does not object. Conversely, upper management may object in the interest of achieving a below-forecast current cost.

What is needed to facilitate leadership is a financial system that allows management, at every level, to have sufficient authority to commit to a level of expenditure that permits expeditious decision making that appears reasonable to employees—the followers of would-be leaders.

Different organizations, both because of their differences in size and because of differences in the nature of their business, have need for differences in dollar authorization levels appropriate at various management levels in order to facilitate managerial leadership. In fact, not all dollars are equal. Authorization to do work with existing employees commits no new expenditures. Such authorizations merely place a claim on the existing work force, increasing the backlog of unfulfilled work orders that await scheduling. Scheduling determines the sequence in which work gets done, not the level of expenditures. The size of the existing work force determines the level of expenditures. Some authorized work may never get accomplished because it simply cannot compete successfully in the scheduling process.

Authorization to contract for outside labor is a much more significant action. Doing so establishes a commitment to new or additional expenditure of funds. When outside contracting is used as a routine extension of the employers' work force, this distinction may become blurred. The result can and has resulted in a "loss of control" of expenditures. It is important that this distinction be recognized. Establishing a fixed level of expenditure for outside contracting that can be treated as though the work were being done by the employers' own employees, while any excess over this amount must be handled as an "outside contract," can facilitate the control of expenditures arising from routine reliance on outside contractors.

Capital expenditures differ significantly from current expenditures. Capital expenditures are "capitalized" as assets, not "expensed" as current costs. The costs associated with capital expenditures are future, not current, costs. The costs appear as depreciation or amortization charges. Authorization to expend funds for capital assets commits future managers, not current managers. For this reason, decisions regarding capital expenditures should be vested in those managers whose time horizon is, properly, longer than the next monthly cost sheet—that is, higher management.

In addition to having the authority to expend funds, all managers need to know the procedures for securing authorization for expenditures of funds larger than they themselves can authorize. Thus, such procedures must exist and exist in specific terms. By knowing these procedures, the manager/leader can act at the time action is called for or expected. The action can simply be to commit to subordinates that the manager has or will seek the desired funds, although he or she cannot authorize expenditures of the type and amount required, personally. Having made such a commitment, the manager is then obligated to carry out the commitment and to let subordinates know the outcome and why the outcome is what it is. These steps keep the process "clean" and helps keep the decision making process in particular connected directly to those individuals who have made the decision.

All of the above procedures suggest that an explicit schedule of expenditure authority be established which enhances the opportunity for every member of supervision to demonstrate responsible leadership of his or her own organization. Table 14-1 illustrates such a schedule.

Of course, the actual numbers appropriate to such a schedule will depend on the scale and nature of the enterprise. The point is that such a schedule needs to be established so that members of management can take action on a timely basis. They need the freedom to project a reality that they can "make things happen."

The authorization numbers need to be high enough to clarify that upper management trusts members of lower management. Spending authority should not be restrained by reasons related to lack of trust. They should be formally restrained only because of the need of higher levels of management to understand the situations for which money is needed and to allow these upper level personnel to bring their broader perspectives and possible alternative courses of action to bear on the situation. It is not lack of trust but narrowness of perspective that should be reflected in these authorization numbers.

Table 14-1 shows a schedule of authorization levels for individual pieces of work—work orders, purchase requisitions, projects, and so forth. The numbers for capital authorization can be higher than they otherwise might be in financial systems

Table 14-1

Authorization of Funds Schedule

(Individual Work Orders or Projects)

Level of Management	*Type and Amount of Expenditure*			
	Employee Labor (hrs. or $)	Materials ($)	Contract Labor ($)	Total Contract ($)
First-line Supervisor	8 hrs.-E* 0 hrs.-C**	100-E 0-C	- 0 - - 0 -	- 0 - - 0 -
Area Supervisor	200 hrs.-E $2000-C	1000-E 500-C	1000-E 500-C	2000-E 1000-C
Superintendent	Unlimited-E $10,000-C	5000-E 5000-C	5000-E 5000-C	10,000-E 5000-C
Site Manager	Unlimited-E $100,000-C	Unlimited-E 25,000—C	Unlimited-E 25,000-C	Unlimited-E 50,000-C
Headquarters Management				
Level 3	Limited to $250,000 on capital expenditures			
Level 2	Limited to $1,000,000 on capital expenditures			
Level 1	Limited to $5,000,000 on capital expenditures			
Finance Commitee	Limited to $25,000,000 on capital expenditures			
Bd. of Directors	Unlimited, except by articles of incorporation			

* E indicates expense
** C indicates capital

in which a formal capital forecast or budget scheme exists. Such a capital budget provides the total authorization level for all capital authorizations during a specified time period for each individual organization for which a top manager exists—plant, laboratory, or marketing organization. This arrangement provides for controlling the total capital funds authorized without the necessity that upper management sees and approves each individual piece of work. The capital budget scheme provides local managers the freedom to act in situations through which leadership is demonstrated, while providing full accountability for all monies authorized. This process requires managers who authorize expenditures of funds to pick and choose carefully under a system that requires full disclosure. Upper management should be provided with after-the-fact records of such authorizations. These will enable them to make judgments regarding the stewardship of company funds demonstrated by their subordinates, that is, judge the performance of these subordinates.

Once established, the figures in Table 14-1 do not normally need frequent changing. Inflation must be reflected periodically. Total expenditures must be responsive to the general business cycle and the specific needs of the business. The capital budget, therefore, is subject to change as these factors change.

My point here is not to outline a financial control or budgetary process, but rather to illustrate that accounting systems can and should be established which recognize the need for managers to lead. Accounting systems should provide for this need, holding managers responsible for results while requiring them to operate within specified boundaries (budgets).

A similar restraint can and should be established for operating expenditures—expenditures that will be "expensed" in the current accounting period, normally monthly or four-week periods. Such restraints can be expressed in absolute dollar terms, or in relative terms—dollars per unit of output. The objective to be achieved is comparatively greater freedom to authorize expenditures in individual cases but restraint and oversight regarding total expenditures.

LINKAGE BETWEEN EXPENDITURES AND BENEFITS

The second significant feature of accounting systems that relates directly to safety is the way in which expenditures and the benefits from these expenditures are related. These two items should be coupled as closely as possible, even to the point of erring on the "too close" side. Two examples illustrate the point.

In order to improve safety performance, supervision needs to spend time, effort, and perhaps some recognizable money on safety-related matters. These costs, when well spent, should be expected to reduce injuries and their attendant costs, for example, worker's compensation costs and medical costs. (See Chapter 1 for further details on injury-related costs.) An accounting system that charges the costs incurred by lower supervision, say a warehouse supervisor, to the operating costs for which the supervisor is held accountable, but charges worker's compensation and medical costs to an overhead account, does not serve the organization well. Supervision may spend their time, effort, and dollars on safety for altruistic reasons, but an accounting system that deprives them of the financial rewards associated with achieving reductions in injury related costs robs them of something very personal—positive influence on their work performance appraisal. Because, in fact, resources are finite in the short-run, supervisors who spend time and effort on safety in the absence of financial recognition do so at the apparent expense of their other responsibilities.

What financial incentive does a warehouse supervisor have for conducting safety meetings, perhaps on an overtime basis, if the benefits do not reduce the costs for which he or she is held responsible? What incentive does a line supervisor have for getting an employee back to work on a modified work basis, if the costs of the employee's being absent are not a part of his or her operating costs? How much time and effort is a line supervisor going to invest in trying to reduce employee time-away-from-work if the costs do not affect the measures by which his or her performance is measured? Supervisory participation in process hazards reviews (process safety management), Central Safety Committee and its subcommittees, injury investigations, and management safety audits are all costs of doing business—costs of doing business safely. These costs are operating costs; they should be accounted for as such. They should not become a "cost of safety" and thereby become an overhead cost.

The only overhead costs that should be charged to safety are the direct costs of operating the safety office. To do otherwise is to act as though safety were something "extra" or separate from the work of the organization. It is not; it is an integral part of every operation and should be accounted for accordingly. There should be no operating budgets for safety. But why should supervision participate in these activities if they are to be denied the benefits expected to flow from these efforts?

Even though effort spent on safety undoubtedly has beneficial effects on other performance parameters, to deny a supervisor some of the more tangible cost benefits resulting from his or her effort provides a considerable disincentive in regard to achieving improved safety performance. Although worker's compensation and medical costs are significant cost elements for most organizations, many organizations charge these costs to an overhead or burden account. The consequence of this accounting treatment for these costs is that no one is held accountable. There are no points at which managerial attention can be applied. Lower level supervision has little to no financial incentive to act more responsibly, and upper management is too far away from the point at which decisions that can affect the costs involved are made—that is, at the first-line supervisor's level. These costs should not be treated as "uncontrollable" costs; they respond to proper management incentives. The accounting system should facilitate generating these incentives, not impede their development.

The second illustration relates to a specific accounting system designed to achieve "close coupling." In practice, the coupling was judged to be "too close." In an attempt to enhance an accounting system to provide the correct incentives to first-line supervisors and to increasingly treat them as managers, an operating cost account was provided each first-line supervisor. All costs associated with the supervisor's operation were charged to this operating account. These costs included allocated space costs (depreciation, heating, lighting), allocated costs of upper supervision, actual material and labor costs for which he or she was directly responsible, actual costs of "benefits" received by the employees he or she supervised, and pension accrual costs. A real attempt was made to have each individual supervisor understand the costs that flowed with the people he or she supervised. This provided a clear understanding of why a mechanic who was paid $14.00 per hour cost $20.00 per hour to employ (addition of benefits), and why the work order to which he was charging his time was charged $25.00 per hour. It helped everyone to understand that an unproductive mechanic was costing the organization $25.00 per hour, not $14.00 per hour.

While analyzing his monthly cost sheet, a supervisor quickly recognized that his charges from the medical insurance carrier had escalated substantially. He knew his people and kept informed regarding employee family members. He believed the charges contained an error. He dutifully began to make inquiry to the site medical coordinator who, on this occasion, was uncooperative in explaining the numbers. Thus, he did not find out what he wanted to know—why his charges were "out-of-line." He went to his supervisor, who ran into the same problem, as did, in turn, his supervisor. This third-level supervisor quickly recognized that a conflict had developed between the supervisor's need to understand the charges being made against his account and the need to preserve confidentiality of sensitive medical information.

In this instance, a family member was involved, not an employee. Supervision within the Human Resources department who dealt with the insurance carrier did not think line management needed to know "who" or "what" about the medical charge that had attracted the supervisor's attention. The medical coordinator verified the correctness of the charges, but provided no additional information. Upper management, upon reviewing the confidentiality consideration, not the details of the source of these particular charges, confirmed that confidentiality must prevail. Confidentiality of medical records had been a long-standing policy and practice that everyone understood and recognized as correct. However, in this case, the accounting system had provided a backdoor route by which confidentiality could be breached. Fortunately, it was not. Long-standing recognition of the appropriateness of real confidentiality had served the organization well.

Following this experience, the accounting procedures were altered. The new procedure provided that medical costs be charged at the second level of supervision and then prorated to the first-line supervisors reporting to this second-level supervisor. This diminished the relative size and, hence, attraction of unusual charges and reduced both the risk of breaching confidentiality and the perception of its having been breached. Nevertheless, the system continued to keep supervisory expenditure of effort and the benefits derived from these efforts close to those who have the maximum opportunity to favorably influence the total costs involved—first-line supervisors.

SUMMARY

Accounting systems should facilitate leadership development, not impede it. They should closely couple expenditures with the benefits of these expenditures. Many accounting systems fail on both counts.

CHAPTER 15

CREW SAFETY MEETINGS

Safety meetings are an integral part of establishing a work environment in which employees work safely free of injury and damage to health or the environment. The existence of safety meetings alone will not produce such an environment, but good safety meetings have been found to be an essential part of a safety management process that produces such an environment (see Chapter 4).

Meetings in which safety is discussed take many forms, as has been discussed in previous chapters. One meeting that has not been specifically discussed is the "crew safety meeting." A crew safety meeting is a meeting of an individual group of employees who work, as contrasted to supervise, together as a recognized work group having a sense of identity as a group. This includes the supervisor and all the people for whom he or she is directly responsible. In workplaces in which employees are organized as self-directed work groups, management participation can be determined by the work group. A sense of identity or "team" is essential to successful crew safety meetings.

One purpose of crew safety meetings is to enhance the sense of "team" or community within the work group. A well-conducted crew safety meeting accomplishes this by clearly focusing on the central theme of the safety of each member of the crew. Personal safety, if nothing else, is one common interest that all members of the crew are likely to share. As this interest in personal safety is used to develop shared values and ideas of acceptable behavior by members of the group, the other areas in which common interests are desirable will emerge, if not already present, and develop—to the benefit of all involved, including the larger organization and its "bottom line."

CREW SAFETY MEETING—BROAD CHARACTERISTICS

There are several characteristics of a good crew safety meeting.

1. **Direct, active, involvement of crew members is assured.** One of the objectives of crew meetings is to secure the individual commitment of crew members to any action, recommendations or procedures that may be developed during the meeting. Commitment is enhanced by assuring that each member has had a real opportunity to have his or her ideas heard and considered by the group. This is not easily accomplished. Leading a good crew meeting is a demanding task that can be made easier by properly structuring the meeting and defining participant's expectations. Participation also requires the number of participants to be appropriately small. Groups should not be combined in the name of efficiency. In any event, teams really exist only in small numbers. "Community" only exists when each member of the group actively interacts with other members of the group while performing work. An interdependency of group members exists. It is essential that this element of crew safety meetings be maintained and not forfeited by enlarging the size of the group in a mistaken effort to be efficient.

The purpose of crew safety meetings is not to hold a meeting. The purpose is to enhance directly employee performance in safety, and indirectly other aspects of their work. It has been said that "four to seven participants is generally ideal, ten is tolerable, and twelve is an outside limit."[1] In today's world of flattened organizational structures, many organizations find these criteria "challenging." However, subgrouping can achieve these group sizes, leaving the task of integrating the findings, conclusions, and actions to subsequent resolution and communication, as necessary. My personal experience supports a group size of ten to twelve as appropriate for balancing the opportunity to be heard with the opportunity to directly hear what others have said. The crew safety meetings I conducted more than thirty years ago would have been much more effective if the crew, approximately twenty people, had been divided into two groups. Although this would have required more work for me, it would have been significantly more effective and cost no more to the company. I simply did not know any better, and apparently neither did anyone else in the organization.

2. **Assured upward communications.** Another characteristic of a good crew safety meeting is that the meeting be structured in such a way as to assure that information flows up the organizational chain. This goal provides the opportunity for upper levels of supervision to keep themselves aware of what is happening in these meetings. By keeping abreast of the results of these crew meetings, upper management will gain a better understanding of employee concerns and the solutions being developed for their resolution. This is not just "nice-to-know" communication. It is essential communication in a safety management process designed to seek excellence. Assured upward communication contributes in a number of ways:

a. It provides an opportunity for upper management to react regularly to events happening in the organization—granting approvals, nonobjecting, or suggesting alternatives when important to do so.

b. It provides the basis for communicating across organizational lines in situations in which this cannot be readily accomplished by the group itself—for example, between sites or divisions.

c. It also provides upper management the opportunity to pass along deserved recognition to the team for their contribution.

The upward communication channel needs to be formalized to assure its routine use. Conversely, routine use will institutionalize such communications and the channel will no longer be recognized as a formal one; it will become "one of the things we do around here." These crew meetings represent the end of the chain in the Central Safety Committee system for organizing the safety management process. Similar meetings, at each level within the organization provide the connecting links, bottom-to-top.

3. **Communication on safety matters is as important top-to-bottom.** Crew safety meetings provide this vital, institutionalized top-to-bottom connection directly through the supervisory organization. This arrangement permits intermediate levels of supervision to put their personal stamp or imprimatur on these communications, thereby enhancing "closer to the workplace" interpretation of the "message." Some upper management will view this channel of communication as too risky, too full of holes that will result in too little being received at the end of the channel. In lieu of using the line organization, they turn to the safety staff to communicate the message from the top across the organization via a "safety bulletin" or a "safety corner' in the site newspaper, or simply by issuing a new or altered safety rule. Such communications are doomed to failure; they fall on barren ground. Subordinates should pay attention to their direct line management, not staff personnel. Bypassing the line organization contributes to the deterioration of its ability to communicate. The line organization should be expected to communicate, and to communicate well. Its performance in doing so can and should be measured and be a part of its performance evaluation.

4. **Intermediate levels of supervision must communicate both up and down.** Of course, intermediate levels of management are not just message carriers providing connecting links between the two ends of the organization. Intermediate levels of management should be expected to originate messages both up and down, based on their analysis and judgment.

Crew safety meetings provide the forum through which these various operational messages can be discussed, evaluated, and adopted. They provide the basis for establishing what the "crew" needs to *do* to reduce new requirements or emphasis to day-to-day practice.

CREW SAFETY MEETING—CONTENT

Good crew safety meetings have three parts: (A) what comes in from above, (B) what is developed for crew use, and (C) what goes up from below.

Part A—What Comes in from Above

On a routine basis, four items of safety interest should be provided from the top—the Central Safety Committee. These are:

1. Safety performance statistics for the larger organizational unit covering the previous reporting period (monthly)—Lost-time and Total Recordables.

2. Information from incident investigations that needs more emphasis than it might get from simply reading the incident investigation report. The recommendations may need to be particularized for some crews.
3. Summary results from the Management Safety Audits for the preceding period (monthly).
4. Any new broadly applicable safety rules or procedures, including new governmental regulatory issues.

Part B—What Is Developed for Use Within the Crew

Crew contributions can vary from the team's response to information from above to what needs to be done to assure that outlying eye-wash fountains get activated on a daily basis in order to keep water from getting "rusty." New safety procedures that apply to all members of the crew are frequent topics for this portion of the meeting. Seasonal off-the-job safety hazards and techniques for avoiding injury from these hazards can also be productively discussed—for example, seat belt use, helmet use by bicyclers including children, and hazards of sunshine at the beach.

Part C—Communications Up the Line

Anything the crew wants the boss to know about falls in this category. The crew may need help in implementing something it would like to do. It may want to communicate a difficulty it is having interpreting some down-from-the-top message or difficulty in applying it to its situation. It may have developed alternative ideas on a subject that it wishes to pass up the line. It may have tried some new procedure or safety program that it thinks warrants broader dissemination. The key idea here is to establish the fact that the organization *expects* upward communication.

CREW SAFETY MEETING—CONDUCTING THEM

Conducting crew safety meetings is no different from conducting any other meeting in which participation is desired and which is expected to generate commitment in support of specific organizational objectives. They do have a clear advantage over many other organizational group meetings. They focus primarily on the personal health and safety of the participants in very real, tangible, and easily recognizable terms.

Crew safety meetings are best restricted to thirty minutes. This limit requires real discipline on the part of the supervisor or discussion leader as well as the participants. The content of the meeting should largely be predetermined. Discussion must be based on well thought out ideas. Achieving this prior thinking should be expected for that portion of the meeting whose topic of discussion has been made known well before the meeting itself. Crew safety meetings should not be "group therapy sessions" that are open-ended and unfocused. Maintaining the focused character of these meetings can be achieved when a topic has been announced ahead of time.

For discussion related to communications coming *down* through the organization, the meeting leader needs to decide whether to simply communicate and leave discussion for a subsequent meeting for which group members can prepare, or attempt to guide the group through discussions on an ad hoc basis. Time lines are, of course, a dominant factor conditioning this decision. The skill, knowledge, and leadership qualities of the leaders are also of significant importance. Productive use of the thirty-minute time limitation is a major objective. By providing for a specified, short time frame, the leaders can focus these meetings on a limited subject while providing for active participation by avoiding an all-to-frequent aspect of some meetings—degeneration into a complaint meeting.

Step 1—Part A

The meeting should open with communication items for the crew, as outlined earlier: Central Safety items, injury performance statistics, audit results, and incident report items. Meeting leaders should state these items and take only those questions that help clarify the message. The meeting leader should defer questions that lead to discussion of the subject to a later meeting, unless he or she is prepared to handle an ad hoc discussion of the subject. Such ad hoc discussions are difficult to guide to productive end points and should normally be avoided.

Step 2—Part B

Following this communication of items brought to the group, the portion of the meeting devoted to an item to be developed by the crew can begin. This should open with the presentation of the statement of the subject for discussion, on a "blackboard" or "flip-chart" so that the subject is continuously in view of the group. In addition, the group can easily recognize any comments or discussions not related to the subject as such and not allow them to consume their attention or time. By use of such discipline, all parties to the discussion become trained to respect this aspect of the meeting and the insistence of "keeping to the subject."

Step 3

The leader, another designated member of the crew, or perhaps a guest should then present a brief background as to why the subject is relevant and any facts that might guide the ensuing discussion. These two items should appear on the blackboard or flip-chart, constantly in view of the group.

Step 4

Now the leader presents the specific question to be discussed, again in full visual display. He or she should frame the question in terms of action to be taken. For example, "What specific action should be taken to reduce injuries from foreign bodies in the eyes of mechanical craft personnel?" The question should not be, "Why do mechanical crafts personnel have more eye injuries than other employees?" The first question drives the discussion toward an action step; the second question leads to speculative discussions with no end-point or need for corrective action. It is surprising how attention to this kind of detail in conducting crew safety meetings determines their usefulness and the resulting sense of accomplishment of the crew.

Step 5

The time has now come to secure group participation. It is time for the leader to stop talking and listen. He or she should accomplish this by asking crew members for their suggestions regarding the question previously put before the group. These suggestions should be received and recorded in abbreviated form by an appointed crew member, in full view of the group. No discussion at this point. Recording these suggestions not only "captures" but also controls the pace of the meeting. After a number of suggestions have been recorded and it appears that no additional ones will be offered, these suggestions should be consolidated into a shorter list containing those having the greatest relevancy to the question before the group. The skill and credibility of the meeting leader now becomes crucial. He or she must consolidate the suggestions yet maintain the support of the group in arriving at what appears to be the main points of agreement within the crew.

Step 6

The next task is to solicit crew evaluation of these restated suggestions. The merits and flaws of each should be noted for all crew members to see and think about.

Step 7

Following the evaluation of a narrowed list of suggestions, a list of specific actions to be taken should be developed, in some order of priority. Throughout this process, consensus should be sought. Crew members should be encouraged to discuss the merits and flaws of each suggestion. The role of the meeting leader is not to direct the group to a preselected outcome. The role of the meeting leader is to keep the group focused on the subject at hand and to channel discussions to some conclusion—an action step.

Failing to establish an agreement sufficient to secure crew support, the successful leader does not gloss over this fact and act as though an adequate agreement has been reached when, in fact, agreement has not been reached. A skilled leader acknowledges the lack of agreement and recognizes the need to back up, perhaps reformulate the question, or ask a subgroup of the crew to study the problem independently before proceeding further. The subgroup should report its results at the next meeting.

Throughout this entire process the objective is to reach understanding and support for purposeful action, mitigating or avoiding entirely the not-invented-here (NIH) syndrome and securing enthusiastic support for change. These can be achieved only if the leader allows and encourages the group to "work its way through" the problem. This "working through" can be a painstaking endeavor. The process takes time, but it takes less time if the leader keeps the meeting "on track."

The leader should recognize subjects that do not coalesce as such and not treat them as though adequate agreement has been reached when, in fact, it has not. To do so destroys the process and undermines the safety effort and morale of the crew in general. Failure to reach agreement adequate to provide a basis for well-supported action is usually the result of having chosen a question too broad to be addressed in the available time. Careful selection of a meaningful but sufficiently narrow question is a fundamental aspect of successfully conducting these meetings.

It may not be possible, however, to reach agreement, even though the question is appropriate in scope. This result is almost always the consequence of inadequate development of background material—facts regarding the issue. In the absence of sufficient facts, individual crew members operate on their own knowledge or supposed knowledge, which varies enough between the members that no common knowledge base exists. In either case, a good leader recognizes these deficiencies and steers the discussion to reformulate the question to a more manageable scope or to secure recognition by the crew that additional basic data are needed. The meeting must not be allowed to degenerate; the leader must salvage a useful product from the meeting. It is important that the group feel some sense of accomplishment.

Step 8

After determining various courses of possible action, evaluating their pros and cons, establishing priorities, and ultimately selecting specific actions to take, the group must accomplish two more goals: to establish who is to take each action and to delineate a timetable for each action.

The discussion part of the meeting is now finished. The group should devote the remaining portion of the meeting to any items thought worthy of communicating upwards, Part C of the meeting, Step 9.

Step 9—Part C

Upward communications can take many forms, but most relate to problem identification. Because recommendations for resolution should accompany these, the group should have done some work before it communicates up the line. Upward communication, to be effective, cannot simply be a list of things that "someone needs to think about or fix." With this restraint, Part C usually moves along orderly and quickly. There may arise situations of such importance that upward communication is appropriate independent of developing recommendations, but these should not be "saved" for presentation at a crew safety meeting. The meeting does provide a back-up communication system, in the event that day-to-day communications have failed.

CREW SAFETY MEETING—FREQUENCY AND TIMING

Experience in what is required to achieve excellence in safety strongly suggests that crew safety meetings should be held on a monthly basis for all employees. This frequency matches the frequency established for meetings of the Central Safety Committee. Actual timing should reflect regularity of schedule and convenience for employees. Attendance should be mandatory, if this question arises, for safety meetings are essential elements of the work environment. They are an integral part of work. Production requirements may make it necessary that these meetings be held on an overtime basis. Arbitrators and courts have held that reasonable overtime is a justifiable job requirement. Of course, excused absences for reasons acceptable for other work absences should be granted.

CREW SAFETY MEETING—OTHER CONSIDERATIONS

All of the parts of a crew safety meeting require some preparation on the part of the crew leader, the first-line supervisor or "resource person," and others in the absence of a conventional supervisor. Perhaps the most significant, but least visible, preparation a leader must make is understanding before-the-fact possible outcomes of the crew meeting. By doing so, he or she can avoid being surprised to the extent that the meeting is allowed to become contentious or otherwise unproductive. To accomplish this, a skilled leader gets some input from individual crew members who are known to be vocal, have strong opinions, or have demonstrated unusual insight in understanding problems and their solutions.

When union representation is present, the shop steward should not be overlooked. He or she needs to be provided an opportunity to constructively contribute and not become part of the opposition. Union representatives have an important, legitimate role to play. Safety of employees should be a common union/management goal. Safety should not be allowed to become a point of contention. Safety is a management responsibility; it should not be inadvertently compromised or abdicated. A crew safety meeting is not the appropriate forum for a union/management discussion.

Well-conducted crew safety meetings can and should represent an important part of the fabric of a successful safety management process. Most supervisors need specific instructions and hands-on training if they are to accomplish this aspect of their leadership function. It will not happen by simply requiring first-line supervisors to have safety meetings. They must be trained to be effective meeting leaders. Left to their own intitiatives, a large majority of first-line supervisors simply turn to the safety office in search of the latest video on safety.

Upper management must demonstrate its commitment to improved employee safety and the process by which improvement can be achieved if improvement is actually to be achieved. Providing both the finances and a reasonable means for accomplishing supervisory training is an important way by which upper management can demonstrate its commitment to safety.

Successful crew safety meetings typically result not only in improved safety, but also in improvement of other important areas: (1) commitment to common goals, (2) development of a sense of personal responsibility toward continually trying to improve an operation, (3) increased use of the minds and experience of all employees in the problem solving process, (4) reduced obstacles to change, and (5) enhanced cooperation among all members of the organization.

For these reasons, it is commonplace for those supervisors who have developed good skills in conducting crew safety meetings also to have crews that excel in other aspects of work-cost, customer satisfaction, and such attributes as loyalty, quality, and productivity.

SUMMARY

Crew safety meetings are an important and integral part of a successful safety management process. They should be held on a monthly basis and should normally be restricted to thirty minutes in length. To be effective, crew meetings must be carefully structured to provide for:

1. Communication *from* upper management
2. Discussion of a safety topic specifically applicable to the crew
3. Formulation of communication *to* upper management

Competence in leading a crew safety meeting is a skill required of all competent first-line supervisors.

NOTES

1. Anthony Jay, *How to Run a Meeting,* Video Arts Limited, Dumbarton House, 68 Oxford Street, London, W1N 9LA, England, June, 1989.

CHAPTER 16

AN AUDIT LIST FOR ASSESSING A SAFETY MANAGEMENT PROCESS

In some sense, every organization has a safety management process. A process that has been developed through years of dedicated effort and that has a track record of achieving truly outstanding success has been described in the foregoing chapters. This chapter provides an outline of criteria useful in comparing an existing safety management process with the model described. The usefulness of this auditing checklist can be maximized if responses are written and supported by factual statements regarding the existing safety management process. The benefits derived from the use of this audit list will be maximized if it is used by a team composed of at least two people: the auditor and a line manager from the organization being audited. The audit should be conducted in the spirit of identifying areas of opportunity for improving the safety management process, not for the purpose of measuring management performance. The well-being of employees, the public, and the environment is the proper measure of management performance. The process should not be confused with the product.

A SAFETY MANAGEMENT PROCESS ASSESSMENT AUDIT LIST

1. Management Motivation

Why is management (at any level of inquiry) interested in safety?

- Costs?
- Well-being of employees?
- Concern for the public?
- Interest of superiors?
- Continuity of operations?

- Governmental regulations?

What evidence exists to support responses to above question?

Identify the visible safety-related activities of the "top" of the organization during the past thirty days.

Suggestions for enhancement?

2. Safety Policy

Does a safety policy statement exist for the organization being audited? Should a policy statement exist for this organization?

To whom is the policy addressed? Correct audience?

Is it a statement of principles? Only principles, or does it contain rules? Any significant principles missing?

Does the policy have influence in the organization? Cite specifics.

How has the policy been communicated to employees? In their working language?

Is policy applicable to contractor personnel? Part of contract?

Suggestions for improvement?

3. Organization for Safety

Does a Central Safety, Health, and Environment Committee exist?

- What is its membership?
- Is every employee represented in the CSHEC?
- How is contractor representation achieved?
- What is its meeting schedule?
- What standing subcommittees exist? Active?
- What ad hoc committees have existed in the past 12 months? Results?
- What reports are made at CSHEC meetings? Attach an agenda. Injury statistics? Incident reports? Subcommittee reports? Disability reports? Audit reports? Medical? Safety staff?
- How are decisions made at CSHEC meetings communicated? How do front-line employees learn of these decisions? Is this communication channel verified by sampling among front-line employees?
- How do mid-level supervisors view the effectiveness of the CSHE Committee?

Suggestions for improvement?

4. Standards of Performance

Does a Safety Manual exist?

- Is it readily available to all employees? How?
- Is it maintained on a current basis? How?
- Is it written by safety staff or prospective users? Procedure for changes well established? Used?

Does the Safety Manual contain:

- A set of general *safety rules* applicable throughout the organization? Are these adequate?

- A set of rules applicable to specific types of work wherever performed? Adequate?
- A set of rules uniquely applicable to specific physical areas of the facilities? Adequate?
- A requirement that all injuries or suspected injuries, regardless of how slight, be reported to supervision and medical immediately?

Does the Safety Manual contain:

- A set of *safety procedures* that are applicable throughout the facility (organization) wherever the *tasks* (activities) to which they apply are performed? Including contractors? Exceptions? Appropriate? Controlled? How? Adequate? List these procedures.
- A set of *safety procedures* that are applicable throughout the facility (organization) wherever the *hazards* (materials) to which they apply may be encountered? Including contractors? Exception? Appropriate? Controlled? How? Adequate? List these procedures.

Do Standard Operating Procedures exist?

- By whom have they been prepared—staff or users?
- Has work activity been divided into reasonable increments?
- Do SOPs specifically cite safety requirements and considerations as integral parts of work procedures? Are rules and procedures stated as requirements or recommendations? Mixture? Appropriate mixture? Cite examples. Are SOPs binding on contractor employees? How achieved?

Suggestions for improvement?

5. Management Safety Audits

Does a formal schedule exist? Followed?

Are audits team audits? Appropriate team composition?

Do audits focus on things or people behavior? Document with statistics.

Do audits require talking with employees who have been audited?

How are audits perceived by front-line employees? Determine by actually sampling.

Are audit reports prepared, summarized, and results regularly reported to Central SHE Committee?

Do observations remain anonymous? If not, why not?

Do safety audits include review of portions of Safety Manual? Of Process Hazards Reviews?

Are contractor personnel audited? Adequately? By whom?

Suggestions for improvements?

6. Goal Setting

Do organizational safety goals exist? Identify goals criteria. Fatalities? Lost workday cases? Total recordables? Any others?

- Are these appropriate in regard to both criteria and target values?
- How are goals set?

- Have goals been communicated? Adequately?

What forms of recognition for goal achievement exist? Adequate? Appropriate?
Is contractor performance included? How? Appropriate?
Suggested changes?

7. Incident Investigations

Are all injuries and illnesses investigated?

Are all injuries more serious than first-aid cases investigated by investigation teams?

- Is composition of teams appropriate?
- Is focus of investigations on fact development and corrective actions?
- Are injury investigation reports openly and widely available to all employees?

Are first-aid cases and events without injuries but which had the potential for serious injury or environmental damage investigated?

- Are the reports of these incidents openly and widely available to all employees?

Has upper management participated in an incident (injury or noninjury) investigation during previous 12 months? Explain.

Does the CSHEC follow up on incident recommendation completion? On all or only selected categories? What categories? Appropriate?

How are contractor employee injuries reported? Investigated? Adequate?

Are there recommendations for improving the usefulness of incident investigation and reporting?

8. The Role of Medical Personnel

Does the employment process reveal that candidates have been noncompetitive for medical reasons?

Do medical personnel participate in CSHE meetings?

Must employees "check in" through medical personnel prior to returning to work following a medical related absence?

Are injured employees normally seen by site medical personnel prior to being treated by off-site medical personnel? Contractor personnel?

Do medical personnel determine employee work restrictions? Or simply fitness to work? Are employee health records confidential? Current? Are health monitoring programs on schedule? Adequate? List programs, e.g., hearing conservation program.

Suggestions for improvement?

9. Accounting Procedures

Do accounting procedures inhibit development of leadership in safety? How?

Do accounting procedures charge the costs of work-related injuries and illnesses to operating accounts?

How are costs of off-the-job injuries and illnesses charged?

Suggestions for improvement?

10. Crew Safety Meetings

Are meetings passive or participative?

How are meetings viewed by front-line employees? Determine by sampling front-line employees.

What is frequency of crew safety meetings?

Suggestions for improvement?

11. Safety Office

Personnel adequate in number and talent?

Personnel supportive to line management? Have some safety responsibilities been vested in safety personnel? Cite examples.

Suggestions for improvement?

12. General Items

Are governmental requirements being met? List programs and current status.

Are injuries classified and reported as required by government and company regulations?

Does a progressive disciplinary procedure exist? Is it creditable?

Are employee training programs adequate?

Suggestions for improvement not previously noted?

INDEX